About the Author

(photo by Carmen Ronan)

Jerome Clark is a prize-winning author of the multivolume *UFO Encyclopedia* (1990–1998) and other books, including *Unexplained! Strange Sightings, Incredible Occurrences, and Puzzling Physical Phenomena* (Visible Ink Press, 1998) and *Unnatural Phenomena* (2005). A former editor of *Fate* magazine, he serves on the board of the J. Allen Hynek Center for UFO Studies and co-edits its magazine, *International UFO Reporter.* In June 2008 the Society for Scientific Exploration, an organization of professionals in the physical and social sciences, gave him its Dinsdale Award for "significant contributions to the expansion of human understanding through the study of unexplained phenomena ... which have brought to the general public comprehensive and trustworthy information presented from a sophisticated perspective."

Clark is also a songwriter (Emmylou Harris, Mary Chapin Carpenter, Tom T. Hall, Seldom Scene, Mary Black, and others) and a prolific writer on roots music. He pursues a wide range of interests—political, historical, and literary—from his home in Minnesota.

Hidden Realms, Lost Civilizations, and Beings from Other Worlds

Hidden Realms, Lost Civilizations, and Beings from Other Worlds

Jerome Clark

VISIBLE
INK
PRESS

Detroit

Hidden Realms, Lost Civilizations, and Beings from Other Worlds

Visible Ink Press®
43311 Joy Rd., #414
Canton, MI 48187-2075

Visible Ink Press is a registered trademark of Visible Ink Press LLC.

Most Visible Ink Press books are available at special quantity discounts when purchased in bulk by corporations, organizations, or groups. Customized printings, special imprints, messages, and excerpts can be produced to meet your needs. For more information, contact Special Markets Director, Visible Ink Press, www.visibleink.com, or 734-667-3211.

Managing Editor: Kevin S. Hile
Art Director: Mary Claire Krzewinski
Typesetting: Marco Di Vita

ISBN 978-1-57859-175-6

Cover images: (front cover) Fortean Picture Library; (back cover) iStock.

Library of Congress Cataloging-in-Publication Data

Clark, Jerome.
    Hidden realms, lost civilizations, and beings from other worlds / by Jerome Clark.
        p. cm.
    Includes bibliographical references and index.
    ISBN 978-1-57859-175-6
    1. Lost continents. 2. Geographical myths. 3. Extraterrestrial beings. I. Title.
GN751.C6 2010   398.23'4—dc22
                                          2010000785

Printed in Singapore by Imago
10 9 8 7 6 5 4 3 2 1

For Arthur & Vivien Larson

Contents

Acknowledgments

To Chris Aubeck, Henry H. Bauer, W. Ritchie Benedict, Lucius Farish, Kevin Hile, Theo Paijmans, Mark Rodeghier, Nick Sucik, David Sutton, Michael D. Swords, and Robert Wood, who all, in one way or another, knowingly or unknowingly, made this book possible. And especially to my publisher, Roger Jänecke, for his saintly patience and splendid ideas, and to my wife, Helene Henderson, for putting up with years' worth of an author's complaints and frustrations. And finally, to two great men, the long-gone Charles Fort and the longer-gone Rev. Robert Kirk, for setting the thoughts in motion.

Introduction

At most given moments, human beings live in two worlds. One is pedestrian reality, the other the one we experience in dreams and speculations. Each world has its wonders and its horrors, and each can elevate or bring us down. Both are tricky to negotiate. To the unwary, both offer false certainties that, just as we are most sure of them, can fall out from under our feet.

Tricks of certainty respect no educational level or social class. Anyone can become obsessed with a belief that seems sensible, even empirically grounded, and some go to their graves unabused of a notion even when most other observers think it has been conclusively discredited—for example, Percival Lowell and his Martian canals. So unyielding was his advocacy, even in the face of what others saw as growing disconfirmation, that it lived on decades past his death and was at last abandoned in the face of evidence that even the most resolute could no longer deny. On the other extreme, many followers of flying-saucer contactee George Adamski, who claimed associations with Venusians, Martians, and Saturnians, refused to be persuaded by clear and specific indications that his stories were conscious fabrications.

If some things are purely imaginary—and no less interesting and revelatory for that—other things are something else, something not quite wholly real and something not quite wholly dreamed up. Something, in other words, that can be experienced vividly in ways that resist both prosaic explanation and lazy categorization. Call them encounters of the liminal kind, visions on the threshold of possibility, or—as I prefer—experience anomalies, as opposed to anomalous events. The latter can be demonstrated, or at least potentially demonstrated, to have occurred in consensus-level reality. They exist in the world, and you can prove as much, even if not always easily.

Experience anomalies, on the other hand, are visions of the otherworldly, and nothing brings them into or keeps them inside this world in any but an experiential sense. They are preserved in memory and testimony and nowhere else. That, however, makes them no less mysterious. Indeed, they are *highly* mysterious, so much so that they transcend language itself. To the extent that vocabulary tries to encapsulate them, it conjures up the noun and adjective "visionary," which translates as "powerful hallucination," except that hallucinations by definition are subjective and personal. The contents of experience anomalies are subjective—in the sense that (as this book will demonstrate) they tend to be culture-specific—in other words, in forms that are at once supernatural and recognizable—but they are also collectively observed. More than one person can have the experience of "seeing" a strange being, creature, object, or landscape. Ordinarily, collective perception settles the issue of whether or not the perceived something is "real," but not in this third world. Here, we learn that an experience of the otherworldly can be, indeed, experienced. We also learn that an experience is not automatically an event, and it is all the more mind-bogglingly puzzling for that.

Among the consistent themes of the human presence in all times and places is the longing for fantastic places with populations of fantastic beings to match. Such realms may well exist on extrasolar planets astronomers are now discovering almost daily and in parallel universes about which physicists continue to theorize. But if they exist as so-far-unproved possibilities, we human beings are not content to await validation from authority. In the meantime, we do as we have always done: explore those hidden realms of the imagination. Even more evocatively, those realms enigmatically continue to open themselves to our experiences of them, and for a brief time, before they fade back into mist and memory, we live them.

—Jerome Clark
Minnesota
August 31, 2009

PART ONE

EARTH'S SECRET PLACES

Lemurian Mountain: Outpost of the Lost Continentals

Situated near the southern end of the Cascade range, in Siskiyou County, Mt. Shasta rises 14,161 feet (4,316 meters) above the landscape of northern California, 40 miles (64 kilometers) south of Oregon and midway between the Pacific Ocean and the Nevada border. It is a volcano which, according to geological evidence, erupts every 600 to 800 years. It has been alleged that the most recent eruption—or so some have inferred from the testimony of an observer looking to land from a ship at sea—occurred in 1786. The witnessed eruption, however, may not have been of Shasta; the issue is in dispute. (White people did not start settling in the area until 1827.) The lakes, rivers, and forests surrounding the mountain make Shasta a major tourist destination.

Whatever its distinctive beauty and natural features, Mt. Shasta is best known around the world for the curious lore associated with it. Its most celebrated legends, which owe more to conscious fabrication than to traditional folklore, are barely more than a century old. Older supernatural myths and tales, which come from the American Indian tribes who live or lived in the area, are just as interesting and in some ways more intriguing. For example, besides the ubiquitous belief in a race of supernatural, often invisible little people—a worldwide fairy tradition with cultural variations—natives spoke of their fear of cave-dwelling hairy giants, the Shupchers, who dispatched their victims by embracing and crushing them. As Bigfoot and Sasquatch such creatures, albeit minus murderous impulses, would survive, at least in supposition and testimony, into modern times.

Dwellers on Two Continents

Shasta as international occult landmark is in good part, however, the consequence of the imagination of Frederick Spencer Oliver, born in 1866. Two years later his par-

According to some occult chroniclers, California's Mount Shasta houses an advanced race of survivors from the sunken Pacific continent of Lemuria (*iStock*).

ents and he migrated from Washington, D.C., to Yreka, California, just north of Shasta, where the family sought to secure its fortune in prospecting. In 1883, while engaged in surveying the boundaries of the Oliver mining claim, the young man—while "in sight of the inspiring peak of Mount Shasta," he would later state—experienced a sudden urge to start scrawling sentences in his notebook. Confused and alarmed, he hastened home. There he sat down and watched his hand, clutching a pen, fly across the page. Known to both occultists and psychologists, this automatic writing sometimes produces whole books, as often as not said to be dictated by superior discarnate intelligences, and this is how, it is claimed, *A Dweller on Two Planets* came to be.

Oliver continued to write—the narrative arrived in spurts, no more than a few pages at a time—and completed the manuscript in 1886. Afterwards, he tried without success to get it published. When one copy of the manuscript burned in a train wreck on the way back from New York, Oliver expressed these ominous sentiments in a November 22, 1897, letter to a correspondent: "Many months ago Phylos [who evidently channeled his thoughts through Oliver] informed both myself [sic] and Mr. Putnam [presumably publisher G.P. Putnam] that from then on there were evil opponents in his [Phylos'] own realm that would make every possible effort to defeat the appearance of his book. It would seem as if this train wreck, if by it the MS. is lost, was the crowning effort of the opposition."

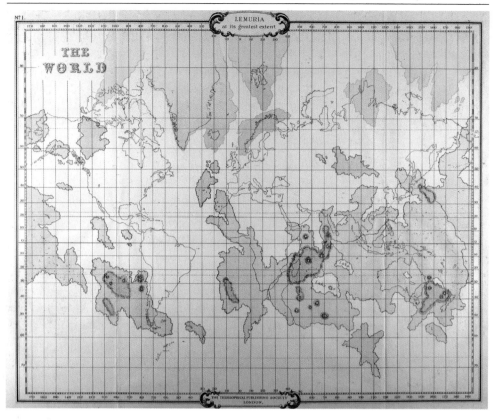

A 1904 map depicts what some believed to be the greatest extent of the Lemurian world (*Mary Evans Picture Library*).

The manuscript, which was gathering dust when Oliver died before his time at age 33, in 1899, may well have been lost if his mother, Mary Elizabeth Manley-Oliver (with assistance from family friends), had not paid for its publication as a 423-page work in 1905. It bore the by-line "Phylos the Thibetan." (Speaking in the novel's characteristically obese prose, one character intones, "And some day the world shall hear of him [the central character] as Phylos the Thibetan, yet shall he not reside in Thibet in Asia, but shall be so called because he shall for a time live on the soul plane of the occult adepts of Thibet.") Phylos, "an adept of the arcane and occult in the universe," one of whose past lives was spent on the lost Pacific continent of Lemuria, psychically communicated the words Oliver had transcribed.

Whatever else may be said of him, Phylos—presumably a confabulation of Oliver's unconscious mind—is not a great novelist or even a limply gifted one. But whatever its literary shortcomings—the book, ripely written, pompous, and preposterous, makes for what politely may be called a challenging read—it has become something of a metaphysical standard, read even today at least by individuals of a New Age bent. A fair number of modern Shasta legends can be traced back to it.

Dweller's plot, such as it is, concerns the past and present life of its narrator, Walter Pierson. After the Civil War, Pierson moves to California and becomes a partner in a gold-mining company in the Shasta area. The work force he supervises includes a number of Chinese men on whom Pierson looks down with racism and contempt—except for one, Quong, who, unlike his fellows, is a "real man," of high character and intelligence. Because of his superior nature, Quong eschews the company of his countrymen but works with the white laborers and soon has their respect because of his energy, wisdom, and compassion.

One day, as Pierson and Quong are on an outing in the wilderness, a grizzly bear rises up, about to attack Pierson, who is armed only with a knife. Suddenly, Quong appears, walks calmly toward the bear, and orders it to lie down. He sits on it and pets the creature, which licks his hand and then departs into the woods.

Soon Pierson learns that Quong is an ancient master of the mystic arts, a member of a secret brotherhood that lives inside the mountain. The two enter through a hidden door and meet other masters inside a luxurious temple. Pierson is initiated into the occult mysteries, and another of the masters takes him in his astral body to Venus (known to its inhabitants as Hesper). On that planet Pierson learns of his previous lifetime in Atlantis, where much of the story is set. Eventually, Pierson is transformed into Phylos, a cosmic guardian.

✳

Lemurian Colony

Though neglected by modern writers on Shasta, Eugene E. Thomas' 1894 novel, *Brotherhood of Mt. Shasta*, helped shape the evolving occult beliefs that *Dweller* set in motion. The protagonist, young Donald Crane, finds that a colony of masters, descended in part from Lemuria, lives secretly inside the mountain. Crane goes through seven steps on his way to mystical enlightenment before joining the "Sacred Brotherhood."

If Frederick Spencer Oliver and Eugene Thomas first put forth the idea of Mount Shasta as a hideaway for a lost colony of mystical adepts with sunken-continent connections, a man who shared a middle name with Oliver—Harvey Spencer Lewis (1883–1939)—did much to fill in the details and to reinforce the link between Shasta and Lemuria. In his early adult life, Lewis, a journalist and editor in New York, developed interests in psychical research and occultism, much of it focused on Rosicrucianism. In 1909, in France, he was initiated into the order. On his return to the United States he became First Imperator of the Ancient and Mystic Order Rosae Crucis (AMORC), founded in 1915. In the 1920s AMORC moved to San Jose, California, where the organization, which still exists, remains headquartered.

Writing as "Selvius" in the August 1925 issue of the Rosicrucian magazine *The Mystic Triangle,* Lewis declared, "For fifty years or more the natives of Northern California and tourists, explorers, and government officials have contributed facts, and some fancies, to the accumulating mass of evidence proving the existence of the 'mystic village' (a name used by common agreement) and supplying the most astounding facts ever attributed to human beings." These "facts" included numerous observations of mysterious phenomena on the mountainside as well as the regular appearances of odd individuals, dressed in pure white robes, "gray-haired, barefoot and very tall," paying for goods with nuggets of pure gold. Moreover:

A symbol of the Rosicrucians, a mystical organization that believes in many occult practices. Some followers of this faith believed that there was a link between Lemuria and Mt. Shasta (*Mary Evans Picture Library*).

At midnight, throughout the whole year, a ceremony is performed in this village, called the "ceremony of adoration to Guatama." This latter word is their name for America; and the real purpose of the ceremony is to celebrate the arrival on this continent of their forebears when the continent of Lemuria disappeared beneath the quiet waters of the Pacific. At such ceremonies wonderful lights are used to such an extent that the whole southern side of Mt. Shasta is illuminated and made visible at great distances. These same lights are used at sunrise, daily[,] and are often seen by passengers on the *Shasta Limited* [train] which passes Shasta at about sunrise in certain seasons.

Though inclined to reclusiveness, the Lemurians—numbering no more than a few hundred—were good neighbors, helping farmers grow bumper crops with their advanced agricultural knowledge and making generous charitable contributions. On one occasion, apparently unremarked upon in the local press, a Lemurian walked all the way down to San Francisco, where he was given the key to the city, "much to the embarrassment of the simple soul who came to bring greetings on the anniversary of the establishment of their community in California."

Either Lewis was extraordinarily credulous, or he was simply imaginative and making it up as he went along. (Needless to say, actual residents of the Shasta area knew nothing of any of this until occult pilgrims started showing up and asking them questions.) In any case, his piece completed what Oliver had begun, linking lost continents and survivors holed up at Shasta. In 1931 AMORC published a book titled *Lemuria: The Lost Continent of the Pacific*, its author identified as one "Wishar Spenly Cervé," in fact a clumsy anagram of Harvey Spencer Lewis. The book, essentially a considerable expansion of the original "Selvius" piece, identifies coastal California as the product of a collision of the

The end of Mu (another name for Lemuria) came when volcanic action and floods overwhelmed the continent, as shown in this illustration from James Churchward's *The Lost Continent of Mu* (*Mary Evans Picture Library*).

eastern edge of the broken-up, sinking Lemuria with the North American continent. Just before that catastrophe, however, a group of wise Lemurians had already relocated to the top of Mount Shasta, knowing they would be safe there from the rising waters.

True Lemurians—in this account anyway—did not, and do not, look exactly like us. Seven feet (2.1 meters) tall, they have large foreheads topped with short hair, but thick and long in the back (in other words, mullets). A walnut-sized lump in the middle of their foreheads represents what amounts to a third eye, through which they sense distant sights and images and engage in telepathic exchanges with their fellows. The third eye also gives them access to all knowledge of time, space, science, spirit, and history. Not all Lemurians perished in the cataclysm—the others scattered and lost their distinctive characteristics to become the ancestors of the present human race—but the Shasta colonists, by keeping to themselves and discouraging outsiders from any but the most minimal interaction (if that), have preserved the otherwise-lost race in its original form.

An article in the May 22, 1932, edition of the *Los Angeles Times*'s Sunday magazine electrified occultists with what appeared to be independent confirmation of a Lemurian Shasta. Writer Edward Lanser reported that on a recent trip from Los Angeles to Seattle aboard the Shasta Limited, he had awakened early to catch the sunrise. The distant mountain's southern slope, he noticed, was eerily illuminated with a "strange, reddish-green light." The light apparently did not come from a forest fire because no smoke accompanied it. Awhile later, as he was eating breakfast, he spoke with the conductor, inquiring if he knew anything about the curious phenomenon. "Lemurians," the conductor replied matter-of-factly. "They hold ceremonials up there."

On his return trip, Lanser said, he drove to Siskiyou County and spent the night in Weed. Lanser related:

> I discovered that the existence of a "mystic village" on Mt. Shasta was an accepted fact. Business men, amateur explorers, officials and ranchers in the country surrounding Shasta spoke freely of the Lemurian community, and all attested to the weird rituals that are performed on the mountainside at sunset, midnight and sunrise. Also they freely ridiculed my avowed trek into the sacred precincts, assuring me that an entrance was as difficult and forbidden as is an entrance into Tibet.
>
> It appeared that, although the existence of these last descendants of the ancient Lemurians have [sic] been known to Northern Californians for more than 50 years, only four or five explorers have penetrated the invisible protective boundary of this Lemurian settlement; but no one has ever returned to tell the tale…. It's safe to say that fifty out of a hundred people living within a reasonable distance of Shasta have at some time or other tried to approach the Lemurians, yet many—who are known to have penetrated at least part of the mystery—will vehemently deny, perhaps out of some well-founded fear, having much such an investigation or having any knowledge concerning the Lemurians.

Lanser also cited the alleged telescopic observations of Lemurian activity by "the eminent scientist Prof. Edgar Lucien Larkin, for many years director of the Mt. Lowe Observatory in Southern California." Larkin is also mentioned in Lewis' Lemurian chronicles. Owned and run for public-relations purposes by the Pacific Electric Railway, "Mount Lowe Observatory" was more tourist attraction than scientific establishment, and Larkin was no scientist, eminent or otherwise, but a Hearst newspaper contributor, inventor, and Atlantis buff who had died in 1924. Moreover, as William Bridge Cooke demonstrated in a later article in the *Mount Shasta Herald* (June 27, 1940), for optical and geographical reasons, Larkin could not have seen what some accounts claimed he saw from his vantage point 800 miles (1,287 kilometers) to the south. In any event, the whole issue is surely moot, since there is no reason to believe that Larkin himself ever made these claims. As far as anyone can determine, they first saw print in 1925, when Lewis publicized them and Larkin was conveniently not around to dispute them.

Though frequently cited in esoteric literature, Lanser's story appears to be either a parody or an outright hoax. It seems to have drawn in equal parts on Lewis' writings (especially the "Selvius" piece) and on Lanser's own freewheeling imagination. We can only infer as much, because the *Times* story was his one and only, if lasting, contribution to Shasta/Lemuria lore.

In its August 1935 issue the *Rosicrucian Digest* warned readers of fraudulent mystics—unnamed, but possibly the emerging psychic charlatans Guy and Edna Ballard (see below)—claiming to have discovered Lemurian temples at Shasta and offering to lead deep-pocketed pilgrims to them. "The naïve believer will lose time and money as well," the magazine predicted.

The following year AMORC went further in a letter to the Mount Shasta City Chamber of Commerce. On May 28 the *Mount Shasta Herald* reprinted portions of the communication, which accompanied a copy of the AMORC-published book on Lemuria. AMORC declared it was "amused by the rumors that we originated these tales [about Lemurians] or merely accepted them as facts.... We are no more responsible for the facts than is the publisher who publishes Anderson's Fairy Tales or the Arabian Nights." In other words, the book was never intended to be anything other than a collection of colorful folktales. The letter warned of phony expeditions whose unnamed guides always managed to find an excuse for their failure to deliver the promised goods. Presumably, AMORC's fear of potential legal liability was such that it was willing to jettison its own book, certainly not issued initially as an anthology of yarns and myths—though Lewis can only have been a conscious fabulist who created much of the lore out of his own head, not out of pre-existing Shasta traditions.

AMORC was already moving away from its founder's claims of flesh-and-blood Lemurians on the mountain. In the *Rosicrucian Digest* for January 1936, John P. Scott recounted his inquiries in the area. "No storekeepers in the vicinity," he wrote, "have ever exchanged merchandise for gold nuggets with any strange inhabitants of this mountain. There are no Lemurian temples or ruins on the mountain." Nonetheless, though many of the stories AMORC itself had promoted were, strictly speaking, hooey, the Lemurians still exist, if not here, then there on "other planes." He explained, "Many earthbound spirits from the old civilization which once existed in this locality are still there, held closely ... by their materialistic ideas. Mt. Shasta seems to us to be a so-called 'sensitive spot,' in which it is easier to contact those on the other planes than most other places."

This notion echoes a concept that figures in Oliver's book—not in the novel's narrative but in an interlude within the text, "Seven Shasta Scenes":

> A long tunnel stretches away, far into the interior of majestic Shasta. Wholly unthought is it that there lie at the tunnel's far end vast apartments, the home of a mystic brotherhood, whose occult arts hollowed that tunnel and mysterious dwelling: "Sach" the name is. Are you incredulous as to these things? Go there, or suffer yourself to be taken as I was, once! See, as I saw, not with the vision of flesh, the walls, polished as by jewelers, though excavated as by giants; floors carpeted with long, fleecy gray fabric that looked like fur, but was a mineral product; ledges intersected by the boulders, and in their wonderful polish exhibiting veinings of gold, of silver, of green copper ores, and maculations of precious stones. Verily, a mystic temple, made afar from the madding crowd.

Oliver, however, does not tie this "mystic brotherhood" to a remnant Lemurian colony, a connection made subsequently by Eugene Thomas.

Lewis Spence (1874–1955) was not yet another pseudonym of Harvey Spencer Lewis. He was a Scottish journalist, political activist, folklorist, and occultist. Among his

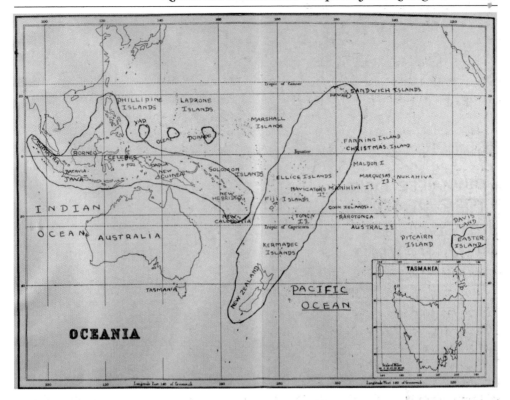

The location of Lemuria, according to Lewis Spence (*Mary Evans Picture Library*).

fascinations was the subject of lost continents, on which he wrote several important books. One of them was *The Problem of Lemuria* (1933). Spence cited Lanser's account of Shasta Lemurians in the context of Lemurian survivals. "The proof that a native white race once dwelt in the Pacific area and that its vestiges are still to be found there is, I am convinced, of the highest moment to the whole study of a difficult question," he wrote.

✳

Meetings on the Mountain

Retrospectively, typically years after the (supposed) fact, several individuals claimed to have met mystic masters on the mountain in the early 1930s. The most notorious of them, Guy Warren Ballard (1878–1939), anticipated the post–1947 flying-saucer contactees who allegedly interacted with wise, beautiful Venusians—though with Ballard those encounters were in Wyoming's Grand Tetons.

As related in *Unveiled Mysteries* (1934), which he wrote under the pseudonym "Godfré Ray King," Ballard's mystical adventures began, however, on Shasta one day in

(Continued on page 13)

LEMURIA

The other legendary lost continent, Atlantis, is a genuinely ancient one, close to 2,500 years old. It cannot be traced past Plato's telling of it in works thought to date from around 355 B.C.E., when it was used for purposes not of history but of political allegory. Whatever its pretensions to the contrary, Lemuria, on the other hand, has a history less than a century and a half in age.

Though in occult tradition it would become the Pacific's equivalent to the Atlantic Ocean's sunken civilization, Lemuria began in the Indian Ocean as a speculative, if scientifically grounded, effort by the English zoologist Philip Sclater to explain how lemurs (primitive primates) could exist both on the island of Madagascar and the southern tip of the Indian continent, two widely separated locations. He speculated that this land bridge, which he called "Lemuria,"

had once linked them. Later, German evolutionary biologist Ernst Haeckel put forth the idea that *Homo sapiens* came into being on that sunken land bridge. Others thought that, perhaps millions of years ago, Lemuria was a land mass connected to an immense continent, called Gondwanaland, which occupied most of the Southern Hemisphere.

It bears noting that none of these scientists thought these landscapes harbored civilizations, advanced or otherwise. Progress in geology, including the discovery of continental drift, rendered such guesswork obsolete. The name and concept Lemuria survives because the celebrated occultist Helena Petrovna Blavatsky picked up on it in her *The Secret Doctrine* (1889), where Lemuria was represented as being the home of humanity's third "root race." The Lemurians were apelike creatures that laid eggs and had three eyes, one in the back of the head. They were also hermaphrodites.

Theosophical visionaries reported their own experiences of Lemurians. W. Scott-Elliot claimed that humans entered physical bodies for the first time on Lemuria. Venusians known as Lords of the Flame helped guide evolution, and Lemurians came more and more humanlike and spiritually developed. The continent broke up during the Mesozoic era, and one peninsula became Atlantis.

Working with Mayan hieroglyphics in the Yucatan late in the nineteenth century, archaeologist Augustus le Plongeon claimed to have found references to Mu, a

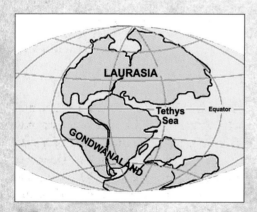

About 200 million years ago there were two supercontinents, instead of today's seven smaller ones. Those who believe in Lemuria think that it might have been connected to Gondwanaland.

lost civilization that he believed must be Atlantis. When he died, his papers fell into the hands of James Churchward, who wrote four books based in part on them. According to Churchward, Mu was not Atlantis but a South Pacific continent and the "motherland of man." The people of Mu were white (of course, as suited the racial sensibilities of Churchward's time), numbering 64,000,000. They built great cities, and when they were not doing that, they worshipped the sun. Churchward claimed that he learned much of this history from tablets written in the no longer extant Nazcal language, but when challenged to produce them, he grew oddly— or revealingly—elusive. In any case, he argued the case in four books, most famously the first, *The Lost Continent of Mu* (1926). Before long, Mu was assumed to be just another name for Lemuria.

In the decades since then, Lemuria has become a staple of mystical thought. Efforts to prove its consensus-reality existence in any geographical, archaeological, or other scientifically grounded sense are rare. It is now almost entirely the province of mystics and New Agers. Lemurians are rumored to survive in colonies at Mount Shasta, inside the hollow Earth, on other planets, and elsewhere. Some people report physical or psychic visits to these hiding places. Channelers record long-winded messages from discarnate Lemurians, the contents varying from messenger to messenger.

Further Reading

De Camp, L. Sprague. *Lost Continents: The Atlantis Theme in History, Science, and Literature.* New York: Dover Publications, 1970.

Scott-Elliot, W. *The Story of Atlantis and the Lost Lemuria.* London: Theosophical Publishing House, 1925.

Sheppard, Jack. "Lemuria Did Exist." *Fate* 4, 3 (July, 1950): 18–25.

(Continued from page 11)

1930, when he was thirsty and looking for a spring. In the course of his search, he met a handsome young stranger whom he first took to be a fellow hiker. The young man asked for Ballard's cup, which he filled with a richly textured liquid. On drinking it, Ballard felt something like an electrical shock run through him. Within a few minutes Ballard saw his companion's "face, body, and clothing become the living breathing tangible 'Presence' of the Master, Saint Germain.... He stood there before me—a Magnificent God-like figure—in a white jeweled robe, a Light and Love sparkling in his eyes that revealed and proved the Dominion and Majesty that are his."[1]

Saint Germain told Ballard that he had been directed to initiate the Seventh Golden Age. He spent centuries roaming Europe trying to find an embodied human being sufficiently advanced to receive the Great Law of Life and to lead the effort on

The continent of Lemuria is swept under the ocean waves in this illustration (*Mary Evans Picture Library*).

earth. Unsuccessful, he shifted his operation to the United States, where he encountered Ballard, whom Saint Germain designated—along with Ballard's wife and son—the Accredited Messenger of the Ascended Masters.

Ballard experienced other dramatic metaphysical diversions, though not at Shasta, over the several years that remained to him. With his medium wife, Edna, and son, Donald, he spent the rest of the 1930s on the road promoting I AM [Ascended Master] Activity, a sect which, outside its following, was reviled for its authoritarian structure, fascistic ideology, and dubious financial dealings.

Channeler Nola Van Valer (d. 1979) reported that she and her husband, Jerry, met masters at Shasta as early as 1930. That spring Jerry had traveled by train to the area, where he met Mol Long in the town of McCloud. In a story reminiscent of Ballard's, the mystic master produced a bowl of soup "which tasted like nothing I have ever tasted upon this Earth. I drank the soup and became so alive with vibration that I was at complete peace and rest within myself." In June his wife joined him, and the two underwent occult education at the feet of Shasta masters.

In *Mysteries of Mount Shasta* (1949) Maurice Doreal—born Claude Doggins (c. 1898–1963) and founder (in 1929) of the Brotherhood of the White Temple—recalled his 1931 encounters at the mountain, not with Saint Germain or Lemurians but with Atlanteans. In Doreal's telling he was lecturing in Los Angeles when two persons from Mount Shasta came to hear him. After a few days they whisked him to Shasta. First, they drove him to the city's outskirts, then covered his face with a thin, transparent mask. Doreal would write:

Then they gave me a belt with two little pockets on the side and a row of buttons. I did not know what was going to happen.... Each one took me by the arm and told me to press certain buttons and I went through the air like a rocket plane and we rose until the earth looked like it was almost fading out[.] [I] breathed perfectly because something in that mask over my face condensed the breath and it seemed that around us there was a shell of some kind of force, because I could hear a humming noise all the time. When we came down it seemed like almost no time had passed; probably, fifteen or twenty minutes. We landed about two thirds up the side of Mt. Shasta—we landed in front of a small building.

There Doreal entered a great city encased within a cavern illumined by a "giant glowing mass of light ... condensed from a blending of the rays of the sun and moon." Atlanteans there lived in white marble mansions amid vast gardens. He learned that evil Lemurians are kept under the watchful eyes of the good Atlanteans, who have them imprisoned on remote Pacific islands. It should surprise no one that Doreal was the owner of a massive library of science-fiction books and a contributor to the letters section of *Amazing Stories* and other SF pulp magazines.

In *The Golden Goddess of the Lemurians* (1970) Abraham Joseph Mansfield devotes a chapter to someone else's alleged 1931 Shasta experience. On a hunting expedition with Mansfield, the unidentified "friend" shot and wounded a deer on the northeast side of the mountain. As he searched for it, he lost his bearings, and darkness fell. Eventually, exhausted, he lay down. Around 3:30 AM a voice roused him with the question: "Why don't you come with me?" The speaker, seven feet (2.1 meters) tall, identified himself as a Lemurian. The man was led deep into the bowels of the mountain into the Lemurian's residence, a beautiful golden cave. He slept there on a golden bed, his head pressed against a golden pillow. The Lemurian spoke of a vast network of tunnels connecting Shasta and other surface locations to the center of the earth, where most Lemurians reside. "I saw plates and gold-lined shafts, and tables and chairs unbelievably monstrous in size." In due course the man returned to the mountainside and found his way to Mansfield and the car they had arrived in.

Not to be outdone, Mansfield outlined his own experiences with Lemurians. He viewed their Plates of Time, "assembled for future generations to preserve the knowledge they had about atomic power so that a new generation would use it wisely and respect the powers of God." In 1934 the Lemurians, he reported, anointed him chief of their gods, a position he held until his death five decades later.

The previous chief of the Lemurian gods, according to Mansfield, was a certain J.C. Brown. Again according to Mansfield, Brown was the assumed name of a British mining engineer, Lord Arthur J. Cowdray. (Another source says that Brown was merely an employee of the Lord Cowdray Mining Company of London.) Be that as it may, somebody calling himself J.C. Brown really existed, showing up in Stockton, California, in 1934 as a 79-year-old man. He had a fantastic tale to tell.

12,000 YEARS AGO The most fascinating legend of man is the legend of the lost continent of Lemuria. It is the firm belief of many authorities and archaeologists, that approximately 12,000 years ago, a great civilization flourished in the Pacific, mother country of many colonies all over the globe, among them Yucatan, Egypt, Babylon, and many others. All of today's civilizations are supposed to be the results of Lemurian colonization.

Could a thriving, highly advanced civilization called Lemuria have existed as far back as 12,000 years ago? Scientists say no, but some occultists maintain the Lemurians may have civilized the ancient world (*Mary Evans Picture Library*).

Exactly 30 years earlier, he told enraptured listeners, he had come upon a curious patch of rock on a Shasta cliff. As he examined it closely, he discovered that it blocked the entrance to a cave. He dug through the rocks and found debris and brush at the cave mouth. The more he dug, the more interesting things got, and soon he was looking down into a tunnel going down deep into the mountainside. Eventually, he found rooms of copper and gold plates as well as shields, swords, and statues. From the look of things, the occupants had left in a hurry. In due course he came upon the skeletons of giants, the smallest a mere six and a half feet (two meters) tall, the largest more than 10 feet (three meters). There were 27 in all.

Brown was vague about what he did during the next three decades, except to note that he had learned the artifacts were of Lemurian origin. He had come to the decision that they should be shared with the larger world, and now he wanted to organize an expedition—at his own expense—to recover the materials at the place only he knew. So every night for six weeks prominent and other Stockton residents—80 of them—met with Brown to plot the expedition, as visions of untold riches danced in their heads. Brown promised them a yacht so that all could go north by water. They would leave at 1:00 PM on Tuesday, June 19.

Brown didn't show, and he was never seen again.

A 1957 advertising brochure distributed by the Chambers of Commerce of three Shasta-area towns (including the municipality of Mount Shasta) took note of the tradition as it had evolved by mid-century: "It is a part of the legend that a druggist in Weed is [the Lemurians'] contact for necessary supplies"—though one suspects fakelore here—an inside joke for the amusement of local business operators. The article goes on, "The entrances to their caves are supposed to be in Bolam Canyon on the north side of Mount Shasta."

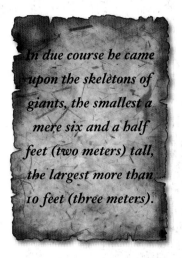

In due course he came upon the skeletons of giants, the smallest a mere six and a half feet (two meters) tall, the largest more than 10 feet (three meters).

The Black City

In a rambling feature published in the *Winnipeg Free Press* in March 1941, Charles W. Montrose wrote that a "Black City of the Clouds" figures in the legends of American Indian tribes in northwestern Canada. Not only that, according to Montrose, but living persons reported that they had seen it themselves. The city sits atop a peak in the Mackenzie Mountains, along the Yukon Territory-Northwest Territories border, over valleys that are lush and tropical in spite of its location. These valleys, like the city, are unknown to conventional geography because they are hidden in vast unexplored territory "between the 55th parallel and the Arctic circle." Among Montrose's supposed informants was a trapper who, though he had since "mysteriously disappeared," had raised vegetables of an immense size over a matter of a few weeks.

The Black City of the Clouds gets its color from the volcanic rock—basalt—from which it is constructed. The individual buildings are "architectural marvels," occupied by beautiful golden-haired, golden-skinned people who are advanced in science and spirit. They have ready access to a rich variety of precious and semi-precious metals. Witnesses—unnamed—have seen "strange, multicolored lights that at certain times of the year, or under particular conditions, blaze from these mountain tops with great brilliance and a fierce intensity—of airships of strange design which, minus roaring motors and blasting propellers, rose vertically into the air from the depth of the valley and disappear with incredible speed."

If Montrose's larger story is unbelievable, no other available source mentions legends or reports of a Black City of the Clouds in the area in question (perhaps his is an embellished or garbled version of the Silent City, see below)—the reference to strange flying objects is interesting. Precisely similar phenomena have been reported in abundance as UFOs since the early summer of 1947 but were almost entirely unknown to any except direct witnesses before that. So perhaps Montrose picked up on *something* with a degree of factual content.

An enthusiastic, uncritical consumer of occult literature, Montrose linked the Black City and its golden residents to Lemuria, though affording them more physical beauty than other accounts conceded (see above). The Black City was tied to another Lemurian outpost, Mount Shasta. "The same type of airship that legend has rearing silently out of the Shangri-La of the Mackenzies has often been reported as having been seen by settlers living in the vicinity of California's sacred mountain," he noted. "The same invisible force or wall of invisible resistance which is reported to guard and block the passes leading to the Black City has actually been experienced ... [by] the curious who sought to view the sacred rites or festivals conducted by original Lemurians in the vicinity of Mount Shasta." Even forest fires could not penetrate the invisible shield.

Around 1937 the mysterious gentle, bearded men who came down the mountain to purchase supplies (paid for with pure gold) in the nearby small town of Weed ceased appearing. Area residents also stopped seeing weird lights and other odd manifestations on the mountain, leading Montrose to surmise that "the Lemurians have gone north ... to join their brethren and the 'golden ones' in the Black City of the Clouds."

The Secret City

The era of flying saucers started with a June 1947 sighting of a fleet of nine shiny discs over the northern Cascade range (Shasta, as noted, is on its southern edge). As saucers entered the imaginations of, among others, mystically inclined Americans, it was inevitable that they would be fully incorporated into the evolving Shasta (and larger occult) mythology.

Like everywhere else, the Shasta region had its share of UFO sightings, of mysterious nocturnal lights and puzzling close encounters, but for the occultists they were somewhere between validation of pre-existing beliefs or just a kind of background noise. The hard-core Shasta lore would draw on terrestrial lost race and extraterrestrial beings in equal measure, and most of all, it would focus on contact and communication. As with some saucer contactees who identified themselves as space visitors, the latter twentieth century would produce self-identified Lemurian inhabitants of the mountain.

"Commander X"[2] sums up the major threads of current Shasta-focused New Age lore:

> The Lemurians ... are often seen wandering in the region. They can be recognized due to the fact that they are quite tall in the eight and nine feet (three meters) tall range. They even have their own underground city here, and it's all made of gold. Even the nature spirits—the knomes [sic], the elves and the fairies—run about here non-disturbed, and many "outsiders" will tell you that they've heard the sound of far away flutes, which are the favorite instrument of the elemental kingdom. The only "unusual dweller" around these parts I might be the least cautious about would be our hairy friend Bigfoot, who has been known to scare the living hell out of hikers

who go away not being such "happy campers," mainly due to the somewhat nonappealing scent he has been known to toss off....

Mt. Shasta has a highly charged aura which prevents the forces of darkness from penetrating anywhere nearby. Teams of Lemurians, Space Brothers and elementals[,] working jointly, meditate daily underground here to heal the planet and to keep this sacred spot safe from either physical or mental attack. Those that have been in the tunnels underground are never the same, their whole life so changed by what they have seen and heard!

In the original draft of the Lemurians-in-Shasta narrative, only a few hundred lost continentals resided within the mountain. Now, however, the Lemurian population numbers more than a million. According to a self-described Lemurian, a young blond woman named Bonnie, the actual population is a million and a half. There is a vast city, five stories high, called Telos. It, or in any event its bottom floor, is located approximately a mile under Shasta—notwithstanding the earlier tradition that Lemurians live in a few small, isolated villages.

(The first floor, by one account, is devoted to government, education, and commerce. The second comprises both factories and houses. The third consists of hydroponic gardens which produce fruits and vegetables for the entire population; Lemurians do not eat meat. On the fourth level gardens, factories, and nature parks coexist. The last floor is a vast natural refuge, where animals, some extinct on the surface, coexist peacefully. "Those that might be carnivorous on the surface," veteran New Age promoter Timothy Green Beckley reports in *The Smoky God and Other Inner Earth Mysteries* [1993], "now enjoy soy steaks.... Here you can romp with a Sabor [sic] Tooth Tiger.")

Bonnie—a real person, as opposed to the usual, in other words, a vision, a voice in the head, or a disembodied entity pushing a pen in an automatic writer's hand—was interviewed by contactee-oriented saucer enthusiast Bill Hamilton. He notes her "almond-shaped eyes and small perfect teeth" and "sincere, cheerful, and rational" manner. She told him she was born in 1951. According to Hamilton, "Bonnie, her mother, her father, Ramu [also the name of a Saturnian friend of California contactee George Adamski], her sister Judy, her cousins Loræ and Matox, live and move in our society, returning frequently to Telos for rest and recuperation." Via an intercontinental subterranean transit system they keep in touch with other Lemurian and Atlantean colonies, including an important one under the Brazilian jungle. The Lemurians control an advanced technology, including spacecraft; some UFOs are actually Lemurian vehicles. In fact, the Lemurians, extraterrestrials by ancestry, arrived here 200,000 years ago from the planet Aurora.

A channeled entity named Princess Sharula ("love" in Solara Maru, or the Solar Language, spoken by Lemurians) Aurora Dux, 267 years old in 1990 (she "looks 30"), also lives in Telos, one of more than 100 cities inside the earth. In her capacity as official ambassador to the surface world, she has related that interstellar spaceships from the "Ashtar Command," with which Telos is allied, come to the mighty city on a regular basis. "The typical Telosian," Sharula says, "has a slightly golden tone to his skin....

In "The Lemurian Documents" by J. Lewis Burtt, published in a July 1932 issue of *Amazing Stories,* Burtt imagined what Lemurian technology and architecture might have looked like (*Mary Evans Picture Library*).

The men are generally 7' to 7'6" in height and the women are generally 6'6" to 7'1" in height. When we come to the surface we have a process of altering the molecules in our bodies so that we are able to appear the same height as people here on the surface."

Telosians enjoy a perfect social order without conflict, hunger, or pollution. The United States government has known of them, according to Sharula, "since the country's conception. It is only near the turn of the [last] century that they started taking action. This action"—the attempt to persuade Telosians to share their technological secrets—"did not get real aggressive until the 1950s."

An alleged experience in September 1993 takes the legends back to the traditional supernatural lore of elvin folk known to the region's original tribal peoples. In *Fate* magazine (September 1994) Karen Maralee wrote of a three-day camping trip to Shasta. On her last evening, as she was walking alone, she heard tinkling sounds and the voices of singing children to her right. She strolled quietly through the trees toward the source. In a small clearing she observed "11 tiny blue fairies, perhaps one foot tall, and seemingly transparent.... The blue color was electric, seeming to pulsate or flicker.... The wings were larger than the fairy bodies themselves."

As she watched, the figures continued to dance, first clockwise in a circle, then counterclockwise, singing all the while, though the words, if words they were, seemed indecipherable. Maralee observed all this literally breathless. When finally, however, she had to exhale, the sound startled the figures who, suddenly realizing they were being observed, turned to stare at her. Then they leaped upwards and vanished.

Maralee claims to have found "fairy dust"—or anyway, 11 piles of blue dust—at the site. "The substance felt like fine sand and was slightly warm to the touch," she stated.

Further Reading:

Commander X [Jim Keith]. *Underground Alien Bases.* New Brunswick, NJ: Abelard Productions, 1990.

Karen Maralee described seeing dancing, blue-colored tiny fairies whose singing was like that of children (*iStock*).

Frank, Emilie A. *Mt. Shasta: California's Mystic Mountain.* Hilt, CA: PhotograFix Publishing, 1998.

Kafton-Minkel, Walter. *Subterranean Worlds: 100,000 Years of Dragons, Dwarfs, the Dead, Lost Races and UFO from Inside the Earth.* Port Townsend, WA: Loompanics Unlimited, 1989.

Leadabrand, Russ, "That Legend," *Pasadena* [California] *Independent* (October 2, 1957).

Montrose, Charles W., "Black City of the Clouds," *Winnipeg Free Press* (March 1, 1941).

Robbins, Dianne. *We Are Not Alone: Messages from the Hollow Earth and the Subterranean City of Telos.* Mount Shasta, CA: Mt. Shasta Light Publishing, 2000.

Walton, Bruce, ed. *Mount Shasta: Home of the Ancients.* Mokelumne Hill, CA: Health Research, 1986.

A Sunken Continent of the Mind: Cayce's Atlantis

Edgar Cayce, the "sleeping prophet," was born on March 18, 1877, near Beverly, in Christian County in southwestern Kentucky, a few miles from the Tennessee border. He was the son of Leslie Cayce—also called "The Squire," he was a small landowner and sometime justice of the peace—and his wife, Carrie. Besides Edgar, the Cayces had four daughters. Two others, a boy and a girl, died in infancy.

From a very early age, Cayce was not quite like anybody else. When young Edgar—"Eddy" then—was four, a freak accident killed his beloved grandfather Tom Cayce as the two were out riding horses. Soon, while living temporarily with an aunt and uncle as his parents cared for Tom's widow, Eddy claimed to hold regular conversations there with his grandfather.

In life, according to family tradition, Tom possessed remarkable psychic powers. In death, according to his grandson, he resumed his old habit of watching over farmhands as they hung tobacco to dry in the barn. Though the workers were unaware of his presence and his directions to them now were only—if that—intuitively grasped, Eddy related, he was able to perceive his grandfather's apparitional form in beams of sunlight that shone through cracks between the ceiling rafters. Cayce biographers allege that the boy unnerved relatives when he related obscure, closely held family-history matters which he insisted his grandfather had imparted in their conversations in the barn. His devout relatives feared that he was under the devil's influence.

A Window into Other Worlds

At the age of three, he stumbled and fell on a board with a protruding nail, which penetrated his skull and pierced his brain. Fortunately, his father, who saw it happen, was there immediately to remove the nail, and his mother bandaged him after

After suffering a head injury, Edgar Cayce said he could see a variety of spiritual beings, including fairies and sprites (*BigStock*).

pouring turpentine into the open wound. Eddy recovered soon, at least to appearances, and soon resumed his normal youthful activities. This was not the only occasion in his youth that Cayce would suffer a potential (or actual) brain injury, possibly affording at least a partial explanation of the extraordinary states of altered consciousness and perception that would recur throughout his lifetime.

In his fourth year "little folk" became his frequent companions. Cayce would maintain all of his life that they were not imaginary playmates but spirit entities—mostly, the souls of boys and girls, first only seven or eight in number, awaiting reincarnations into their physical bodies—who were there to prepare him for challenges and difficulties that he would encounter in later years. When he moved in with his uncle and aunt, the number of spirit entities multiplied as relatives, including parents, joined them. They were no longer interested in childish pursuits; now they wanted to teach him. The adult Cayce claimed that while the beings were invisible to everybody else, his friend Hallie "Little Annie" Seay, one year older than Eddy, also saw them. They liked her and enjoyed answering her many questions.

Once they encountered a different variety of little folk. One day, they noticed an unmoored boat that had drifted on to the sand along Little River. On impulse they boarded it and sailed it on the water till they came to a tiny island. They climbed out of the boat and proceeded to entertain themselves with their usual pursuits. In short order their supernatural friends joined them.

At one point, Cayce would write in his autobiography, the spirits showed them some smaller entities of varying colors and shapes. He described them as fairies or sprites. They were unfriendly, evincing no interest in human beings in general and children in particular. Cayce's account accords more closely to the traditional fairies of world folk belief than to the sentimental fairies of popular Victorian children's literature to which young Eddy would have been exposed. Little Annie, who died of pneumonia in January 1892, never provided an independent account, and Cayce's claims about her involvement rest solely on his own testimony.

Another defining early experience took place in 1889, after he'd retired to his bedroom after a day spent in good part reading scripture. In the middle of the night, he found himself ascending slightly into the air as a "glorious light as of the rising morning sun seemed to fill the whole room and a figure appeared at the foot of my bed." Surprised and confused, Eddy could only deduce that it was his mother, but he got no answer when he called out her name. When the figure vanished, he went off to check his mother's whereabouts. She told him she had not been in his room. On his return the apparition made a second appearance. This time Eddy recognized it, surely not coincidentally, as an angel bearing a noteworthy resemblance to one illustrated in his aunt's Bible, with which he was well familiar. The angel told him his prayers had been answered, urged him to be faithful and true, and predicted that he would help the sick and afflicted.

Eddy attracted attention in his area for his keen intelligence, eloquent speaking, and remarkable powers of memorization, sometimes so fantastic as to seem clairvoyant (as when he allegedly committed books and documents to memory by sleeping—or even just laying his head for a few moments—on them). Though most who knew him thought of him as good-hearted and friendly, he was seen by some as different and thus—in their fearful judgment—an intolerable presence. The religious thought he had the devil in him, and the more secular diagnosed him as mentally ill. All of this led to trouble from teachers, classmates, and church folk (though Cayce was a Bible-memorizing Christian, if an unconventional one, to the end of his life). Conflict and hostility drove him from school by the eighth grade, and he never returned. From then on, his education would be an autodidact's, informed by wide if erratic reading as well as by the many and diverse people he would meet in the decades ahead.

One afternoon in November 1892, toward the end of his school career, another pivotal life event occurred. During recess he was playing ball with schoolmates when a baseball struck him in the lower spine. In his sister Annie's account—she was on the playground at the time—Eddy fell over, then got back on his feet, apparently unhurt. Back in his class, however, he began to behave strangely, speaking up, joking, and insulting others, actions uncharacteristic of Eddy in his normal state. On the way home he jumped in front of cars, rolled in the ditches, and smiled maniacally all the while. When he continued to conduct himself in this unusual fashion at home, his mother angrily ordered him to bed after dinner.

As soon as he lay down, he seemed to enter yet another unusual state. While still apparently fully conscious, he embarked on an odd, rambling discourse, covering a range of subjects. One was a secret illicit relationship between two of the county's most respected men—something, his father believed, Eddy could not have known about. Once he shouted, "Hooray for Cleveland!", announcing that Grover Cleveland was winning the Presidential race, as in fact he was, even though news of his victory did not reach the rural district until later. Most significantly, however, Eddy provided specific directions to his parents on how they might cure him of his affliction. They were to gather herbs, corn mush, and other household food items and place them in a poul-

(Continued on page 28)

Robson's Island

The *S.S. Jesmond,* carrying a cargo of dried fruits, was sailing in the open Atlantic on its way to New Orleans one night in early March 1882. Its captain was the Ireland-born David A. Robson. This much of the story seems undeniably true. It may also be true that while at latitude 26° north and longitude 22° west, Robson and his crew noticed masses of dead fish extending all about them for miles. (Independent accounts from the period and location speak of the same phenomenon, presumably the consequence of natural or artificial water pollution.) The dreary, disturbing sight went on and on as the ship plowed through the darkness. An exhausted Robson went to bed.

What is said to have happened next, reported in the *New Orleans Daily Picayune* a month later, is—to put it charitably—less certainly true. Nonetheless the tale, playing to people's fascination with lost lands and civilizations, lives on to this day in alternative-reality literature, sometimes (as in the late Charles Berlitz's 1984 bestseller, *Atlantis: The Eighth Continent*) represented as possible evidence of Atlantis. Modern writer William L. Moore observes that the area is "located on exactly the same extensive volcanic fault as the Azores—islands long associated with the Atlantis legends."

Loud, insistent knocking at his door roused the sleeping Robson the next morning. His second officer excitedly informed him that they were in sight of land, though charts showed nothing there, only 2,000 fathoms of water. After confirming the alert with his own eyes, Robson immediately slowed the ship for fear of collision with reefs. Soundings indicated that the sea bed beneath the *Jesmond* was only 300 feet (91 meters) deep, as opposed to the 12,000 feet (366 meters) of the charts.

Some distance ahead loomed an uncharted island with smoking peaks. At 10 miles (16 kilometers), with the water growing ever more alarmingly shallow, Robson dropped anchor and boarded a boat that took him, a third officer, and a boarding party to the shore. There was no beach, he found, only an extended, apparently lifeless stretch of land littered with volcanic debris and, in the distance, mountains with ongoing volcanic activity. After landing on the island's western edge, the men tried to enter the interior, but rocks, boulders, and steam made the going difficult, dangerous, and finally not worth the effort.

Not knowing what else to do, the crew congregated by the shore and considered the options. One man, nervously picking at the ground with his boat hook, unearthed what looked like a flint arrowhead. This naturally generated considerable excitement. Tools were procured from the *Jesmond,* and frantic digging ensued. In due course the men found two huge stone walls, and between them an entrance. They made their way down into it, walking carefully through the rubble until at length they came to a massive collection of artifacts attesting to the presence of an unknown people who had once lived on or colonized the mysterious island.

It took a day and a half to take the materials off the island and into the mother ship. They included quantities of spears, swords, tools, and vases, sometimes engraved with unrecognizable hieroglyphics-like writing. Most spectacularly, there were the remains of two bodies. One consisted of some bones and a nearly complete skull, and the other was a mummy laid in a stone sarcophagus.

The second evening, the weather turned threatening, and Robson was forced to abandon his plan to continue looting the island of its treasures. The men returned to the ship and sailed off, with Robson expressing the hope that he and his crew would be able to revisit the island on their return trip to England.

On April 1 the ship was safely at harbor in New Orleans. An individual identified as the *Daily Picayune* shipping reporter interviewed Robson at a seaside tavern. The next day the paper ran a story based on that alleged interview, asserting the claims recounted above.

Like many other newspapers of the period, the *Picayune* ran dubious and fictional stories as supposed news. Many such yarns were made up in the editorial offices. Stories published on or near April Fool's Day are particularly suspect. On the first, in fact (or perhaps in fiction), the *Picayune* noted casually that recently a ship arrived at New York had mentioned "having sighted a new volcanic island" at close to the same location claimed for the Robson discovery. (A New York paper, on the other hand, said nothing of such but focused on the stormy weather the ship and crew had endured in the course of their voyage.) The *Picayune* "interview," of course, supposedly occurred on April 1, even if the story ran the next day.

A rival newspaper, the *Times-Democrat*, remarked briefly on the arrival of the *Jesmond* at New Orleans on the first and mentioned it several more times over the week the ship remained in port. It also says its passage had been "ordinary."

Needless to say, the alleged mass of enigmatic archaeological artifacts has proved as elusive as Robson's island. Or, possibly more to the point, just as nonexistent.

Further Reading

Ellis, Richard. *Imagining Atlantis*. New York: Alfred A. Knopf, 1998.

Moore, William L. "Captain Robson's Lost Island." *Fate* 38, 7 (July 1985): 70–75.

(Continued from page 25)

Edgar Cayce (*Mary Evans Picture Library*).

tice to the back of his head. The request, coming from someone who was already making them feel uneasy, so unnerved the Cayces that they refused to comply. More accepting of ostensible psychic communications, Eddy's grandmother Sarah Cayce, however, moved promptly, and by morning the boy was well.

In December 1893 the family moved into Hopkinsville, Christian County's commercial center and largest town, with a reputation as a wide-open place (nicknamed "Hoptown") with gunmen, gamblers, and prostitutes prominent among the citizenry. Reluctant to abandon his rural roots—and still troubled by the memory of a murder he had witnessed on the city's streets when he was visiting as a small child—Eddy moved in with relatives in the country and continued to farm.

Over the next months vivid dreams featuring mystical figures and symbols haunted his nighttime imagination; in a recurring series of images, a veiled woman led him across landscape and stream. Then one day in June 1894, as he repaired a broken plow in an open field, a wave of warmth and comfort suddenly engulfed him. The last time he had encountered that sensation, the angel appeared to him. A voice then told him, "Leave the farm. Go to your mother. Everything will be all right." He was in Hopkinsville by evening and never looked back.

Cayce as Healer and Prophet

Young Cayce's first major job in Hopkinsville was at the Hopper Bookstore, a general-interest establishment and not, as skeptics would subsequently assert, an occult-oriented business. His experience there would mark the beginning of his opening to the wider world, though Cayce would remain at heart a provincial country boy whose worldview, if not one congenial to Southern fundamentalists, and literary tastes were unshakably Bible-centered.

For a few months Cayce and his father entered into a partnership selling insurance. The 23-year-old Cayce did well at his new job until he began to suffer from debilitating headaches. On April 18, 1900, on a business trip to Elkton, 20 miles (32 kilometers) east of Hopkinsville, he sought relief from a local physician. The doctor prescribed a white powder which Cayce was to mix in water and swallow. The young man returned to his hotel room and did just that—with disastrous consequences.

The next thing he knew, he was in bed in the Cayce family home. A family friend had found him, behaving oddly, at the Elkton train station and accompanied him on the trip to Hopkinsville. Cayce had no memory of this, and besides the amnesia, he was nearly without voice, able to speak in no more than a whisper. At first assumed to be temporary, the condition continued, even worsened, in the weeks and months ahead as physicians, family members, and his fiancée, Gertrude Evans, looked on despairingly.

Unable to work as an insurance salesman any longer, Cayce took a job as an apprentice in a photography studio, to learn skills that would serve him well in his later professional life. When a stage hypnotist passed through town, friends urged Cayce to see if the man—Stanley "The Laugh King" Hart—might be able to cure him of his ailment. Remarkably, when Hart hypnotized Cayce, the young man spoke in a normal voice. When out of hypnosis, however, he relapsed back into the whisper. Even with posthypnotic suggestion, the laryngitis stubbornly persisted.

Though others tried to help Cayce, things got only worse. Even brief, whispered speech grew steadily more painful. Then in the winter of 1901 Al Layne, a Hopkinsville man with a mail-order degree in osteopathy and an involvement in hypnotism, began treating him. As before, the hypnotized Cayce spoke without impediment. Again, however, posthypnotic suggestion had no effect. Then a medical consultant offered the provocative suggestion that Layne should address Cayce's unconscious mind directly and ask it to diagnose the affliction.

The experiment was conducted at the Cayce residence on the afternoon of March 31, with Leslie and Carrie looking on (and Edgar's sisters Annie and Mary sneaking a view through the keyhole). Layne put Edgar into a hypnotic state and said, "You are now asleep and will be able to tell us what we want to know. You have before you the body of Edgar Cayce. Describe his condition and tell us what is wrong." After a few moments of inaudible mumbling Cayce's voice came through clearly: "Yes. We can see the body."

Referring to Cayce in the third person, the voice went on to characterize the vocal problems as of psychological origin. "Nerve strain" had paralyzed some of the vocal muscles. The problem could be cured through hypnotic suggestion that blood circulate through the affected area. As soon as Layne spoke the words, the voice replied that the circulation was starting to flow. Layne and the Cayces could see the neck and chest turn pink as the blood proceeded to flow so vigorously that Leslie loosened the collar to help its movement. Twenty minutes into the treatment, Cayce's voice declared, "The vocal chords are perfectly normal now. Make the suggestion that the circulation return to normal, and that after that the body awaken."

Once awake, Cayce spat into his handkerchief and soaked it with blood. Then he said, "Hello. Hey, I can talk."

He would suffer relapses about once a month for the next year, but each time they responded to the sort of treatment he underwent on March 31. Layne remarked that if Cayce could diagnose himself, he surely could do so for others, and he volunteered himself as the first test subject. In trance Cayce told Layne how to treat a persistent gastrointestinal inflammation with exercise and meditation. On awakening, Cayce had no memory of anything, and Layne had to show him his notes. He was subsequently cured.

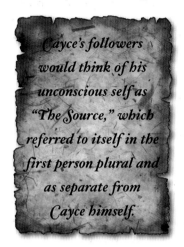

Cayce's followers would think of his unconscious self as "The Source," which referred to itself in the first person plural and as separate from Cayce himself.

Thus was Cayce's career as psychic healer launched. At first those who approached him were confined to family members and local friends, but as time went by, Cayce's fame spread, and soon requests for treatment were arriving in the mail from strangers who had read about his gifts in newspaper articles. Cayce found that he could conduct readings at a distance with persons he had not met or would ever meet. He asked only for voluntary donations and never got rich from his apparent clairvoyance, even when he tried to use it in business ventures, notably in Texas oil fields in the 1920s. As always, he had no conscious memory of what he spoke while entranced.

Cayce's followers would think of his unconscious self as "The Source," which referred to itself in the first person plural and as separate from Cayce himself. In later years alleged discarnates manifested through Cayce in the fashion of a more conventional spirit medium. Most spectacularly, a loud, haughty entity claiming to be the Archangel Michael appeared from time to time.

The stories told of Cayce's seemingly miraculous gifts remain, of course, contentious. Skeptics reject them, unsurprisingly, as inherently impossible, insisting that they amount to no more than anecdotes, regardless of apparent documentation. Only the most extreme critics, however, have judged Cayce anything other than honorably intentioned. He did not get rich from the exploitation of his talents. Numerous individuals swore that he healed them, and it is surely futile to quarrel with their assessments of their own health status. All that can be said with reasonable certainty, perhaps, is that our understanding of the world in some areas is far from firm, that personalities and abilities like Cayce's exist at the fringes of knowledge, and that at this stage conclusions about them ought not to be reached dogmatically.

Cayce died on January 3, 1945, but his work continues in the Virginia Beach-based Association for Research and Enlightenment (A.R.E.), founded in 1931. A small library of books, including several comprehensive biographies (the first published in 1943, the latest in 2000), examines Cayce's life, teachings, and related subjects.

Cayce on Atlantis

From 1923 onward, Cayce's readings often incorporated references to sitters' past lives, though reincarnation plays no role in Christianity. In fact, at first the comments—of which, as always, he had no conscious awareness and which, also as always, were pronounced in the first-person plural pronoun—startled and disturbed him. In due course he came to accept them and to believe that family members and close associates had all experienced numerous incarnations together. Many of these could be traced back to the lost continent of Atlantis.

The Atlantis stories amount to a creation myth, a marriage of Genesis to a fantastic tale presumably manufactured in Cayce's unconscious imagination, inspired in part by occult materials to which Cayce had been exposed. The telling of the epic took place over a period of years and involved some 600 life readings. Allusions to the subject go back to some of the first readings after 1923—with Atlantis referred to also as Alta or Poseidia—but early 1927 readings for Edgar Evans Cayce, Edgar's 14-year-old son, brought the subject into focus and made it clear, at least to those who took The Source at its word, that Atlantis was to be considered a "real" place, evidence for which still could be uncovered if one were willing to engage in the effort, however difficult, to seek it out.

On February 27, 1927, a life reading informed him that his already evident engineering and mechanical skills had come to him in a past life in Poseidia and that they had served him well through all subsequent incarnations. Three days later, in a follow-up reading in which the young Cayce asked questions about the nature of Atlantis, The Source began to provide details which eventually—especially through concentrated readings over a period in 1932—would lay out a rich, complex history of a magnificent kingdom from which all of humanity had sprung. Only Cayce's most devoted followers, some of them still endeavoring to prove the real-world truth of the readings, believe it to represent consensus-level reality. Still, it is quite a story.

It begins with God and, as in Genesis, his command "Let there be light." In this case, however, "light" meant a being named Amilius, the first soul entity God created around 10,000,000 years ago. Other souls, all of light, followed, but Amilius remained the principal one and uniquely close to the Creator. Together the two fashioned spirits in their image; these spirits headed earthward so that they could incarnate in self-generated physical forms. They sought experiences of taste, touch, smell, and sex unavailable to them as immaterial shapes. Unfortunately, contrary to plans, they found themselves trapped in inferior biological bodies, modeled on animals but with embellishments that generated satyrs, mermaids, unicorns, and other creatures preserved in mythological memory. Amilius transformed himself into Adam and, accompanied by "twin soul" Eve, manifested on Earth—in five different places at once with five different skin colors representing the varying races—in "superior" (present-day *Homo sapiens*) physical form, intending to lead the other Earth entities back to God. White people appeared first in the Carpathian Mountains, black people in northern Africa, yel-

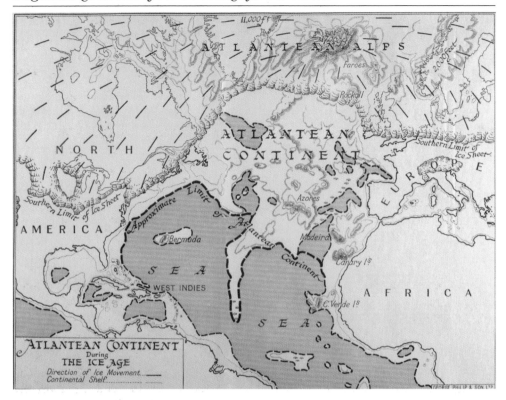

A 1933 map depicts the location of Atlantis during the time of the Ice Age, when the water levels of the oceans were much lower (*Mary Evans Picture Library*).

low people in the Gobi Desert, and brown people in the Andes and Lemuria. The people of Atlantis had red-hued skin.

The earliest civilized order to develop among the new humans—100,000 years ago—was Atlantis, where Amilius/Adam and other followers of God built a temple to celebrate the "law of one," what we would call Christ Consciousness. As large as Europe, Atlantis was a huge land mass stretching from the Gulf of Mexico to the Mediterranean—in other words all across the North Atlantic—with islands scattered around it. Its capital city was Poseidia, open and unwalled, situated on a hill overlooking the ocean.

The Atlanteans were giants whose diets consisted of fruits, nuts, vegetables, and goat's milk. A typical lifespan stretched a thousand years. Atlantis' technology was in many ways advanced even beyond our own. Their principal achievement was something called the Crystal, which provided heat and energy from the sun and the earth's interior. The Atlanteans possessed airplanes and submarines and had cracked the secret of antigravity. Even more spectacularly, they were skilled telepaths.

Conflict broke out between those who followed the law of one and the sons of Belial (a.k.a. those of Belial), the latter a movement centered on religious skepticism, materialism, hedonism, and selfish pursuits. Cayce's readings were usually rendered in a garbled, sometimes nearly incomprehensible prose which at times confounded even his sons, who tried in subsequent writings to explain what their father—or The Source—actually meant. Here is how Hugh Lynn Cayce, writing in 1935, deciphered the account of the dispute:

> Very early in Atlantean history, two factions arose that were deeply split over the issue of how to treat these souls that had become so entangled in matter.... The sons of the law of one were those who believed the soul was a gift from God and strove to keep the race pure, free from animal characteristics and appendages. They wanted to aid those deeply entangled in the physical world and help them regain their positions as creatures of God. The sons of Belial were those without standard or morality and believed in gratification of the senses without respect to others. They looked down on these entangled souls as "things" to be treated as slaves or machines.

Evidently, though, it was not this conflict that led to the first destruction of Atlantis around 50,700 B.C.E. The precipitating event was an attempt to protect the civilized world—which had now spread beyond that continent and into regions such as Egypt and India—against marauding giant land animals, sea serpents, and flying creatures. These monsters destroyed land and crops and menaced human beings, making life unbearable to those who were trying to conduct business. It is not wholly clear what these animals were supposed to be. Some readings make them sound like dinosaurs, others monstrous thought creations. In any event, a gathering of nations was held in Egypt—one country where the bestial hordes had yet to penetrate—where those attending discussed ways to slaughter the beasts into extinction via some sort of "death ray."

In a fashion less than clear, the ultimate consequence—apparently triggered in part by the misuse of the advanced Atlantean weapons technology in the anti-monster war—the earth's axis shifted. Much—albeit by no means all—of Atlantis was broken up, and the climates of the world's various regions changed so radically that the monsters died out. Many human beings fell victim to the cataclysm, too, and many Atlanteans fled to other islands and nations. A number survived on the continent, now reduced to a series of five islands, to rebuild and resume social and technological development over the next 22,000 years. Through Atlantis' history, the entity Amilius continued to reincarnate and, under different names, push his (or her; some incarnations were as a woman) countrymen in positive, productive directions while seeking to frustrate the nefarious schemes of those of Belial.

In 28,000 B.C.E. the second and final destruction of Atlantis took place, this time as a direct result of technology disastrously misapplied. The Atlanteans had developed some sort of enormous crystalline "power station" fueled by a "firestone." After it was "unintentionally turned too high," according to The Source, it ignited a shattering explosion, sparking massive volcanic activity and generating a tidal wave that swept across much of the world, to be remembered in legends of the Great Flood. The climate was altered again, possibly because of a polar shift.

Was the once-great Mayan civilization actually built by Atlanteans? (*iStock*)

Two of Atlantis' remaining five islands vanished beneath the water, leaving only Poseidia, Aryan, and Og. Many Atlanteans fled or migrated elsewhere, to serve the Law of One as religious leaders. Some went to Egypt, others to the Yucatan and Peru and to what would be the states of Nevada and Colorado. The Atlanteans had long since taken on more or less the appearance and height of human beings as we know them today. The Source described the average lost continental as "five feet ten inches [about two meters], weighing a hundred and sixty pounds; color as of gold that is burnished; yet keen of eye, gray in color. Hair as golden as the body. In activity alert, keen, piercing in vision, and of influence on those that approached."

Meanwhile, on the surviving Atlantis islands the dispute between the two factions went on, with one dominating for a period, then another. Laborers and the poor also battled for recognition and a rightful place, further roiling the already unstable social and political situation. Then, by around 11,000 B.C.E., authorities concluded that the remaining islands were also destined eventually to fall apart. Over the next thousand years, until the final disaster occurred, migrations sent Atlanteans around the globe, including into the interior of North America, where they would be remembered as the Mound Builders. In a November 12, 1933, reading, The Source reported:

> Then, with the leavings of the civilization in Atlantis (in Poseidia, more specific), Iltar—with a group of followers that had been of the household of Atlan, the followers of the worship of the *One*—with some 10 individu-

als—left this land Poseidia, and came westward, entering what would now be a portion of Yucatan. And there began, with the activities of the peoples there, the development into a civilization that rose much in the same manner as that which had been in the Atlantean land. [The reference is to the Mayans.] Others left the land later. Others had left the land earlier. There had been upheavals earlier from the land of Mu, or Lemuria, and these had their part in the changing ... when much of the contour of the land in Central America and Mexico was changed to that similar to [what] may be seen in the present.

Cayce, who made many predictions about coming events in the twentieth century, declared that Atlantis would rise from the depths in 1968 or 1969. He said that this extraordinary event would take place in a part of the Bahamas, the three-island chain of Bimini (North Bimini, South Bimini, East Bimini) 50 miles (80 kilometers) from the coast of Florida and a part of the Bahamas.

The Hunt for the Bimini Atlantis

In the 1930s, as the bulk of Cayce's Atlantis readings—remarkably consistent, if nothing else—were conducted, his followers were inclined to take his word, or at least not to search actively for verification. It would be some years before some adventurers were curious enough to go looking. The results would be disappointing. A sympathetic (if not entirely uncritical) observer, K. Paul Johnson, sums it up in a sentence: "There appears to be no case in which historical information in the readings that was not generally known at the time has subsequently been proven true." That, of course, prominently includes Atlantis.

From the 1960s to the present, explorations of the waters around Bimini have sought evidence of the lost continent. Some searchers, perhaps the most vocal of them David Zink, who photographed them, found a series of large, rectangular

(Continued on page 38)

A 1923 illustration from a Swedish journal speculated that the Azores are the last visible remnants of Atlantis (*Mary Evans Picture Library*).

Underwater Civilization

Ivan T. Sanderson (1911–1973) was a bright, articulate man, trained in zoology, botany, and geology at Cambridge University. He became an American citizen in 1947, while retaining his British citizenship. Until the last decade of his life, he traveled widely collecting animal specimens and writing popular books about wildlife around the world. In the 1950s, as a regular guest on television talk and variety shows, he presented specimens of exotic creatures. For a time he was something of a celebrity in the early television age.

There was another, less well-known side to Sanderson. It would come to dominate his life and career in the last decade and a half, though his interest in the world's mysterious and controversial phenomena had been sparked, he would claim, when he attended a lecture by Charles Fort, the influential author of books on anomalies. As early as 1948, in a *Saturday Evening Post* article, Sanderson proposed that dinosaurs still lived in remote regions of the earth. He would write one of the first books linking Sasquatch, Yeti, and related traditions of

Pioneering cryptozoologist Ivan T. Sanderson believed in the existence of the Yeti in the Himalayas, as well as other strange animals and zoological phenomena (*Richard Svensson/Fortean Picture Library*).

elusive hominids. He is recognized as a pioneer of cryptozoology, the protoscientific discipline devoted to studying the evidence for unknown, uncatalogued, and uncertainly extant animals. He closely followed UFO sightings and even conducted investigations in his role as science correspondent for a newspaper syndicate.

Elsewhere, he explored a range of extraordinary claims. These writings combine sometimes thin research with the most extravagant sorts of speculations. In one, for instance, he contended that ants practice teleportation. He also fell victim to a few outlandish hoaxes, including a 1948 case in which a prankster left giant three-toed tracks on a Florida beach. Sanderson's own on-site inquiries failed to uncover the fakery, and led him to the hypothesis that a giant, 15-foot-tall (4.6 meters) penguin was responsible. (The hoaxer confessed in 1988, long after Sanderson was gone.) Most of all, though, the chatty, egocentric Sanderson loved to tell stories, however dubious, and to spin theories, however woolly, for the sheer pleasure of giving expression to an unfettered imagination. Many of his listeners and readers took him seriously when he was simply being playful.

It is perhaps in this context that we ought to consider Sanderson's contention, outlined in one of his last books, *Invisible Residents,* that the earth's oceans harbor technologically advanced civilizations, undetected—

needless to point out—by us surface-dwelling humans. The book's subtitle is "A Disquisition upon Certain Matters Maritime, and the Possibility of Intelligent Life under the Waters of This Earth." He coined the faintly comic acronym "OINTS" from "Other Intelligences." In its conclusion Sanderson wrote with his characteristically droll wit, "That they are for the most part overcivilized and quite mad is, in my opinion, an open-ended question but quite probable."

Naturally, he brought UFOs into the equation, though he preferred "UAO," which could mean either "unidentified aerial object" or "unidentified aquatic object." (Sanderson allows for UFOs coming from other planetary bodies or more exotic places but is most interested in ones that represent shared Earth space.) *Invisible Residents* relates sightings of unidentified structures and lights above seas and fresh-water bodies, on them, and beneath them, and then proceeds to recount allegedly mysterious disappearances of ships and aircraft in areas Sanderson calls "vile vortices."

"Vile vortices" were an expansion of the notion of the "Bermuda triangle," a name invented by the veteran Fortean writer Vincent H. Gaddis (1913–1997) in a 1964 article for the men's adventure magazine *Argosy*. Though it was Gaddis who put those two words together, he did not create the idea of unexplained vanishings between the Florida coast and Bermuda. The first published piece to allege that the area was haunted and dangerous was an Associated Press account dated September 16, 1950, written by E.V.W. Jones. In *Fate* for October 1952, Florida writer George X. Sand detailed what he called a "series of strange marine disappearances, each leaving no trace whatever, that have taken place in the past few years" in a "watery triangle bounded roughly by Florida, Bermuda and Puerto Rico." The claim was picked up in 1950s UFO books by Donald E. Keyhoe and M. K. Jessup and in Frank

The Bermuda Triangle, marked off as the region between the tip of Florida, Puerto Rico, and the Bermuda Islands, has long been feared as a place where ships and planes mysteriously disappear or are destroyed (*Dezsö Sternoczky/SUFOI/Fortean Picture Library*).

(Continued from page 35)

stones, positioned in straight lines and sharp right angles, which they thought were a major archaeological discovery: an Atlantean road. Zink went on to write a whole book on the subject.

But skeptical archaeologists retorted that the stones, while real enough, were not artificially made. They were a perfectly natural formation formed by ordinary geological processes, they insisted. In May 2005 an expedition led by archaeologist William Donato and psychologist Greg Little uncovered artifacts with what appeared to be shaped or

Edwards' best-selling "true mysteries" collection *Stranger than Science* (1959). By the time Gaddis' article appeared, devotees of the mysterious had all the pieces together; all they lacked was a name.

Sanderson held that the Bermuda Triangle is only one of 10 vile vortices (actually a dozen, if one counts the polar regions). These are not actually triangles but lozenge-shaped areas, stretching in parallel bands above and below the equator, exactly 72° apart. In these regions meteorological and oceanic conditions are so radically unstable that they actually disrupt the space-time continuum, allowing visitors from elsewhere—other planets and dimensions—to establish undersea bases. These OINTS do not hesitate to take severe measures if they think someone or something threatens the secrecy with which they surround themselves and their activities. Thus, airplanes and marine vessels vanished from the face of the ocean, never to be heard of or from again. Beyond the jokey "overcivilized and quite mad" observation (perhaps better defined as a wisecrack), Sanderson had little more to say about these hypothetical beings, their natures, or their motives.

Subsequent research by Larry Kusche, Paul Begg, and others effectively discredited the Bermuda Triangle and related legends, which owe more to poor or nonexistent research than sinister OINTS. Overall, there is no evidence that marine disasters happen any more frequently in these areas than elsewhere, and most of the so-called inexplicable incidents turn out to have well-documented prosaic explanations.

Further Reading

Begg, Paul. *Into Thin Air: People Who Disappear*. North Pomfret, VT: David and Charles, 1979.

Kusche, Lawrence David. *The Bermuda Triangle Mystery—Solved*. New York: Harper and Row, 1975.

Sanderson, Ivan T. *Invisible Residents: A Disquisition upon Certain Matters Maritime, and the Possibility of Intelligent Life under the Waters of the Earth*. New York: World Publishing Company, 1970.

manipulated by human beings. Little and Donato are harshly critical of skeptical claims, arguing that the assertions are based on inadequate to nonexistent investigation and, beyond that, misrepresentation of the evidence. Little theorizes that the artifacts are from a "maritime culture" which perhaps 4,000 years ago set up a harbor in Bimini. The issue "doesn't relate in any way to Edgar Cayce, Atlantis, or any other fantastic claims," says Little (notwithstanding his and his wife Lora's long membership in the A.R.E. and involvement in New Age thought)—but in fact needs to be viewed in the context of ongoing controversies over the early dates for the peopling the Americas. "What has been discovered about the ancient past in the Americas since 1997," Little rightly notes, "has almost completely altered the history that had been accepted since the 1930s."

It may well be that revelatory archaeological discoveries await further documentation in the waters off Bimini, but validation of Cayce's Atlantis teachings remains an unlikely prospect.

Further Reading:

Cayce, Edgar Evans. *Edgar Cayce on Atlantis*. New York: Hawthorn Books, 1968.

Cayce, Edgar Evans, Gail Cayce Schwartzer, and Douglas G. Richards. *Mysteries of Atlantis Revisited*. New York: St. Martin's Paperbacks, 1988.

Johnson, K. Paul. *Edgar Cayce in Context: The Readings: Truth and Fiction*. Albany: State University of New York Press, 1998.

Kirkpatrick, Sidney D. *Edgar Cayce: An American Prophet*. New York: Riverhead Books, 2000.

Little, Greg. *Alternate Perceptions Magazine online* (November 2005). http://www.mysterious-america.net/Resources/Bimini%20HarborScreen2.pdf.

Robinson, Lytle, ed. *Edgar Cayce's Story of the Origin and Destiny of Man*. New York: Coward, McCann & Geoghegan, 1972.

Stearn, Jesse. *Edgar Cayce: The Sleeping Prophet*. Garden City, NY: Doubleday and Company, 1967.

Zink, David. *The Stones of Atlantis*. Englewood Cliffs, NJ: Prentice-Hall, 1978.

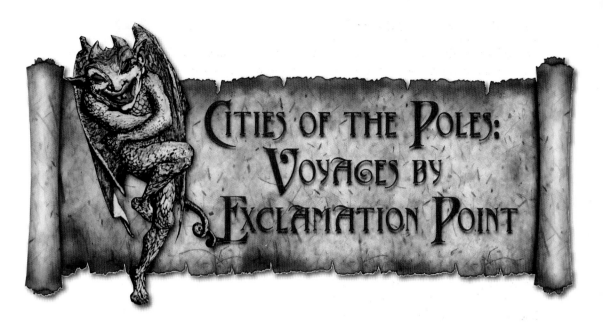

CITIES OF THE POLES: VOYAGES BY EXCLAMATION POINT

Over the course of a long career as editor and writer, Ray Palmer mastered the art of huckstering mystification. He energetically hawked outlandish claims, often having to do with hollow-earth lore. In 1959, when Palmer was editing the small-circulation magazine *Flying Saucers* out of Amherst, Wisconsin, he received two review copies of a vanity-press book titled *Worlds beyond the Poles,* by an obscure theorist/crank named F. Amadeo Giannini.

Giannini championed the unique notion that the earth is more or less splindle-shaped. The universe is not a vast near-emptiness, he argued, but an immense landscape of "physical continuity"; what we think are galaxies, stars, and planets are in truth "globular and isolated areas of a continuous and unbroken outer sky surface." All of this came together, he wrote in what one assumes to have been an unintentional effort to make already dubious notions even less believable, in a vision he experienced while strolling through a New England forest one day in 1926. Even Giannini acknowledged that his concept of the earth's and the universe's shape cannot be visualized except "psychically."

Author and book would have faded even deeper into the obscurity from which they emerged if Palmer hadn't found something in the volume to get his more excitable readers wound up. Giannini had a new wrinkle on the myth of polar openings into the inner Earth. It turned out that no less than the celebrated aviator and polar explorer Adm. Richard E. Byrd (1888–1957) had entered such an opening while on an expedition to the North Pole in early 1947. (He also thought the same had happened on a South Pole expedition in January 1956.)

In the December 1959 issue Palmer took this story but failed to credit Giannini (or hold him responsible) for it, asserting that he learned this extraordinary secret after "years of research." In his "research," Palmer wrote with what passed for a straight face, he had uncovered contemporary reports from the *New York Times* in which Byrd men-

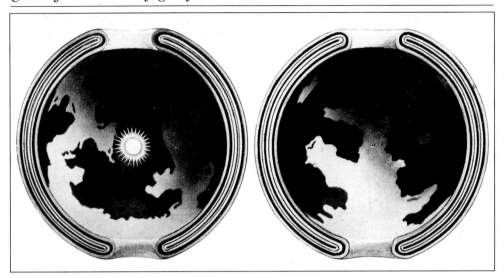

A 1912 illustration by Marshall Gardner shows an interior sun and oceans (*Mary Evans Picture Library*).

tioned seeing ice-free lakes, lush, green forests, mountains, and a giant, unknown animal, apparently a prehistoric mammoth, in a land 1,700 miles (2,735 kilometers) beyond the North Pole. These unexpected sights alerted him to the presence of an undiscovered land beneath the frozen polar region. (In 1956, similarly, Byrd allegedly flew 2,300 miles [3,700 kilometers] beyond the South Pole.) Palmer asserted that all of this is "well-authenticated.... At *both* poles exist unknown and vast land areas, not in the least uninhabitable, extending for distances which can only be called tremendous, because they encompass an area bigger than any known continental area!"

Not all readers chose to be wowed. A number wrote Palmer to point out the small consideration that in February and March 1947 Byrd was at the South, not the North, Pole. Moreover, as they determined easily, the *Times* had reported nothing about forests and mysterious beasts at the pole. Palmer was forced to concede that rather than having researched them on his own, he had taken these claims directly from Giannini. After that brief bow to the merely factual, however, he was off on a new and even more exotic tangent. Palmer suggests in his editorial in the February 1960 issue of *Flying Saucers*:

> Now, as to the HOW of our "serious error." Some time ago, we made a remark that there was a systematic effort being made to render the whole flying saucer story ridiculous. We promised to make this a particular point of attack, in the future, and name names, present facts. That time hasn't come yet. We can only say that we haven't changed our mind about this effort, and now, with the publication of the December issue ... and our claims in it, we are more certain than ever. In short, what we want to say is

that our statement that Byrd made a North Pole flight in 1947 to 1,700 miles [2,735 kilometers] BEYOND it, was a fishing expedition, for which we hope our readers will pardon us.

Not only has it not weakened our theory, it has strengthened it immeasurably, and also strengthened the theory that a systematic effort is being made to render flying saucers a subject of ridicule. In short, there were two alternatives—either Byrd made a SECRET flight over the North Pole in 1947, which NEVER hit the newspapers, or a deliberate effort was being made to build an edifice which could be toppled IF AND WHEN THE TRUTH CAME OUT ABOUT THE SOUTH POLE! There was only one way for this editor to discover if he had, somehow, missed the BIG story, the actual fact of a 1947 Byrd Polar flight as described, and by publication, he could ferret out the missed story. The whole thing was what you might term a "calculated risk."

Palmer continues in this vein of bafflegab for pages more in virtually unparaphrasable rhetoric. He does reject Giannini's cosmology as unworthy of serious consideration, then turns the subject to supposed mysteries of the polar regions, which leaves open the question of whether another world waits to be discovered within the earth. As usual Palmer was simply playing with his readers, and soon he abandoned these for other diversions.

✳
Domain of the Arianni

Palmer's nudge-and-wink twaddle would have left little mark outside the yellowing pages of old, modestly circulated *Flying Saucers* issues if not for the fact—and it is just about the only fact of the whole business—that in the 1970s a retired Marine Corps officer Tawani Shoush, also a member of the Modoc tribe, had not produced a remarkable document. Shoush, a Missouri man, headed something called the International Society for a Complete Earth. Because the organization sported a swastika logo and insisted the inner-earthers are "Nordic," outsiders perhaps could not be blamed for drawing unflattering conclusions about the group's political allegiances, but Shoush insisted he and his associates did not advocate Nazism (though not everybody would believe them). They did, however, hope to sail a dirigible into the North Pole hole, where they would meet the good folks who call the interior home. "The hollow Earth is better than our own world," Shoush told *Chicago Tribune* columnist Bob Greene in 1978, "and we can only speculate that we will feel like coming back." The expedition never happened—just as well, given the potentially fatal consequences to which serious misreadings of geography can lead the confused—and the organization hasn't been heard from in years.

It did, however, make a lasting contribution to fringe literature with a monograph it sold. The monograph purported to be the secret diary of Admiral Byrd from

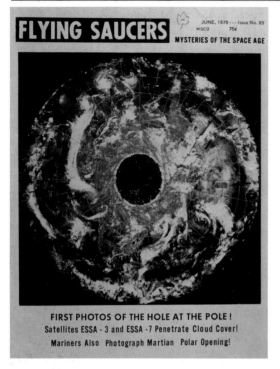

FLYING SAUCERS

JUNE, 1970 --- Issue No. 69
WISCO 75¢

MYSTERIES OF THE SPACE AGE

FIRST PHOTOS OF THE HOLE AT THE POLE !
Satellites ESSA - 3 and ESSA - 7 Penetrate Cloud Cover!
Mariners Also Photograph Martian Polar Opening!

A cover feature illustration from a 1970 issue of *Flying Saucers* **declares that a NASA photo clearly shows a gaping hole at the North Pole** (*Mary Evans Picture Library*).

his supposed 1947 North Pole expedition. Nothing about this is remotely believable, almost needless to say, starting with absurdly overwrought prose (replete not only with exclamation points, which sophisticated writers employ minimally, but multiple ones) bearing no resemblance to the erudite language the real Byrd used in his real writing. The prose reads exactly like ineptly executed pulp fiction, which of course is precisely what it is.

In any event, the bogus diary chronicles a flight starting in the morning of February 19, 1947. At 10:00 AM, four hours later, faux-Byrd notes: "We are crossing over the small mountain range and still proceeding northward as best as can be ascertained. Beyond the mountain range is what appears to be a valley with a small river or stream running through the center portion. There should be no green valley below! Something is definitely wrong and abnormal here! We should be over Ice and Snow! To the portside are great forests growing on the mountain slopes. Our navigation Instruments are still spinning, the gyroscope is oscillating back and forth!"

The plane descends to a thousand feet (300 meters). Byrd and radioman lose sight of the sun, and they see a mammoth and, soon after, green, rolling hills. Then, at 10:30, Byrd lets flies with the exclamation points:

Ahead we spot what seems to be a city!!!! This is impossible! Aircraft seems light and oddly buoyant. The controls refuse to respond!! My GOD!!! Off our port and starboard wings are a strange type of aircraft. They are closing rapidly alongside! They are disc-shaped and have a radiant quality to them. They are close enough now to see the markings on them. It is a type of Swastika!!! This is fantastic. Where are we! [sic] What has happened. [sic] I tug at the controls again. They will not respond!!!! We are caught in an invisible vice grip of some type!

Minutes later, a voice speaks through the radio. In a slight Scandinavian or German accent it welcomes the admiral to "our domain," then promises to land his plane "in exactly seven minutes." The aircraft is no longer under the crew's control. Within the promised period it descends and lands gently.

> I am making a hasty last entry in the flight log. Several men are approaching on foot toward our aircraft. They are tall with blond hair. In the distance is a large shimmering city pulsating with rainbow hues of color [an allusion to another staple of hollow-earth literature, Rainbow City; see below]. I do not know what is going to happen now, but I see no signs of weapons on those approaching. I hear now a voice ordering me by name to open the cargo door. I comply.

It is surely pointless to observe that if all of this had happened in real life, Byrd would have been far too preoccupied to be scrawling in his diary (and, of course, taking extra time to dot his sentences with all those exclamation points) even as events were unfolding. The rest of the story, however, is reconstructed "from memory," faux-Byrd writes.

The two explorers step aboard a platform without wheels and speed toward a glowing crystal city. There they are taken to a big building "out of a Buck Rogers setting!!" After consuming a warm, tasty beverage unlike any with which they are familiar, Byrd sees two men approach. They separate him from his companion and lead him a short distance to an elevator which descends to another floor. They walk down a long hallway until they reach a great doorway. As it opens, one of the men says, "Have no fear, Admiral, you are to have an audience with the Master."

As his eyes adjust to the "beautiful coloration" of a room too "wondrous to describe," he hears the voice of the Master, an elderly, handsome man seated at a long table. Byrd sits and listens, his remarkable memory recalling every word that the Master intones:

> We have let you enter here because you are of noble character and well-known on the Surface World, Admiral.... You are in the domain of the Arianni [better known as Aryans], the Inner World of the Earth. We shall not long delay your mission, and you will be safely escorted back to the surface and for a distance beyond. But now, Admiral, I shall tell you why you have been summoned here. Our interest rightly begins just after your race exploded the first atomic bombs over Hiroshima and Nagasaki, Japan. It was at that alarming time we sent our flying machines, the "Flugelrads," to your surface world to investigate what your race had done. That is, of course, past history now, my dear Admiral, but I must continue on. You see, we have never interfered before in your race's wars and barbarity, but now we must, for you have learned to tamper with a certain power that is not for man, namely that of atomic energy. Our emissaries have already delivered messages to the powers of your world, and yet they do not heed. Now you have been chosen to be witness here that our world does exist. You see, our Culture and Science is many thousands of years beyond your race, Admiral....

Your race has reached the point of no return, for there are those among you who would destroy your very world rather than relinquish their power as they know it. In 1945 and afterward, we tried to contact your race, but our efforts were met with hostility, our Flugelrads [flying saucers] were fired upon. Yes, even pursued with malice and animosity by your fighter planes. So, now, I say to you, my son, there is a great storm gathering in your world, a black fury that will not spend itself for many years. There will be no answer in your arms, there will be no safety in your science. It may rage on until every flower of your culture is trampled, and all human things are leveled in vast chaos. Your recent war was only a prelude of what is to yet to come for your race. We here see it more clearly with each hour....

We see at a great distance a new world stirring from the ruins of your race, seeking its lost and legendary treasures, and they will be here, my son, safe in our keeping. When that time arrives, we shall come forward again to help revive your culture and your race. Perhaps, by then, you will have learned the futility of war and its strife, and after that time, certain of your culture and science will be returned for your race to begin anew. You, my son, are to return to the Surface World with this message.

The forger of the diary has taken the message Space Brothers preached to flying-saucer contactees and put it into the mouth of an inner-earther. This is yet one more of multiple indications that the diary was composed in the 1970s.

The diary ends with a coda dated December 30, 1956, with the observation that "I have faithfully kept this matter secret as directed all these years. It has been completely against my values of moral right.... This secret will not die with me.... I HAVE SEEN THAT LAND BEYOND THE POLE, THAT CENTER OF THE GREAT UNKNOWN."

As laughable as all this may seem, the faux-Byrd diary is firmly ensconced in hollow-earth literature.[1] At least one writer has speculated that "Admiral Byrd's weird flight" was the secret inspiration for the International Geophysical Year, proposed in 1947 though not declared till a decade later. Not all hollow-earth advocates, however, have been fooled.

For example, Dennis G. Crenshaw, editor of *The Hollow Earth Insider,* has remarked that the Master's words are unsettlingly like those uttered by the Dalai Lama of Shangri-La in the 1937 film *Lost Horizon.* Crenshaw does not hide his suspicion that Tawani Shoush and his associates forged the document. Unfortunately, not content to let well enough alone, Crenshaw himself sails off into fantasyland, charging—on no visible evidence—that Giannini's family "*owned* the Bank of Italy and the Bank of America." Moreover, the "Illuminati and ... a New World Order ... John D. Rocherfeller [sic] and his pals" financed Byrd's polar expeditions in the service of a vast cover-up. The "One Worlders' plan" is to "cloud the water" by having "one of their own, an admitted [sic] member of an international banking family, toss in a controversy—such as this phony trip by Admiral Byrd—to make hollow earthers appear ... ridiculous."

Travelers stumble upon a hidden Shangri-La in *Lost Horizon,* a 1933 novel by James Hilton that was adapted to film in 1937 and again in 1973 (*Ronald Grant Archive / Mary Evans*).

One suspects, however, that they can manage that on their own.

Rainbow Quest

The origins of Rainbow City go back millions of years, to a long-forgotten time when the human race conquered and colonized worlds in the Milky Way Galaxy and dozens of other galaxies. Eventually, however, the humans encountered their nemesis: a race called the Snake People. The ensuing conflict dragged on inconclusively for a thousand years until at last events turned decisively in the Snakes' direction. The ancient humans were virtually destroyed, chased through space by vengeful Snakes until finally our ancestors found a few backwater worlds in which to hide and lick wounds. Among these planets was Mars, which sheltered the humans for a long time. Then the planet began to lose its oxygen, and the Great Ruler dispatched an exploratory fleet to the neighboring world, the third from the sun.

(Continued on page 51)

SILENT CITY

In the latter half of the nineteenth century, press accounts highlighted observations of what they called the "Silent City." The Silent City was a mysterious presence supposedly encountered, usually in the summer, typically between June 21 and July 10, in the sky over the Muir Glacier 150 miles (241 kilometers) north of Juneau, Alaska. Dubious-looking photographs of it or something similar (allegedly seen along the Alaska-Yukon border) were printed and sold as postcards. The latter are widely judged to be fakes, but the sightings comprise something of a historical and meteorological enigma.

In late 1890 the *Juneau Times* featured the testimony of a miner identified as George H. Kerson. (The article was reprinted in other newspapers all over North America.) "I think I am the first white man who ever gazed on the frozen city of the north," he said. And he did not mean the mirage; he insisted that he had seen the original two years earlier, while in northern Alaska on his way to a prospecting trip to the Yukon Territory. In Kerson's telling, at one point the party, traveling on the river, arrived at a fork. Kerson wanted to go one way, the rest the other. So he set off on his own after hiring two American Indian guides.

Weeks later, the three reached the foot of a mountain range where they set up camp for the winter. Soon the cold weather set in, sometimes with winds so bitter that the campers dared not leave their immediate location. One day when the temperature was relatively mild, Kerson suggested that they find something interesting to do, such as scale a nearby mountain. When one expressed interest, they embarked along the frozen river, following it for 20 miles (32 kilometers) until they reached their destination. Then:

We reached a plateau between the foothills and high range. Here the stream ended and we started to climb one of the big hills. After a lot of hard work we reached a point near the summit. A wonderful view was had from here, but the strangest thing was a city in one of the valleys....

At first I thought it was some fantastic arrangement of the ice and snow which had assumed the form of a city, but examination with a glass showed that such was not the case, it being too regular in appearance. It was a city, sure enough.

Determined to see more of it, I commenced to work downward.... After several hours of hard work I reached the outskirts of this mysterious city, and found that this place was laid out in streets, with blocks of strange looking buildings, what appeared to be mosques, towers, ports, etc., and every evidence of having been built by art.

The whole was of solid ice, or seemed to be, but blows from a hatchet on one of the walls disclosed the fact that beneath this barrier of ice was some sort of building material. It looked to be wood, but of stonelike hardness, and apparently petrified.

The silence around the place was something ghostly. Not the slightest sound broke the awful stillness of the place, which, added to the weird look of the empty streets, made it gruesome enough. I soon got tired of investigating the city, as the streets were blocked in many places with huge masses of ice, rendering passage almost impossible. [My companion], too, became uneasy, and we started on the return trip, reaching camp the next day, tired, but satisfied that we had been the first men to gaze on that silent city for centuries.

In an 1895 issue the *New York Sun* noted that "at least half a dozen white men profess to have seen the city, while the natives of the Alaska coast cherished the tradition of its existence." One witness, John M. White, "solemnly declares that he saw it on June 21 some years ago." According to the *Sun*:

He declares that he studied the mirage for nine hours through a powerful glass as it was spread above the glacier on the side of Mount Fairweather. He affirms that the city is walled; that its houses are battlemented and the chimneys surmounted by chimney pots; that within the walls there is

In 1895 a dozen men supposedly saw a spectacular walled city on the side of Mount Fairweather in Alaska (*iStock*).

a tall monument surrounded by the sculptured figure of an Indian in full headdress and feathers. His glass revealed to him some of the inhabitants, men in knee breeches and jackets. The only beast visible was a donkeylike creature, with a body as large as that of a horse.

The mirage appeared at first about 11:30 AM as a mist, and out of this rose the towers and battlements of the city as did those of ancient Troy. By noon the city was as clearly outlined as New York is from the Jersey heights.

White theorized that the city whose image was being reflected into the air existed "at the north pole on the edge of the traditional open polar sea." As evidence he pointed to a native Alaskan legend about a race of savage warriors who had passed through the region, on a rampage of murder and destruction. They became the ancestors, White speculated from no apparent evidence, of the present-day American Indians. The unknown race left behind others who lived, and continue to live, in a warm region near the North Pole. Since then these mysterious people have built a huge city.

Other, relatively more prosaic, but still problematic hypotheses tied the Silent City to Montreal or even Bristol, England (the latter an impossible 2,500

miles [about 4,000 kilometers] distant). In the summer of 1889, an investigator from Chicago, L. B. French, reportedly saw it near Mount Fairweather. "We could see plainly houses, well-defined streets, and trees," French told the *New York Times*. "Here and there rose tall spires over huge buildings, which appeared to be ancient mosques and cathedrals.... It did not look like a modern city—more like an ancient European city." He thought it could house as many as 100,000 residents.

As an 1897 expedition explored the wilderness near Mount St. Elias, its members spotted a vivid mirage above a glacier. One member, C.W. Thornton, wrote, "It required no effort of imagination to liken it to a city, but was so distinct that it required, instead, faith to believe that it was not in reality a city." It was clearly visible for half an hour, then slowly faded away, leaving a rocky ridge in its place.

The Silent City is little heard of these days, except as an example of a mirage-generated legend. No earthly city plausibly fits witnesses' descriptions, so efforts to explain the phenomenon now insist that the city's reported features amounted to no more than optical illusions and imaginings, if not outright fiction.

Further Reading

X. "Cities in the Sky." *Whig-Standard Magazine*, 12, 14 (January 19, 1991): 22.

(Continued from page 47)

On their return the visitors informed the ruler that they had found a pleasant, fertile place that would sustain human life. Some thousands sailed from Mars to Earth, settling in the area that is now Antarctica, then a warm and tropical land, to construct seven cities, each with its own color in the Martian fashion. Each was named after its color—Red City, Blue City, and the like. The greatest of the seven, Rainbow City, consisted in its entirety of plastic colored like the rainbow. The colony was governed from here, with the son and daughter of the Great Ruler, along with the daughter's fiancé, himself the son of a leading political figure. The ancients were giants, seven to eight feet (2.4 meters) tall. They developed a kind of teleportation system to move cargo around the globe and as far as the moon. They also constructed an immense subway infrastructure, with trains shooting at 2,000 miles (3,218 kilometers) per hour through vast tunnels that spanned the earth.

A golden age followed, but it ended when the Snakes attacked the earth, flipping it on its side. That caused Antarctica to become the frozen wasteland we know today. The residents of the seven cities were scattered, left to find their way northward toward more temperate climes. Over time—the calamitous event occurred a million years ago—they lost their advanced knowledge and technology and even an awareness of their own history. All that remained were vague myths of a magical era when wise and benevolent gods ruled the earth.

Today, Rainbow City lies under 10,000 feet (3,048 meters) of ice, unknown and inaccessible to all but a handful of persons who are reincarnated ancients from the ruling family. The Ancient Three were, many incarnations ago, the son, daughter, and fiancé, "the Ancient Three, 'Who were, Who are, Who will be, Always.'" They live in a community of mystical masters beneath Tibet.

Or so claimed a Livingston, Montana, couple named William C. and Gladys Hefferlin, who surfaced in the September 1946 issue of Palmer's *Amazing Stories*. The Hefferlins, however, failed to impress the magazine's editor and readers, and they turned to the California-based occult organization Borderline Sciences Research Foundation. BSRF issued a series of writings under the rubric "Hefferlin Manuscript."

The Hefferlins related that in 1927, while living in San Francisco, they met Emery, who shared their fascination with metaphysical questions. After moving to Indiana, they lost track of him for a time, then learned that he was in New York. After some initial correspondence they began communicating by telepathy, with Gladys a medium, handling ESP chores on the Hefferlins' end. They learned that Emery was often absent from New York, off on unexplained errands. He eventually explained that he was doing the work of Tibetan masters, who introduced him to the Ancient Three. The trio recognized him as a reincarnated ancient engineer. At their direction he built models of a circle-wing aircraft. The Ancient Three wanted him to construct a fleet of 350 full-sized versions.

When those were completed, Emery and an expedition flew to Antarctica to search for the remains of Rainbow City, which they found in late November 1942.

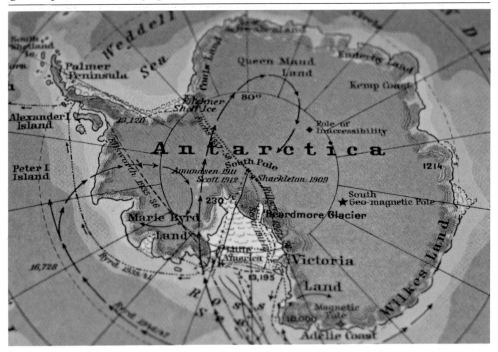

Antarctica wasn't always a frozen continent, according to one tale. It was located in a more fertile climate and settled by Martians until the Snake aliens attacked Earth and rotated the planet (*iStock*).

From Emery's continuing telepathic communications, they were informed of the city's long history. Over the next several years Emery roamed the earth uncovering remnants of the tunnel system. He also uncovered caches of nuclear weapons. Meantime, the circular aircraft continued their search for ancient remains. Persons who saw the planes called them "flying saucers" and thought they were from another planet.

The Hefferlins wrote that the Ancient Three now—as of the late 1940s—were secretly in control of much of the world, with only the white race refusing to recognize or to be guided by them. "Thought machines" set in seven temples around the world beamed teachings to people in the Third World, urging them to cut their ties with the "European Empire Nations." Soon the white nations would be forced to accept the role of the Ancient Three, who would usher in a utopian society based on the political model of the United States. Aggression, war, and racism would cease. The new order was not far away. The Hefferlins had been appointed North American spokespersons for the Three, but even they could not enter Rainbow City, or so they explained to individuals who wanted them to take them there.

Walter Kafton-Minkel, the leading chronicler of hollow-earth lore, argues that these yarns take their inspiration in good part from H.P. Lovecraft's 1936 novella *At the Mountains of Madness*. He writes:

In the tale, a scientific expedition bores a hole into the Antarctic ice crust and discovers a tunnel filled with the well-preserved corpses of alien life forms. Nearer the South Pole, the expedition discovers a great deserted city hidden behind mountains higher than the Himalayas and finds carvings telling the story of a race of "Elder Things" which settled at the Pole nearly a thousand million years ago and created the earth's life forms. When the "great cold" came, the Old Ones settled first in the oceans, and then traveled down to a sea in the interior of the earth.

In 1960 Michael Barton, writing as Michael X, published *Rainbow City and the Inner Earth People,* based on psychic communications from astral entities speaking on the "Telethot" channel. Barton fused Shaver Mystery (see p. 55) material and hollow-earth theories with the sort of material the Hefferlins, long faded from the scene ("now believed to be living in Rainbow City," according to fringe chronicler Jim Keith), had peddled. Rainbow City is a kind of base for the Ancients and the Guardians as they enter the earth's interior through the South Pole. The Ancients and the Guardians—wise Venusians—are cleaning out "both the astral and physical levels of the inner Earth ... in preparation for the coming Golden Age."

Further Reading:

Kafton-Minkel, Walter. *Subterranean Worlds: 100,000 Years of Dragons, Dwarfs, the Dead, Lost Races and UFOs from Inside the Earth.* Port Townsend, WA: Loompanics Unlimited, 1989.

Standish, David. *Hollow Earth: The Long and Curious History of Imagining Strange Lands, Fantastical Creatures, Advanced Civilizations, and Marvelous Machines Below the Earth's Surface.* Cambridge, MA: Da Capo Press, 2006.

Living Hell: The Demons Beneath Us

"I always wonder what people would do if they knew there was real evil underfoot," said Richard S. Shaver, "and that Hell was a genuine ancient city with genuine ghouls in it." Shaver was speaking from firsthand experience. He had seen the evil that is—literally—underfoot. He had been there personally and met the ghouls and the demons. Or so he would insist at voluminous length in print—and, over the years, to a smaller and smaller but still deliciously creeped-out audience—for more than three decades, ceasing only with his death.

One of five children, Shaver was born in Berwick, Pennsylvania, in 1907. On graduating high school and moving to Philadelphia, he worked manual labor jobs which provided no outlet for his fertile imagination. He found one finally in Detroit, where he moved in 1929 to join his relocated family. There he signed up at the Wicker School of Art, where he took instructions in drawing. He worked as a nude model on the side and even made enough money to employ a model to work for him. He took up bootlegging. In 1930 he joined a Communist group, the John Reed Club, but his tenure there was brief, though just long enough to get his attention-grabbing presence at a May Day parade noted the next day in the *Detroit News*. He went back to the Wicker School for a part-time teaching job, supplementing his income by sketching people in the city park. He got romantically involved with a student, Russian émigré Sophie Gurivitch, whom he would marry in 1933.

In 1932 an unemployed Shaver managed to find a job on the assembly line at Briggs Body. It was a tedious, dangerous occupation. Years later, that period of Shaver's life would figure prominently in the mythology of his life, but nearly a decade would pass before the story of what supposedly happened as he worked the line became a subject of spirited controversy. It is certain, however, that in the wake of the death of his beloved older brother Tate, he suffered an emotional breakdown. By the time he was taken to the Detroit Receiving Hospital Emergency Ward in mid-July 1934, his behav-

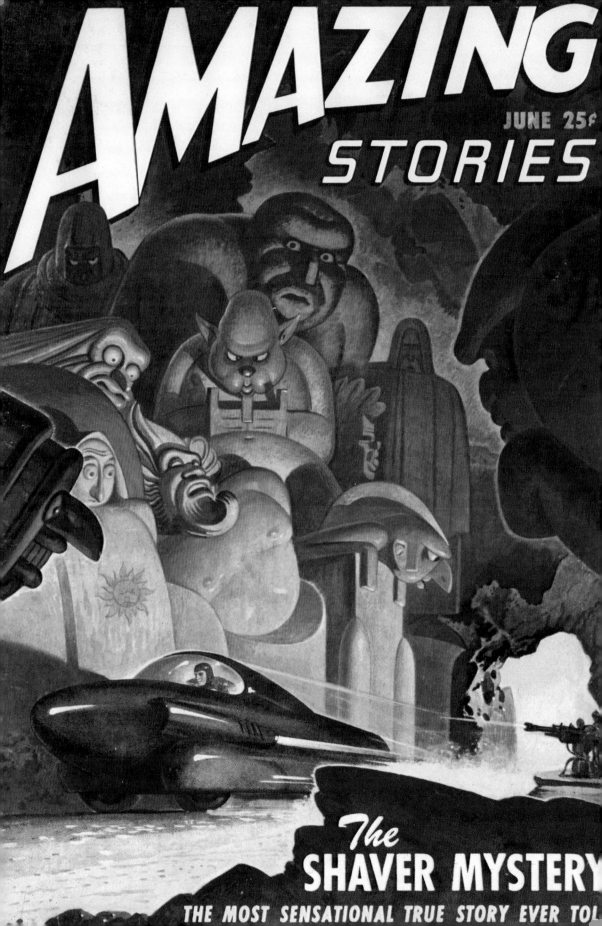

ior had become agitated and violent, and he needed to be forcibly restrained. Besides accusing attending physicians of trying to poison him, he complained that mysterious, sinister strangers were shadowing him. Concerned for herself and their young daughter, Sophie insisted that he be placed in a mental institution. On August 17 papers were drawn up to have him committed to the Ypsilanti State Hospital.

In later years Shaver would claim that the episode amounted to little. He had suffered "heat stroke" and been hospitalized a scant two weeks. Not even those who would become friends or followers believe this to be true. According to persons close to Shaver, the hospitalization lasted as long as eight years. (Writer Doug Skinner states matter-of-factly, "Shaver was released from the Ionia State Hospital in Michigan in 1943.") Pressed on the subject, Shaver responded with conflicting stories. Though the details tended to contradict each other, they generally agreed that these were lost, unsettled years in which he lived in a fog of fear and confusion. Separated from her husband, Sophie died in an accident in her apartment in December 1936. Their young daughter was given to Sophie's parents to raise, and she would grow up knowing nothing of her biological father until, years after his death, she came upon his name in a magazine article.

At some point Shaver moved to Pennsylvania, landed a job as a crane operator, and remarried. His new wife left him a few months later, Shaver would report vaguely, after "finding some papers indicating I had been in a mental hospital." Subsequently, Shaver married his third and last wife, Dorothy Erb, who would be with him until his death in 1975.

Whatever else was happening to Shaver between his hospitalization and his emergence into the wider world, it is evident that he was immersed in fantasy literature, including A. Merritt's popular novel *The Moon Pool* (1919), which is about good and evil ancient races living in caverns beneath the earth. Besides that, Shaver was trying his hand at writing, seeking without success to get published in the flourishing pulp science-fiction, horror, and adventure magazines of the period. He was also working on a language he called "Mantong," which he would later represent as the oldest in the world. He took his inspiration from an article he had read in a 1936 issue of *Science World*. There, Albert F. Yeager wrote of "The True Basis of Today's Alphabet." According to Shaver biographer Jim Pobst, "Yeager claimed that six letters in the alphabet stood for concepts, and that each word in the language could be deciphered, with the use of his concepts.... Shaver ... [went] further than Yeager, taking 26 letters in the alphabet, assigned them his own meaning and developed what he believed to be a language."

The "Shaver Mystery," as it would be called, got its start in September 1943, when one "S. Shaver" of Barto, Pennsylvania, wrote a letter to the editor of Ziff-Davis' *Amazing Stories,* based in Chicago and founded in 1926 by Hugo Gernsback as the very first magazine of "scientifiction" (soon to be renamed science fiction—SF to its devoted

◄ Richard S. Shaver told remarkable stories of his alleged subterranean adventures in a series of wild tales published in *Amazing Stories* magazine (*Mary Evans Picture Library*).

readership, later "sci-fi" to the less engaged). The editor of that publication was Ray Palmer, a colorful figure who had risen from the ranks of SF fandom to anointment, in June 1938, to *Amazing*'s helm. An accident in his youth, followed by a disastrously botched operation, left Palmer with an unfixable spinal injury. His back permanently curved, he never attained normal height (he stood no more than four feet eight inches [1.5 meters])—but his energy seemed never to flag as he lurched from one enthusiasm or promotion to the next. Palmer, one might say, had the instincts of a carnival barker. From the arrival of the Shaver letter onward, Ray Palmer and Richard Shaver would be linked forever in the lore of the outlandish.

As he liked to tell the story, Palmer overheard *Amazing*'s managing editor, Howard Browne, the one who actually opened the envelope, muttering something about "crackpots" as he directed the letter to the wastebasket. (According to some reports, Browne found the letter sufficiently hilarious to read aloud for the amusement of the editorial staff before he disposed of it.) Not ready to let it go at that, the intrigued Palmer retrieved it from the oblivion to which otherwise it would have been destined.

When he read it, he decided that Shaver had something—or, as the cynics have had it, spotted a potentially lucrative new promotion—and the two entered into correspondence, with Shaver pouring forth his thoughts and experiences in multi-paged, literally daily communications. Shaver said he feared that if he did not get it all down, the truth would be lost. Palmer would recall that the letters looked as if they were composed on a "toy typewriter with several keys missing." The alphabet appeared in the January 1944 issue. Eventually, Palmer would visit the Shavers at their farm, where he allegedly had a strange and unsettling experience (see below).

Subsequently, Palmer took a 10,000-word Shaver manuscript, *A Warning to Future Man,* and expanded it (deleting the strong sexual content, for one thing) into the 31,000-word SF novella "I Remember Lemuria!", published under Shaver's by-line in the March 1945 issue. (Lemuria here was an ancient name for Earth, not the fabled Pacific lost continent.) With difficulty—or with unearthly assistance, as Shaver asserted—Palmer, preparing for what he suspected would be significantly enhanced sales, managed to push the print run from 135,000 to 185,000, this during the wartime paper scarcity. Again, in Palmer's not automatically credible version of events, the issue sold out, and a "flood of letters began to come in that totaled, in the end, more than 50,000." Even the hyperbolic Palmer rescinded that assertion, later characterizing the letter total as in the thousands—still impressive if true.

In his editorial in the issue, Palmer wrote that "Lemuria!" grew out of "racial memory" from 12,000 years ago. "The strange fact of the matter," he stated, "seems to be that all over the world there are more people than we might imagine who have a firm faith in a memory of past civilizations, and remember such vital things as Mr. Shaver." Of course, he added (capital letters in the original):

> IT COULD be a hoax! IF MR. SHAVER WERE THE CLEVEREST MAN THE WORLD HAS EVER KNOWN! But we can't believe this is so. The alphabet alone is too much to explain away in such a manner. We

confess we are bewildered, impressed, and excited. And at the very least, we are delighted at the series of stories from the typewriter of Mr. Shaver.... But Mr. Shaver has not been the only source of a great deal of material on Lemuria since we published his first letter. We have been deluged by a storm of corroboration from all over the country.

Shaver provided a brief foreword to the story, insisting, "I know only that I remember Lemuria! Remember it with such a faithfulness that I accept with a faithfulness of a fanatic. And yet, I am not a fanatic.... What I tell you is not fiction!"

✳

Nightmare Underground

Shaver was always—no doubt necessarily—unspecific about dates (surely in the interest of obscuring his actual whereabouts in the periods in question), but the alleged experiences in which he is introduced to the reality of the Cavern World are apparently set in the late 1920s or early 1930s, though Shaver's claim cannot be incorporated into any real-world chronology.

In the version he usually told, he had spent an evening reading Lord Byron's Gothic dramatic poem *Manfred* (1816). The hero is a tormented soul who is seeking death. Shaver's eye fell on lines like these:

Ye spirits of the unbounded Universe
Whom I have sought in darkness and in light!
Ye, who do compass Earth about, and dwell
In subtler essence! ye, to whom the tops
Of mountains inaccessible are haunts,
And Earth's and ocean's caves familiar things....

Finally, he dies, and as evil spirits descend to claim his soul, the ghost of Astarte, the woman he had loved in life, rescues him. Highly popular in the nineteenth century, the poetic drama inspired compositions by the heavy-duty likes of Schumann and Tchaikovsky.

In Shaver's account, he found himself thinking that "Byron was not, strictly speaking, writing fiction"; more likely, the poet was hinting at some deep, sinister reality he could not reveal outright. After turning out the lights, he impulsively beamed a telepathic message into the ether. To his shock, an apparitional woman appeared to him on what looked like a screen. As she gazed at him with an expression of supreme assurance, he sensed that she was reading his thoughts, and then her confidence buckled. "She seemed suddenly to realize that she had made a mistake in answering my call," Shaver would write, as her telepathic probing told her that he was not, as she presumed, one of those in the know. She vanished in an instant.[1]

The encounter with the apparitional woman in the night had catastrophic consequences. It tipped off evil forces to Shaver, who was quickly seen as what might be called a security risk—in other words, as one with the potential to expose their secrets. In the weeks and months that followed, inside his brain he felt dim presences weighing, judging, probing, and talking about him. In time, specific presences, both benevolent and malign, came to the fore and grew ever more tangible.

While he was employed as a welder on the assembly line at a Highland Park, Michigan, auto plant, voices began sounding clearly and audibly inside his head. It took him awhile to realize just what they were: the private, unspoken thoughts of his fellow workers. As he would write, "The welding gun was, by some freak of its coils' field attunements, *not* a radio, but a *tele*radio, a thought augmentor of some power." Before long, he was hearing other voices, frightening and unpleasant ones, coldly vicious and cruel. There were screams, evidently of human beings, most of them women, undergoing hideous torture. Less alarmingly, but no less mystifyingly, were references to spaceship flights—actual, not imaginary, ones.

The encounter with the apparitional woman in the night had catastrophic consequences. It tipped off evil forces to Shaver....

Unnerved, Shaver quit his job, but the torment did not end. He allegedly hit the road, wandering and taking jobs wherever he could find them, all the while undergoing persecution by underworlders, who he now believed had murdered his brother and were determined to destroy him as well. This period of his life was also subject to varying recollections, and Shaver historians and fans tend to the presumption that in reality he was institutionalized. Shaver, however, had it that he was arrested and imprisoned for "many years"—a hard-to-credit chronological claim, as we shall see—for some shameful crime which the malevolent invisibles caused him to commit.

In his correspondence with Palmer, in the series of stories he would publish in *Amazing,* and in the anecdotes he would relate the rest of his life, a complex and not entirely coherent alternative reality unfolded. Few would believe that it literally existed, and even some of those few were inclined to the view that the Cavern World must represent an alternative, astral or visionary reality, though Shaver, firmly materialist and atheist in outlook, always insisted that the caves and their inhabitants were no less physical than the familiar world. But one thing on which just about everybody, skeptic or believer, agrees: for all the contradictions in his testimony, for all the wildly implausible, frankly crazy tales he told, Shaver was basically, almost inexplicably, sincere. The bulk of the controversy about sincerity has focused less on Shaver than on Palmer, his—one might say—enabler.

To understand Shaver's story, one has first to appreciate his notion that "all matter—all things—are a mixture of energy, part of which is integral and part of which is disintegrant." Shaver chronicler Bruce Lanier Wright summarizes the concept: "Detrimental energy, variously called de, der, dis, or d, represents entropy, evil, destruction; integrative energy, called te, ter, or t, is the life force, health, youth, vitality, sexual potency. Shaver's key discovery was that entropy is not a universal, unavoidable phenomenon. All winds down, it seems, only near a degenerate sun. Like ours."

But it was not originally degenerate. In fact (or at least in Shaver's imagination, leaving unaddressed the question of what its own sun was), it was once a planet whose atmosphere was dense with clouds. Finally, when a meteor struck, the effect was to ignite the world, turning it into an immense fireball—a sun, in other words. Out of this cosmic collision a solar system was formed. The resulting planets, including Earth, basked in its health-giving, warming energies. The earth caught the attention of the Atlans and the Titans, two Elder races passing through space, and tens of thousands of years ago

Memory of the Titan race was preserved in human mythology, including the story of the Titan Enceladus, buried beneath Mount Etna for defying Zeus (*Mary Evans Picture Library*).

they settled here. The dis-free Atlans and Titans never stopped growing over the course of the years, decades, and centuries of their all-but-immortal lives, and many were gigantic in stature. They possessed beam technologies with various functions: healing, creativity, sexual stimulation, remote viewing, telepathic communication, teleportation, and more. In other words, they lived in something of a paradise. But as with all good things, this one was not to last.

When the "carbon shell" protecting the sun collapsed 20,000 years ago, the sun began shooting out dis rays. As they washed over the earth, generating death and disease, the Elders were driven into a vast subterranean Cavern World—as Shaver had it, "tier on tier of cities, endlessly vast, the homes of giants ... a maze, a catacomb, labyrinth"—which at its height housed 50,000,000,000 Atlans and Titans. Even here the deadly energies penetrated, and as the centuries passed, life grew ever more intolerable. Finally, 12,000 years ago as many Atlans and Titans as could boarded spaceships and departed from Lemuria to seek out younger stars or "dark worlds"—sunless planets artificially heated—where another cosmic race, the Nortans, dwelled.

Those who remained on Earth suffered three fates. One group became us: humans who had adjusted to the rays sufficiently to roam the surface, even at the cost of death and disease. These people, our ancestors, lost access to the supertechnology of the ancients and would recall the Titans and Atlans only in legends of the gods who had once ruled Earth. Two other groups—the tero and the dero—lived on in the Cavern World as damaged goods.

The dero were and are a loathsome bunch: sadistic idiots devoted to debauchery and torture enhanced by the "stim rays" from the machinery left behind in the cosmic exodus thousands of years ago. They also kidnap surface humans and are the cause of misery among surface humans, ranging from nightmares to airplane crashes. They live "mostly in caverns close to cities," according to Shaver. "The dero get much, if not all, of their supplies from the surface, particularly food. Meat especially"—from their human prey.

The tero, an embattled and shrinking minority, are the good guys who, against immense odds, do battle with the dero and their evil schemes. The tero still have their own human forms, but abuse of stim rays and the effects of dis rays from the sun have combined to turn the dero into mutants of hideous appearance, resembling, Shaver wrote, "fearfully anemic jitterbugs, small, with pipestem arms and legs, pot bellies, huge protruding eyes and wide, idiotically grinning mouths."

✳

Shaver's Adventure

For the first part of his extended prison stay, so he related, Shaver suffered incessant mental torment courtesy of the dero. ("I know those dero only let me live because my life was a burden to me," he declared, "and because my torture was a delight to them and they feared no retribution.") Finally, however, the harassment ceased suddenly. He felt better but still was uneasy about the prospect of its resumption. Then he had a vivid dream of a woman who sat on the edge of his coat as he slept. "Her features were not out of the ordinary," Shaver related, "but strangely and beautifully exaggerated.... She had that strange, wise quality men have sung of as the witch maid's alone since Time began." Shaver realized that she was blind.

In their conversation she promised him freedom if he did her bidding without question for a year. In the morning, when Shaver woke up, he found on his bed the pale ribbon she had worn in her hair—proving that she was a real woman who in some unexplained fashion had been able to get past the prison walls and bars. She returned frequently, sometimes "just a kind of protection," but at other times "her sweet, actual body lay in my arms, I swear." He called her Nydia, after the blind heroine of a Bulwer-Lytton novel (*The Last Days of Pompeii*) that he had once read. Shaver learned that his situation had changed because the tero had succeeded in driving out a dero colony which had been situated immediately beneath the prison.

Just before dawn one day soon afterwards, Nydia showed up in apparitional form with a hypnotized prison guard, who unlocked Shaver's cell door. Shaver was led into a nearby forest, through which the two passed for miles until they reached the side of a mountain. There they came upon a door, well concealed behind bushes, and on the other side, they entered the cavern where Nydia and her fellow tero lived.

He met the real, physical Nydia—of whom the "Nydia" he had known was only a psychic replication—and consummated their relationship in the tero equivalent of a marriage. She was one of 20 tero and one of six who were blind because of the darkness and dim light to which they were constantly exposed inside the cavern. "We are different from the kind of human you are used to," she told him. "We need men like you to aid us in our constant struggle with the living devils that inhabit [many] of these underground warrens."

Shaver was shown the wonders abandoned by the ancients. They included distance-ray beams which could see through miles of rock. In the first demonstration, Shaver observed a "scene of utter horror ... a real Hell," with scenes of stomach-turning torture of human victims of the dero. "From immemorial times,"

Shaver had a dream of a beautiful, but blind, woman, who asked him to do her bidding for one year without question (*iStock*).

Nydia said, the dero "have had such Hells in the underworld.... You see, you surface Christians are not so far wrong in your pictures of Hell, except that you do not die in order to go there, but wish for death to release you once you arrive." Via abuse of the ancients' "beneficial rays"—"ben rays" for short—the dero are able to keep their tormented victims alive for as long as 20 years.

Much more pleasantly, Shaver explored the ancient thought records, stored in a library elsewhere in the cavern. There, he was sat in a chair and a helmet placed on his head. As powerful stored mental images poured into his brain, he "became" a real Atlan named Duli. (Shaver wrote, "Duli became an Elder of the ruling council of the city of Barto on the planet Mu [Lemuria]," without mentioning the surely not coincidental fact that Shaver had lived in the city of Barto, Pennsylvania.) Another thought record allowed him to relive the life of Mutan Mion, whose story became the basis of "I Remember Lemuria!"

Shaver lived in the Cavern World with Nydia and her tero band for eight years. At last, however, the dero reclaimed their old base, killing everyone but Shaver, who managed to escape to the surface to write letters to Ray Palmer.

It is, of course, to state the painfully obvious that none of this could have happened. Still, that point duly made, it is perhaps worth pointing out that the story is impossible *even by Shaver's own account*. Put aside the consideration that Shaver's absence from the world for eight years could not have gone unnoticed. Forget that no one has ever produced evidence of an extraordinary prison break of which both the authorities and the press would certainly have taken notice. Simply consider Shaver's claim to having been jailed for "many years," and then being housed in the Cavern World for eight. We have already seen that Shaver's known biography and whereabouts unambiguously undercut any such assertion. It is virtually certain that in reality Shaver resided in a mental institution during most or all of the mid–1930s and into the early 1940s.

Shavermania

To the end of his days, Ray Palmer stuck to the story of the strange experience that allegedly befell him when he first met the Shavers. Like Shaver, Palmer tended to be vague about dates, but apparently the incident took place at some point before *Amazing* ran "I Remember Lemuria!" and Palmer was trying to figure out exactly what he had in Shaver's peculiar claims. One presumes, then, that the visit occurred sometime in 1944 or, at latest, early 1945.

Palmer recalled that he arrived at the Shavers' Pennsylvania farm near midnight after a long trek from Chicago. He chatted with the couple for a couple of hours, while Dick Shaver spoke frankly as if he thought Palmer already knew the secrets of the caves. Before he was shown the guest bedroom, he would write, "I was sure of one thing at least—Mr. Shaver was not consciously perpetrating a hoax."

As Palmer lay in bed, he heard voices emanating from the room to which Shaver had retired. (Dorothy Shaver had stayed up to wash dishes and feed pets.) Though Palmer was sure Shaver was sound asleep, voices—from Shaver's mouth, to all

RAYMOND A. PALMER

Editor and author Ray Palmer (1911–1977) helped the Shavers and other authors publish their outlandish stories in books and magazines; he also published his own incredible tales (*Mary Evans Picture Library*).

appearances—began to speak. There were five of them: "a woman's voice; a child's voice; a gruff man's voice; and two other male voices of varying pitch and timbre." They were talking in distressed tones about a horrible incident they had seen earlier in the day—a woman's being physically ripped apart—at a location four miles away and four miles beneath the surface.

"What's all this about?" Palmer allegedly blurted. "Let me in on the secret!"

In response the childlike voice said coldly, "Pay no attention to him. He's a dope." (Apparently, tero speak in 1940s American slang.) Then the voices switched to one Palmer did not recognize, and they were all speaking excitedly at once. Palmer swore, "What I heard could not have come from Mr. Shaver's lips—it was humanly impossible!"

Even in private, Palmer, whose actual personal beliefs were usually hard to read, even for those who

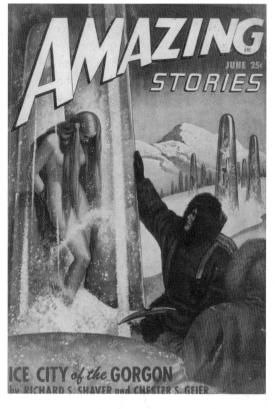

A Shaver tale published in a 1948 issue of *Amazing Stories* (*Mary Evans Picture Library*).

thought they knew him, would cite this experience as a major reason he believed the Shaver Mystery to be based in reality, however defined. In an interview a few years before his death, he defined that "reality" as an astral one. "Mentally," he said, Shaver "entered a very real world. And I don't believe it's in actual caves in the earth.... If he went anywhere, it was into the astral." Of course, the astral notion solved all difficulties, geographic, chronological, and evidential. Shaver didn't have to be anywhere except in his head, which kept its own time.

Until 1948 *Amazing* carried regular Shaver Mystery material, variously credited solely to him, to him as co-author, or to another writer assigned to write stories based on the Shaverian vision. The letters-to-the-editor section was filled with communications from excited readers, either pushing the speculations forward or relating their own anecdotes of encounters with the unknown. Little of the latter directly "confirmed" the Shaver Mystery, and the few letters that did are sometimes suspected, fairly or unfairly, to be Palmer concoctions.

While some readers were thrilled, others were outraged at what they judged to be a shameless hoax. That hoax, they charged, not only insulted their intelligence but discredited the emerging science-fiction genre as it sought literary respectability. In September 1947, at its meeting in Philadelphia, the World Science Fiction Convention denounced the Shaver material as a "serious threat to the mental health of many people" and a "perversion of fantasy fiction." Palmer, however, didn't care; he was indifferent to the genre's desire for respectability. He had never been known as a champion of literary SF. His was a purely pulpish heart, his SF crude and loud. The Shaver Mystery, in other words, fit right in, except for the small detail that it purported to be true.

The June 1947 issue was devoted entirely to the mystery. It would be the last to afford such extended space to the subject. By this time, though, *Amazing Stories*'s owners, Ziff-Davis, were losing patience with what they judged an embarrassing debacle, not to mention a potential pain in the pocketbook, as organized SF fandom threatened a boycott. Shaver, who had ambitions to success as a pulp-fiction writer, continued to contribute stories that made no authenticity claims, but the mystery itself was turned over to a small fan organization, the Shaver Mystery Club, which had its own bulletin under the editorship of Ziff-Davis employee Chester S. Geier. By 1948 Shaver was out of *Amazing* altogether, and soon Palmer was out of a job, replaced by Browne. Accounts differ as to whether he fell or was pushed.

It is certain that Palmer had minimal enthusiasm for Ziff-Davis' plan to relocate its editorial offices to New York City; so had Curtis Fuller, the editor of another Ziff-Davis magazine, *Flying*. The two launched their own periodical, the digest-sized *Fate,* the first issue dated Spring 1948, under the rubric of Clark Publishing Company. Its inspiration was the sustained public interest in flying saucers, following the first widely publicized sightings (and the invention of the term) from the previous summer. *Fate* also covered a range of "true mysteries," most prominently psychic phenomena, but Shaver merited only a single article in 1950. *Fate* readers who expressed an opinion made it clear that they desired no more ("entertainment for morons," as one miffed reader sniffed). Fuller privately thought that Shaver was a nut.

✳

Horlocks of Lassen

Before Shaver and Palmer introduced them to the world, nobody had ever heard of the tero and the dero (or their equivalent as high-tech, super- or sub-human combatants representing subterranean good and evil forces), but as noted, others would step forward to tell tales of them once the news was out. Such yarns gave Shaver's stories credibility, at least if one didn't judge them manifest nonsense. A word of caution is in order here, however. As already noted, Palmer was not above manufacturing bogus material under other people's names, as Fuller learned in the early days of *Fate.* So while we may note that a man signing his name Ralph B. Fields published a letter in the December 1946 issue of *Amazing,* we may not automatically presume that a man named Ralph B. Fields existed.

Nonetheless, whatever may or may not be said about Mr. Fields, there is a Lassen Peak, also known as Mount Lassen. It is at the extreme southern edge of the Cascade

Mount Lassen, like Mount Shasta, in the Cascade Range is associated with lore about Lemurian survivors who settled there (*iStock*).

Range. Situated in Shasta County in northeastern California, it stands at 10,457 feet (3,187 meters), a volcano that last erupted in 1921. To the north is the better known Mount Shasta, which has its own mystical lore dating back to the late nineteenth century. Much of that lore centers on allegations that survivors of the lost continent of Lemuria live within Shasta. Occasionally, almost as an aside, it is remarked without elaboration that another, smaller colony of lost continentals dwells within Lassen.

This is the context in which Fields' supposed experience occurred. He did not make clear when the alleged encounter took place, but his letter states that he and a friend, Joe (no last name), living in the general vicinity of Lassen, decided to go searching for guano (bat droppings used as fertilizer) in caves inside the mountain. On the evening of the third day, having reached an altitude of 7,000 feet (2,134 kilometers), they set up camp beneath a rock outcropping. Fields took the food out of their bags, while Joe went looking for brush with which to get a fire going. A few minutes later Joe returned, an excited expression on his face, to report that on the other side of the rock was a cave entrance.

They ate quickly, then found their way to the cave. They entered it through a small opening. Twenty feet (six meters) in, the cave expanded so that it was now 10 feet (three meters) wide and eight feet (2.4 meters) high. One hundred yards (about 91 meters) later, the tunnel took a turn to the left. The two continued for another mile or two. Their surroundings never changed, which led them to observe that it appeared to

A poster for the 1960 film adaptation of H.G. Wells' *The Time Machine*. Wells called his subhuman creatures "morlocks," which is suspiciously similar to the word "horlocks" in a supposedly true story (*MGM / GEORGE PAL PRODUCTIONS / Ronald Grant Archive / Mary Evans Picture Library*).

have been artificially created. Then Joe thought he had seen a light deeper in the cave. As they walked in that direction, the light returned, shining in their faces and briefly blinding them. When they had regained their sight, Fields pointed his flashlight in that direction. The beam caught three approaching men, dressed in working clothes, thick-soled shoes on their feet. Fields and his friend were shocked and frightened to discover that they were not alone in the cave.

One of the strangers asked what they were doing there. The answer did not seem to persuade him, and a tense exchange followed. Fields suspected that they had come upon a criminal gang in hiding. Two other strangers joined the first three, and the two explorers were led deeper into the cave and, where the walls expanded, to a toboggan-shaped device. The device flew them silently and rapidly into the cave world. Finally, a similar vehicle, moving fast in their direction, appeared, forcing the one which the original party occupied to come to an abrupt halt. Fields wrote:

> One machine had no sooner stopped than our captors leaped from the machine and started to dash away. A fine blue light leaped from the other machine in a fine pencil beam and its sweep caught them and they fell to the cavern and lay still. The figures dismounted from the other machine and came close to us. Then I noticed they carried a strange object in their hands. It resembled a fountain pen flashlight with a large, round, bulb-like affair on the back end and a grip something like a German luger. They pointed them at us. After seeing what had happened to our erstwhile captors I thought that our turn was next, whatever it was.

Instead, one of them inquired if they were surface people. Then he asked, "Where did the horlocks find you?" He went on to say, "You are very fortunate that we came this way. You would also have become horlocks, and then we would have had to kill you also." Fields improbably quotes verbatim a long paragraph, the core of which is, "The people on the surface are not ready to have the things that the ancients have left.... There are a great many evil people here who create many unpleasant things for both us and the surface people. They are safe because no one on the surface world believes in us or them."

Fields and Joe were then flown up the cave, and they then made their way to the exterior world by foot. "What is the answer to the whole thing?" Fields asks. "I would like to know."

Possibly, the answer is as much H.G. Wells as Richard Shaver. In Wells' famous *The Time Machine* (1895) the violent, evil underearthers of the distant future are called "morlocks," a single consonant away from "horlocks."[2]

Brodie's Deros

Not all dero-related stories are of an origin as uncertain as the alleged Fields'. John J. Robinson undeniably existed, a figure on the East Coast UFO scene and an associate of New Jersey-based *Saucer News* publisher/editor James W. Moseley. Robinson had no reputation as a spinner of yarns, which makes his story no less hard to credit. It rests solely on his testimony. If we take him at his word, one possible explanation for the strange narrative is that he was the credulous victim of an elaborate prank.

In the mid–1940s, so the account goes, Robinson lived on the third floor of a house in Jersey City. A reclusive artist named Steve Brodie occupied the second floor. Eventually, Robinson befriended Brodie, who nonetheless continued to behave eccentrically. He had a pronounced disdain for meat, and he seemed to live in fear that, as Robinson put it, "someone might be attempting to sneak up behind him." He did two kinds of paintings: some depicting conventional scenes, the others capturing eerie, otherworldly visions. As he painted the latter, Robinson observed, he appeared to enter a trance state.

On glimpsing an *Amazing Stories* issue in Robinson's pocket, Brodie looked startled. Robinson proceeded to detail Shaver's claims, to Brodie's visibly mounting unease. "He writes of the dero!" he exclaimed with obvious disapproval. With much coaxing and a promise that he would not be ridiculed, Brodie spoke of a terrifying experience he had undergone seven years earlier.

He and a friend had gone out west to prospect for semiprecious stones. Locals warned them to stay away from a particular desert mesa; several individuals had vanished there, they said. Naturally, the young men laughed off these words of caution. Just as predictably, they would pay the consequences.

A few days into the expedition, hearing a cry from his companion, Brodie took startled notice of a cowled figure standing at the base of the mesa. Soon another appeared beside it. The first produced a rod-shaped device which it directed toward Brodie, who abruptly felt himself paralyzed. As Brodie's friend took to his heels, the second figure aimed its own device at him. The next thing he knew, Brodie's nostrils were thick with the sickening scent of burning flesh. That was the last he ever saw of his friend.

A third figure approached Brodie, then placed something just below his ears, rendering him unconscious. "At this point in his narrative," Robinson said, "Steve showed me why he wore his hair long at the back of his head. Behind each ear at the base of the parietal bones of his skull were bare, seared, scarred patches of skin upon which no hair could grow. Both of these areas behind the ears were a little smaller than the size of a silver dollar and were perfectly circular. Steve said they were the marks of a dero slave."

Of what followed from the initial encounter, Brodie had only nightmarish intermittent memories, flashes of recall in which he saw himself sharing a cave with other human beings. They were inside a cave, imprisoned by the deros who could kidnap any surface dweller they had a mind to take. As soon as one of his captors noticed that Brodie was conscious, he would be zapped into blackness.

Then one day he woke to find himself walking the streets of New York City with no idea how he got there. He had on his prospecting clothes and a hundred dollars in his pockets just as he had on the day his life changed. That day, he soon learned, had been two years before.

Brodie added that the scent of meat had nauseated him ever since. For his part, Robinson saw no evidence that Brodie read much of anything, least of all Shaver material out of which he could have concocted this implausible tale.

Soon afterwards, Robinson moved from the apartment, losing contact for a time with the people there. On a return visit six months later, he learned that Brodie was no longer there. A mutual acquaintance claimed that he had spotted Brodie on a train passing through Arizona. Brodie, who appeared to be in a "stupor" (though he was not a drinking man), did not respond to a greeting. He disappeared after the train stopped at a small town. Robinson inferred from this anecdote that Brodie was back in the deros' clutches.

✳

Into the Cavern World

Surely the most curious—certainly the most convoluted—post-Shaver tale is set at a real place, Blowing Cave, located near Cushman, Arkansas. In November 1983 a man named Charles A. Marcoux died there in a bizarre accident. These things are undeniable. Just about everything else beyond these facts is peculiar and unbelievable.

Marcoux's interest in weirdness commenced in his youth, when he was exposed to Palmer's pulps *Amazing* and *Fantastic Adventures*. That exposure puts into context Marcoux's testimony about an alleged incident that happened to him on December 24, 1945, as he stood at a stoplight in Flint, Michigan, waiting to cross the street on his way to a shoe store. At that moment his gaze was inexplicably directed to a drab, unfash-

Experienced cave explorers have yet to stumble upon any evidence of subterranean civilizations (*iStock*).

ionably dressed couple under the opposite light post. His mind was flooded with thoughts seemingly not his own. "Telepathically," Marcoux would write, the couple "impressed me that they were 'Teros' and that I KNEW THEM PERSONALLY." When the light changed and they crossed, heading toward him, he wanted to speak to them but felt prevented from doing so. The two passed by without looking at him. When he turned to follow them, they disappeared—almost literally—into the crowd.

Marcoux spent the rest of his life seriously, even fanatically, committed to Shaverian beliefs. In 1957, at a UFO lecture, he met another Michigan man, David A. Lopez of Saginaw, who happened to be an experienced cave explorer (spelunker). Lopez had never heard of the Shaver Mystery. When Marcoux explained it to him, Lopez coolly replied that nothing in his experience and specialized field of knowledge suggested that any such thing was possible. Lopez had been exploring caves since he was 14, a result of meeting his future brother-in-law, a resident of Cushman, Arkansas. Lopez was introduced to Blowing Cave, and for years afterwards he traveled to Cushman to pursue activities there.

He started a mimeographed saucer magazine, *UFO Journal,* announced as the publication of the grandly titled UFO Investigations Bureau Civilian Intelligence. Marcoux had a column in it, and—at Marcoux's urging—so did George D. Wight of Benton, Ohio. Lopez would not meet Wight personally until 1960. Meanwhile, Marcoux moved to Glendale, Arizona, where he started a small group called the Subsurface

Research Center. Lopez remained unconvinced of Shaver's claims but managed to stay generally friendly with Marcoux. "His insistence on the existence of a subworld and my years of cavern explorations and knowledge to the contrary did much to strain our tempers," Lopez would write. (In a February 1958 letter Marcoux privately told Lopez, "I have been invited into the 'cavern world' where I will spend a few days.") Wight also rejected Shaverism, but like Lopez maintained mostly cordial relations with the obsessed seeker.

Lopez organized a group of friends and acquaintances who wanted to become spelunkers. They would begin their forays with Blowing Cave, then expand their area to others in Missouri, Kentucky, and Tennessee. Lopez folded his *UFO Journal* in August 1961 and thereafter abandoned ufology altogether for speleology.

In 1966 the spelunkers, now expanded to a dozen, journeyed from the Upper Midwest to Arkansas, intending to spend a week exploring Blowing Cave. There, so they later recorded in letters to Palmer (who did not acknowledge them for reasons we can only speculate about), they encountered teros—or, anyway, their equivalent. Lopez would prefer to call them subworlders, holding that "teros" was a word of Shaver's invention. Lopez would provide no detailed account, but he did indicate that these beings are human but blue-skinned and white-haired (even the children). As descendants of Noah, they do not speak English; their languages are Hebrew, Sanskrit, and Greek.

In any event, Lopez would assert, "I did owe Marcoux a long and deserving apology and I felt that it was time he knew that his hypothesis was correct. However, when I tried to communicate I was unable to locate him."

Meantime—details here are vague—Wight must have joined the expeditions and met the entities he continued to call the tero. He returned alone to the cave, coming back briefly in 1967 to hand over to Lopez a diary to be given to Marcoux. Wight said he, too, felt guilty about ridiculing Marcoux's beliefs when they had turned out to be right after all. That was the last Lopez or anyone in his circle ever saw Wight.

After 13 years Lopez came upon Marcoux's name and tracked him down. Marcoux finally had the diary in his possession. It is said to have related the spelunking group's experience at Blowing Cave, beginning with the sighting of a light at the end of a long tunnel. Members crawled through a narrow crevice and found artificial steps on the other side. According to Wight, "Suddenly we came into a large tunnel corridor, about 20 feet [6 meters] wide and just as high. All the walls and the floor were smooth, and the ceiling had a curved dome shape. We knew that this was not a freak of nature, but manmade. We had accidentally stumbled into the secret cavern world."

They soon met blue-skinned humans who told them that the tunnels went on for hundreds of miles, leading eventually to cities populated by assorted entities, including reptile beings and Sasquatch-like creatures. The blue-skinned men identified themselves as direct descendants of Noah, who had gone underground in the wake of the Flood. In due course they discovered an advanced technology and the remains of the civilization that had created it. Wight and his friends boarded an elevator that took them deeper into the earth. At the end of the descent, they entered a city of glass where the Noachians lived.

During subsequent visits the explorers met the tero, who had been there all along. But no one would believe them. Hoping to prove their bizarre story, they captured a giant cave moth, but when they reached the surface, the sunlight turned it instantly to dust.

Wight decided that he wanted to live permanently with his inner-earth friends. Subsequently, claims one account, "all evidence of [his] ever existing began to mysteriously disappear from the surface. Birth certificates, school records, computer records, bank records, etc., all seemed to vanish, apparently the work of someone in a very influential position." The remaining members of the group took one last trip inside the cave and bade their farewells to Wight, who came up once after that to give his diary to be passed on to Marcoux. Within the diary Wight wrote, "Yes, Charles, all that you told me is true.... I owe you a debt of gratitude, because the Teros healed my crippled leg, instantly. I am grateful for more than just that, and I have left these notes and somewhere a map so that you, too, can visit with these people.... Maybe we'll meet here some day." The diary, perhaps no surprise, is said to have disappeared long since, presumably expunged as surely as evidence of Wight's existence.

Marcoux reported seeing blue-skinned people living among Sasquatch-like and reptilian beings in cavern cities (*BigStock*).

It is, of course, impossible not to think of the above as some combination of science-fictional tall tale and mad prank, but unfortunately for him, as it turned out, Marcoux was profoundly impressed. He spent his last year or so soliciting volunteers for an expedition to Blowing Cave among readers of inner-earth publications such as *The Hollow Hassle* and *Shavertron*. In September 1983 he and his wife moved to Cushman. In November, standing outside the cave, he was attacked by a swarm of bees, suffered a heart attack, and died on the spot.

That, however, is not quite the end of the story. After Marcoux's death, fellow expedition member and *Hollow Hassle* editor Mary Martin consulted a psychic in California. Martin alleged that she had told the psychic only Marcoux's name and the fact of his death. Supposedly the psychic channeled this message from the deceased would-be subterranean explorer: "Tell her I am unable to find the way to the underground tunnel at this time. Tell her to look into the Cucamonga wilderness area for what she seeks. She must be very wary, for the guardians are quite jealous.... They won't let me talk to you anymore. They are forcing me away.... Help me."[3]

✳

The End of the Affair

In the mid 1950s, Palmer sold his share in *Fate* to Curtis and Mary Fuller. He had long since moved to rural Portage County, Wisconsin, where he lived until his death in 1977. The Shavers were already living there (they would relocate to Arkansas in 1962). Palmer started a variety of magazines, none of which ever garnered circulations of more than a few thousand, but he had a loyal following. He regularly featured Shaver-mystery material in the pages of *Mystic* (later *Search*) and *Flying Saucers*. Between 1961 and 1964 he published 16 issues of *The Hidden World,* a quarterly magazine in trade-paperback format, dedicated exclusively to Shaver matters. *Hidden World* reprinted old stories, presented new writing, and provided forums for Shaver fans.

From his home in Summit, Arkansas, Shaver marketed agate stones, which he claimed to believe contained images from the ancient world, though some of the more keen-eyed customers thought they detected evidence of a purely terrestrial hand in their creation. In other words, not many were convinced. Doug Skinner writes:

> Shaver turned to painting to show the pictures that nobody else seemed able to see.... A sheet of cardboard or plywood was first coated with a variety of chemicals, chosen to simulate the texture of rock and to "respond easily to the minute light forces." Shaver had no set mixture, but experimented with different combinations of laundry soap, wax, Windex, glue flakes, dye, and diluted paint.... A rock was then sawed open and set on an opaque projector. Once the image was focused onto the cardboard, he sprinkled water over it and gave the picture time to form. Only then did he get out his paints to carefully touch it up and clarify it.

> The resulting paintings were fluid and hallucinatory, distorted dreamlike visions of faces, battles, mermaids, and strange creatures. And, as always, naked women.... He insisted that the paintings weren't his own creations, but strictly documentation.

Following Shaver's death on November 5, 1975, the paintings got some recognition and praise as folk art, resulting in exhibitions in galleries in New York City, San Francisco, and elsewhere.

Pilgrims regularly showed up at the Shavers' door. A friendly, outgoing man for the most part (though subject on occasion to radical mood swings that caused him to turn unpredictably on associates), Shaver usually welcomed them. Over time the

Shaver Mystery was incorporated into the lore of the hollow Earth, even though Shaver himself rejected the concept and insisted that the Cavern World is just under the earth's surface, not deep down in its interior.

Shaver lives on, both in the memories of a very small number of believers and as a sentimental figure in debunking literature, where he and Palmer are often depicted—implausibly and hyperbolically—as the true fathers of the UFO craze. British writer Roger Ford once went so far as to declare that the "UFO Phenomenon in general might well be the Shaver Mystery materialized." There is, in fact, practically nothing to link Shaverian ideas with subsequent reports and theories of UFO visitors, but in the 1950s a handful of fringe individuals connected with the contactee movement brought the dero and the tero into their already crowded cosmos. In the early 1950s the ubiquitous channeling entity and starship commander Ashtar

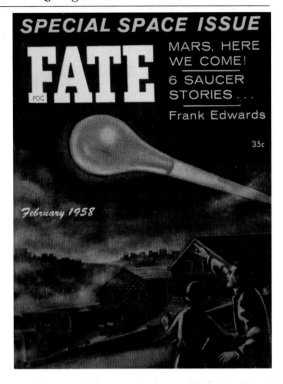

A lightbulb-shaped UFO appears in the sky in this 1958 issue of *Fate Magazine*. Palmer sold his stake in the magazine and moved on to work on other similar magazines (*Mary Evans Picture Library*).

informed occult author Trevor James Constable that the dero "are the forces of Eranus, whom you call Satan." The dero, Ashtar added, reside in the astral realm.

Curiously, after devoting so much effort to laying out the nature and history of the dero, late in life Shaver radically contradicted nearly everything he had said prior to that. In 1973 he waxed oddly hazy on an issue on which he had been quite precise for many years. "I wish I knew where the dero come from," he said in an interview. "I don't think they ever grew on Earth.... I think they came in from space as a kind of vermin chased away from other planets." It was not his only contradiction. Over time there were enough of them to cause exasperated disciples to speculate that the dero were using their telaug (telepathic) rays to befog Shaver's memory.

The sheer strangeness and audacity of the Shaver affair continues to fascinate some historians of American popular culture, as does interest in Palmer as a kind of bush-league P.T. Barnum. Those who charge that Palmer exploited a mentally ill man have a point, but since both men lived relatively happily ever after, it is futile to argue that any real harm was done except to the insulted intelligences of unsympathetic observers. There were, of course, always more of them than there were actual believers.

Further Reading:

Commander X [Jim Keith]. *Underground Alien Bases.* New Brunswick, NJ: Abelard Productions, 1990.

Goulart, Ron. *Cheap Thrills: An Informal History of the Pulp Magazines.* New York: Arlington House, 1972.

James, Trevor [Trevor James Constable]. *They Live in the Sky.* Los Angeles: New Age Publishing Company, 1958.

Kafton-Minkel, Walter. *Subterranean Worlds: 100,000 Years of Dragons, Dwarfs, the Dead, Lost Races and UFOs from Inside the Earth.* Port Townsend, WA: Loompanic Unlimited, 1989.

Palmer, Ray. "The Observatory." *Amazing Stories* 19, 1 (March 1945): 6, 8, 10–11.

Palmer, Ray, ed. *The Hidden World* A–1 (Spring 1961). Amherst, WI: Palmer Publications.

Shaver, Richard S. "I Remember Lemuria!" *Amazing Stories* 19,1 (March 1945): 12–70.

Skinner, Doug. "What's This? A Shaver Revival?" *Fate* (June 2005).

Steiger, Brad, and Joan Whritenour. *New UFO Breakthrough.* New York: Award Books, 1968.

Steinberg, Gene. "The *Caveat Emptor* Interview: Ray Palmer." *Caveat Emptor* 1 (Fall 1971): 9–12, 26.

———. "The *Caveat Emptor* Interview: Richard S. Shaver." *Caveat Emptor* 10 (November/December 1973): 5–10.

Wright, Bruce Lanier. "From Hero to Dero." *Fortean Times* 127, 1999: 36–41.

PART TWO

THE ALTERNATE SOLAR SYSTEM

By the Light of the Moon: Lives of the Lunarians

At least 4.5 billion years old, the moon is generally thought to have been formed out of debris from the young Earth's collision with a slightly smaller celestial body, perhaps about the size of Mars. Its mean distance from the earth is 238,000 miles (382,942 kilometers), and it is 2,160 miles (3,475 kilometers) in diameter. A flurry of meteoric impacts and, later, volcanic activity shaped the bulk of its surface features between 4 and 2.5 million years ago. Since then, the moon has remained essentially stable except for the now much rarer encounter with a meteorite or comet. In 2009 lunar scientists announced the surprising discovery of small amounts of water on the surface.

Speculation about lunar life, including proto-science fiction literature on the subject, goes back to the ancients, who observed the moon's face and discerned what they inferred to be oceans, land masses, and vegetation. The first to do so was the Greek philosopher Anaxagoras (500–428 B.C.E.). Subsequent theorists held that since the moon's days are 14 times as long as the earth's, its inhabitants must be 14 times taller.

In the late Middle Ages, after telescopes were directed toward the moon, the debate did not end; if anything, it intensified. In 1638 the clergyman and amateur scientist John Wilkins (1614–1672) wrote in his book *The Discovery of a World in the Moone:*

> That those spots and brighter parts which by our sight might be distinguished in the Moon, do show the difference between the Sea and Land of that other World....
>
> The spots represent the Sea, and the bright parts Land....
>
> That there are high mountains, deep valleys, and spacious plains in the body of the Moon....
>
> That there is an atmosphere, or an orb of gross vaporous air, immediately encompassing the body of the Moon....

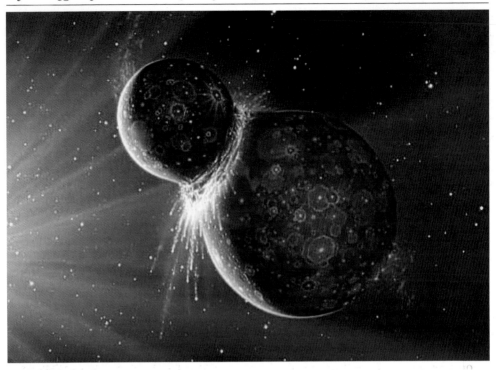

There are several theories of how the Moon was formed, including that a Mars-sized planet may have collided with Earth, the resulting debris eventually becoming the Moon (*illustration by Joe Tucciarone, NASA*).

That it is probable there may be inhabitants in this other World, but of what kind they are is uncertain.

Though many educated and influential men of his time agreed with the premise, others scoffed. The Italian astronomer and lunar mapmaker Giovanni Riccioli (1598–1671) declared bluntly, "No man dwells on the moon," and held that the moon is dry, dead, and inhospitable to life. On the other hand, Riccioli's contemporary Johannes Hevelius (1611–1687), a German astronomer and cartographer of the moon, argued for oceans and "Selenites," as he called the beings who he believed lived on the land areas or continents.

A number of moon-life advocates came from a more or less explicitly theological premise that embraced—sometimes demanded—the presence of intelligent entities on all worlds, not necessarily excluding asteroids and comets. In the words of James Ferguson (1710–1776), the Scottish autodidact and popular writer on astronomy, God created "an inconceivable number of suns, systems, and Worlds, dispersed through boundless space.... From what we know of our own System, it may be reasonably concluded that all the rest are with equal wisdom contrived, situated, and provided with accommodations for rational inhabitants ... ten thousand times ten thousand Worlds ... peopled with myriads of intelligent beings, formed for endless progression in perfection and felicity." In a multi-volume biblical commentary published between 1817 and 1825, the Methodist clergyman Adam Clarke infers from Old Testament references that there "is scarcely any doubt remaining in the philosophical world, that the moon is a *habitable globe*.... All the *planets* and their *satellites* ... are inhabited; for matter seems only to exist for the sake of intelligent beings."

Among the greatest astronomers, honored for his discovery of Uranus in 1781, often thought of as a model empiricist, Sir William Herschel (1738–1822) is less known for his obsessive interest in intelligent extraterrestrial life in the solar system and beyond. In the assessment of historian of science Michael J. Crowe, who examined many of Herschel's unpublished papers, "pluralism was a core component in Herschel's research program and as such influenced many of his astronomical endeavors." Herschel believed that life existed on the moon; he also thought—first certainly, then less so—that he had observed evidence of it through his telescope.

German astronomer and cartographer Johannes Hevelius speculated that an alien race of Selenites inhabited the Moon. The idea was used in the 1901 science fiction novel by H.G. Wells, *The First Men in the Moon* (*Mary Evans Picture Library*).

In the mid–1770s Herschel turned his telescope to the lunar surface and began writing journal entries in which he detailed sightings of immense trees, forests, and pastures. By 1778 he was seeing "circuses"—circular formations—which in his estimation represented cities, towns, and villages. Through 1783, after which his attentions were attracted elsewhere, canals, roads, and patches of vegetation caught his eye, or at least his imagination. None of this appeared in any of his published work, however, probably because in time Herschel grew more sensitive to the limitations of the telescopes of his time and experienced doubts about what he had actually seen. Telescopes had played "many tricks" on him, he confided to a friend, and it was only after considerable experience that he felt confident of accurate observations through them. From then on, when he talked of extraterrestrials, he made no claim to eyewitness validation of his own.

Less restrained, the German astronomer Franz von Paula Gruithuisen (1774–1852) got so carried away that even colleagues sympathetic to the idea of a populated moon recoiled. In an 1824 paper boldly titled "Discovery of Many Distinct Traces of Lunar Inhabitants, Especially of One of Their Colossal Buildings," he argued (in part one) for vegetation, which he said he had seen, and for animals (in part two). He did not claim to have seen the latter but to have observed the paths they left in their migrations; the animals travel "from 50° northern latitude up to 37° or possibly 47° southern latitude." Gruithuisen reserved the most sensational revelations for the third part, where he outlined observations of lunar structures: walls, forts, roads, cities. A structure with a star-like shape was surely a "temple," he judged, and an indication that the people of the moon are religious.

Colleagues such as Carl Friedrich Gauss (Göttingen Observatory) and Johann Joseph von Littrow (Vienna Observatory) thought that Gruithuisen's imagination was running away with him, but—even if more cautious in stating so publicly—they took the idea of lunar intelligences seriously, even proposing methods with which to communicate with them. Another Gruithuisen critic, Bremen astronomer Wilhelm Olbers, judged the presence both of vegetation and of sentient entities on the moon to be "very probable."

Many (albeit not all) astronomers agreed, enough to inspire a notorious series of pieces in the *New York Sun* published between August 25 and 31, 1835, and written—as revealed subsequently—by Richard Adams Locke (1800–1871). The first story bore this headline:

GREAT ASTRONOMICAL DISCOVERIES
Lately Made
By Sir John Herschel, LL.D, F.R.S., &c
At the Cape of Good Hope

Sir John Herschel, a real-life astronomer (1792–1871) and the son of Sir William, was actually conducting telescope observations from the Cape of Good Hope at the time—he was there from 1832 to 1838—which in an age of slow-moving international communication ensured no speedy rebuttal. Locke credited Sir John with a telescope of such power that it could discern objects on the lunar subject as little as 18 inches (46 centimeters) long. The astronomer saw animals, one like a goat with a horn, the other a rolling, spherical-shaped amphibian, then bipeds with both human and bat features (he was even able to observe them in conversation with one another), and, finally, a superior species of man-bats "of infinitely greater personal beauty" and angelic aura.

The press of the time picked up the stories, and some leading newspapers expressed full confidence in their veracity. Credulity was rampant, according to the celebrated critic and fantasist Edgar Allan Poe (1809–1849). "Not one person in ten discredited it," he wrote with something between amusement and outrage, "and (strangest point of all!) the doubters were chiefly those who doubted without being able to say why—the ignorant, those uninformed in astronomy, people who *would not* believe because the thing was so novel, so entirely 'out of the usual way.'"

As the story spun out of control, Locke quietly put the word out that he had written it and that it wasn't, in point of fact, true. After that, denunciations were ringing as

A VIEW OF
THE INHABITANTS OF THE MOON,
AS SEEN THROUGH THE TELESCOPE OF SIR JOHN HERSCHEL.

In a notorious 1835 journalistic prank, Richard Adams Locke reported that astronomer Sir John Herschel's telescope was powerful enough to detect animals and intelligent beings on the lunar surface (*Mary Evans Picture Library*).

resoundingly as endorsements had been just days before. In a mostly ignored and forgotten public statement a few years later, Locke was to insist that he had not meant to fool anyone, that his purposes were satirical. In other words, he had simply poked fun at exotic, unfounded speculations about the moon's inhabitants and at popular gullibility. In any event, Locke's tales were destined to be called ever after the "moon hoax." Ironically, Sir John Herschel, the real one, was later to champion (in an 1858 book) the likelihood of "animal or vegetable life" on the far side of the moon.

Camille Flammarion (1842–1925), the French scientist, popular author, and "leading advocate of extreme pluralism" (in the words of modern astrobiological chronicler David Darling), dismissed those who argued that with no atmosphere the moon could not sustain life; they possessed, he sniffed, all the reasoning powers of "a fish." To the contrary, he insisted in an 1877 work, changes on its surface visible from Earth may be "due to the vegetable kingdom or even the animal kingdom, or—who knows?—to some living formations which are neither vegetable nor animal." Interpretations like these were far from universally embraced—many astronomers by now deemed them nonsensical, and those who thought otherwise found themselves more and more on the defensive—but they were surprisingly persistent.

(Continued on page 86)

HIDDEN REALMS, LOST CIVILIZATIONS, AND BEINGS FROM OTHER WORLDS **[83]**

METON

Elizabeth Klarer (1910–1994) had three children: a son named David, a daughter named Marilyn, and another son, Ayling. The last of these is not someone you are likely ever to meet. He is an astrophysicist who lives on the planet Meton, like so many planets unknown to terrestrial science, but one on which his mother lived for a short time back in the earthly 1950s.

Born on a farm in Natal, the South African Klarer claimed to have sighted her first UFO in October 1917 as the spacecraft saved the earth from an onrushing giant meteorite. A second, less dramatic sighting occurred in 1937, when she and her husband witnessed the pacing of their small airplane by a mysterious luminous object. On a third occasion, on December 27, 1954, she glimpsed a handsome man through the porthole of a saucer hovering not far away. The fair-haired occupant studied her with a hypnotic stare before his spacecraft shot off in a blast of heated air.

Klarer met that spaceman on the morning of April 7, 1956. She and her two children had left Johannesburg for a holiday on the Natal coast. While there, she felt an odd compulsion that caused her to return to the family farm. She went to "Flying Saucer Hill," site of the previous sighting, and there greeted Akon and another extraterrestrial, who resembled his companion except for darker features and a more muscular build. Both were scientists, Akon an astrophysicist, the other a botanist. They flew her a thousand miles into space to a huge "carriership," where she met other space people.

In an interview years later, Klarer recalled the interior of the ship as "simple but completely beautiful." It was home to 5,000 residents of all ages. Compared to Earthlings, the adults were "taller, better looking, more considerate and gentle, not aggressive and violent." On a giant screen (known as an "electric mirage") she viewed scenes of the home planet, known as Meton, four light years from Earth in the Alpha Centauri system. She ate a vegetarian meal on the ship, learning there that Meton houses a utopian society. She also was told that Metonites do not have names, only "mathematical harmonic numbers," though for the sake of convenience and comfort Akon provided her with a spoken name.

Klarer's photographs of the departing spaceship thrilled some South African ufologists, who boasted that they now had their own George Adamski, a Polish-American man from southern California who had electrified the international occult community with his claims of contacts with angelic "Space Brothers."

Though many rejected Adamski's stories and photographs as manifestly bogus, he had a fierce supporter in Klarer's countryman Edgar Sievers. Sievers hailed what he deigned her validation of Adamski, even though the latter had said nothing about a planet named Meton. Still, both spoke of attractive aliens from a peaceful, superior society, here on earth seeking to turn Earthlings from their destructive ways. Sievers crowed, "Through her experience she is able to substantiate many of Adamski's claims, both as regards more detailed knowledge as well as the wider implications." In his excitement he failed to consider the obvious possibility that Klarer patterned her stories after Adamski's.

It is certainly true that even to the untrained eye Klarer's spacecraft photos do not appear compellingly authentic. At least one formal photoanalysis, conducted by an American UFO group in the 1970s, concluded that the "spacecraft" was in reality a small model. Still, where even the most implausible extraordinary claims are concerned, it is not always possible to judge sincerity or even to define it. Her defenders, including the late Zimbabwean ufologist Cynthia Hind, who was generally more critical-minded than Sievers, held

that Klarer seemed to believe what she was saying (though Hind acknowledged that "we have only her word for it and some questionable photographs"). If her ambition was to make money from it, she failed. She died, Hind wrote, "in comparative poverty." Even if her space contacts were in some sense "real" to her, they certainly did not occur in consensus reality.

What set Klarer apart from most other contactees of the period was her story's departure from the asexual sterility of the competition. The Metonites, she reported, do not marry, though they remain faithful to partners with whom they enjoy robust sexual relationships. Not long after meeting Akon, Klarer became his lover. (At some point Akon remarked unromantically that the Metonites needed new blood and he had chosen her for a "breeding experiment." He insisted, though, that he loved her.

Meton is described as a paradisiacal world of green oceans and islands, but no continents (*iStock*).

For her part, Klarer recorded, "I surrendered in ecstasy to the magic of his love making, our bodies merging in magnetic union as the divine essence of our spirits became one.") After Akon's departure Klarer found that she was pregnant. He returned and took her to Meton.

She lived on that planet for four months, long enough for Ayling to be born and to receive some initial maternal care. She had to return to Earth because of health problems: her heart could not adjust to Meton's distinctive magnetic-field vibrations. From then to the rest of her life, she said, she kept in touch with Akon and Ayling by telepathy and through a holographic device which would project their images into her house.

According to Klarer, the earth-sized Meton is awash in great oceans. There are no continents, only islands of various sizes on which the inhabitants dwell in happiness, harmony, and security. The climate is controlled and therefore perfect, and technological advances have eliminated all bodily disease and environmental pollution. Metonites live in houses that are transparent from the inside out (though not in the opposite direction). They communicate with each other via telepathy, and they don't have or need books because all instruction is delivered by thought. The living, Klarer reported, is easy:

> There are no chores.... It is all done with a light ray. For example, a beam of light will bring you your food on a tray. Families are larger—most families have about seven children. You could have children while thousands of years

(Continued from page 83)

For example, in 1902 American astronomer William H. Pickering (1858–1938), an outspoken proponent of alleged Martian canals then at the center of a furious international scientific controversy that seems inexplicable from this distance, reported changes in the lunar landscape—best explained, he wrote in *Century* magazine, as evidence of an atmosphere containing water vapor. If there was water vapor, then surely there could be vegetable life, at least. He acknowledged, however, that intelligent beings living under lunar conditions would be unimaginable and unworthy of consideration. Nonetheless, he characterized the vegetable life as "crops," by definition the product of cultivation, necessitating the presence of cultivators. In a meant-to-be confidential communication to his older, skeptical brother, Harvard College Observatory director E.C. Pickering, he reported that he had been tracking lunar "canals"—which he attributed to strips of vegetation—for more than a decade. "I have seen everything practically," he declared, "except the Selenites themselves running round with spades to turn off the water into other canals."

old, as there is no problem with age. They use a natural contraceptive, a type of vegetable which they put in their food. There is no marriage and divorce. They simply find their mate and stay together for life. If there is an accident and a loss of life, the person simply reincarnates and comes back to the same mate.

"Breeding experiments" with Earthlings are possible because the Metonites are genetically linked to us from previous visitations. We are their direct descendants. (Metonite civilization is 400,000,000 years old.) Atlantis was their principal base when they were here thousands of years ago. Another base was located in South America. "They have also come back to create bases on the Moon and Mars," Klarer said. "They can bring back to life Mars as well as Venus, and this they plan to do since their main work throughout the galaxy is to prepare star systems for human habitation."

Further Reading

Bord, Janet, and Colin Bord. *Life beyond Earth? Man's Contacts with Space People.* London: GraftonBooks, 1991.

Hind, Cynthia. *UFOs—African Encounters.* Salisbury, Zimbabwe: Gemini, 1982.

Klarer, Elizabeth. *Beyond the Light Barrier.* Cape Town, South Africa: Howard Timmins, 1980.

Sievers, Edgar. "Encounters in South Africa." *Uranus* 3, 3 (December 1956): 46–49.

William Pickering voiced no such assertions in any public forum, but in the mid–1920s he did theorize that changes heretofore laid to seasonal changes in vegetation now evinced the migrations of vast insect swarms or—he also thought possible—migrations of seal-like animals. He remained an advocate of lunar life well past his retirement as astronomer and was writing about it almost up to his death. No scientist of any repute since then has associated him- or herself with any comparable notions.

Mystic Moon

Naturally, not just scientists have had their say about who may abide on the earth's satellite. The Swedish scientist-turned-spiritual pilgrim Emanuel Swedenborg (1688–1772) visited the moon in a visionary or out-of-body state, returning to relate

The Selenites (shown in a 1918 illustration) were a sophisticated, advanced species, according to some observers, who may have been wiser in their use of technology than Earthlings (*Mary Evans Picture Library*).

that its inhabitants are "as small as children of six years old, their voice proceeds from the stomach, and they creep about."

In 1837 Joseph Smith (1805–1844), founder of the Church of the Latter Day Saints (otherwise known as Mormonism), is alleged to have given a blessing, or perhaps merely expressed a personal opinion, in which he pronounced—as Oliver B. Huntington, who heard it, would recall, paraphrasing Smith's words—"The moon [is] inhabited by men and women the same as on this Earth, and ... they [live] for a greater age than we do—that they live generally to near the age of 1,000 years." The men, averaging a height of six feet (two meters), wear clothing in the "Quaker style" and lead simple lives, often going about barefoot. For longer trips they drive buckboards and carriages. Their society is a communal one without hierarchies.

Mormon apologists have furiously disputed Huntington's account, but the views attributed to Smith of a moon inhabited by intelligent, human-like beings reflected widely shared popular, and even scientific, opinion of the time, and if true, they hardly make him any more misguided than many of his fellow citizens.

During the Spiritualist craze of the nineteenth century, some mediums reported communications with lunar inhabitants or even astral voyages to the moon's surface. In a book published in English translation in 1847, H. Werner related his experiences with a medium who, in a trance state, found small, humanlike beings, "on a much lower grade of cultivation," dwelling in stone structures. Elsewhere, hidden within the moon's huge mountain chains, were individuals forced into exile because of their atheism. These "unhappy beings" are in a state of incessant conflict. "They are wretched creatures," the medium reported, "and a torment to themselves."

Though scientists had grown ever more doubtful about the presence of intelligent life on the moon, as late as the early decades of the twentieth century a few of them—most prominently the above-mentioned William H. Pickering reported that they had observed evidence of something like vegetative patches in some small craters. Pickering dismissed theories—surely correct—that these were artifacts of light and shadow. Speculations about lunar vegetation continued well into the 1950s, along with the possibility (albeit a minority view) of a thin lunar atmosphere sufficient to sustain life. In 1960 a young University of Chicago astronomer, Carl Sagan (1934-1996), proposed that primitive micro-organisms may survive under thick layers of moondust.

Popular speculations about intelligences on the moon would attain new life after World War II, when sightings of puzzling sky objects ignited widespread interest in flying saucers (later called UFOs) and eventually theories about alien bases. Transient lunar phenomena (TLPs), as they are called, have played a significant role in all of this as well. TLPs consist of unexplained changes in the lunar surface, sometimes including unusual lights, shadows, and moving objects. Though some astronomers attributed such sup-

The late popular astronomer Carl Sagan believed that life likely existed somewhere on other planets in the cosmos (*NASA/Cosmos Studios*).

posed occurrences to mere optical illusions, others regard them as genuine anomalies and over time have prevailed. In December 2005 geophysicist Gary Olhoeft, citing recent NASA research, wrote, "It may be that TLPs are caused by sunlight reflecting off rising plumes of electrostatically lofted lunar dust."

TLPs—not called that until the mid-twentieth century—interested Charles Fort (1874–1932), chronicler of unexplained physical phenomena and pre-UFO-era theorist of extraterrestrial visitation. Fort, who had an unquenchable sense of humor, noted observations of changing geometric shapes in the crater Linné and remarked wryly:

> Astronomers have thought of trying to communicate with Mars or the moon by means of great geometric constructions placed conspicuously, but there is nothing so attractive to attention as change, and a formation that would appear and disappear would enhance the geometric with the dynamic. That the units of the changing compositions that covered Linné were the lunarians themselves—that Linné was terraced—hosts of the inhabitants of the moon standing upon ridges of their Cheops of the Serene Sea, some of them dressed in white and standing in a border, and some of them dressed in black, centering upon the apex, or the dark material of the apex left clear for the contrast, all of them unified in a hope of conveying an impression of the geometric, as the product of design, and distinguishable

from the topographic, to the shining god [Earth] that makes the stars of their heaven marginal.

Less mirthful notions show up in 1950s UFO books, such as *Flying Saucers on the Attack* (1954; *Flying Saucers on the Moon* in its original British edition) by Harold T. Wilkins (1883–1960), where it is stated as simple fact that "the moon ... long has been a stopover for what we call flying saucers." Wilkins predicted that the first astronauts to land there would find "massive portals" leading to "great sublunar tunnels" housing "beings of other unknown worlds in space." These beings would not be pleased to see the intruders, as the subsequent unleashing of their superior firepower would attest.

Another Wilkins, respected amateur astronomer Hugh Percy Wilkins (1896–1960), head of the British Astronomical Association's Lunar Section, would make a remarkable claim which gave impetus to UFO-based theories about intelligences on the moon. Its genesis was in a July 29, 1953, telescopic observation by *New York Herald Tribune* science editor John J. O'Neill of what O'Neill believed to be an immense bridge—a natural one, he stressed in a public statement—linking two mountain tops on the western Mare Crisium (Sea of Crises). Because his four-inch refracting telescope was a relatively modest instrument, he wrote Wilkins, who worked with a larger instrument, to ask him to examine the designated region. On the evening of August 26, when a doubtful Wilkins scrutinized the site, he was surprised to see—or at least think he saw—the bridge. Sadly, O'Neill died before he received Wilkins' letter of confirmation.

That, however, did not end the matter. On December 23, interviewed on British radio, Wilkins stated flatly, "Now this is a real bridge. Its span is about 20 miles from one side to the other, and it's probably at least 5,000 feet [1,524 meters] or so from the surface beneath." He went on, "It looks artificial. It's almost incredible that such a thing could have been formed in the first instance, or if it was formed, could have lasted during the ages in which the moon has been in existence. You would have expected it either to be disintegrated by temperature variations or by meteor impact.... It looks almost like an engineering job.... Yes, it is most extraordinary." On June 17, 1954, visiting southern California, Wilkins studied Mare Crisium with the 100-inch reflecting telescope at Mount Wilson Observatory and sighted the bridge again.

But other amateur astronomers were seeing something different, namely the effects of light from a low sun upon this particular part of the lunar landscape. Subsequent viewing, for example from the Lunar Orbiter in the 1960s, has conclusively established that no such object, whether natural phenomenon or engineered structure, exists. But at the time, even in the face of ridicule which soon led him to resign from the BAA, Wilkins stuck to his conviction.

Donald E. Keyhoe (1897-1988), a retired Marine Corps major and the most famous UFO proponent of his time, reported the observations of O'Neill and Wilkins (who in fact harbored heretical UFO sympathies), along with others of (more genuinely anomalous) TLPs, and from them spun some fanciful theories. In his book *The Flying Saucer Conspiracy* (1955) he wondered if an intelligent lunar race, a few centuries ahead of its counterparts on Earth, grew alarmed as it saw that Earthlings would soon bring their

NASA's Lunar Reconnaissance Orbiter (LRO) is designed to find safe landing spots and to locate sources of water and other resources that might be used for a future base. No evidence of any kind has been discovered about a lunar civilization (*NASA*).

bombs, wars, and violent ways to the moon; consequently, the aliens launched observational vehicles—UFOs—to monitor terrestrial activity. Or maybe the "moon race have been enslaved and forced to build the space base for outsiders.... It was even possible that a strong moon race, perhaps with unknown weapons, could have overwhelmed the space visitors and might be in control. As to which was the right answer, I could only speculate. But the evidence of some intelligent race on the moon seemed undeniable."

There was also Morris Ketchum Jessup (1900–1959). Jessup had an educational background in astronomy and experience as a working scientist. He conducted undergraduate and graduate work at the University of Michigan, where he attained an M.S. degree in 1926. In the late 1920s he and associates from the university set up a large refracting telescope in South Africa, employing it to discover many double stars. By 1931, Jessup had abandoned the work necessary for an astrophysics Ph.D. (though in later years he was often identified as "Dr. Jessup"), and he left astronomy to pursue his own archaeological interests in Mexico and Peru. When flying saucers came along, by which time he was working ordinary jobs outside the sciences, Jessup would write four books, distinguished both because one (*The Case for the UFO*, 1955) was the first to use the new phrase "UFO" in the title and also because they contained some strikingly original ruminations on the nature and origin of UFO intelligences.

In *The Expanding Case for the UFO* (1957) archaeological artifacts meet lunar anomalies (authentic and otherwise) and wed in a shotgun marriage uniting goofy guesswork to staggering silliness. In general outline, if not in specific detail, it anticipates the "ancient-astronaut" craze generated by Erich von Däniken (*Chariots of the Gods?*) and his imitators in the late 1960s and 1970s. Jessup stated, "There are 'little people' in African and New Guinea jungles today. They have been written about, photographed, measured and studied. But *nobody* knows their origin or ancestry. They are, perhaps, one of the 'erratics' of ethnology. Were these people, these isolated tribes, 'planted' in the tropical African jungle from UFO [sic] thousands of years ago? Did UFO [sic] land, or crash, and establish racial germs or colonies?"

After noting the occurrence of TLPs over the centuries, he proceeds to decree it arguably possible that these pygmies either arrived originally from the moon or colonized it from here, having developed an advanced technology based on levitation and antigravity. "We have reason to believe," he wrote, "that space flight may have been in existence for 70,000 to 100,000 years, [and] there is reason to believe that space flight derives from a time in the pre-cataclysmic era which developed a first wave of civilization.... If we do, indeed, have 'little people' within the UFO, as reported by observers of varying responsibility, then we may assume that the Pygmies, at some remote epoch, developed a civilization which discovered the principle of gravitation and put it to work." They reside on the earth, the moon, and in giant spacecraft located in space between the two in a zone of gravitational neutrality.

No one picked up on Jessup's moon-connected super-pygmies, but some UFO and related literature continued—up to the present—to explore the connection between the moon and extraterrestrials based there. The *NICAP Bulletin* for January 1959, reporting the observation of domelike objects on the moon, wondered if these were "possibly structures built by unknown space travelers." Writing in England's *Flying Saucer Review,* W. Raymond Drake advanced the notion the moon's surface appears as it does because long ago the lunarians blasted it in a nuclear conflict, either with each other or with hostile invaders. Surviving lunarians crawled into "deep caverns with air and water," and it is from there that they dispatch saucers Earthward. As it happens, the moon is not quite what it appears to be. "Our belt of atmosphere hundreds of miles thick may have some of the properties of a giant lens, which magnifies the Moon to twenty times its real size," according to Drake. In Ray Palmer's *Flying Saucers* magazine, Guy J. Cyr, a Catholic priest, imagined a moon awash in life and oceans and, of course, spaceships, and Robert W. Russel conjured up lunarians residing in great numbers under crater floors.

As pictures of the lunar surface proliferated, from improved photographic and telescopic technology on Earth and from shots taken from spacecraft near or on the moon, enthusiasts pored over them in search of alien artifacts. A hoax published in a September 1969 issue of the now-defunct supermarket tabloid *National Bulletin,* which concocted the story in its editorial office and gave it a phony by-line, purported to show censored transcripts of communications between NASA's Mission Control and the Apollo 11 moon landing (the first) on July 20, 1969. The discussion concerned sight-

Though apparently no other civilization has occupied the Moon, in coming decades human beings may establish a colony there (*illustration by Rick Guidice, NASA*).

ings of extraterrestrial spacecraft in the astronauts' vicinity. In the mid–1970s, in the pulp newsstand magazine *Saga's UFO Report,* Joseph Goodavage published sensationalistic material, cited in most subsequent writings on the subject, supposedly demonstrating evidence of lunar extraterrestrial activity.

Books by Don Wilson (*Our Mysterious Spaceship Moon* [1975] and *Secrets of Our Spaceship Moon* [1979]), Jean Sendy (*The Moon: Outpost of the Gods* [1975]), and George H. Leonard (*Somebody Else Is on the Moon* [1976]) put forth variations on the theme of moon-as-ET-colony-and-launching-pad, drawing their inspiration largely from creative interpretations of ambiguous photographic images. Wilson championed an especially outlandish allegation, namely that the moon itself is a hollow spacecraft. "The greatest UFO in our skies is there for everyone to see," he proclaimed, possibly seriously.

Fred Steckling of the George Adamski Foundation was responsible for another notable book in the genre. In *We Discovered Alien Bases on the Moon* (1982) he sought to prove that the contactees' claims of an extraterrestrial presence there (see below) were not, as critics thought, childish fiction. Itself absurdly fictional, the book sparked a devastating refutation by well-informed amateur astronomer and moon-watcher Francis G. Graham, head of the Pennsylvania Selenological Society. Graham's monograph opens with these wry words:

Fred Steckling believes the US moon program discovered aliens on the moon, and the lunar program is continuing under great secrecy, in order to

Contactee Howard Menger claimed to have spotted a dome on the surface of the moon (*BigStock*).

establish contact with the UFOs; further, some people in the government have in fact duplicated a crashed UFO ... and are using that for transport to the moon. It is not clear [to] which George Pal movie Mr. Steckling has been tuning his cosmic Interrossiter, but it is certainly not tuned to reality, if one compares his book to the main body of scientific knowledge as a yardstick of what constitutes his view of the reality of the moon.

But perhaps conventional lunar science is wrong and Mr. Steckling is right. What evidence does he produce? Mr. Steckling shows 150 photos and drawings. One of these, of himself, we can believe. The remaining 149 demand critical appraisal. Of those 149, 15 are of Earth UFOs, postage stamps, and pond water.

More recently, a small band of advocates have conducted their own lunar observations and studied NASA photographs, from which they argue that evidence of buildings and construction is visible to those willing to see it. They include Michael Bara and Steve Troy, who for several years ran a "Lunar Anomalies" website which scoured official photographs for depictions of alien activity, launched colorful attacks on doubters and deniers ("twits," "jackasses"), and carried screeds condemning "radical, America hating far-leftists who have little use for a space program or anything that would make America safer," otherwise known as Democrats and liberals.

Travelers' Tales

"As my space friends had promised, they took me on my first trip to the moon the second week of August, 1956," New Jersey sign painter and contactee Howard Menger relates matter-of-factly in the first sentence of a chapter of his *From Outer Space to You* (1959). The trip, however, ended up something of a disappointment. Menger and his friends, both space people and Earthlings, orbited the moon but did not land on it. Through a screen, however, he managed to see dome-shaped structures.

Fortunately, Menger was granted a return trip the next month, and this time he was permitted to step onto the surface—with a camera yet. In his book, of one photograph showing a saucer approaching a dome he notes, "The author was permitted to take only a few photographs" but was still keeping several under wraps, while others "did not come out well." He reported, "For some reason I was never allowed to take photographs of surface detail, people, their mechanical installations and the like." Sadly, the result was that none of the published photographs looks like anything that could not have been created on a kitchen table. One critic observed at the time, "These photos are so evidently faked that it is almost foolish to even criticize them."

He and hundreds of other Earthlings from an assortment of nations were led on a guided tour which took them from dome to dome.

Unlike other contactees Menger did not aver that the lunar landscape is livable (though he does give the moon an atmosphere which, of course, more prosaic astronomical doctrine does not afford it), but that the space people from other planets (primarily Venus) who reside there live inside the domes. He and hundreds of other Earthlings from an assortment of nations were led on a guided tour which took them from dome to dome. "All of us were shown musical instruments, samples of art and architecture, and other interesting things," Menger vaguely recalled. Going on even less helpfully, if that's conceivable, he added, "In fact [sic] one building was like an interplanetary world's fair, with each planet represented by some sort of contribution in art, technology and so on."

If anything, contactee Buck Nelson, an Ozarks farmer who may fairly be characterized as a hillbilly, had even fewer details about his lunar adventure, which took place nearly a year and a half before Menger's, in April 1955. Nelson's principal contact was Little Bucky, an Earthling expatriate who now considered Venus home.

Little Bucky and two extraterrestrial associates (one the oddly monikered "Bob Solomon") showed up at midnight on April 24 to fulfill a promise to take Buck Nelson into space. In return, as Nelson would write, "I would tell about it to the world." Buck held up his share of the bargain, writing and peddling a not fully literate booklet with the to-the-point title *My Trip to Mars, the Moon, and Venus* (1956).

What the world learned was that after a stopover on Mars, where he and his dog Teddy, who accompanied him on the epic voyage (Little Bucky's dog Big Bo was there, too), had a good meal and met some nice folks, the ship zipped him off to the moon for another excellent meal and a good rest. On the moon Nelson saw a "building." Some lunar "children played with several sized dogs. They rode Big Bo like a pony." Then Bucky and band were off to Venus.

While aboard a mothership from Saturn on April 22, 1953, contactee and space traveler George Adamski (who had first come to public attention with photographs, allegedly taken through his telescope, of flying saucers near the moon) conversed with the pilot, an individual named Zuhl. In his *Inside the Space Ships* (1955) Adamski does not mention tape-recording the exchange, but perhaps he had a remarkable memory; at any rate, he quotes the Saturnian's words about the moon:

> The side of the Moon which you can see from your planet is quite comparable to your desert areas on Earth. It is hot, as your scientists correctly claim, but its temperature is not so extreme as they think. And while the side which you do not see is colder, neither is it as cold as they believe. It is strange how people of Earth accept statements from those they look up to as men of learning without questioning the limitations of that knowledge.
>
> There is a beautiful strip or section around the center of the Moon in which vegetation, trees and animals thrive, and in which people live in comfort. Even you of Earth could live on that part of the Moon....
>
> Many of your scientists have expressed the idea that the Moon is a dead body. If this were true ... it long ago would have vanished from space through disintegration. No! It is very much alive and supports a life which includes people. We ourselves have a large laboratory just beyond the rim of the Moon, out of sight of Earth, in the temperate and cooler section of that body.

Shortly thereafter, Adamski got a look for himself through a viewing instrument aboard the craft. He spotted a small growth of vegetation and, more dramatically, a small animal. "It was four-legged and furry," he wrote, "but its speed prevented me from identifying it." Adamski fails to explain how he would have been able to "identify" a moon animal.

✳

The Contactees' Moon

On a website devoted to contactee lore, English saucerian Jimmy Goddard summarizes the moon as envisioned in the claims of space communicants:

> The Moon has a substantial atmosphere—6 pounds per square inch in its lowest elevations.... [It] has a much higher gravity than has been theorized—a value greater than 50% of Earth's.... [It] has water and known vegetation.... There are large variations in environment, between the side that always faces the earth, and the far side that only can be seen from lunar orbit. (*This is only because the Moon is not a true sphere but is bulged on the side facing Earth, causing this side to be in effect higher altitude land. While, as Adamski admitted, this is a hostile desert area for the most part, people can live there if they undergo suitable decompression*) [italics in original].... The Moon is occupied by space people. There are artificial bases on the front side, and more natural bases on the far side. The evidence has been photographed and verified.

In an October 10, 1952, automatic-writing communication to a contactee group in Prescott, Arizona, two Uranus residents reported that besides the known Earth moon, there is a "dark moon" which the "magnetic field" renders invisible to terrestrial observers. Moreover, "your first Moon is not as far away as you think.... [It] has an atmosphere and water.... There are even inhabitants on the Moon! We have many bases of interplanetary nature there, too."

Sadly, not so. As Giovanni Riccioli knew as long ago as the 1600s, the moon is dead. So, too, are the dreams humans dreamed as they rambled the lunar landscapes of what turned out to be no more than their imaginations. This line from an eighteenth-century Scottish lyric folk song (which Lord Byron later incorporated into a famous poem) says it all:

> We'll go no more a-roving
> By the light of the moon.

Further Reading:

Adamski, George. *Inside the Space Ships.* New York: Abelard-Schuman, 1955.

Corliss, William R., ed. *The Moon and the Planets: A Catalog of Astronomical Anomalies.* Glen Arm, MD: Sourcebook Project, 1985.

———, ed. *Mysterious Universe: A Handbook of Astronomical Anomalies.* Glen Arm, MD: Sourcebook Project, 1979.

Crowe, Michael J. *The Extraterrestrial Life Debate: The Idea of a Plurality of Worlds from Kant to Lowell.* New York: Cambridge University Press, 1986.

Cyr, Guy J. "Life on the Moon?" *Flying Saucers* (August 1964): 12–28.

Drake, W. R. "Is the Moon Inhabited?" *Flying Saucer Review* 6, 1 (January/February 1960): iii, 30–32.

Ford, A. E. *Guardian Spirits, A Case of Vision into the Spiritual World, Translated from the German of H. Werner, with Parallels from Emanuel Swedenborg.* New York: John Allen, 1847.

Fort, Charles. *The Books of Charles Fort.* New York: Henry Holt, 1941.

Graham, Francis G. *There Are No Alien Bases on the Moon.* Burbank, CA: William L. Moore Publications and Research, 1984.

Grego, Peter. "Alien Moon." *Fortean Times* 112 (1998): 26–27, 29.

Heinerman, John. *People in Space: Documented Extraterrestrial Life on Other Worlds.* San Rafael, CA: Cassandra Press, 1989.

Jessup, M. K. *The Expanding Case for the UFO.* New York: Citadel Press, 1957.

Keyhoe, Donald E. *The Flying Saucer Conspiracy.* New York: Henry Holt and Company, 1955.

Menger, Howard. *From Outer Space to You.* Clarksburg, WV: Saucerian Books, 1959.

Nelson, Buck. *My Trip to Mars, the Moon, and Venus.* Mountain View, AR: privately printed, 1956.

Oberg, James E. "Myths and Mysteries of the Moon." *Fate* (September 1980): 38–46.

Rickard, Bob. "Lunar Construction Site." *Fortean Times* (1998) 112: 28.

Russel, Robert W. "Intelligences in the Moon?" *Flying Saucers* (February 1968): 24–28.

Steckling, Fred. *We Discovered Alien Bases on the Moon.* Vista, CA: George Adamski Foundation, 1982.

Williamson, George H., and Alfred C. Bailey. *The Saucers Speak! A Documentary Report of Interstellar Communication by Radiotelegraphy.* Los Angeles: New Age Publishing Company, 1954.

SHROUDED IN MYSTERY: VENUSIANS IN ALL THEIR VARIETY

Only slightly smaller than the earth and once called its sister planet, Venus is the second planet from the sun. Often likened to hell, it is no place you would want to live or even visit. Its dense atmosphere, shrouding the entire planet under a cloud cover and consisting of 96 percent carbon dioxide and a minute amount of water vapor, traps surface heat in a fierce greenhouse effect. The average temperature is a tropical 840 °F (449 °C)—blistering enough to melt lead. The atmosphere also produces surface pressure 90 times what we experience on Earth, unless we happen to be standing on the ocean floor at a depth of 3,000 feet (914 meters). It rains droplets of sulfuric acid. The presence of sulfur-dioxide concentrations may imply ongoing volcanic activity.

This scientific description of the Morning Star and the Evening Star, as Earthlings have called this bright and beautiful presence (which the ancients thought were two separate celestial bodies) in our heavens, would not have been possible if not for space probes and technical advances in astronomy in the mid- to latter twentieth century. Before that, it was possible to imagine just about anything about Venus, including the beings and creatures that lived on it, and human beings did precisely that.

The Dreams of the Scientists

Among the most notable of the early speculators was the philosopher Immanuel Kant (1724–1804). In *Universal Natural History and Theory of the Heavens* (1755) he outlined the hypothesis—astronomically and logically dubious—that the distance from the sun determines the intelligence level of a world's inhabitants; thus, the people who live on Mercury are the stupidest, and Venusians are only dimly brighter. Kant and his contemporaries knew nothing of Uranus and Neptune, which were not discovered until the following century, or Pluto, found in 1930, so in the Kantian cosmic scheme of

A computer-generated veiw of Maat Mons on Venus based on a 1991 photograph by the Magellan spacecraft. Clearly, the surface of this boiling-hot planet is unsuitable for life (*JPL/NASA*).

things, the smartness of the people of Jupiter (fifth in the solar system) was exceeded only by that of Saturn (the sixth and, to mid-eighteenth-century knowledge, the last).

On the other hand, to Bernard Fontenelle (1657–1757), author of a widely read 1686 book on life on other worlds, Venusians are "little black people, scorch'd with the Sun, witty, full of Fire, very Amorous." In the generally comparable imagining of Jacques Henri Bernardin de Saint-Pierre (1737–1814), Venusians live in a paradisal, pastoral realm. The mountain people are shepherds, while "the others, on the shores of their fertile islands, give themselves over to dancing, to feasts, divert themselves with songs, or compete for prizes in swimming, like the happy islanders of Tahiti."

An observer in 1743 reported seeing "ashen light"—mysterious illumination—on Venus' dark side. Since then other astronomers have described the phenomenon, still not conclusively explained though generally thought to be the consequence of electricity in the atmosphere. To German astronomer Franz von Paula Gruithuisen (1774–1852), however, the phenomenon could be explained as light given off by "general festivals of fire" in which the Venusians periodically participate, corresponding with "changes in government" or perhaps to religious celebrations. This and other luminous anomalies led French inventor Charles Cros (1842–1888) to wonder if Venusians were trying to signal the earth and to propose ways of sending signals back.

Using earthly population-density figures as a guide, Scottish clergyman and amateur scientist Thomas Dick (1774–1857) startlingly counted the Venusian population at a densely packed 53,500,000,000. Popular science journalist Richard Proctor (1837–1888) wrote in *Other Worlds than Ours* (1870), "On the whole, the evidence we have points very strongly to Venus as the abode of living creatures not unlike the inhabitants of Earth."

Because the clouds covering the planet rendered telescopic observation of its surface impossible, much about Venus remained unknown in the first half of the twentieth century. Thus, the sorts of speculation in which even mainstream astronomers sometimes engaged looks outlandish in retrospect, more science fiction than science.

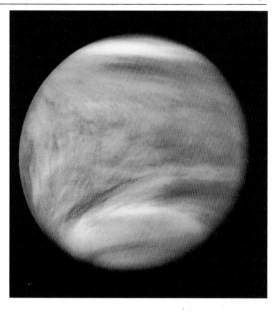

The Pioneer Venus Orbiter took this 1979 photo of Venus' cloud cover, which is too thick to allow a look onto the planet's surface (*NASA*).

For example, in common with his French colleague Edmond Perrier (1844–1921) and others, Harvard University astronomer William H. Pickering—incidentally an ally of Percival Lowell in the Mars canal controversy—argued that Venus is a tropical planet teeming with water and humid swamps, harboring giant reptiles of the sort that roamed the earth during the age of dinosaurs. "As to the question of intelligent life," he added in a 1911 interview with a *Boston Post* reporter, "the question is still open." Around the same time another then prominent astronomer, Thomas Jefferson Jackson See (1866–1962), of the U.S. Naval Observatory at Mare Island, California, declared the issue of intelligent Venusian life a settled one, based on his years of observation.

Astronomer and popular-science writer Garrett P. Serviss (1851–1929) judged the odds of Venusians' existence at 100 to one. Because they live closer to the sun and are subject to its electrical fields—intensified as they pass through the planet's cloud cover—Venusians, humanlike in form, may enjoy the benefits of superior "nervous energies." He theorized, "They may perceive electricity as we perceive light and sound, by means of organs adapted to such a purpose," and communicate through an electromagnetic form of telepathy. "Tall, finely proportioned, handsome, combining the bod-

(Continued on page 104)

MERCURY

Mercury is the first planet and the one closest to the sun. It is second in smallness only to the last planet, Pluto, the one most distant from the sun. Mercury, 3,033 miles (4,880 kilometers) in diameter at its equator, rotates on its axis every 58.65 days and orbits the sun on an elongated path every 87.97 days. It has no atmosphere to speak of, though it may have ice buried in craters at its two poles. Temperature during the days can rise to 800 °F (426.7 °C), then at night sink to –300 °F (–184.4 °C). The chance that intelligent life exists there is, it appears, somewhere between virtual zero and absolute zero.

In common with every other planet in the solar system, however, Mercury was once thought, or at least speculated, to harbor sentient beings, sometimes written about with astonishing specificity. The eighteenth-century visionary Emanuel Swedenborg, who wrote of out-of-body visits to other planets, noted that the people of Mercury disapproved of the expression of ideas via words, judged too material; their language depended on communication via eyes. Though possessed of excellent memory and insatiable curiosity, they are a pompous lot, "principled in a species of haughtiness ... puffed up with self-conceit." Their high self-regard notwithstanding, they are lousy analysts, "little distinguished for their judgments ... and the deducing of conclusions from knowledge."

In 1837, the Rev. Thomas Dick published *Celestial Scenery*, which pegged the population of Mercury at 8,960,000,000, which would make that little world a seriously crowded one. When angels flew the Spiritualist minister Thomas Lake Harris (1823–1906) through the cosmos, they made a stop at Mercury, where Harris observed a "world of Christian Platonic Philosophers ... the good, the useful, the beautiful and the true ... far transcended."

More serious and influential from a scientific point of view were the efforts of the prominent Italian astronomer Giovanni Schiaparelli. In the 1880s Schiaparelli sought to map the surface of Mercury, in the process coming to the erroneous conclusion (though not decisively disproved until the 1960s) that Mercury is in a gravitational lock which keeps one side forever directed toward the sun. This interpretation allowed for a twilight-zone area, bordering the too-hot side and the too-cold dark side, with a presumably life-friendly temperate climate.

Like other astronomers of the period, Schiaparelli thought Mercury has an atmosphere, and he took note of observations of dark spots (in reality craters carved by meteorites) which he declared "analogous to our seas." Though he measured his words, the astronomer—whose reported sightings of *canali* on Mars in the previous decade sparked the canal debate that would consume international astronomy for nearly half a century—left the clear impression that conditions favored the presence of intelligent beings.

Some other late nineteenth-century astronomers took up the idea, though none claimed to have detected direct evidence of living Mercurians. In a newspaper interview in 1902, the prominent Prof. George W. Hough, head of Northwestern University's astronomy department, told a reporter that after decades of observation through the Dearborn Observatory telescope, he had found Mercury, Venus, and Mars to be Earth-like planets. "The inhabitants of Venus or Mercury or Mars, after a process of evolution begun millions upon millions of years before the earth even assumed its present form, must be ages in advance of us in civilization," he said.

Decades later, the contactees of the 1950s had an obsession with Venusians, Martians, and—for some reason—Saturnians. In contactee lore all planets of the solar system are inhabited, but it has relatively little to say about the residents of Mercury. What follows are two of the rare exceptions.

In his telling of the story, Dan Martin was driving on a rural Texas road one night in August 1955 when he felt unwell. He pulled over and stepped outside to recover his strength. As he was doing so, a flying machine, 60 feet (18 meters) long and shaped like a diesel locomotive, landed nearby. He glimpsed several men inside, but it was a woman who came out of the craft to engage him in conversation. The men couldn't speak English, she explained. She promised him that he would be contacted

Mercury, like all of the planets in our solar system, was also thought to harbor life, when actually it has no atmosphere and its surface temperatures range from about 840 °F (450 °C) during the day down to –275 °F (–170 °C) at night (*iStock*).

again and this time allowed to fly inside a larger ship.

That contact occurred 10 months later, in June 1956. Martin answered a knock at his door and met an attractive-looking couple. "We have come to take you for a journey on a spaceship," the man announced. "We will return you to your home within about seven hours." The two positioned themselves on either side of him, gripped him above his elbows, and floated him through the air until they entered a small craft which then took them to a larger one. He was introduced to the captain, who informed him that the ship he had boarded was called the "Michiel," present in the earth's atmosphere for 6,000 years and responsible for biblical miracles and other wonders.

After a tour of the ship and a big meal in the dining room, during which crew members peppered him with questions about Earth and humans (the aliens, one infers, having learned little from 6,000 years of observation), all concerned repaired to a lecture room where the captain droned on about the history of the solar system, conditions on Mercury (where this particular group of space people hailed from), and matters Martin judged, so he averred, too sensitive to reveal to readers of his little-heeded monograph on his supposed experience.

If Martin's yarn seems a tad half-hearted, there is the epic saga of Latin American contactee Enrique Castillo Rincón. It began in June 1963 in the Central American republic of Costa Rica and followed him in later years to Colombia, Brazil, and Venezuela, and then back to Colombia. It was there, in the early morning hours of November 19, 1973, that he encountered the crew of a spacecraft from Mercury, only a little more than two weeks after he had boarded another ship, this one from the Pleiades. (The Pleiades crew told him that the Third World War could be expected in four years or thereabouts.)

Castillo had gone to a region of rural Colombia to meet the space people, who obligingly showed up at 3:00 AM. His space friend Cyril came to greet him, and after a short delay, during which Castillo was bathed in a "very bright blue flash of lightning" before being allowed to pass

(Continued from page 101)

ily qualities of Apollo, Jupiter, and Adonis," a Venusian adult male, Serviss rhapsodized, "would possess powers apparently supernatural."

On the other hand, a 1927 writer for the *Fresno Bee* imagined Venusians as enduring a hellish existence. The anonymous theorist argued that half of the planet's surface is frigid, the other half blistering, with the halves switching places after the 225 Earth days it takes the planet to orbit the sun. Consequently, Venusians are forced to seek refuge in two widely separated mountain ranges, where they can dwell, if only temporarily, in temperate climes covering a slender zone between the two extremes. Engaged in this constant travel and struggle, Venusians are unable to maintain a stable, lawful social order. "Blood-thirsty competition and individual self-protection" define their interaction with their fellows.

Beginning in the 1920s, however, a handful of astronomical investigators were collecting more realistic data which suggested, first, fierce surface temperatures and then (in 1932) the absence of oxygen and water vapor, plus an abundance of carbon through the door, he was introduced to two short humanoids, around four and a half feet (1.37 meters) tall, with "avocado-shaped heads." Castillo related, "I got up to greet them, but they just bowed, without extending their hands." They appeared shiny as if coated with a film of oil, "well-proportioned, with large normal eyes, normal ears, Greek nose, and prominent jaw. They [wore] short sleeves that exposed their shiny arms."

When Cyril identified them as residents of Mercury, Castillo protested that no such thing could be possible, given the fierce surface temperatures of that planet. Cyril coolly responded, "You would be astonished at the civilizations that have flourished there."

In the course of his extended stay in the vessel, Castillo met other aliens, including a gray-skinned, hairy, spatula-fingered, but otherwise human-looking 10-foot (three meter) giant from Jupiter, seen shuffling through one of the corridors

Years later Castillo, still an active contactee, acknowledged to British ufologist Timothy Good that Mercurians, Jovians, and the like are pretty much impossible, most likely false identities of deceitful extraterrestrials.

Further Reading

Good, Timothy. *Unearthly Disclosure: Conflicting Interests in the Control of Extraterrestrial Intelligence.* London: Century, 2000.

Martin, Dan. *Seven Hours Aboard a Space Ship.* Detroit, MI: privately printed, 1959.

dioxide in Venus' atmosphere. This sparked an inevitable skepticism about life, even vegetable life, among scientists who were paying attention.

Even so, others acted as if oblivious to the new developments, treating the planet as it had always been depicted: as a warmer Earth. In 1922 Salt Lake City meteorologist Alfred Rordame, speaking before the American Meteorological Society, argued that spectroscopic findings which appeared to show no oxygen or water vapor could not be trusted; in reality, he contended, the "spectroscope is incapable of penetration below these clouds around Venus, as the light is reflected from the upper surface of them. The bulk of whatever oxygen and water vapor exists must be beneath this veil in the stormy atmosphere nearer the planet." That same year Charles G. Abbot of the Smithsonian Institution remarked that Venus is the only other planet in the solar system likely to harbor intelligent life because it has, he claimed, both "water vapor and water clouds." As late as 1946, Abbot fantasized about radio communication with Venusians "brought up completely separate [from Earthlings], having their own sys-

THE MAN FROM VENUS

by PAUL

A scientific conception of life on earth's nearest neighbor. Science says Venus is a sister world and human forms of life are more possible than on any other planet.

(For further details see page 97)

Copyright, FANTASTIC ADVENTURES 1939

tems of government, social usages, religions, and surrounded by vegetation and animals entirely unrelated to any here on Earth."

In his best-selling *Astronomy* (1935) astronomer/clergyman (and, in subsequent decades, creationist hero) Arthur M. Harding wrote, "No one would imagine for an instant that after the Creator had constructed this magnificent solar system ... He would have neglected our little globe to be the abode of life and overlooked its twin sister and neighbor, Venus. Surely there must be some forms of life on Venus that are not so very different from what we find on the earth. The objection has been raised that Venus is too near the sun to have life on it. It is true that Venus is a little warmer than the earth, but this is no barrier. We have life at the tropics and also life at the poles."

Still, because no one had glimpsed Venus' surface, those inclined to do so continued to imagine everything from a massive dust bowl to lush vegetation to a planet-encircling ocean. Writing in *The Universe We Live In* (1951), John Robinson revived the venerable vision of Venus—most prominently put forth more than three decades earlier by Swedish chemist and Nobel laureate Svante Arrhenius (1859–1927)—as a place like "the far-off Carboniferous Period of the Earth's geological history" with "seas and swamps and the steamy, heavily carbonated atmosphere.... Venus has every appearance of being a world something like our world hundreds of millions of years ago."

Donald H. Menzel (1901–1976), of the Harvard Observatory, had a reputation as an uncompromising debunker of UFO reports, but he was also a wild-eyed theorist about Venus, in one instance in the same book (*Flying Saucers,* 1953). He envisioned "warm seas" in which life forms of all kind, from the microscopic to large invertebrates and vertebrates, flourish. "It is somewhat interesting to note that, had we ourselves developed on Venus instead of on the earth," he reflected, "it is not at all unlikely that we might have developed into a race of mermaids and mermen." On the other hand, in the same decade Soviet astronomer G.A. Tikhoff pictured Venus as a world of glimmering, ray-emitting flowers. In a December 1959 presentation to the year-old National Aeronautics and Space Administration (NASA), the California Institute of Technology's Harrison Brown spoke of a mostly marine Venus harboring jellyfish-like creatures.

From February 1961 and through the next two decades, the United States and the Soviet Union launched a series of space probes. Some sailed near the planet, others entered its atmosphere, and a few successfully landed on its surface. The discoveries ended all talk that intelligent Venusians, or even life forms larger than microbes, populate that world.

✳

The Occultists' Venus

In his fiftieth year the Swedish scientist Emanuel Swedenborg, the author already (in the words of one biographer) of "160 works and [founder of] six new sciences,"

◀ **There has been considerable speculation in the past, such as in this 1939 book, on what life on Venus could be like because the planet's size is similar to Earth's and it has cloud cover (*Mary Evans Picture Library*).**

In this 1911 illustration, a Venusian is depicted as a menacing giant; usually, however, when people thought of aliens, they came to Earth from Mars (*Mary Evans Picture Library*).

began experiencing mystical visions that occupied him the rest of his life. Among other spiritual adventures he traveled to the moon and all the planets known in the eighteenth century. All of these bodies, he reported in *Earths in the Solar World* (1758), are populated by intelligent beings, sometimes by more than one kind.

Venusians, he wrote, "are of two kinds; some are gentle and benevolent, others wild, cruel and of gigantic stature. The latter rob and plunder, and live by this means; the former have so great a degree of greatness and kindness that they are always beloved by the good; thus they often see the Lord appear in their own form on their Earth." The bad guys not only rob their victims but eat them.

Another influential mystic who spoke with certainty of Venusians was Helena Petrovna Blavatsky (1831–1891), founder of Theosophy. Blavatsky, with Swedenborg one of the most important figures in the history of Western occultism, proposed an enormously complex cosmic order and alternative history, including "Lords of the Flame" on Venus. Blavatsky had not much to say about them, perhaps because she had so much else to invent.

It was Martians, not Venusians, whom people of the nineteenth century were more likely to claim they had met or heard from. Martians either communicated through mediums or, as dubious late-century newspaper accounts alleged, flew, sometimes landing, airships. For the most part, Venusians existed only as abstract possibilities, not as entities one might encounter.

In the twentieth century Guy Warren Ballard set a dubious precedent for a later generation of claimants to extraterrestrial contact (by the early 1950s being called "contactees"). Ballard was a man with a checkered past and little claim to personal achievement until in the last decade of his life he came forth with bizarre and escalating stories about his interactions with Ascended Masters, commencing with a 1930 visit to California's Mount Shasta (whose interior, as we have seen, mystical legend has it, harbors survivors of the lost Pacific continent Lemuria).

As he told the story in *Unveiled Mysteries* (pseudonymously bylined "Godfré Ray King," 1934), Ballard—well versed in Theosophical and other occult writings—had decided to take a day off from his job as a mining engineer to investigate the alleged presence of a supernatural group of deities called the Brotherhood of Mount Shasta. He was thirsty and trying to find a mountain stream when a young-looking stranger approached to pour a creamy liquid into Ballard's cup. Ballard drank it without question. The substance had an "electrical vivifying effect in my mind and body," he would report.

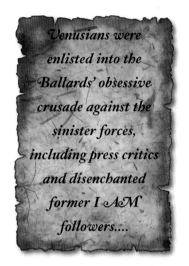

Venusians were enlisted into the Ballards' obsessive crusade against the sinister forces, including press critics and disenchanted former I AM followers....

Soon the mysterious figure introduced himself as Saint Germain, an Ascended Master, and proved it by supernatural demonstrations. Ballard had been chosen, he said, to be the Messenger of the Masters. With his wife Edna (1886–1971) he went on to form the I AM Religious Activity ("AM" standing for Ascended Master), an intensely controversial group, formed in Chicago and later moved to Los Angeles, the Ballards' home base, in 1932. ("I AM" also is an allusion to Exodus 3:14, where God says to Moses, "I am who I am." In the Ballards' Theosophy-based theology—Saint Germain is borrowed from Blavatsky—Ascended Masters are former humans who used the divine energy of God's light that exists in each of us to ascend to God's level.) The group, albeit reduced, survives to the present, even after son Donald's retirement from the movement in 1957 and Edna's death 14 years later. Guy Ballard died on December 29, 1939.

In the 1930s the Ballards roamed the nation with what amounted to a mediumistic road show, producing extravagant pageants, thrilling followers with communications from Saint Germain and others, and enraging others who saw them, with some justice, as charlatans and fascists. The Ballards had both been enthusiasts of American Nazi William Dudley Pelley (1890–1965). In the wake of an out-of-body encounter with Ascended Masters which he detailed in a widely read 1929 magazine article, Pelley had assembled a paramilitary army of pro-Hitler, anti-Semitic lowlifes known as Silver Shirts because they wore, well, silver shirts in their faux-German uniforms. When the Ballards broke with Pelley to form their own organization, they borrowed many of Pelley's far-right political precepts and ambitions but—whatever their other intellectual, philosophical, and moral failings—did not traffic in anti-Semitism.

Prominent among the otherworldly entities with whom Guy Ballard interacted were Venusians. He first met them in Saint Germain's company when the two attended (in out-of-body states) a convention of Masters in their gold-laden retreat beneath the Grand Tetons in Wyoming. Twelve of them—men and women—showed up for the confab, appearing suddenly in a blaze of light. They were beautiful, golden-haired, and violet-blue-eyed, all in all looking very much like the Venusians who would become standard issue in tales of the saucer-contactee era. They entertained the assembled mystical masters with a violin-and-harp concert. As coincidence would have it, in consensus reality Edna Ballard was a harpist.

Venusians were enlisted into the Ballards' obsessive crusade against the sinister forces, including press critics and disenchanted former I AM followers (one of whom remarked dryly that the couple had a "well-defined persecution complex"), who sought to frustrate Guy and Edna's struggle to bring humans to divine light and ascension. A regular communicant in their mediumistic demonstrations was the "Tall Master from Venus," a Lord of the Flame. To rapturous crowds the Tall Master, speaking through Guy, praised Guy and Edna as "the most precious Beings on the face of this Earth today." Another Venusian, Sanat Kumara, grumpily scolded the faithful, "The greatest mistake of mankind today is to think that they must have physical contact in order to express love." The Ballards and their otherworldly associates forbade all forms of sexual expression, even hand-holding and kissing.

Many prophets, even ones who claim experiences of a fantastic and outlandish nature, are sincere visionaries. Some, on the other hand, aren't. More than a few observers think that the Ballards consciously and deliberately concocted an elaborate hornswaggle, its particulars cobbled together from Blavatsky and other sources. A particularly prominent influence is the occult novel *A Dweller on Two Planets,* by "Phylos the Thibetan" (the supposed channeler of the contents to automatic writer Frederick Spencer Oliver, composed in the mid–1880s but unpublished until 1905). It is certainly the model—Ballard barely changes the language—for many of Ballard's adventures with the Masters. (Oliver's hero Walter Pierson is taken to Venus whose inhabitants have, it turns out, "splendid physiques ... graceful and perfect [in] every line.")

A second, another 1894 mystical novel, Will L. Carver's *The Brother of the Third Degree,* features as a leading character the Comte de St. Germain. The Comte de St. Germain was an actual historical figure, an eighteenth-century dabbler in the mystic arts and a notorious charlatan who hinted that he was immortal in the most literal sense. Voltaire famously sneered that the attention-obsessed count was "the man who never dies."

Decades later, writing in England's *Flying Saucer Review,* W.R. Drake deduced exactly who St. Germain really was:

> Viewed in our flying saucer context, the appearances and disappearance across the centuries of this fantastic man with phenomenal talents and inexhaustible wealth, without origin or social background, which so baffled his contemporaries, become suddenly illumined in one startling wondrous revelation. Is it not plausible to suggest that Count St. Germain was a missionary from Space, an avatar from Venus with remarkable powers, who throughout the ages has selflessly descended to Earth to direct Man's evolution, and who periodically returns to Venus in spaceships to recuperate? His extraordinary longevity may be normal for that lovely planet, the source of his diamonds; his spiritual ideals and nobility of life, acknowledged by all witnesses, testifying to a civilization there far transcending our own.

Venusians and Flying Saucers

In a little-noticed story published in a Washington newspaper, *Centralia Daily Chronicle*, on April 1, 1950, an elderly man related his recent meeting just days before with the crew of a Venusian spacecraft. Whatever immediate appearances may have suggested to the contrary, it was not an April Fool's Day joke. Soon afterwards, Kenneth Arnold (whose 1947 sighting over Mount Rainier brought flying saucers into public consciousness) and his wife, Doris, interviewed the claimant, an elderly retired railroad worker named Samuel Eaton Thompson, and taped his account.

Thompson, a poorly educated, unsophisticated man, was returning from a visit to relatives when he pulled over to take a break in a wooded area between Morton and Mineral, Washington. As he walked into the trees, he came upon a clearing in which a large globe-shaped structure hovered just above the ground. He noticed several strikingly beautiful children playing on steps that led from a door on the side of the craft. They had a deeply tanned appearance, and long blond hair that came all the way to their waists. They were naked. Soon similar-appearing adults came to the door and watched him, apparently uneasy about his intentions. Thompson managed to persuade them that he meant no harm.

He ended up, he said, spending some 40 hours (including one overnight) in their company over the next two days, interrupted only by a quick trip home for a camera (which recorded nothing except a bright glow as if from overexposure). The Venusians were innocents who seemed to have stepped out of an interplanetary Garden of Eden, without sin, shame, or even technological knowledge; all they knew about their ship was that its four buttons took one up or down or to Earth from Venus or the reverse. The Venusians had come to spread peace and good will, though they had not received it from Earthlings, whose aircraft had shot at their ship. All planets of the solar system are inhabited, the Venusians told him, but only Martians are more warlike than the people of our world. Thompson's companions consumed only nuts, vegetables, and fruits, and their exemplary dietary habits kept them from ever suffering illness; they died only of old age. They lived not by intellect but by instinct, yet "they're really smarter than we think they are. They've got a gift that is so much greater than ours that there is no comparison." According to them, Jesus Christ will return in 10,000 C.E.

The Arnolds did not believe Thompson had a literal physical encounter. Kenneth Arnold, who considered much of the story absurd to the point of comedy, thought it was something like a vivid dream or hallucination. They did not doubt, however, that Thompson believed every word he was saying. Anyone who hears the tape-recorded interview is likely to agree. It is hard to overstate Thompson's naivete, evinced for example in his struggle to describe concepts (vegetarianism, reincarnation, and sun signs) for which he lacked a vocabulary.

(Continued on page 116)

KAZIK

Though alleged to be a real one, Kazik—pronounced *Kay*-ik—is a fictional planet. It came into being not through natural cosmological processes but in a murky incident that took place in the early history of ufology. But for the energetic exploitation of a flying-saucer promoter, it would never have been invented.

Among the first groups to be formed in the early days of the UFO controversy was the International Flying Saucer Bureau (IFSB), announced in April 1952 and headquartered in Connecticut. In a statement circulated to attract members, its head, Bridgeport factory worker Albert K. Bender, expressed the desire to "get all Flying Saucer minded people acquainted with each other.... We would like to be considered 'Friends of the Flying Saucer Occupants' providing they decide to land on Earth with a friendly attitude."

Soon IFSB claimed 600 members, including a branch in Great Britain. The first issue of its magazine *Space Review* was released in October. In those days— it would not be the case in later years— there was a large overlap between science-fiction fans and UFO buffs. *Space Review*, which ran amateurish science-fiction stories along with saucer news, was much like the SF fanzines that proliferated in the 1950s.

Bender, a bachelor who lived with his stepfather and was perhaps not the most mature of 31-year-olds, had converted his dwelling into what he called a "chamber of horrors," with monster pictures on walls, shrunken heads, artificial bats, and the like everywhere else. He would write that at night he imagined leaving his body and traveling through space, while "thousands of eyes ... from the blackness" watched him.

In September 1953 something happened. Exactly what it was has never been clear, but whatever it was, its effect was to frighten Bender badly. He confided the outlines, and no more, to close associates. As he told it, three men in black suits had called on him, threatened him, and imparted the secret behind the UFO mystery. The visit and attendant revelations so upset him that he was sick for three days. At first Bender said the men were government agents, though in later, cryptic accounts he grew vaguer about who exactly the three men were. One plausible interpretation, though unproved, is that they were FBI agents. In those days saucer buffs were sometimes suspect as subversives in effect or intent. If so, Bender presumably exaggerated the incident beyond recognition.

In any event, Bender closed down IFSB with an announcement in the October issue of *Space Review* that flying saucers were "no longer a mystery" but he was not at liberty to say more. "We advise those engaged in saucer work to please be very cautious," he warned.

Gray Barker, a movie distributor from Clarksburg, West Virginia, had been particularly active in the IFSB, serving as the organization's chief investigator. Barker, who died in 1984, would go on to become notorious as a publisher of out-landish saucer materials and promoter of outright hoaxes, a few of which he helped launch. Bender's sudden silence may or may not have intrigued him origi-nally. After some exchanges, in person and by mail, with Bender, Barker came to suspect, at least in more skeptical moments, that there was less than met the eye. In one of those, he wrote New Zealand ufologist Harold H. Fulton on November 20, 1954:

> There is little mystery connected with it other than the mystery of Al's own mind and imagination. I think that it was a persecution complex, developed, perhaps, out of being unable to cope with the administrative details of his large organization, his inability to solve the saucer mystery, and pos-sibly some deep seated psy-choses.... I could be "all wet" but I have spent more time on this than anyone else I know of, and have scads of material and notes on the thing.

In other private correspondence, though, Barker expressed what appears to be genuine puzzlement. In any event, ambivalent views don't sell, and they did-n't stop Barker from taking these "scads of material and notes," padding them with paranoia-drenched speculation, and producing a best-selling book with the lurid B-movie title *They Knew Too Much about Flying Saucers*. It laid the ground-work for the pop-culture image of "men

Albert K. Bender illustrated this 1953 cover for the magazine founded by Gray Barker (*Mary Evans Picture Library*).

in black" as menacing figures linked to a sinister official "Silence Group" or per-haps even to hostile otherworldly intelli-gences. The book generated fervent dis-cussion on ufology's fringes for years to come. Barker, now editor of his own peri-odical (*The Saucerian*) and a fledgling saucer/New Age book publisher, milked the "Bender mystery," as he fashioned it, for all it was worth.

The ultimate prize—a tell-all volume by Bender himself under Barker's Saucer Books imprint, initiated in 1959 with the publication of contactee Howard Menger's *From Outer Space to You*—eluded him. In December 1958 Bender agreed to com-pose the book that Barker had been pressing him to produce. As he would tell

Barker, he had produced one chapter, and then "something happened," and that was that. For a while, anyway. In 1962 Barker let his customers know that Bender was ready to spill everything in a book titled *Flying Saucers and the Three Men*.

The result, which disappointed everybody (including Barker, who eventually confessed his own sense of anticlimax), read like the mediocre science-fiction novel it clearly was. Bender's account did not even conform to what limited information he had given out in the weeks after his supposed silencing, but took a whole new direction.

Now, as Bender had it, eerie forces—strange lights, glowing eyes, and sulfur stenches—were manifesting in his house as he engaged in his IFSB labors. Things took a serious turn to the sinister, however, after he urged his membership to try to contact space people via telepathy at the same time on March 15, 1953 ("World Contact Day"). Bender lay down on his bed that evening to concentrate on his own psychic communication attempt. An intense headache, followed by odd sounds and visual sensations, drove him into unconsciousness. He revived soon to find himself in an out-of-body state floating above his bed, while his physical body remained where it was. A voice spoke through the dark room, warning him (like nothing so much as a character in a comic book) to "discontinue delving into the mysteries of the universe." When Bender protested that his intentions were friendly, the disembodied

voice explained, "We have a special assignment and must not be disturbed by your people." Then it was gone, and Bender was back in his body.

One night late in July, three shadowy figures, floating just above the floor, showed up in Bender's room. "All of them were dressed in black clothes," he would write. "They looked like clergymen, but wore hats similar to Homburg style." They told that they wanted to keep in touch with him and "have you come with us at a time to be announced to you soon." They left him with a small piece of metal through which he could let them know he wanted to speak with them. He was to hold it tightly in his palm and repeat the then-meaningless word "Kazik" over and over gain.

When Bender used the device soon afterwards, he felt himself leaving his body again, finding himself inside a circular room covered by a glass dome. A humanlike figure entered through a wall panel and gave Bender a slide show in which the latter was shown pictures of the aliens' home planet, "many, many light years from your small system of planets." He went on, "All ... systems of planets ... have been formed from a central source so powerful that you could not even approach it.... It is a vast glowing body so immense one cannot calculate its density. It is the creator of all of us, and more families of planets are constantly being formed and thrown off into orbits."

One picture showed a hideous-looking creature. It turned out that this was the true form of the "man"—who had stepped out while Bender's attention was elsewhere and who now spoke through the image. The monstrous entity said that on Kazik there are three sexes, male, female, and hermaphroditic, the last of them the "exalted ones who become our leaders."

Soon, after a floating feeling, Bender found himself in his own bed. After due reflection "I decided the best possible thing would be to discontinue publishing *Space Review* in its present form," he wrote in his book, "for I already knew the secret of the UFOs, and no one would believe the story anyhow if it were published." That much, at least, is prescient.

In August three black-clad alien men with glowing eyes visited Bender. The next thing he knew, he was in an enormous cavern, apparently in some hidden realm on Earth. The figures, who were still with him, led him to a large cigar-shaped spacecraft. Inside the ship they met an alien, in his actual monster form, who told Bender that he was "at a spot on your planet known as Antarctica. We have chosen this area because it is uninhabited and there is no one to disturb us in our task." Not coincidentally, Bender in real life was engaged in what he called "Project X," in which selected American, Australian, and New Zealand members were to try (by surveying UFO flight paths) to determine if the saucers had a base at the South Pole.

His alien contacts told Bender that they were here to "obtain water from your

According to Albert K. Bender, who made this drawing, sinister Men in Black convinced him to stop looking for aliens (*Mary Evans Picture Library*).

vast bodies of sea," for reasons they would not specify. They had arrived in 1945. "We have carried off many of your people to our own planet for means [sic] of experimentation and also to place some of them on exhibit for our own people to see."

When Bender asked about other inhabited planets, one of his contacts replied, "At one time people existed on the planet you call the Red Planet, or Mars. They were destroyed by people from a passing planet similar to ours. They were exploited and ravaged by these visitors. The other planet nearest you, called

Venus, is covered in shroud, because it is going through a prehistoric stage similar to the one your planet experienced so many years ago." Bender also learned that God does not exist and that human beings do not live on after death.

Some weeks later, sitting alone at home, Bender smelled the familiar sulfur odor which always heralded visitations. The three men materialized, and as usual, when they touched him, he passed out, to reawaken in the glass-domed room he had entered on other occasions. Three silver-haired, beautiful-appearing women showed up ("I wonder if they appeared in their natural forms or if they were in reality monsters such as the males I had seen"). After removing all of his clothing, they poured a liquid on his body and "massaged every part ... without exception." After they left, a hooded alien appeared to tell him that the procedure he had just undergone would

"ensure your continued good health for years to come."

One day in 1960 Bender discovered that the metal disc the Kazikians had given him was gone. He took this as evidence that the beings had left. "Since then," he wrote (not exactly accurately), "flying saucer reports have decreased."

Bender never explained why, if "Kazikians" was pronounced "Kayik," he knew that, or why the aliens, whose spoken and written language was not English, would spell it that way—in the unlikely event they spelled it at all.

Further Reading

Barker, Gray. *They Knew Too Much about Flying Saucers.* New York: University Books, 1956.

Bender, Albert K. *Flying Saucers and the Three Men.* Clarksburg, WV: Saucerian Books, 1962.

(Continued from page 111)

After the newspaper article and the Arnolds' interview (the contents of which were not released until three decades later), Thompson disappeared from history, his vision—arguably literal as much as metaphorical—of Venusian visitors casting no shadow on the saucer tall tales that would surface in the next few years. Unlike Thompson's, the Venusians of the contactee movement would be technologically sophisticated and scientifically advanced.

No evidence indicates that George Adamski (1891–1965) ever heard of Thompson, but as a longtime figure on the California occult scene he knew of Blavatsky and was conversant in Theosophy, and he may or may not have known the Ballards personally. What is certain is that the golden-haired, peace-loving, long-winded Venusians he claimed to have encountered had been heard of before, but this time there was the additional element of flying saucers, heretofore unmentioned even in mystical literature dealing specifically with interplanetary intelligences. The UFO controversy that erupted in the summer of 1947 and continued uninterrupted to the present changed forever the landscape of alternative realities; from then on, no talk of people from other worlds could fail to mention the nuts-and-bolts vehicles in which they arrived.

Adamski came to modest public visibility in the 1930s as a kind of low-rent guru, founder of the Royal Order of Tibet and the teacher of a doctrine he called "Universal Progressive Christianity." Known to his followers as "professor," he set up a tiny observatory, with 15-inch telescope, on the southern slope of Mount Palomar, causing him to be mistaken—or perhaps that was the intention—for a professional astronomer from the Palomar Observatory a few miles away. His emergence on the international scene awaited the saucer craze, however. By 1949 he was adding juicy items about official cover-ups of UFO flights from "the other side of the moon" and about secret government knowledge that

In this 1953 work by George Adamski and Desmond Leslie, Adamski recorded his 1952 visitation by Venusians in a remote part of California (*Mary Evans Picture Library*).

all planets are inhabited. That same year he published a didactic novel, *Pioneers of Space,* which previewed interplanetary tales sometimes much like those he would soon peddle as actual events.

In 1950 and 1951, in *Fate,* a digest popular among enthusiasts of the paranormal, Adamski published pictures of alleged spaceships. The photographs stirred considerable interest, but nothing compared to what would happen in late 1952—November 20, specifically—when Adamski, accompanied by six "witnesses," watched a saucer land in the California desert near Desert Center; alone, he went on to speak with its occupant, the Venusian Orthon. Orthon's essential message was that Earthlings' warring ways were generating concern throughout the solar system.

That was only the start. There were other photographs, other contacts with Venusians, Martians, and Saturnians, a trip into space and around the moon, and finally (and unacceptably to his followers) voyages to Venus and then Saturn. He reported most of this in three books, in pamphlets, in private conversations, on lecture platforms around the world. To some he was "Earth's cosmic ambassador," and to others he was a shameless con man. He did not get rich, but he did get famous in a way. Soon enough a small army of contactees joined him in friendship and solidarity with Venusians.

Initially, Adamski had to be content with pictures of the Venusian surface. In his remarkably tedious *Inside the Space Ships* (1955) he recounts his travels in "Scouts" from Venus and Saturn and conversations—whole pages of droning (all of it inexplicably transcribed verbatim) by assorted spacemen. In the last chapter he boards a Venusian craft one August day in 1954 to meet with, among others, Orthon, who—using laserlike images—shows him scenes from Venus. "I saw magnificent mountains ... some not very different from those of Earth," Adamski wrote. "Some were thickly timbered and I saw water running in streams and cascades down the mountainsides." Orthon noted that Venus has a system of canals that link the planet's seven oceans and many lakes. (In the science-fictional *Pioneers of Space* the "Venetians" tell the narrator that they have "nine oceans, many lakes and rivers, majestic, towering mountains.") Adamski also saw cities consisting of dome-shaped buildings and houses "radiating in prismatic colors that gave the impression of a revitalizing force.... The people I saw on the streets of these cities seemed to be going about their business in much the same manner as Earth folk, except for the absence of rush and worry so noticeable with us." Cylinder-shaped cars glided just above the ground. (*Pioneers:* "Venetian" cars "seem to be gliding right over the surface of the ground.")

He also observed an ocean and a beach, animals and flowers. The clouds surrounding the planet, Orthon explained, are a "filter system" counteracting "the destructive rays which otherwise would enter its atmosphere." That is why the average Venusian lives a thousand Earth years. The Venusian political system consists of a one-world democratic order, arranged in approximately 50 states or provinces.

In his last four years Adamski's claims grew even more outlandish, if that is imaginable, so extreme that even those who had embraced in their entirety all the previous yarns started to suspect that he was now making up stories. Either that, or the CIA was setting him up. Or maybe it was evil space people; after all, Adamski had acknowledged that lately a "new set of boys" had come onto the scene, replacing the beloved and always trustworthy Orthon and associates. In 1961, in any event, Adamski reported that he finally got to make the trip to Venus. After a 12-hour flight the ship landed on the surface. Its earthly passenger wandered about for five hours before boarding the Venus–California express for the return trip.

Naturally, this was all exhausting. Adamski felt fatigued after a short walk, but that was not just because of his tiring travel schedule and his advanced age. It also had something to do with the atmospheric pressure, which was comparable to what one might encounter "at the altitude and in a comparable location with Mexico City." He noted that "80% of the planet is covered with water. The cloud cover that does not permit us to see the surface of Venus is caused by constant evaporation of moisture. This permits a large tropical area where fruits and vegetables are plentiful." In an ever more egregious whopper, Adamski gave the Venusian day a length of 23 earthly hours, when in fact it is 243 *days*.

An illustration depicting George Adamski's encounter with Orthon in 1952 (*Mary Evans Picture Library/Michael Buhler*).

Though many contactees have told tales of adventures with Venusians, only a relatively small number have claimed actual visits to Venus. None have had much, if anything, of interest to say about it, though one anonymous American wrote to the *Australian Saucer Record* in 1961 to state that his space friends denied Adamski's contacts; Venusians do not exist, they said, and to prove it they flew the writer to Venus, where he saw a swampy planet with oceans and jungles. "The reason there is no human life on Venus is that a human being could only live for a few days on that planet," he said. "Everything grows very fast and dies fast."

Another Venusian traveler, who reported the more typical inhabited, paradise-like world, was 1950s contact claimant Buck Nelson. An Ozark farmer, Nelson attracted even more ridicule than most with his stories—always related in a kind of backwoods English—which fused a naïve homoeroticism (beautiful Venusian men who shed their clothing for reasons that never quite make sense) with racist notions (a Venus segregated by skin color) and laughable swindles (the marketing of packets of Venusian dog hair).

The more obscure John Langdon Watts interacted with Venusians, who he learned live 2,500 years because, like Thompson's friends, they eat good vegetarian food. They are here, he wrote in the 1970s, to prepare us for a planet-wide cataclysm that will occasion massive damage in the seminal year 2000. He took up residence for a time on Venus, living in a domed city with a female resident, Mara. From his earthly home in Florida, he published books detailing cosmetic and diet tips he had picked up from the lovely Mara.

The Englishman George King zipped to Venus in his astral body, arriving in the Valley of the Sun at the Temple of Solace. A guide named Patana took him to another temple, from which spiritual vibrations were beamed into the brain of every Venusian. For his part King experienced "a supreme, pulsating, scintillating, living brilliance which knew me more completely than I had ever known myself." King subsequently moved to Los Angeles, where he continued to channel assorted space communications. His Aetherius Society—named after his principal contact, a Venusian—is one of the most successful and long-lasting of the contactee sects. King himself died in 1997.

Another astral visitor, Allen Noonan (whom a cosmic voice had asked to be "Savior of the World"; he assented), noticed architectural marvels that somehow escaped the attention of other pilgrims to Earth's sister planet. "There is a city on Venus that would be called the New Jerusalem if it were here," he told journalist Lloyd Mallan. "The cities of our own planet are obsolete. On Venus there is [a] most striking city. The City of Spirals. It has no streets. Everything is built of beautiful spirals. The people and the traffic move around on elegant spirals."

Few peddled Venusians tales more colorful than the yarns spun by a young chiropractic student from Inglewood, California, named Lee Crandall, who called himself "the first man to visit another planet." Crandall's adventures began early one early evening in May 1954 when, as he was sprinting to catch a bus, he plowed into the back of a tall man clad in a brown suit. Moments later, the man vanished. On a subsequent evening, August 31, the stranger showed up at Crandall's trailer house. After introducing himself as Brother Bocco from Venus, he invited Crandall to travel with him—then and there—to his home planet. The young man scrawled a note, "Folks: Gone to Venus. All is well."

A luminous, multicolored spaceship sat in the driveway, just behind his car. After Bocco knocked on its side, a door revealed itself, and three steps lowered to the ground. The two men were off on an interplanetary jaunt—in a ship constructed out of "magnetized dove feathers" and covered inside by a white quilted material. In no time they had landed on the Venusian surface. Bocco took Crandall on a whirlwind tour, one stop on which was a saucer factory at which Crandall learned how feathers are magnetized (though his subsequent explanation to fellow Earthlings would remain suitably vague).

Two other trips soon followed. For several years before he dropped out of sight to pursue a more conventional career, Crandall was a regular on Southern California's contactee circuit. Yet his Venusians, aside from their benign nature, little resembled the more popular Venusian stereotype (blond and attractive in the fashion of models and Hollywood actors). In Crandall's account Venusians "have pointed ears, large feet, and a duck-like gait." They also have no bones, explaining why "when you shake hands with them, their hand just seems to melt into your own." The appearance of a Venusian will literally stop a clock, but it will resume as soon as the spaceperson has disappeared into thin air (with a sound like air hissing from a tire); even better, the clock will have been moved forward to the correct time.

A particularly odd contactee doctrine held that Nikola Tesla (1856–1943), the celebrated and accomplished electrical scientist, hailed from Venus, to which he returned when Earthlings thought he had died. According to occult writer Margaret Storm, the infant Tesla was brought from Venus and deposited at a remote provincial location in Yugoslavia, his task to bring scientific advancement to the earth. Storm's associate Arthur Matthews, in Tesla's company, visited nearby planets in a Venusian spacecraft on a number of occasions.

A Nightmare of Venusians

The contactees' Venusians have been a tediously virtuous lot, with very, very rare exception. The unsettling stories told by a Swedish man known only as Helge, whose apparent sincerity, his highly implausible testimony notwithstanding, puzzled some observers, including investigator Håkan Blomqvist, are perhaps the sole exception. Helge's alleged adventures are hard to read as either literal truth or deliberate fiction, but whatever their ultimate epistemological nature, they are undeniably more interesting— quite a lot more interesting—than the competition in the ET-contact section. Like Thompson's tale, one is led to the uneasy reflection that some things are neither exactly true nor exactly false; perhaps "visionary" will have to do. The story is long and complex, and what follows necessarily skips over a great deal of detail to get to the core.

Born in 1913, Helge (not his real name), a rock blaster by profession, lived with his wife, Anna, in Uddevalla, near Gothenburg, Sweden. Said to have been an atheist and an outspoken scoffer at UFO reports, he nonetheless believed he possessed a talent for telepathy. In the late autumn of 1965, kidney stones were causing him discomfort, and he was to undergo an operation on December 10. On impulse he abruptly left the house with his dog and took a walk along a nearby frozen lake.

Something disturbed the animal, which began running in circles and acting up. Helge put it on a leash, and then he heard a whirring sound above him. Looking up, he spotted a disc-shaped object with a translucent surface through which he could glimpse moving figures. The UFO descended until it was a few feet above the ice. A tube dropped from the bottom, and through it four humanlike entities floated as if on an invisible elevator. Once outside, they approached him. They were one older man, two younger men, and a woman, all covered in transparent overalls that revealed their nude, unblemished bodies. Entirely hairless, they had big dark, slightly slanted eyes and perfect teeth. Their ears were pointed, the openings inside so big that Helge thought he could see inside their heads. On their wrists each wore a broad dark bracelet with a yellow button on it. The men were thick-necked and built like wrestlers.

Over the next hour the beings communicated with Helge via drawings in the snow. They were curious about such earthly activities as hunting and dancing, and at

In 1965, a Swedish man reportedly saw a UFO from which a tube descended, carrying four aliens (*BigStock*).

one point the oldest of the group retrieved a cylinder-shaped device from the ship, then glided it along Helge's back. Helge felt a warm sensation, followed by a cessation of the pain from his kidney stones. The four then returned to their craft, which shot off at a dizzying rate of speed.

The next day, when Helge was X-rayed prior to his operation, medical personnel were puzzled to discover that his physical problem had been cured. Not long afterwards a Stockholm ufologist interviewed him about his encounter.

In August 1966 Helge experienced a second contact. Again drawn outside by some mysterious instinct, he once more observed the UFO hovering above the lake. This time, however, the older man stood outside in mid-air, and he spoke, but his words were not coordinated with his lips; they seemed to emanate from the ship moments after the mouth movement. Helge was given a metal plate and instructed to wear it always. The being instructed him to go to the Bahamas (and specifically to the Bahamian island of Little Exuma) as their representative. Helge declined on the grounds that he could not speak English, was uneducated, and had a wife to care for. All to no avail—he was told that he had no choice in the matter.

Afterwards, Helge buried the plate, a small rectangle made of an aluminum-like material, about three inches wide by two inches thick, with three rows of symbols on one side. The following March, leaving it behind, he and Anna nonetheless went to the Bahamas to live. On the flight there, they noticed 14 men who, because of their black dress, they assumed were Catholic priests. The "priests," however, were nowhere in sight when everyone else left the airliner. Beyond that curious little incident, nothing of significance happened. Too embarrassed to return to their hometown, Helge and Anna moved south of Stockholm to an apartment arranged for them by a small UFO group that knew something about his experience. A wealthy member of the club offered to finance further trips to the Bahamas.

Helge drove to Uddevalla and dug up the plate. Heading back to Stockholm, he stopped at a gas station, where an oddly dressed old man, sporting black slouch hat and black cape, approached and asked if he could accompany him. Helge agreed to take him. On the way the stranger revealed himself to be one of the "priests" on the flight, identifying himself as Father Rapas ("Ra Paz" in one account). He worked for the "overlords," as he called them, who had contacted Helge earlier. He directed Helge to return to the Bahamas and to bring along the plate this time. Rapas took over the driving, and Helge dozed off. When he awoke, the car was parked near its destination, and the driver was gone.

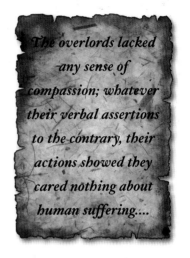

The overlords lacked any sense of compassion; whatever their verbal assertions to the contrary, their actions showed they cared nothing about human suffering....

The couple stayed at a hotel in Nassau as 1967 turned into 1968. This time Helge was taken alone in a boat with two others to a small Bahamian island. Through an opening they entered a mountain, and inside it they found themselves in an extraterrestrial base where they observed several kinds of entities, including giants, dwarfs, and hermaphrodites. From then on, however, Helge would deal with the sorts of Venusians who occupy more typical contactee literature: beautiful and golden-haired.

Helge came back with orders to found a group to be called the New Generation, which was to attract young people to work for peace and justice. The core was the small UFO group that had formed around Helge, who showed its members what he alleged was a letter from Rapas. Its language was blunt to the point of rudeness: "We detest you. That is why we believe in the youth; they are the only ones whose hands are not soiled with the blood of others.... Your catchword shall be: Freedom from violence—from hunger—we are all brothers and sisters.... You who have supported [Helge] shall not be forgotten; you shall reap a hundredfold, but if someone hurts him or his devoted wife, I say, they shall be revenged sevenfold." Rapas also produced a list of 65 rules members were obliged to follow—or else. Helge himself was to stay in the background.

The New Generation fell apart within months. Its members, unenthusiastic from the start, felt anxious about the threats, and the group's wealthy benefactor expressed displeasure at being asked for large sums of money whose purpose was never explained to him. The New Generation did generate some coverage in the Swedish

(Continued on page 125)

HIDDEN REALMS, LOST CIVILIZATIONS, AND BEINGS FROM OTHER WORLDS   **[123]**

THE SUN

In 1440 the Christian philosopher Niko-laus Krebs (1401–1464) reflected, "Of the inhabitants then of worlds other than our own we can know still less, having no standards by which to appraise them. It may be conjectured that in the area of the sun there exist solar beings, bright and enlightened denizens, and by nature more spiritual than such as may inhabit the moon."

To many who believed in the exis-tence of intelligences on other worlds, the sun was considered as likely a place to house inhabitants as any other extra-terrestrial body. In the early eighteenth century, the English mathematician William Whiston (1667–1752) judged it possible that the sun, like the earth, har-bors people who live inside its interior. Other writers in the same century imag-ined solarians as angelic. The astronomer Johann Elert Bode (1747–1826)—remem-bered for Bode's law, which provided a mathematical estimation of the distances between planets—held that the sun is earthlike, protected by an atmosphere from the light and heat it spread out toward the rest of the solar system.

Sir William Herschel wrote in 1795, "The sun ... appears to be nothing else than a very eminent, large, and lucid planet, evidently the first, or in strict-ness of speaking, the only primary one of our system.... Its similarity to the other globes of the solar system ... leads us to suppose that it most probably ... inhab-ited ... by beings whose organs are adapted to the peculiar circumstances of that vast globe." What human observers saw as sunspots were actually, he theo-rized, hollow spots in the atmospheric layer; if one could look down to its bot-tom, one could glimpse the true surface, cool and hospitable to life.

Even more fantastically, Thomas Dick thought—according to his 1823 book, *Christian Philosopher*—that the sun con-tains "a number of worlds," all inhabited. According to Michael J. Crowe, a leading historian of the extraterrestrial-life debate over the centuries, "life on the sun was championed in the late 1850s and in the 1860s by a number of Ameri-can, Belgian, British, French, and German authors," some of them respected scien-tists. As late as 1894 journalist and edu-cator Sir Edwin Arnold (1832–1904) char-acterized as foolish the views of those who denied that hydrogen-eating crea-tures may live on the sun. If these were not mainstream opinions, they were con-sidered, even if only barely, within the boundaries of acceptable discourse.

According to French Spiritualist Allan Kardec, "The sun is not a world inhabited by corporeal creatures, but a rendezvous of superior spirits that by thought radiate from there toward other worlds, which they direct through the mediation of less elevated spirits."

Advances in astronomy, however, effectively removed solar life from even highly speculative consideration. Such musings were left to cranks, such as the ancient-astronaut theorist W. Raymond

Drake. Drake subscribed to many out-landish ideas, among them the suspicion that the standard scientific description of the sun might be no more than a "leg-pull," he wrote. "Is the sun inhabited?" he asked. "Who knows? Should we not be really scientific and suspend judgment until man gets there?"

While living in Prescott, Arizona, in 1952, George Hunt Williamson recorded communications—mostly via automatic writing and telepathy—from assorted aliens living on other planets in the solar system. One, Regga of Masar (Mars), is said to have remarked, "Your Sun, which is our Sun also, is not a hot flaming body. It is a cool body. One of our great astronomers believed this and stated it. The so-called solar prominences are as cool as your aurora borealis (northern lights). You do not necessarily have to have heat just because you have light. Look at your firefly. You think your Sun gives off great heat because you can 'feel' it. Certain forces come from the Sun, and when they enter the earth's magnetic field this resonating field causes friction. And from friction you get heat. There are other facts about the Sun I cannot tell you now. In outer space The Sun does not appear bright as it does to you on Earth."

Further Reading

Crowe, Michael J. *The Extraterrestrial Life Debate: The Idea of a Plurality of Worlds from Kant to Lowell.* New York: Cambridge University Press, 1986.

Drake, W. Raymond. "Is Our Sun Inhabited?" *Flying Saucer Review* 5, 6 (November/December 1959): 15–17.

Williamson, George H., and Alfred C. Bailey. *The Saucers Speak! A Documentary Report of Interstellar Communications by Radiotelegraphy.* Los Angeles: New Age Publishing Company, 1954.

(Continued from page 123)

press, but its origins in space-contact claims were kept secret. Following the movement's collapse, Helge withdrew into seclusion and cut off ties with nearly everyone.

His adventures continued, and he traveled to the Bahamas and to Mexico doing the work of the spacemen (there were no women involved past the first incident in 1965). Sometimes he flew in spacecraft. He met other humans, including an American who was murdered soon afterwards; the space people explained that the man had either been a CIA agent or leaked information about their whereabouts to the agency. Helge hated and feared the overlords, characterizing his association with them a "hell." He was afraid to cut himself off from them because he was sure they would kill him if he did. The overlords lacked any sense of compassion; whatever their verbal assertions to the contrary, their actions showed they cared nothing about human suffering, even if it was occurring right in front of them. Helge felt like no more than an animal when he was around them. They never slept, as far as he could tell, and they lived on no more than liquid sustenance. They were either ignorant or disingenuous; when asked a question, they would not respond immediately but would come back up with a vague answer 24 hours later. Helge came to suspect that they harbored sinister intentions on the human race, perhaps planning to infiltrate the population until they could take over.

At one point, noting that contactees such as Adamski and Howard Menger, who purportedly worked with good space people, also spoke of evil aliens who opposed them, Helge said he had fallen in with the wrong group. He died of a heart attack on October 23, 1977, at the age of 64.

The Swedish ufologist Håken Blomqvist spoke with Helge only once, in 1973, and the phone conversation was brief. Helge said little more than that he was forbidden to talk about his experience. Over a period of years, Blomqvist pieced it together from informants who knew Helge. After the contactee's death he was able to track down the Stockholm doctor who had treated him between 1968 and 1972. The physician saw no evidence that Helge suffered from any mental disorder; yet he spoke from time to time of his dealings with extraterrestrials. Most of all, the doctor had the impression of a badly frightened individual.

Blomqvist interviewed Helge's widow Anna in June 1984. "Like her former husband," the investigator wrote, "she is very down to Earth and practical. She confirmed almost all the details of the contact and added several interesting pieces of information. What startled me somewhat was her almost total lack of interest in the subject of UFOs."

She recalled that her first meeting with an ostensible spaceman was during the third trip to the Bahamas. Insisting that he was supposed to meet one of his contacts there, Helge led her to a Nassau disco. There she encountered a short, peculiar-looking man with hypnotic eyes. At one point the stranger produced a photograph which he said depicted his family who lived on Venus (or maybe it was Saturn; Anna was not sure about the precise planet of residence). After that Anna stayed home while her husband traveled alone to the islands. He sometimes would be gone as a long as a month, returning with a deep tan. The spacemen frequently came to the couple's place in Sweden, however, and she witnessed—at least peripherally—some of their interactions with Helge.

After years of monitoring developments to the best of his ability, Blomqvist was inclined to the view that everyone was sincere and that something very strange had indeed taken place. On the other hand, he confessed, "sometimes I get a feeling of unreality, like reading a science fiction novel." More specifically, Helge's tale has the resonance of a tale written by the late Argentine fantasist Jorge Luis Borges.

It also is consistent with a notion argued in the writings of the controversial occult journalist John A. Keel (1930–2009), author of *The Mothman Prophecies* (1975)—on which Mark Pellington's 2002 film starring Richard Gere was based—and other books. In Keel's judgment Venusians and other ostensible space people exist as extraordinary entities but are not who they say they are. Beneath their friendly extraterrestrial exteriors, they are sinister "ultraterrestrials"—demons by another name—from an invisible realm Keel calls the "Superspectrum," known in traditional mystical lore as the astral or etheric world. In *UFOs: Operation Trojan Horse* (1970) he puts it this way:

> Suppose a strange metallic disk covered with flashing colored lights settled in your backyard and a tall man in a one-piece silver space suit got out. Suppose he looked unlike any man you had ever seen before, and when you asked him where was he was from, he replied, "I am from Venus." Would you argue with him? Chances are you would accept his word for it.... Buried within the context of all the contactees' messages there are clues to an even more complex threat. A direct threat to us.... The endless descriptions of peaceful far-off worlds and shining cities of glass are only subterfuges.

Even those taking a more benign view of Venusians have been forced to bow to the reality that the planet cannot support intelligent life. While Venusians no longer comprise the leading extraterrestrial faction in contact claims, they still make the rounds, almost always these days as channeling spirit entities rather than as physical saucer pilots. Contactees and their followers now say that the "Venus" of Adamski and his successors was and is a sort of parallel-universe—or higher-vibrational—counterpart to the planet of our lower-vibrational place on the vibrational scale.

Further Reading:

Adamski, George. *Inside the Space Ships.* New York: Abelard-Schuman, 1955.

Blomqvist, Håkan. "The Helge File: Men in Black in Sweden?" *AFU Newsletter* 20 (October-December 1980): 7–13.

Clark, Jerome. "The Coming of the Venusians." *Fate* 34, 1 (January 1981): 49-55.

Crandall, Lee. *The Venusians.* Los Angeles: New Age Publishing, 1955.

Crowe, Michael J. *The Extraterrestrial Life Debate: The Idea of a Plurality of Worlds from Kant to Lowell.* New York: Cambridge University Press, 1986.

Drake, W.R. "Count St. Germain, the Man Who Never Dies." *Flying Saucer Review* (March/April 1961): 15–17.

Good, Timothy. *Alien Base: Earth's Encounters with Extraterrestrials.* London: Century, 1998.

Keel, John A. *UFOs: Operation Trojan Horse.* New York: G. P. Putnam's Sons, 1970.

Menger, Howard. *From Outer Space to You.* Clarksburg, WV: Saucerian Books, 1959.

"New Theories about the Cruel Life on Venus." *Fresno* [California] *Bee* (September 25, 1927).

Phelan, Jim. "Now, If Earthlings Just Can Learn to Magnetize Feathers—Whoosh!" *Long Beach* [California] *Independent-Press-Telegram* (April 24, 1955).

The Not-So-Dying Race: Martians Envisioned and Encountered

Of all the planets beyond the earth, Mars has inspired by far the most speculation about its inhabitants. Aside from thousands of science-fiction stories and novels (most famously H.G. Wells' *War of the Worlds* [1898] and Ray Bradbury's *The Martian Chronicles* [1950]), a broad range of literature has treated life on Mars, intelligent and otherwise, as if it were a reasonable possibility or even an established fact.

If Mars harbors a population of sentient beings, those beings have managed to remain remarkably well hidden from modern space probes and the searching eyes of today's telescopes. More realistically, the planet may house microscopic life that, like comparable entities on Earth, thrives in extreme conditions. So far, however, even this modest—though surely interesting and significant—biological phenomenon has yet to be demonstrated conclusively. The major undisputed facts about consensus-reality Mars follow:

It is the fourth planet in the solar system, 4,222 miles (6,793 kilometers) in diameter (compared to the earth's 7,926 [12,753 kilometers]), and it has two small moons: Phobos and Deimos. Its long elliptical orbit brings it as close to us as 35,000,000 miles (56,315,000 kilometers; when it is in opposition, meaning the opposite side of the earth to the sun) and as far away as 250,000,000 miles (402,000,000 kilometers). A Martian day lasts 24.7 hours, a year 686.98 days. Mars' thin atmosphere is 95.3 percent carbon dioxide, 2.7 percent nitrogen, 1.6 percent argon, 0.15 percent oxygen, and 0.03 percent water vapor. Temperatures range from 80 °F (26.7 °C; in the equator during the summer) to –207 °F (–132.7 °C; during polar winter nights). The mean temperature is a crisp –67 °F (–55 °C). Some billions of years ago, geological evidence suggests, the planet may have been warmer and wetter, but today its atmospheric pressure is so feeble that it cannot sustain liquid water. If any such exists—and if it does, it would be the place where tiny life forms are most likely to be found—it lies under the surface.

As late as the mid-twentieth century, not a few mainstream planetary astronomers were convinced that vegetation existed on Mars and that it and its asso-

Hollywood adapted the H.G. Wells novel *The War of the Worlds* in 1953, and again in 2005. Such fictional accounts have kept the idea of Martians vivid in the popular imagination (*Paramount Pictures/Ronald Grant Archive/Mary Evans Picture Library*).

ciated seasonal changes could be observed from Earth. "It is almost certain that there is some form of vegetation on Mars," British Astronomer Royal H. Spencer Jones wrote in 1940. The next year the American astronomer Fred Whipple, expressing a more expansive but still generally respectable view that went beyond theories about plant life, speculated, "Intelligent beings may have protected themselves against the excessively slow loss of atmosphere, oxygen and water, by constructing homes and cities with the physical conditions scientifically controlled.... [Or] evolution may have developed a being who can withstand the rigors of the Martian climate. Or the race may have perished."

※

The Early History of Martians

The visionary Emanuel Swedenborg, who encountered a wide range of supernatural entities while in trance states, described the inhabitants of Mars as gentle souls, literally the creatures of thoughts (their outer shape expressed their inner nature). They worshipped God, who occasionally appeared on their planet. Swedenborg, whose claims were manifestly earnest if ungrounded in consensus reality, did not meet with the living occupants but the spirits of dead ones. Living or otherwise, Martians look like us, according to Swedenborg, though they may have different colors, sizes, or ways of walking.

Such allegations made little impression on scientists who were seeking astronomical evidence bearing on the question of Martian life. In that regard the observations of the great German-born British astronomer William Herschel would set in motion ideas that would influence generations of mainstream thinking about the biology of the red planet.

Respected in the history of astronomy for his discovery of Uranus (which he initially mistook for a comet), Herschel is much less well known for his obsessive convictions about intelligent life in the solar system, not excluding the sun and the moon, and beyond. He held that Mars is so earthlike that "its inhabitants probably enjoy a situation in many respects similar to ours." Telescopic observations of what he believed to be ice caps, seas, and vegetation-covered dry land—plus an atmosphere with sufficient water vapor to generate clouds—persuaded him that the planet was brimming with life of all kinds.

The presence of oceans and plants would be a given to subsequent generations of Mars-watchers and theorists, though there would be some dissenters. But in 1870, in his *Other Worlds Than Ours,* the widely read popular-science author Richard Anthony Proctor (1837–1888) pronounced, "If we admit that the vaporous envelope which occasionally hides parts of Mars is aqueous, we must believe in the existence of aqueous oceans on Mars.... The Martian lands are nourished by refreshing rainfalls; and who can doubt that they are thus nourished for the same purpose as our own fields and forests—namely, that vegetation of all sorts grow [sic] abundantly?" In 1878 Proctor even opened for the discussion on the possibility of sentient beings—"no larger than flies or ants"—on the recently discovered Martian moons Deimos and Phobos.

✳

From Canali to Canals

In 1877, with Mars in opposition, astronomers around the world turned their telescopes as the planet rolled close to Earth. No viewing that year would have the historical resonance of those made at the Brera Observatory, in Milan, by Italian astronomer Giovanni Schiaparelli (1835–1910). Ironically (and, as it would turn out, significantly), his telescope—a refractor with an eight-inch aperture—ranked among the most modest in use by a professional in the discipline. Yet in 1877 Schiaparelli was a highly regarded scientist of international reputation, winner of an award from Britain's Royal Astronomical Society (RAS) for his work on meteors and comets.

In a technical memoir published the following year, he devoted a portion to his alleged sightings of *canali* (singular *canale*) on the Martian surface during the opposition. *Canali* translates into English as either "channels" or "canals." Both imply life. Channels, ordinarily regarded as natural features, carry water, and water is one prereq-

The landscape of Mars was once thought to have canals running through it, the result, it was deduced, of construction by intelligent beings (*Mary Evans Picture Library*).

uisite to living things. Canals, of course, unambiguously suggest intelligent beings with engineering skills. Schiaparelli did not claim credit as the first to see *canali*—they had been observed at least as far back as 1830, he wrote—but he did assert discovery rights to a planet-wide system of them. Beyond that, he was cautious in what he speculated publicly about the nature of the *canali*. He was, however, deeply interested in the prospect of intelligent extraterrestrial life, and this fascination would lead him to be privately more sympathetic to the extraordinary theories about "Martian canals" that soon would tear the astronomical world apart.

English speakers were alerted to Schiaparelli's reported discovery at an April 12, 1878, RAS meeting when a letter from the Italian was read and drawings shown. The largely skeptical presenter, mapmaker and artist Nathaniel E. Green, suggested in effect that the supposed *canali* were most likely optical illusions. Soon other astronomers who expressed an opinion were echoing that view. But with the 1879 to 1880 opposition and a raft of new observations, a few astronomers stepped forward to back Schiaparelli, and even Green changed his mind. Particularly influential was the report from Irish astronomer Charles E. Burton, who stated that he had "independent-ly detected" some of the same *canali.*

In 1882, reporting on his own studies conducted during the previous opposition and confirmed that same year, Schiaparelli described a new and remarkable phenome-non: "gemination." By that he meant that at least 20 of the *canali* known to him had doubled since he had last seen them. As he put it, "To the right or left of a pre-existent line, without any change in its course or prior position, another line is produced equal and parallel to the first.... Between the lines thus generated the distance varies from ... 350 to 700 kilometers." These, he insisted firmly, were not mere tricks of the eye. "I am absolutely sure of what I have observed," he said.

In the wake of these revelations, a spate of articles in the press and in scientific journals such as *Nature* and *Scientific American* brought the controversy to the forefront of scientific discourse that spring. It also brought forth a suggestion, quickly withdrawn as "rash," from the already mentioned inhabited-Mars proponent R.A. Proctor. In a letter to the *London Times,* Proctor noted that perhaps the *canali* were indeed canals, "engineering works on a much greater scale than any which exist on our globe." More cautious Mars observers argued that they were no more than "boundaries of differently tinted districts."

The 1884 opposition, which occurred during poor viewing conditions, did nothing to settle the seething controversy. Still, Schiaparelli's supporters were growing in number, and some were aggressively asserting that the debate had now been settled. "The 'canals' of Mars," Agnes Clerke wrote in her book *Popular Astronomy during the Nineteenth Century* (1885), "are an actually existent and permanent phenomenon." The 1886 opposition, which Schiaparelli met with a brand-new 18-inch refractor, produced a sighting of only one new gemination, but more important, "confirmation" from French astronomers at the Nice Observatory of the *canali* and doublings that Schiaparelli had mapped four years earlier. Other astronomers were similarly impressed, and references to "large engineering works" on the Martian surface began to appear in the popular press.

Over the next few years observers reported bewilderingly inconsistent and sometimes blatantly contradictory results—occasionally by the same observers. Even the popular French astronomer and extraterrestrial-life advocate Camille Flammarion fretted, "The more one dedicates time, study, and care to the analysis of the numerous and varied observations made of this mysterious planet, the more one is obstructed from arriving at a definite opinion." Yet where the question of intelligent life there was concerned, Princeton astronomer Charles A. Young noted, "Probably there is no astronomical subject concerning which opposite opinions are so positively and even passionately held."

The 1892 opposition, in which viewing conditions were the clearest they had been in years, produced a wealth of papers in scientific journals. Many affirmed the presence of canals, however interpreted, and even—if not in all cases—some doublings. Among the boldest claimants, William H. Pickering, who had done his observing from an observatory he had set up in Arequipa, Peru, for Harvard University, produced papers for *Astronomy* and *Astro-Physics,* declaring that the "so-called canals exist upon the planet, substantially as drawn by Professor Schiaparelli." There were also clouds, lakes, and vegetation. For his efforts, Pickering was sent packing by his disapproving Harvard astronomer brother E.C., who had dispatched him to South America in the first place. William, however, would be heard from again.

Lowell and the Dying Race

A recurring issue of interest to Martian-life possibilities concerned the question of whether water vapor existed in the atmosphere, and thus ultimately of whether

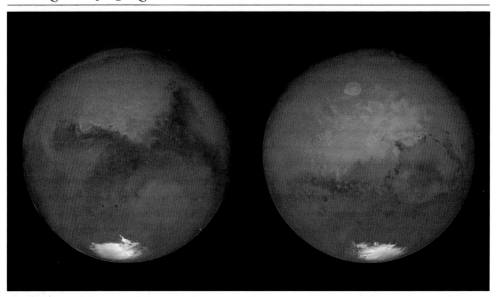

An image taken by the camera aboard the Hubble Telescope clearly shows Mars' southern ice cap, once thought to be strong evidence of drinkable water on the planet. We now know it mostly contains frozen carbon dioxide (*NASA*).

Mars is more like the earth or the moon. Conflicting analyses of spectroscopic readings collided in the scientific literature of the latter nineteenth century, with much of the discussion focused on whether Mars' polar caps—one natural feature whose reality no one disputed—were composed of water or carbon dioxide. But even some canal skeptics, notably the English astronomer E.W. Maunder (1851–1928), still considered channels, water vapors, and aqueous polar caps to be settled matters.

This was the state of affairs when Percival Lowell (1855–1916) arrived on the scene. Born into one of Massachusetts' most prominent families, heretofore a caretaker of the Lowells' Asian business interests and author of four books on what was then called (at least by Occidentals) the "Oriental mind," he had left Japan in 1893 to pursue a longstanding interest, dating back to his days at Harvard, in astronomy. Early the next year he proposed to Harvard that his deep pockets and its co-sponsor an astronomical observatory, to be located in the Southwest. Harvard agreed, but Harvard Observatory director E.C. Pickering rejected him as a dilettante, "a man without good judgment"—a view widely shared, he said, by those who knew Lowell. Nonetheless, the university leased Lowell a 12-inch telescope (to be supplemented by an 18-inch refractor borrowed from another astronomer), sending William Pickering and Andrew Douglass with him to the chosen site, the high mesa near Flagstaff, Arizona.

As early as May 1894 Lowell was telling scientific colleagues that his observatory intended to watch Mars not sporadically but nightly, on the likelihood that Schiaparelli's canals were "the work of some sort of intelligent beings." These words generated unease among some who heard them, though probably none was prepared for what was to come, a controversy that future historians of science would characterize as astronomy's "most famous folly."

Before the year was out, Lowell claimed to have viewed no fewer than 184 canals, including eight doubles. By July he had devised a theory from which he never deviated until his death 22 years later. In Lowell's belief, Mars, its atmosphere one-seventh the thickness of the earth's, is a dying world whose inhabitants depend upon a vast system of canals to divert water from the polar ice caps for irrigation purposes. At the intersections where the canals cross are small dark regions, "oases" where plant life grows and all of life is sustained. Of the physical forms of the Martians themselves, Lowell refused to speculate beyond the suggestion that they are giants, far more physically efficient than their terrestrial counterparts, and technically brilliant—in other words, they are superhuman. A Social Darwinist by political inclination, Lowell thought that wealthy oligarchs direct Mars' social order; "only the fittest have survived," he maintained.

Lowell's book *Mars,* published in December 1895, met with frigid responses in many quarters but warmly welcoming ones in others, especially in Britain. Schiaparelli quietly supported Lowell's theories, while carefully weighing his public pronouncements, which ran to the nuanced likes of statements holding, for example, that theories about canals as "due to intelligent beings ought not to be rejected as an absurdity." The Italian, befitting a personal politics more liberal and optimistic than Lowell's, contended, "The institution of a collective socialism ought indeed result from a parallel community of interest and of a universal solidarity among the citizens, a veritable phalanstery which can be considered a paradise of societies." Suffering failing eyesight and distaste for the growingly rancorous dispute, however, Schiaparelli withdrew from the controversy in the mid–1890s.

After expanding his staff and setting up a temporary observatory in Mexico for viewing Mars during the end-of-the-year observation in 1896, Lowell himself fell victim to health problems—neurasthenia, specifically—and retired for four years. Meantime, supporters and detractors continued to fight it out. Among the latter, whose ranks came to include no less than Lowell's assistant Andrew Douglass (who was fired for his indiscretion), the conviction grew that the so-called canals were merely "illusions of vision" (Douglass' phrase).

The influential European astronomer Eugène M. Antoniadi (1870–1944) monitored developments as head of the British Astronomical Association's Mars Section. When he compared astronomers' sketches of alleged canals from the 1896 opposition, he found them wildly variable and incredible on their face. The observations of another fierce critic, the Italian Vincenzo Cerulli, persuaded him that "the canals of Mars are themselves only simple alignments of spots similar to those which the telescope shows us on the moon"; when more powerful telescopes became available, "the canals ... will lose that linear form which presently makes them so mysterious and so interesting."

Spectroscopic analyses conducted during the 1896 opposition found, according to American astronomers W.W. Campbell and J.E. Keeler, no difference between water vapor on Mars and that on the moon. In other words, Mars is lifeless except to

Martians have taken many forms in our imaginations over the years, sometimes being friendly (as in this depiction from 1924), and other times hostile (*Mary Evans Picture Library*).

those suffering the sorts of optical illusions that caused them to believe they were seeing canals.

In June 1903, speaking before the RAS, E.W. Maunder, who years before (see above) had accepted the existence of channels even if not of extraordinary interpretations of them, reported on experiments with schoolboys who had "seen" canals on drawings of Mars when none were present. One listener, the leading American astronomer Simon Newcomb, was moved to join the anti-canal forces. For his part, Lowell would return, in 1905, with what he identified as the first photographs ever taken of the canals, making the statement so forcefully that some were at least temporarily swayed. The photographs—of 38 canals and one double—were taken at the Lowell Observatory on May 11 by staff member Carl Otto Lampland. Thousands more were taken from Flagstaff and from the Andes (where Lowell had sent an expedition) during the 1907 opposition. Despite confident pronouncements by Lowell and his supporters, others failed to detect the claimed images in the photographs and attendant negatives.

Even so, theories about Martians abounded even as, in the judgment of most scientists, the evidence was—almost literally—drying up. In *Nature,* not ordinarily thought of as a science-fiction magazine, E.H. Hankin put forth the most fantastic of all: "Perhaps on Mars there is only one living being, a gigantic vegetable the branches or pseudopodia of which embrace the planet like the arms of an octopus, suck water from the melting ice caps ... and are visible to us as the Martian canals."

But canal theories were in retreat, the subject of ever more devastating criticisms by some of the most important scientific figures of the time, including Alfred Russel Wallace (1823–1913), with Darwin the co-discoverer of evolution via natural selection. In various forums, including one full-length book, Wallace argued against the unlikelihood of intelligent Martian life on biological grounds. Other scientists continued to stress the evidence that the "canals" were no more than optical illusions, and telescopic scrutiny—with ever more refined instruments—of the red planet during its 1909 close approach gave little encouragement to the dwindling band of Lowellians.

The controversy staggered on for another two or three years before effectively concluding. In 1913 Antoniadi wrote that though "the discovery of new canals" would continue to be announced, "the astronomer of the future will sneer at these wonders; and the canal fallacy, after retarding progress for a third of a century, is doomed to be relegated into the myths of the past." On the other hand, the unbowed Lowell retorted before his death in 1916 that "every new fact discovered has been found to be accordant to it."

Lowellism did not entirely pass with Lowell himself. His ally and associate William Pickering continued to champion Martian-intelligence theories until his own death in 1938. A 1935 astronomy textbook by Arthur Harding treats Martians and their canals matter-of-factly as if a still-open possibility. Some astronomers accepted Lowell's observations of water and vegetation, if not of canals. A few astronomers, such as Wells Alan Webb, held to canal hopes into the 1950s. In 1947, when flying saucers entered public consciousness and many wondered if visitors from space had arrived, Mars was at the top of suspected places for their point of origin. Not only many lay people but also some Air Force investigators and scientists thought as much.

Martian Signals

In 1892 and again in 1901, according to *Metropolitan Magazine* in 1907, "the receivers of the wireless telegraph stations ... registered, and for a long period at a time, the signal three dots ... persistently repeated." The dots allegedly had no demonstrable earthly origin, it was claimed, but the "three dots singularly recall three points of light which were observed on the planet Mars in 1901."

During the heyday of speculation about intelligent Martians, some thought it might be possible to communicate with red-planet residents, while others wondered if communication weren't already being attempted from the other direction. Among them was the great electrical scientist and inventor Nikola Tesla, who wrote an extraordinary article in the February 9, 1901, issue of *Collier's*. It began:

> In some experiments I have been conducting for some time I have been noticing disturbances that have had a peculiar effect on my instruments. What these disturbances are caused by I am unable to say at present, but I am firmly convinced that they are the results of an attempt by some human beings, not of our world, to speak to us by signals.

> I am certain of some points.... I am convinced that these [disturbances] are not caused by something terrestrial. I know, too, that they are not caused by the sun or moon, and hence I am forced to the belief that they come from some other planet....

> I have observed electrical actions which have appeared inexplicable.... How long these attempts have been going on is, of course, problematic. It is possible they have only just begun. It is possible, also, that they have been going on for centuries.... [F]rom their nature, I am completely given over to the

conviction that they are the first attempts of some other planet to open up communication with us.

Tesla's remarks did not go over well with scientists, who protested that Tesla had provided no evidence to support his sweeping assertions. But theories of Martian communication continued. Camille Flammarion speculated, according to a 1907 pronouncement, "The Martians tried to communicate with us hundreds of thousands of years ago" and "may have tried again a few thousand years ago, and never having obtained a response, they concluded that the earth was uninhabited or that its denizens did not trouble themselves about the study of the universe or the search after eternal truths."

The 1909 opposition, however, brought into view what some hopeful astronomers took to be lights signaling from the Martian surface. In October 1913, from a Geneva observatory, Fritjof Le Coultre—described as an "undistinguished astronomer" in one press account—reported 17 consecutive nights' worth of bluish white flashes, "like the light of powerful electric arc lamps." He thought they were signals to Earth, and so did Lowell Observatory astronomers, who believed they had seen the same thing the same night. A colleague at the Paris Observatory, on the other hand, preferred "auto-suggestion" as the explanation.

In 1919 electrical genius Guglielmo Marconi (1874–1937) claimed—though without providing details—that he had detected signals from Mars. The signals were subsequently traced to an experiment conducted by Irving Langmuir from the General Electric Laboratories in Schenectady, New York. (Apparently embittered by the experience, in 1924 Marconi denied that the incident had ever happened, dismissing Martian signals as a "fantastic absurdity.") An attempt to hear otherworldly radio messages at a wireless receiving station near Omaha over a week in April 1920 produced "nothing that could by any stretch of the imagination be construed as a message from Mars," said the experimenter, electrical scientist Frederick E. Millener.

On the night of August 22, 1924, when Mars passed within 34,500,000 miles (55,510,500 kilometers) of Earth, a "radio photo message continuous transmission machine," recently invented by C. Francis Jenkins of Washington, D.C., recorded film of a "fairly regular arrangement of dots and dashes along one side" and on the other "at almost evenly spaced intervals ... curiously jumped groups each taking the form of a crudely drawn human face," in the words of one account. A retired astronomer, David Todd, who participated in the experiment with Jenkins, told a reporter, "It may not be a message from Mars, but if it isn't from Mars, where is it from?" Army specialists tried to detect a code but failed to do so. Astronomer F.E. Fowle of the Smithsonian Institution thought they were no more than "disturbances introduced by solar or terrestrial causes not yet understood." At an observatory in Dulwich, England, Prof. Norman Edwards picked up "long, harsh dots at regular intervals in groups of four, five and three at a wavelength of 30,000 meters," but dismissed suggestions that they were intelligent messages from Mars. Something comparable was recorded at radio station WOR in Newark, New Jersey.

According to the *Washington Post* (August 23, 1924), a city employee named F.H. Signor was listening to WOR when it went off the air at 10:00 PM. For some reason he kept the radio tuned to the station's wavelength, and soon he heard what sounded like dice clattering and fingers snapping. Signor suggested—the article does not make clear if he meant it seriously; surely not—that he had heard something like a "Martian craps game."

By the next opposition, in 1926, disillusionment with the concept of communication with Mars had set in, and most who had once been interested were abandoning the quest. A spokesman for the Royal Astronomical Society told United Press, "Although a few cranks ... still appear greatly excited over the hope of the establishment of communication with Mars, we are no longer interested in the subject. It is possible that life in some form does exist on Mars, but whether this life could comprehend any kind of communication from other parts of the universe is very doubtful."

Astronomers have given up communicating with possible Martian intelligence, but a few are still actively searching for signs of advanced beings elsewhere in the galaxy (*iStock*).

Still, later that year a Columbia professor suggested—one presumes he was joking—that radio interference, then a significant problem for listeners to the new medium, happened because Martians trying to signal Earth messed up the signals.

In January 1929 a French astronomer would make a curious claim that in some ways anticipated the speculation that would emerge less than two decades later: that interplanetary spacecraft—to be dubbed flying saucers, then the more formal unidentified flying objects (UFOs)—were visiting Earth from Mars. In a statement to the press, Henri Pensa remarked that on each of three successive nights the previous winter, and again the past November, a silvery object trailing fire had been observed in the same position of the sky and moving in the identical direction in the Rodez Mountains in Auvergne. Pensa deemed the behavior of these phenomena to be uncharacteristic of meteors, but arguably consistent with the intelligent behavior of Martians signaling this planet via what he termed "interplanetary bombardment." He said the objects had fallen from the sky, and he and colleagues had collected "fragments," their nature unspecified. Unfortunately, Pensa would be heard from no more, but somewhat comparable assertions would be made, also in France, seven years later.

Scientists were not the only ones reporting interplanetary communications. On January 10, 1935, Charles Spayde, the operator of a telephone and telegraph station just west of Lima, Ohio, informed the *Lima News* that he had been "receiving a series of strange, unintelligible signals. They differ from ordinary telegraphic, high frequency signals ... because of the odd flat or dull tone.... The peculiar new signals ... are exceptionally broad in wavelength and come in all over the dial. I have attempted to work out a translation code, but so far have been unable to decipher it. But I am convinced the signals are not static or mechanical disturbances. It is my opinion that they do not originate on this planet."

From an observatory in the lower Alps, French astronomer Robert Damion gave this statement in early spring 1936:

> This winter during several nights which were pitch dark for the absence of the moon and stars I noticed a certain portion of the sky in the vicinity of Mars suddenly lit up by a strange light of a deep bluish tint. That light while it lasted, some 40 seconds each time, was so strong that one could easily read a newspaper by it. Similar phenomena have occurred before in France, and been remarked upon by my fellow astronomers. The last time was some eight years ago in the vicinity of Lyon.

> I am convinced that Mars is trying to signal our planet by some means unknown to us. If they really are signals, we should be quite unable to answer them, not having yet been able to design searchlights powerful enough to throw a beam even a quarter of the way to our nearest planet neighbor.

That same month Damion spoke of seeing bluish lights on the Martian surface. On May 30, 1937, "a series of bright flashes was seen extending across the south polar cap" north of the southern rim of the disk. They were "irregularly intermittent and were estimated to be about one magnitude brighter than the rest of the cap," Latimer J. Wilson, one of the observers, wrote in *Popular Astronomy* not long afterwards. He noted, "The flashes extended almost midway between the northern edge of the cap and the southern rim of the disk. A line of tiny white dots seemed to extend across the cap, some of the spots coalescing to swell into a brilliant white spot which quickly became yellow, then red-yellow, the phenomenon passing from left to right across the polar cap." He offered no theories about their nature and cause. By this time theories about Martians, much less ones sending messages toward Earth, were evaporating from respectable discourse.

✳

Psychic Martians

In the nineteenth and twentieth centuries, as astronomers and biologists debated the existence of Martians, a number of individuals spoke of personal

Amateur medium Catherine Elise Müller believed that she was not only communicating with Martians, but projecting herself onto the planet's surface, which was not unlike this 1930 depiction (*Mary Evans Picture Library*).

encounters or communications with people from the red planet. Most of these claims from the former century were associated with the Spiritualist craze that swept the world in those years, and the contacts were effected through mediumship or out-of-body travel. For example, in the course of a series of trances in late 1853, spirit beings led American occultist Thomas Lake Harris on a guided tour of heaven and other planets. One of the latter was Mars, on which he saw the Garden of Eden, located on a small island on the planet's equator. (See Brinsley le Poer Trench's later beliefs in this regard below.)

The most famous such case concerned an amateur medium, Catherine Elise Müller (1861–1929), studied by the University of Geneva psychologist Théodore Flournoy, who recorded the episode in a classic work of anomalistic psychology published in English as *From India to the Planet Mars* (1899). Assigned the pseudonym "Hélène Smith" in the book, Müller grew up in a mystically inclined family and herself had strange experiences. Eventually, she became the principal figure in a Spiritualist circle, channeling messages first from prominent dead persons before graduating to more fully formed, dramatic visions of the Martian landscape. These came about after one of the sitters voiced the hope that one day human beings and Martians would be able to speak freely with one another. In due course that started to happen; not only that, Müller often found herself on the planet itself. Mars became so vivid to Müller that, as Flournoy observed, she appeared in some sense to be living her Martian life each moment of her day, switching easily—in various states of consciousness—from earthbound consensus reality to her imaginative one on another world. In today's clinical language, she possessed a fantasy-prone personality.

Müller befriended Martians and even produced over time what purported to be a Martian language—in truth, in Flournoy's words, "an infantile travesty of French." Hardly needful to say, Müller's Mars had canals.

The American psychical researcher James H. Hyslop investigated a case of automatic writing from 1895. A clergyman's wife identified only as Mrs. Smead recorded communications from her three dead children and brother-in-law. One of the children, Maude, told her that some spirits stay on Earth, while others are dispatched to other worlds. Soon thereafter, Mrs. Smead learned from another of the children that Maude and her uncle now resided on Mars, from which the little girl subsequently communicated. She provided a map, which—no surprise—showed the canals.

Writing in 1959, Nandor Fodor, a psychoanalyst and psychical researcher, remarked, "Since Emanuel Swedenborg ... at least a dozen well-known mediums have been involved with the planet Mars." Among them was the British clergyman and Theosophist Charles Webster Leadbetter (1847–1934), who claimed to have visited the planet in an astral state on several occasions.

Leadbetter's Martian surface is Lowellian, with great canals (built by previous colonists from the earth's moon) and vegetation along their banks. The dwindling civilized population, which lives along the equator (where the daily temperature averages 70 °F [21 °C]), consists of beings who resemble Earthlings but are shorter, barely reaching five feet (1.5 meters) in height, and have broader chests to encase larger lungs, since the air is thinner. (Scattered bands of "savages" live elsewhere, in less hospitable regions of the planet.) Most educated Martians, he wrote, "have yellow hair and blue or violet eyes—somewhat Norwegian in appearance." They dress colorfully and have a particular fondness for flower gardens. Mechanical devices and trained animals do most of the work, allowing Martians to live long, disease-free lives of leisure under an autocratic monarchy and a communistic social order, in which sexual infidelity is assumed and the state raises the children who are its by-product. Martians, or the bulk of them, adhere to a strictly materialist philosophy.

The rigid cultural and intellectual orthodoxy that dominates most of the populace is challenged by a "secret brotherhood" that formed several centuries ago and is now widespread. According to Leadbetter, "Some at least of the members ... have learnt how to cross without great difficulty the space which separates us from Mars, and have therefore at various times tried to manifest themselves through mediums at spiritualist séances, or have been able, by the methods which they have learnt, to impress their ideas upon poets and novelists."

The Dentons and the Martians

Among the nineteenth-century American Spiritualists who reported Martian visions were members of the Denton family. William Denton (1823–1883), an Ohio-based geologist and political activist, believed he had been blessed with the gift of psychometry, which enabled him discern the nature and history of objects he either held in his hand or, when that was impossible, simply focused his concentration upon. His wife, Elizabeth, their son, Sherman, and William's sister, Anne Denton Cridge, laid claim to comparable talents.

In 1874, with his wife's assistance, William Denton published an interesting book on psychic exploration of outer space. He addressed an obvious problem with such efforts: the testimony was contradictory, and it often conflicted with "known astronomical facts." "How are we to know," he asked, "which account ... is the true one? Or whether any is true? The only way, it seemed to me, by which we could arrive at the truth, would be to obtain independent examinations of a planet by various parties, no one of which should know anything, previous to the examination, of what the other had said." The idea was certainly a sound one, but Denton's "independent" examiners turned out to be his son, his wife, and his sister, though he insisted that each had been kept ignorant of the others' discoveries. Indeed, the results do not suggest collusion, conscious or otherwise, or even innocent contamination. On the other hand, they don't suggest real Martians, either.

Male Martians are beardless, and all are dark-skinned, yellow-haired, and blue-eyed. They wear red pants and blue jackets.

For our purposes we consider the experiments, conducted in the latter 1860s and early 1870s, with Mars as the target.

Of the three explorers, Sherman was the most active. On multiple occasions, from January 1867 into September 1869, he visited Mars in a trance state in which spirit body or clairvoyance allowed him to observe the planet's surface at close range. On his first trip, he came upon a thriving population of human-like inhabitants, their "faces not as pleasant as ours," owing perhaps to wider mouths and catlike eyes. Male Martians are beardless, and all are dark-skinned, yellow-haired, and blue-eyed. They wear red pants and blue jackets. They are "very honest people." On subsequent trips Sherman encountered a different race with five fingers and otherwise more closely Earthling features. These Martians fly small and large aircraft, and sometimes they attach springs to their feet and hands to enable them to walk faster. William Denton inferred that these beings "live in a region extending from south of the equator high into the north temperate zone." Sherman also reported seeing Martian people engaged in religious, industrial, agricultural, leisure, and other activities, and he observed large Martian animals vaguely reminiscent of horses and elephants.

Anne Denton Cridge, who conducted her examination in the summer of 1869, first noticed Mars' dense, life-sustaining atmosphere, then its great mountains and lush valleys where huge, crocodile-like reptiles lived. Her first trip exposed her to a Martian race whose members look like us except for their pinker skin and mostly red hair. They were a spiritually advanced lot. Elsewhere on the planet, however, there was a less developed race that was small, black, and hair-covered. On her second expedition she explored mansions in a lovely suburban landscape. A later trip brought into view Martians whose eyes held an iris like a many-sided lens, and yet another tall, thin Mar-

(Continued on page 151)

MALDEK

Asteroids—some astronomers prefer to call them minor planets or planetoids—can be found in a belt on the other side of the orbit of Mars. More than 100,000 have been photographed through powerful telescopes, and more are known or suspected to exist.

In the seventeenth century astronomers wondered why—though otherwise in a numerically predictable progression in their paths outward from the sun—no planet could be discerned where one would have been expected between Mars and Jupiter. This progression, formulated in Bode's Law, was discovered by Berlin Observatory director J.E. Bode and reported in 1772. Astronomers embarked on a search for the missing planet. In early 1801 Sicilian astronomer Giuseppe Piazzi found it by accident while mapping the section of the sky occupied by the constellation Taurus. Before the year was out, another observer confirmed his discovery, and Piazzi named the planet Ceres, after the goddess of agriculture and protector of Sicily. In March 1802, however, a second "planet"—Pallas, about two-thirds the size of Ceres (485 miles [780 kilometers] in diameter)—was documented, then others in 1804 and 1807 and, later, through the latter 1840s. By 1890 astronomers had recorded as many as 300. At that point it had long since become apparent that the missing planet as such was not there, just an enormous amount of debris, of which Ceres remains the largest piece.

Today the solar debris field otherwise known as the asteroid belt is thought to consist of an accumulation of materials—more than 10,000 pieces of them large enough to be individually catalogued—of assorted origins. Some of them date back to the formation of the solar system; Jupiter's gravity prevented them from growing and evolving into a larger body, though if compacted into one entity, the resulting world would be only one-third the size of the earth's moon. Over many millions of years, some of these small bodies have crashed into each other and broken apart, further reducing their sizes. (Some pieces end up in the earth's atmosphere as meteors or meteorites.) Burned-out comets and passing meteoroids also have been captured in the asteroids' orbit and now travel with them around the sun. Asteroids that have more highly elliptical orbits than their companions may pass relatively near the earth, sometimes close enough to pose a significant menace. Sixty-five million years ago, for example, an asteroid five to 10 miles (16 kilometers) in diameter crashed into our planet and initiated catastrophic atmospheric and climatic changes that caused mass extinction, most prominently of the dinosaurs.

For some decades after its discovery, a respectable, astronomically mainstream theory held that the asteroid belt represented the wreckage of a destroyed planet. In one reading, the planet broke apart after it and another large body collided. Another proposed a far more radical hypothesis: Extraterrestrial beings had blown it up. In his 1823 book, *Christian Philosopher*, Thomas Dick declared that the explosion that had created the planetoids "would seem to indicate, that a moral revolution has taken place among the intelligent beings who had originally been placed in those regions." According to the Rev. James Wills (1790–1868), an Irish Anglican, the asteroids evinced a "planetary wreck ... an impressive memorial ... telling an awful history of rebellion, revolt, and Divine justice, to the eyes that are privileged to read it."

In the latter nineteenth century most scientists turned from the notion of a planetary catastrophe to the still-current view described above. A very few maverick scientists, such as Thomas Van Flandern (1940–2009), still champion what is now known as the EPH (exploded-planet hypothesis), but at the moment they are in a distinct minority. Even these dissenting scientists, however, link the explosion to natural forces (massive volcanic activity, collision with another body in space) and not to the destructive actions of extraterrestrial weapons technology.

In the years after World War II, a small, quasi-religious subculture of contactees grew into an international movement. Among the most influential figures was George Hunt Williamson, educated in anthropology. He lived with Indian tribes in North Dakota, Minnesota, and New Mexico. When flying saucers caught his interest in 1950, he would wed tribal traditions and biblical revisionism to space

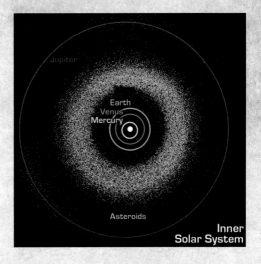

The Asteroid Belt between Mars and Jupiter may once have been a planet, which some have named Maldek, that broke apart into thousands of pieces (*NASA/JPL-Caltech/R. Hurt*).

visitations to put together an alternative history of the human race, described in a trilogy of books that anticipated the emergence, almost two decades later, of the "ancient-astronaut" genre associated with Erich von Däniken. Before that happened, however, Williamson sought personal contacts with extraterrestrials while living in Prescott, Arizona, in 1952. He, his wife, Betty, and several other local saucer enthusiasts would assert that in the summer of that year they began receiving messages—first through automatic writing and then by code through ham radio—from beings from the solar system and beyond. The contacts ended in February 1953.

Among the messages was this one, channeled from a Neptune resident named Zo: "Your so-called Hydrogen Bomb could make an asteroid belt out of you. This happened many years ago to the planet of what you would call the fifth orbit.... After [that planet's] destruction there were terrible disasters on Masar [Mars]." In his *Other Tongues— Other Flesh* Williamson writes that the ancients knew the destroyed planet by the name Lucifer and that "outer space intelligences" call it Maldek. The first syllable, "Mal," means "tongue" in "Solex-Mal," in Williamson's visionary universe the "Universal Mother Tongue of Creation," once spoken by all human beings and still spoken by all space people. Though Maldek is never mentioned in the Bible, Williamson—using logic that the uninitiated will find hard to follow (for example, every use of "tongue" actually refers to the exploded planet), deduced that both Hebrew patriarchs and New Testament chroniclers knew of Lucifer/Maldek's destruction. Or, in this reading of Holy Writ, in Williamson's words:

> Maldek was a world of iniquity that exploded and burned and was a planet in our solar system that defiled all the other planets because of its evil, and Maldek (tongue) set on fire its vortex, the power of its birth and being, and therefore was set on fire of the unseen state ... because Maldek released the terrible hydrogen power she broke her vortex and was thereby reduced to an unseen state.... Maldek ... was

an undisciplined child of the solar system; it wished to have power over all other planets.

Williamson placed Maldek's destruction at the time of the Tenth Plague, as chronicled in Exodus, as death spread through Egypt, the skies and waters were choked with red dust, and stones—meteorites, presumably—rained from the sky and Moses led the Israelites in flight into Canaan. These disasters were one consequence of Maldek's cataclysmic fate. Most scholars place the Exodus—an event only inferentially attested to in surviving historical records—at around the mid-thirteenth century B.C.E. (Williamson also professed to discern Maldekian allusions in Navajo mythology and in the writings of Emanuel Swedenborg. "All other worlds go through space in majesty, but Lucifer [Maldek] didn't even have a final resting place," Williamson wrote. "The blasted fragments of a once beautiful and proud planet were left to float endlessly in space that others might know what Lucifer had done. It would be a warning to all that this should not be.")

If, strictly speaking, this is nothing but science fiction, the contactee underground took it as gospel, albeit not strictly speaking. In the fashion of a folktale motif, Williamson's Maldek would function as a template on which three fundamental notions would be imprinted: Maldek = populated; Maldek = blown up; and Maldek = present-day asteroid belt. On occasion Maldek is said either to have the alternate name Malona or to have a moon by that name. From there, contactees, channelers, and cosmic occultists freely have recreated their own Maldeks.

George King (1919–1997) founded the Aetherius Society, among the most long-lasting of the contactee groups. An Englishman deeply interested in yoga and the paranormal, he entered the realm of space contact on a Saturday morning in May 1954. While he was washing dishes in his bachelor flat, a voice with no visible source boomed, "Prepare yourself. You are to become the voice of Interplanetary Parliament." In King's account of it, an Indian yoga master entered his apartment some days later, interrupting King's meditation to inform him that he was passing on a message from Cosmic Intelligences: King was to become their "primary terrestrial mental channel."

Soon, in deep meditative states, he was communicating with the Venusian Aetherius, also a Cosmic Master and a member of the Interplanetary Parliament, which meets on Saturn. In due course, other Cosmic Masters came through, most controversially Jesus, another Venusian. In early 1955 King gave his first public channeling, and the society formed not long afterwards, quickly gaining an international membership. Though accused of being everything from a charlatan to a Communist, he attracted and kept a loyal following. (Today the society's membership numbers, according to best estimates, around 2,000.) Before his death, King had channeled some 600 communications, which outlined a com-

plex cosmology, theology, and history. Only the part that deals with Maldek concerns us here.

"Hundreds of thousands of years ago" the earth-sized planet Maldek hosted a civilization that had a modestly sophisticated technology, enough to keep the population content while robots took care of pedestrian tasks. Maldek was sufficiently advanced that it could launch ships into space, but not advanced enough to keep them there for very long. Over time the people grew ever more inward-looking and finally unbalanced enough to engage in self-destructive pursuits, such as blowing up a "hydrogen bomb" and themselves and their world with it. They left more than asteroids in their wake, however.

The Maldekians were now a massive number of souls needing bodies in which to reincarnate. The peoples of the other solar planets refused the mass of would-be immigrant souls. But happily for them, they found a home on Earth, whose inhabitants—the race of Adamic Man—kindly stayed long enough to tutor the newcomers before departing what had been their home planet. The first great Maldekian civilization was on the continent of Lemuria in the Pacific Ocean. Unfortunately, Maldekians only repeated their sorry history, falling into conflict and nuking the continent into nonexistence. A sufficient number of Lemurians survived, though, eventually to create Atlantis, in the Atlantic Ocean, which they blew up, too. But in this instance Martians took pity and swooped in to

GODS AND SPACEMEN
THROUGHOUT
HISTORY

Sequel to the best-selling
«Gods & Spacemen
in the Ancient East»

W. Raymond Drake

In this 1975 book, W. Raymond Drake chronicles the alleged history of extraterrestrial races in Earth's past (*Mary Evans Picture Library*).

save some right-thinking Maldekians/Lemurians/Atlanteans, and after that the cycle was stopped. Even so, the earth remains under threat by dark forces from elsewhere, and on its present course the earth is likely to resume the destructive cycle of past ages.

In *Gods or Spacemen?* (1964) W.R. Drake, declared, "Some of the asteroids are said to be controlled by Space Beings who are now propelling these floating islands near Earth. These Intelligences are reported as coming to warn us that misuse of Nature's forces locked in the hydrogen-atom could blow our own planet to pieces like their own Maldek."

Maldek is still a ubiquitous theme in channeled communications. Channeling entities offer no single, coherent version of the planet's history and fate. Here is a representative sampling:

- "Male aggressors from another solar system" invaded Maldek, dominated by powerful women, with a timid male population doing their bidding. The invaders sought to establish a patriarchy. A destructive war ensued until at one point beings from a third solar system produced a ceasefire and negotiations to end the conflict, urging a settlement in which "one side would control [Maldek's] three satellites while the other would rule Maldek itself." When that compromise was rejected, the war resumed, and then Maldek was no more.

- "Long ago," in the course of an interstellar war, forces from the Pleiades and Sirius A attacked and destroyed Maldek, believing that it had bombed Sirius B and turned it into a "water planet ... due to the shattering of the protective ice shields that surround her." Later, it was determined that evil Andromedans had actually been responsible for the unprovoked assault of Sirius B; the Andromedans had framed the people of Maldek. In an effort to make amends for the tragic mis-understanding, "it was decided by the humans upon Sirius A to reseed human life into [our] solar sys-tem.... Earth became the chosen planet, and the only one with third dimension life remaining within the third dimension.... And indeed, 50,000 years ago, human life was seeded upon Earth through Sirian intervention."

- Ten million years ago Maldek and Mars harbored "crystalline life-forms." On Maldek the entities were able to move in and out of matter, thus escaping such body-bound experiences as birth, death, and rebirth. The sudden altering of its molecular structure, owing to a "solar-level curse between the Logos of Maldek and the then-Logos of our sun, Helios," froze Maldekians who happened to be temporarily in physical form into that state perma-nently. At some point afterwards "Maldek was ... shattered in a psy-chic attack orchestrated by Sanat Kumara ... related to a curse between Sanat Kumara and the planetary Logos of Maldek."

- "Our Moon, according to the Andromedans, is an artificial moon.... [O]ur Moon originally came from a star system in Ursa Minor, called Chauta ... one of four moons in a solar system that had 21 planets. Our Moon was brought from an orbit around the

17th planet. It was brought here, with others, during a war. Our Moon's first location in orbit in our solar system was around a planet called Maldek, which has completely been destroyed during that war and which is now the asteroid belt.... Now, apparently our Moon was one of two moons in orbit around Maldek. The other moon orbiting Maldek we know today as Phobos, which is now orbiting Mars.... The beings that were on the Moon in the domed cities were known as Ari-ans—the 'white race.' The Pleiadians appar-ently were responsible for moving our Moon to an orbit around Earth. So, the Ari-ans that came here on our Moon were in fact humans from the destroyed planet of Maldek, one of the lost tribes of Lyrae[;] some of the reincarnat-ed souls of them today are living underground on Earth in Tibet."

- "Next I had several lives on Malona or Maldek. Some of my lives there were as Reptilians again. Again there were quite a few lives there, then one more time a major inter-planetary war broke out. This war was between the 'Lemurian' descendants from MU who had set-tled on Malona, and the Atlantean descendants who had settled on Earth. The Reptilians and the Sirius A humanoids were also involved in this war.... Ashtar and the Sirians had planted crystals all over the planet and had planned to set up some kind of energy grid or shield. Once again, a Reptilian take-over appeared imminent, and the Sirian Humanoids were attempting to make the planet uninhabitable for them. Whether or not they truly intended to destroy the planet I do not know, but I would like to think not. I had had considerable spiritual powers in that life, and I believe that I had attempted to intervene in their plans to try and save the planet. So I attempted to re-program these crystals to ... deflect the energy back to the Sirian ships, but was not successful, and may have inadvertently contributed to the problem. Because when the Atlanteans and Sirians energized these crystals with some kind of high energy beam, the energy was too strong and it destabilized the planet's energy grids, and it was completely blown apart, and again a couple billion people died in that explosion. The remnants of Malona or Maldek formed the Asteroid Belt. But before Malona exploded, about 13,000 years ago, a group of us had evacuated and came to Earth.... As far as a time frame for these events goes, my sense is that Malona was destroyed about 13,000 years ago...."

- "Space Intelligences are reported as asserting that Lucifer was the evil planet, Maldek, whose blasphemous inhabitants aspired to conquer the Solar System using the terrible sidereal force known to the Atlanteans as Mash-Mak.... Some of the asteroids are said to be controlled by Space Beings who are now propelling these floating islands near Earth. These intelligences are reported as coming to warn us that misuse of Nature's forces locked in the hydrogen-atom could our own planet to pieces like their own Maldek."

Further Reading

Aetherius Society. *The Aetherius Society: A Cosmic Concept*. Hollywood, CA: Aetherius Society, 1995.

Crowe, Michael J. *The Extraterrestrial Life Debate: The Idea of a Plurality of Worlds from Kant to Lowell*. New York: Cambridge University Press, 1986.

Williamson, George Hunt. *Other Tongues—Other Flesh*. Amherst, WI: Amherst Press, 1953.

(Continued from page 143)

tian race with big hands and feet. Her final exposure to Mars, on August 19, led her into a vast church where Martians worshipped "monstrous forms."

According to Mrs. Denton's excursions in the summer of 1869, Martians have beautiful buildings and statues, and they are "purer white than Anglo-Saxons." Living in peace and harmony, they devote themselves to artistic and scientific endeavors, including telescopic observation of Earth. They share the planet with a darker race, inferior and temperamentally "more like the people of this planet."

From these varying, not obviously cohesive narratives, William Denton inferred—or rationalized—the presences of four Martian races that differ from each other more than human races do. He thought that the three travelers had not alighted at the same regions of the planet, and since the races live separately, they saw different entities. More likely, the three psychics conjured up generally human-like Martians out of then-popular speculations from astronomy, proto-science fiction, and mediumistic communications.

✴

Airships from Mars

In any event, the Dentons may have given the world the first printed reference, at least in English, to Martian aerial machines. The Dentons did not contend that such devices were flying through space to our planet, but it would not be long before earth-bound humans were claiming to have encountered Martian ships and their crews.

From late 1896 to mid–1897 American newspapers regaled readers with stories, of widely varying plausibility, of sightings of mysterious airships. Most readers who took the tales seriously suspected that they were the creations of unknown inventors who soon would announce their aviation triumph, but a minority—five decades before UFOs entered popular lore—took a more fantastic view: that these were craft built and flown by Martian visitors. This sort of speculation spurred hoaxers and pranksters. As early as November 27, 1896, a letter in a California newspaper, the *Stockton Evening Mail,* related correspondent H.G. Shaw's supposed encounter, near Lodi two days earlier, with an airship and "three strange beings ... nearly or quite seven feet high [2.1 meters] and very slender." The beings' speech sounded like "warbling," and each of the entities carried a bag with a nozzle, from which he, she, or it would take an occasional breath. After unsuccessfully trying to abduct the writer and his companion—weighing only an ounce apiece, they lacked the strength—they floated into their hovering ship and sailed away. Shaw was certain, he said, that they hailed from Mars.

Though it is unlikely that anyone failed to recognize that this story was a barely concealed joke, a yarn published in the *Dallas Morning News* for April 19, 1897, managed to generate excitement among the unsuspecting decades later, when the article was rediscovered and not immediately recognized as a local correspondent's tall tale. An

ATOMIC AIRSHIP OF MARS

The highly scientific Martians had conquered the atom. Their airship travels through the stratosphere at projectile speed under atomic power (See page 271 for details)

A fiction story from 1942 describes Martian airships using nuclear power and suggests that humans also use nuclear energy for peaceful purposes (*Mary Evans Picture Library*).

airship appeared over the tiny north-Texas town of Aurora at 6:00 AM on the seventeenth, the *News* recounted in a brief piece, and crashed into a windmill owned by a local judge. Amid the remains residents found the "badly disfigured" body of a being, not further described, thought to be a Martian. The story concluded with the information that a funeral would be held the following day.

On April 16, according to a letter from him appearing in the *St. Louis Post-Dispatch* three days later, traveling salesman W.H. Hopkins witnessed a landed airship in a clearing in the hills east of Springfield, Missouri. Its two occupants, a woman (the most "beautiful being I ever beheld") and a handsome, bearded man with shoulder-length hair, stood nearby. Though neither was wearing a stitch of clothing on a cool spring day, both appeared uncomfortable, as if too warm. When Hopkins made himself known, the woman acted frightened, the man threatening, but he soon convinced them that he meant no harm. Though they spoke no English and communication took place via gestures, Hopkins eventually inferred to his satisfaction that they were Martians. They examined him "with great curiosity.... They felt of my clothing, looked at my gray hair with surprise and examined my watch with the greatest wonder." After giving him a tour of the ship's interior, they waved good-bye and flew away.

Waves of mystery-airship reports erupted at various times and places in the early years of the twentieth century. A rash of sightings excited and baffled New Zealanders in 1909, leading one letter writer to suggest in the *Otaga Daily Times* (July 29) that "atomic-powered spaceships" from Mars could be responsible. This may be the first time someone attached the specific word "spaceship" to observations of anomalous aerial phenomena.

In three books published between 1919 and 1931 the American anomalist and iconoclast Charles Fort drew on his collection of oddities recorded in newspapers and scientific journals to document a worldwide phenomenon of strange aerial phenomena. Though Mars figures on occasion in Fort's generally eccentric theorizing, it is not a large theme. Nonetheless, in a letter that saw print in the *New York Times* for September 5, 1926, Fort briefly outlined the evidence for an interplanetary presence to which human beings were blind. "If it is not the conventional or respectable thing upon this Earth to believe in visitors from other worlds," he wryly remarked, "most of us would watch them a week and declare that they were something else, and likely enough make things disagreeable for anybody who thought otherwise." In 1931 friends and associates of Fort formed the Fortean Society, whose magazine kept alive ideas of Martian and other visitors.

The Adventures of Hugh Mansfield Robinson

Hugh Mansfield Robinson brought old-fashioned mediumship into the age of electronic communications. A lawyer who lived in a London suburb, he had a metaphysical bent that led him to an immersion in Eastern religion and Christian mysticism. Out of that background he was directed to Martians, whom he first contacted in dramatic fashion one night in 1918. His son had just asked him how Martians are able to signal the earth (presumably popular lore on that subject spurred the question) when Robinson felt a presence near him. The presence—of a Martian woman whom Robinson soon came to know as Oomaruru (Martian for "loved one"; spelled Umaruru in some accounts)—said, "Come with me. I will show you."

In an interview with Fodor a decade later, Robinson said, "I caught hold of my son's hand to remain earthbound. With my other hand—which was now a hand of my phantom body—I clasped Oomaruru. With the speed of light we flew and flew. Half way I felt jerked back. That was the point where the radio waves from Mars and Earth clashed and created a chaos. The grace of God helped me through. I saw a giant red glow in front of me: Mars. We got nearer and nearer and alighted inside a radio station. Oomaruru called out: 'That man is a medium, and jump into his body.'

"I did so and looked at things through his eyes. I saw many radio towers, with sparks flashing, and antennas for reception. But the revolutions of Mars imposed a terrific strain on the etheric band that tied me to my body. I felt I was in deadly danger. As if drawn back by a snapped elastic, I felt I was rushing back to Earth. In four minutes I was back and told my son of my experience."

Robinson claimed that Martian attempts to signal Earth had started around 1900. With him on their side now, though, they had a new champion who would do his utmost to usher in a new age of interplanetary comity. In 1921, when a London department store got high-powered receivers that could receive signals in the then-unprecedented 30,000-meter-length range, he and radio engineer Ernest B. Rogers asked it to open itself to Martian signals at a specific time. The signals were to repeat certain letters of the alphabet in a sealed envelope Robinson had given to Rogers. Allegedly, the message came in when it was supposed to, with the requested letters. According to Robinson, "A schoolmaster in Ilfracomb, Devonshire, who had the proper apparatus and with whom

I made plans to experiment, received the same mysterious signals, this time a complete sentence in Martian: UM GA WA NA. It means God is All in All. It was my birthday, and Oomaruru wanted to please me. I asked for one more test: a signal that would last for a quarter of an hour. We got it, twice in sequence, with terrific energy."

In telepathic exchanges—Robinson always sensed them coming when he felt a pain in his left temple—Oomaruru revealed that she had a husband and son and, moreover, lived on Earth long ago in Egypt (as, of course, no less than Cleopatra). She and her fellow Martians wanted to help Earthlings but would not force more on them than they could grasp at their state of scientific and ethical development. "There are different races on Mars, just as on this Earth," he told reporters. "The cultured ones do not differ much from us. But there are Martians who look like rats." Even the "cultured" Martians, however, were an odd-appearing bunch, if one can judge from drawings produced under Robinson's guidance. Their ears are enormous, and their heads slant upwards in long cones with the apparent texture of acorns. The men are seven and a half feet (2.3 meters) tall, the women six feet (two meters) tall. They have "huge shocks of hair and Chinese features," Robinson said. "They smoke pipes and drink tea from the spouts of kettles." They have airships, trains, and cars, and their diets consist of three "electrified" apples a day.

Robinson's curious beliefs—which included knowledge of other inhabited planets, for example Venus, whose people are "particularly nice"—attracted only limited attention until October 1926, and again two years later, when they were the subject of international press coverage, most—though not quite all—of the tongue-in-cheek variety. If nothing else, Robinson would prove himself to be a committed publicity hound who left a remarkable paper trail as he drove himself from one folly to another.

The first widely publicized episode concerned a telepathic message Robinson allegedly received from his Martian friends, who promised to send three words (*opesti nipitia secombra*) via radio signal to a London receiving station at an agreed-upon time. He put the words into a sealed envelope. When the story leaked to the press and ridicule ensued, the radio station refused to cooperate. If there was a signal, it went unheard. Robinson had a back-up plan, however, and another London radio station heard another message at the appointed moment—not the three words, but two Morse code signs for the letter "M," presumably standing for Mars. A *Popular Wireless* writer, who was present, related in the October 12, 1926, issue:

> Several expert telegraphists were amongst the company that actually heard the "M's" and there is no doubt whatever of their mysterious nature. The coming of the two Morse letters without any accompanying call sign or means of identification was in itself an extraordinary fact. But quite as inexplicable was the uncanny hush that preceded the call. The loud working of the various commercial stations suddenly faded and died down, and it was on a queerly quiet background that the M-M came through. The whole effect of the signals was very weird and mystifying and it certainly created a sensation for the critical crowd of listeners that filled the room.

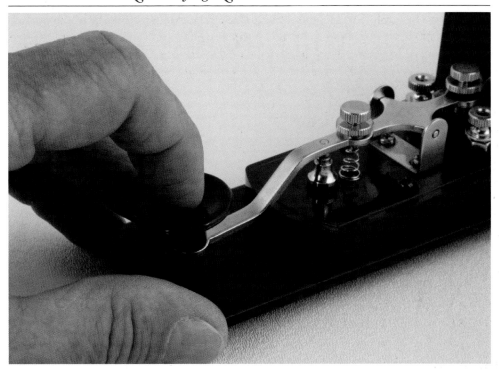

Hugh Mansfield Robinson set up an experiment in 1926 in which Morse code signals from Mars were sent telepathically, some claimed, to a London radio station (*iStock*).

Robinson next hit the front pages in October 1928, when he sent a telegraphic message—at 36 cents a word—from England's Rugby Wireless Station. The coded communication read, "Love to Mars from Earth." Robinson and two others, one of them United Press reporter Henry T. Russell, gathered at the home of scientist A.M. Low, who had encouraged Robinson's experiment, to await the message. At one point, Russell wrote, a seemingly entranced Robinson mumbled, "It's coming, it's through. They tell me they are sending it now. Everything's all right." Just then, eight minutes after the initial message had been sent, a long wireless message arrived, and a few minutes later, another followed. "It was very mysterious," Low asserted, "but it is hardly likely that it was a message from Mars. However, I must confess I do not know who sent it. One striking thing about it was that it was not an ordinary message. It was a long series of undecipherable dots and dashes. For example, at one time there were 11 dots followed by three dashes."

Nonetheless, Oomaruru herself denied that Martians had sent any signals. That was because, she said (in a telepathic communication with Robinson), "Mars received neither message. Do not attempt to use the Rugby station again, but make the next attempt from America."

At the same time, Robinson was touting a recording of the Martian national anthem, received through a medium friend. To Fodor he said that the Martians "speak like giants. Their voices roll and rock the room." Fodor went with Robinson to see the medium—Mrs. St. John James, wife of a London clergyman—and was underwhelmed. All he heard, he wrote, was "loud gibberish ... the worst imitation of mediumship I ever witnessed." (Robinson also worked with American medium Suzanna Harris. On the afternoon of the radio experiment, he sat in on a séance during which she "emitted an ectoplasm.... That ectoplasm ... raised two trumpets.... The Martians then blew on the trumpets.") Fodor was also present at a failed wireless contact attempt in January 1929, when Robinson was to receive a "recessional Swan Song" from the Martians as their planet spun out of opposition for two years.

In December, Robinson tried radio messages again, this time from a station in Rio de Janeiro. The already comical grew farcical when he announced that this time he would have the assistance of a psychic dog named Nell. In August 1932 an article in *The Guardian* reported that Robinson had perfected an "instrument," undescribed and possibly nothing more than Mrs. James' mediumship, which enabled him to effect easy communication with his Martian friends. He said they were monitoring events on Earth with much interest. According to Oomaruru, the world would soon face a great crisis. In that regard, at least, she was certainly prescient.

But Robinson, whose ambition clearly had been to be a world figure, was slipping into obscurity. A last press-wire story about him appeared on March 3, 1933, when he repeated his claim of continuing contacts. The evening before, he said, he had talked—through Mrs. James—with Oomaruru and two other Martians. Robinson played a recording in which Oomaruru sternly urged Earthlings: "Forsake mammon, lust, and luxury. Turn to God in your troubles. Return to the simple life, and your former greatness will return."

Reviewing the forgotten episode a quarter-century later, a still-amused Fodor recalled Robinson to be "as slippery as a human eel."

✳

Flying Saucers from Mars

The coming of the UFO age in 1947 brought romantic ideas about Mars and its space-faring population from the fringes and into the mainstream of popular culture. Within a couple of days of the first widely publicized sighting on June 24, an anonymous press-wire reporter had both coined the term "flying saucers" and called them "Martian planes," neither a phrase pilot-witness Kenneth Arnold had used.

Curiously albeit coincidentally, theorizing about visitors from the red planet had already commenced. Two days prior to the sighting, on the evening of June 22, Lyman Spitzer, Jr., associate professor of astrophysics at Yale University, had appeared on New Haven's WTIC radio to suggest that Martians may have lived on their planet for millions of years. Thus, they may have "visited the earth.... Unless they had spent some time in a large city or had landed sufficiently recently to be photographed, we would have no record of their having been here.... Any few men who had seen them would

The idea that flying saucers may actually be spacecraft occupied by extraterrestrials did not gain popularity until the 1950s (*iStock*).

probably not be believed by anyone else." Spitzer's thoughts were recorded in the *Hartford Courant* the next day, but nowhere else, and thus did not influence the flying-saucer scare about to erupt on the other side of the country. In the heady days and weeks following Arnold's sighting and others that came in its wake, a Detroit meteorologist wondered if perhaps the saucers were "signals from Mars," and R.L. Farnsworth of the American Rocket Society thought they might be "remote-controlled electronic eyes from Mars."

Still, though sightings of flying saucers ("UFOs" did not enter popular parlance for another decade or so) continued unabated, only a relative handful of Americans (mostly those familiar with Fort's writings) believed they were extraterrestrial spacecraft, a notion that did not take a firm hold in the national and world imagination until at least the mid–1950s. The first Gallup poll ever taken on popular assessment of the subject, in August 1947, uncovered no measurable embrace of spaceships; they do not show up as a category at all.

Most Americans who credited the reports—who did not dismiss them as natural phenomena, misinterpretations, and hoaxes—suspected that the United States or Soviet military were secretly testing advanced military airplanes. Within official circles, where that was known not to be the case, military agencies, or at least individuals within them, seriously contemplated the possibility of interplanetary vehicles. That almost became the official conclusion of the Air Force's first UFO-investigation group, Project Sign, in 1948, but Air Force Chief of Staff Gen. Hoyt S. Vandenberg rejected a Sign-sponsored estimate of the situation advocating that explanation, and extraterrestrial theories fell out of fashion in favor of more prosaic approaches focusing on witness error and deceit.

Among mystery-minded civilians, however, saucers and Mars were closely linked from the beginning. The first four issues (1948–1949) of the true-mystery/alternative-reality magazine *Fate,* besides prominently featuring saucers, carried no fewer than three articles on possible Martian intelligences. As early as 1950, Mars oppositions and saucer reports held sufficient interest so that the *Los Angeles Herald-Express* (March 21) was telling its readers that "scientists advised observers not to strain their eyes looking for 'flying saucers' zooming off the surface of the planet." The proximate cause of such hopes was a hugely popular article, "The Flying Saucers Are Real," in the January 1950 issue of the mass-market men's magazine *True.* The article, by aviation journalist and retired Marine Corps Maj. Donald E. Keyhoe, concluded that well-intentioned travelers from a Lowellian Mars were studying the earth in preparation for eventual open contact.

Mars figured largely in the first three UFO books. Keyhoe expanded the *True* piece into a best-selling paperback of the same title. Frank Scully followed with the wild-eyed *Behind the Flying Saucers,* which presented as true stories—manifestly dubious (and subsequently proven false) to all but the most credulous—detailing fatal crashes of Martian and Venusian spaceships in southwestern American deserts. A third title, *Is Another World Watching?,* by a mystical English immigrant to California named Gerald Heard, identified the saucers' pilots as Martian superbees "of perhaps two inches in length ... as beautiful as the most beautiful of any flower, any beetle, moth or butterfly." Heard's theories would prove the least influential of the three.

By the early 1950s an active subculture of enthusiasts was following sightings, forming into clubs, and publishing newsletters and magazines. The growth of such organized interest mirrored the varying—and sometimes fundamentally incompatible—approaches available to persons intrigued by reports of ostensible otherworldly visitors. One faction, dubbed ufologists, held that the nature of UFO reports remained undetermined and that theories about UFOs must necessarily be speculative. Most ufologists, at least in the first two decades of the UFO controversy, were fairly confident that scientific investigation would eventually validate the reality of extraterrestrial visitation, but they acknowledged that such visitation had yet to be decisively established.

The most articulate ufologists were read in popular-science writing, and their theories about intelligence elsewhere borrowed from ideas being circulated by astronomers who still deemed such life on neighboring planets to be at least marginally possible. The ufologists also carried forth the nineteenth-century notion that oppositions were the most opportune times to look for evidence of Martians. Convinced that they had documented a correlation between sighting waves and Martian approaches—such waves erupted during the opposition years 1950, 1952, and 1954—they predicted a mammoth eruption of UFO activity in 1956. That did not happen, but late the next year, when Mars was nowhere near the earth, sighting numbers skyrocketed. In the September 1958 issue of *Fantastic Universe,* the group Civilian Saucer Intelligence of New York took note of these developments and drew the logical conclusion:

> [M]any saucer researchers considered it as virtually a proven fact that there was an association between UFOs and the near approach of *Mars* [italics in the original], but the sighting lull in late 1956 ... and the sighting wave in late 1957 ... knocked that idea on the head. At present, the existence of any simple, predictable cycle in saucer phenomena is open to question.

On the other hand, at the same time French ufologist Aimé Michel was reluctant to abandon Mars theories about UFOs. Whatever the distance at any given moment, why shouldn't Martians be able to send spacecraft here? After all, he wrote, they had already built "canals more than 1,000 miles [1,600 kilometers] long, and, perhaps, of launching satellites of 40 miles [about 75 kilometers] in diameter, such as Phobos and Deimos, weighing several hundred million tons."

Nonetheless, Martian speculation largely disappeared from ufological literature after the late 1950s. It was not revived even after an April 24, 1964, report by Newark Valley, New York, farmer Gary T. Wilcox—judged sober and credible by family, friends, and investigators notwithstanding the bizarre character of his account—claimed to have encountered two squat, space-suited UFO occupants on his property. "We are from what you know as the planet Mars," Wilcox was told.

The second stream of organized interest in aerial anomalies was more mystical and religious in its direction than the pragmatically oriented ufologists were. To the contactees and their followers, there were no UFOs—unidentified flying objects—but known extraterrestrial spacecraft, piloted by benevolent beings from planets in our solar system and beyond. Contactees claimed to have encountered these beings either physically or psychically, or both. As we have seen, contactees—a word coined in the 1950s—were not unique to the flying-saucer era; all that made the interplanetary communicants of that period different was their explicit connection of the contactors with saucers.

Among the first communicants with Martians was a tiny band of saucer enthusiasts from Prescott, Arizona. In 1952, as they were conducting experiments in automatic writing, they received messages from various space people housed in passing saucers. One of the most prominent, "Nah-9," hailed from Mars. Nah-9 warned the group of a "destructive blast to be felt on Saras," the extraterrestrial name for earth. "Evil planetary men, who abound, will attempt contact with evil men of Saras for destruction! The good men of Saras must unite with the ben [good] men of Universe."

One member of the group, George Hunt Williamson, soon emerged as a leading figure in the emerging saucerian movement, a "witness" to contactee George Adamski's initial meeting with a Venusian (an incident that has become legendary in the occult subculture) in the California desert on November 20, 1952, and the author of a trilogy of

George Adamski stands next to a painting by Gay Betts that shows the androgynous-looking Venusian man he claimed to have met in 1952 (*Mary Evans Picture Library*).

books in what would later be called the "ancient astronaut" genre. In the third of these, *Road in the Sky* (1959), Williamson brought Lowellian notions into a whole new arena:

The key in the legend is the fact that the happy life in the former world of the Hopis ended when the crops failed due to a lack of *rain* [Williamson's italics]. Remember, the planet Mars is known to be covered with desert areas, and Dr. [sic] Percival Lowell believed that Mars was a dying planet. He theorized that the Martians were forced to construct their great canal system in order to retard the progress of water evaporation and save their civilization. Did the dwindling water supply on Mars force some of her people to migrate in space ships to another world? Did the colonists on their arrival upon Earth pick the deserts of the American Southwest because they only understood the economy of an irrigated area and a desert environment? When the descendants of the original colony later constructed the great figures on the desert to attract the "rain gods" they must have been impelled by a racial memory that stemmed back to the fear of an insufficient water supply—a fear that constantly overshadowed the lives of their ancestors on "dying" Mars.

Adamski's primary contact was a Venusian named Orthon, but in *Inside the Space Ships* (1955) he recounts meetings with Firkon, a Martian. Even more outré tales were told by Ozark farmer Buck Nelson in a crudely written monograph (*My Trip to Mars, the Moon, and Venus* [1956]) and on the contactee circuit. Nelson regaled the impressionable with an account of a pleasant visit via saucer to Mars with his dog, Teddy, and noted approvingly that racial segregation is practiced there.

In what is surely the silliest episode in the history of contactee-era Earth–Mars interactions, the Martian Monka—or at least his earthly representative, Dick Miller—produced a tape recording in which he announced, "I am what you would call the head of my government." Like Mansfield Robinson's friends three decades earlier, Monka promised to deliver a statement over earthly radio, in this case a Los Angeles station, at 10:30 PM on November 7, 1956. Massive hoopla notwithstanding, Monka failed to deliver on his promise. Meanwhile, the *Los Angeles Mirror-News* reported that earlier Miller had been caught faking a space radio message in his native Detroit. Still, Monka would live on in channeled communications for many years to come, sometimes as a Martian, sometimes as an entity from some other planet or dimension.

✳

Garden on Mars

B rinsley le Poer Trench (1911–1995)—later (as of 1975) the Eighth Earl of Clancarty— was a nearly stereotypical British crank, who combined his interest in UFOs with just about every fringe idea and doctrine with which he came into contact over the course of his long life. Between 1956 and 1959 he edited the popular English magazine *Flying Saucer Review,* championing contactee claims and an occult-tinged approach. He went on to compose a trilogy of books—*The Sky People* (1960), *Men among Mankind* (1963), and *Forgotten Heritage* (1964)—on long-ago extraterrestrial interactions and alien influences on human origins. He did so several years before Erich von Däniken (*Chariots of the Gods?*) and his imitators would generate the "ancient astronauts" craze of the 1970s and beyond.

Like other early saucer writers such as Desmond Leslie and George Hunt Williamson, Trench argued that humans owe their existence to advanced extraterrestrial biological science. In *The Sky People* he wrote of a space race known as the Jehovah:

> Jehovah ... is a name adopted quite recently, as such things go, to designate the People from Somewhere Else in space who deliberately created, by means of their genetic science, a race of human beings peculiarly adapted to perform certain definite and predetermined functions.... They achieved all this in an artificial environment prepared in what was, at the beginning of their project, a desert area. The exact location of this place has always puzzled Biblical students. By means of irrigation they turned this land into a veritable garden. It was an enormous agricultural project.

In short: Long ago, employing techniques that we would now call genetic engineering, they brought us *Homo sapiens* into being. This was not, however, the first creation. That had taken place "in the starry mists of antiquity" through the efforts of the wise and benign Elohim, to whom the less wise and less benevolent Jehovah were at least theoretically answerable. The Elohim created the Galactic Men of the Golden Age— the gods of Greek, Roman, and other mythologies—who roamed Earth and cosmos.

In the second creation the mischievous Jehovah brought Adamic—Animal, or mortal—Men into being. Then, fearing that their creation would be discovered (the

(Continued on page 166)

LANULOS

As he drove near Parkersburg, West Virginia, on the rainy evening of November 2, 1966, sewing-machine salesman Woodrow W. Derenberger saw an unusual-looking dark gray vehicle speed past him on Interstate Highway 77. The vehicle suddenly swerved sideways, covering both lanes, and forced Derenberger to hit the brakes.

The roughly cylindrical structure looked like no car or truck Derenberger had ever seen, so he would relate in many forums over the next few years. Besides its peculiar appearance, it was behaving as no car could, hovering just above the ground as a "small fluttering sound" emanated from it. According to what Derenberger told an early investigator, this is what happened next:

A door opened, and a man stepped directly out and began walking at a normal rate of walk towards the side window opposite the driver's side. At the second he stepped out of the object, the door closed immediately, and the object rose to a height of what I estimated to be 50 to 75 feet [15 to 23 meters] straight up and remained stationed.... I was aware of a voice which said, "Will you open your window?" I leaned over the engine hump, and I had the window down by the time he got directly there. He was standing with his arms folded under his armpits. He was about six feet [two meters] high in height, and

I would estimate weighing about 185 pounds. He was smiling. I did not see his lips move, but I was aware that he was talking to me.

Derenberger soon learned that the stranger's name was Indrid Cold. This was the first of many meetings with this entity, who looked like a dark-haired human with a sun tan. He and his friends, some of whom Derenberger would encounter subsequently, hailed from the planet Lanulos "near the Ganymede star cluster." (Ganymede is actually a satellite of Jupiter.)

Within hours of his first alleged experience Derenberger was busy drawing attention to himself via phone calls to newspapers, radio and television stations, and law-enforcement agencies. He soon was a regular on the then-thriving flying-saucer circuit. In 1971, with Harold W. Hubbard, he published a vanity-press book titled *Visitors from Lanulos*. But by the 1980s he had burned out, living in good part on subsidies from a well-to-do follower, a Massachusetts man who hoped for his own meeting with the Lanulosians. (Derenberger was supplying this highly impressionable individual with letters said to have been composed by Indrid Cold and his wife, Kimi, whose spelling and grammatical limitations were, coincidentally one presumes, identical to Derenberger's.) In 1984, in a final letter to this die-hard supporter, Derenberger tersely asserted:

I am dropping out of sight[;] I am going over seas, I dont [sic] want anything else to do with U.F.O.s, they have caused me to [sic] much worry and trouble. Please dont [sic] try to reach me in any way, for I am thru [sic] with all space people, I have told them never to contact me again.

Derenberger claimed to have traveled through space on a number of occasions. He spent time on Lanulos, a planet whose beautiful inhabitants walk about in the nude. On his initial visit he provoked stares because he refused to shed his clothing. Modesty was part of the reason; the other was that he was embarrassed at being overweight. Soon enough, though, he found his place on the nudist planet. At one point Derenberger gave this account of Lanulosian life for a small flying-saucer magazine:

These people do not have a written record of how their planet began; however, they do have a legend. They believe their forefathers came from Earth in a space ship and after they had landed, somehow lost the art of space travel. It was many, many years before they again learned how to travel in space.

Mr. Cold told me that their religion and their belief in God is the same as our own. They believe there is but one God, who created everything that is good, and is the Father of all. Mr. Cold has told me many times that they would

like to land and come and talk with our people, but he has met several times with hostility, has been shot at[,] and also other ships of his friends have been shot at. At one time in Arkansas, he was shot with a shotgun and he had to have several pellets removed his from leg and thighs. These people are as much afraid of our own people as we are of them. Yet they say they would like to make friendly contact with all our people, and be able to tell us their ways and learn ours.

They would like to be able to trade with our country. Mr. Cold says that they have things that we would like to have, as do we have things that they need. He has told me things that I have no way of knowing whether they are true or untrue, yet in everything he has told me I have never, never in any way learned that he has been untruthful. He has told me that he made an offer to our Government that if they would guarantee safety for both him and his ship, he would land. But for some reason unknown to him, our Government will not grant his request. He said that our Government leaders said that no physical harm would come to him, but otherwise he would have to place himself and his ship in their hands and they would do what was best for him and for us. Mr. Cold has

Sewing-machine salesman Woodrow W. Derenberger tells how he was supposedly contacted by aliens in this 1971 book (*Mary Evans Picture Library*).

declined this offer. I have no way of knowing if this is true.

In their country, they don't have a Government as we know it, but a Guiding Council. Their officials are also elected. There are 56 members in their Council, and they are elected every six years (in our time). Any time one of the officials proves to be unfit for the job, he can be dismissed and another one elected. These people are very friendly and have never had a war on their planet, nor

have they crime, as we know it here. They not only talk with telepathy, but have a language of their own. I know a few words of their language. When a couple is married, it is said that they are "united." The wife calls her husband her "united," and the husband calls his wife his "union."

Their children are very healthy, but they do have sickness. They also have diseases they cannot control, as we do, and have death they cannot prevent. When their children are old enough to know right from wrong, no matter what age, they are sent to school and go until they are 28 years old. At this time, if they have not reached the standard of learning that they should, they go to school until they do. Everyone works at a job that he himself chooses. If a man does not like his work, he can ask for reclassification and can be assigned to something else.

Derenberger found his major champion in John A. Keel, who gave the contactee's claims their widest circulation in his popular book *The Mothman Prophecies*. Keel believed Derenberger to be sincere but deluded, the victim of demonic entities, "ultraterrestrials" in Keel's phrase, which masqueraded as Lanulosians. As Derenberger's tales grew ever more outlandish, Keel rationalized that the ultraterrestrials were trying to sabotage the contactee's credibility and perhaps his sanity as well. (Derenberger may have used notions derived from Keel to cover himself when he elected to remove himself from the no longer tenable pretense of Lanulosian contacts. See above.)

When *Mothman Prophecies* (directed by Mark Pellington) was released as a dramatic film in 2002, character actor Will Patton played a Derenberger-based character given the name Gordon Smallwood. A wink to ufology insiders, "Gordon Smallwood" is borrowed from Gray Barker's *They Knew Too Much about Flying Saucers,* which brought men in black into saucer lore (see "Kazik"). Barker assigned the pseudonym to Canadian Laimon Mitris, allegedly silenced after he gained access to a piece of a UFO. In the movie Smallwood is a contactee clearly based upon Derenberger.

For a time Keel promoted the claims of Thomas F. Monteleone, a University of Maryland student who insisted he, too, had been to Lanulos. Some years later, in a magazine article and elsewhere, Monteleone, today a prominent science-fiction writer, admitted to—more to the point, boasted of—hoaxing the story to confound Derenberger, whom he judged also to be a hoaxer.

Some observers have argued that Derenberger's original experience was in some sense genuine. In defense of that proposition, they point to broadly confirmatory testimony of passers-by who reported seeing a figure along the highway standing near a parked van matching Derenberger's. A local newspaper printed (and researchers from a conservative UFO group investigated) an apparently independent sighting, almost exactly two days later, of a flying object strikingly like the unusual one Derenberger had described. Whatever the truth, Derenberger's later yarns challenged even the most gullible listeners, and he had few defenders.

Perhaps the salient point is that even at their first encounter Indrid Cold reportedly predicted that the two would meet again. One may reasonably deduce that even at this stage Derenberger was already laying plans for a contactee career. The fame and fortune he expected from his career choice, however, managed to elude him.

Further Reading

Derenberger, Woodrow W., and Harold W. Hubbard. *Visitors from Lanulos.* New York: Vantage Press, 1971.

Keel, John A. *The Mothman Prophecies.* New York: Saturday Review Press/E.P. Dutton and Company, 1975.

(Continued from page 161)

In one version of the Garden of Eden biblical story, Adam and Eve are servants to aliens, and they mate with the Serpent People to create the human race (*iStock*).

Jehovah had been acting without permission), they put them on a spaceship and escaped to Mars. On Mars they hid the Adamic Men in a hard-to-find, terraformed location called the Garden of Eden. There, the Adamic Men functioned as the Jehovah's servants but never their equals. Because it was lonely and dissatisfied, the all-male band was soon joined by female equivalents, fashioned out of tissue samples taken from the men. The two sexes performed various menial tasks for their masters, who showed up periodically to check up on them.

Word of the females somehow got to the Serpent People (a Galactic race also known as the "Wise Ones," known by their totemic serpent symbol), who showed up at the Garden one day to the considerable, albeit helpless, distress of the Jehovah. The Serpent People alerted the subject race to a range of issues the Jehovah had kept them from knowing about: the edibility of food in the Garden, knowledge of good and evil, clothing, and—not least—sexual intercourse, in which the Serpent People and the women set about engaging with enthusiasm. The Adamic men soon joined the party. From such interbreeding the modern human race emerged, part Galactic, part terrestrial mortal. "In each and every one of us," Trench wrote, "both these tendencies are present and are the prime source of human conflict, individual and social."

Having incurred the wrath of the gods, Noah-I, the Jehovah who created the Adamics and who remained their benefactor, was exiled from Mars. In their company he piloted a spaceship to Earth, and the adventure of humanity as we know it commenced. Since then, earth's spiritual leaders have sought to restore the "total consciousness" inherent in every human being's psychic heritage from his or her Adamic ancestry.

Face on Mars

Barring unexpected developments, it is likely that the last claim for the presence of intelligent life on the red planet passed with the fading—almost literally—of the

Face on Mars. As a general principle the Face's proponents did not argue for living Martians, just an artifact (and associated structures) left there ages ago either by a vanished race or by extraterrestrials who once had a colony there.

The "Face" appeared in two 1976 photographs taken by Mars-orbiting *Viking* spacecraft. Located in the planet's Cydonia region (latitude 40° north), it resembles an enormous human face (1.6 mile long, 1.2 mile wide) clad in something like a helmet. The form is immediately detectable, which explains the power and fasci-nation it would wield in the coming years. NASA released the pictures in July of that year, identifying them as curiosities caused by a "trick of light and shadow." On April 5, 1998, the

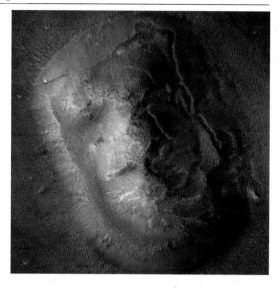

Better photographs of the surface of Mars have shown that the land formation that once looked like an artificially constructed face is actually a completely natural formation (*NASA*.)

Mars Global Surveyor (MGS) took a high-resolution picture which documented that was exactly the case; without shadows, the "Face" turned out to be an ordinary butte or mesa, one of a number on the Cydonia landscape. Critics, however, complained that hazy atmospheric conditions could have covered the truly anomalous features, so MGS conducted a second look on April 8, 2001, and took a photograph from a clear sky. The results were the same. High-resolution stereoscopic pictures from the Euro-pean Space Agency released on September 21, 2006, again failed to document a fantas-tic structure. An even more finely detailed image from the Mars Reconnaissance Orbiter in April 2007 eliminated any remaining possibility—and by now any such was of microscopic proportions—that proof of an extraterrestrial civilization could be found in Cydonia.

Before then, however, the Face had become, if not a genuine Martian feature, a real feature of earthly popular culture. More importantly, it was the focus of research by a small group of technically trained individuals—most prominently ex-NASA con-sultant Richard Hoagland—who insisted that their own analyses had demonstrated the Face to be extraordinary and artificial. Hoagland wrote a book, *The Monuments of Mars* (1987), alleging that the Face was only one unexpected feature of the Cydonian landscape. There were, he said, immense pyramids and mounds indicative of an ancient city arranged geometrically around the Face.

Over the years Hoagland's ideas grew ever more incredible, encompassing ever more labyrinthine conspiracy theories as he sought to explain NASA and other space-exploration agencies' failure to validate the Face as well as structures on the moon and elsewhere. As with all conspiracy theorists, he manages to bring President Kennedy's assassination into the story, in this instance orchestrated by some sinister group that wanted to discourage a joint American-Soviet moon venture, inevitably necessitating the sharing of secrets, especially the ones concerning American officials' knowledge of a lunar civilization.

Though the most publicly visible advocate of the Face, Hoagland was also the most extreme. Other researchers, including Stanley McDaniel, John Brandenburg, Gregory Molenaar, and Vincent DiPietro, produced more restrained and superficially more plausible work. Still, the Face on Mars fell victim, like the Canals of Mars, to technological advances that made possible unambiguous views of the planet's surface. No doubt Mars has more surprises in store, but surely they will not involve massive engineering projects and enormous archaeological structures.

Further Reading:

Brandenburg, John E., Vincent DiPietro, and Gregory Molenaar. "The Cydonian Hypothesis." *Journal of Scientific Exploration* 5, 1 (1991): 1–25.

Case, Justin. "Do Flying Saucers Come from Mars?" *Saucer News* 6, 2 (February/March 1959): 8–9.

Clark, Jerome. "The Extraterrestrial Hypothesis in the Early UFO Age," 122–40. In David M. Jacobs, ed. *UFOs and Abductions: Challenging the Borders of Knowledge*. Lawrence: University Press of Kansas, 2000.

Corliss, William R., ed. *The Moon and the Planets: A Catalog of Astronomical Anomalies*. Glen Arm, MD: Sourcebook Project, 1985.

——, ed. *Mysterious Universe: A Handbook of Astronomical Anomalies*. Glen Arm, MD: Sourcebook Project, 1979.

Crowe, Michael J. *The Extraterrestrial Life Debate: The Idea of a Plurality of Worlds from Kant to Lowell*. New York: Cambridge University Press, 1986.

Denton, William, and Elizabeth M. F. Denton. *Soul of Things; Psychometric Researches and Discoveries*. Volume III. Boston: William Denton, 1874.

Evans, Hilary. *Gods, Spirits, Cosmic Guardians: A Comparative Study of the Encounter Experience*. Wellingborough, Northamptonshire, England: Aquarian Press, 1987.

Fodor, Nandor. *The Haunted Mind: A Psychoanalyst Looks at the Supernatural*. New York: Garrett Publications, 1959.

Jones, H. Spencer. *Life on Other Worlds*. London: Hodder and Stoughton, 1940.

Medway, Gareth J. "Mediums, Mystics and Martians." *Magonia* 99 (2009): 3–9.

Michel, Aimé. "Do Flying Saucers Originate from Mars?" *Flying Saucer Review* 6, 2 (March/April 1960): 13–15.

Rabkin, Eric S. *Mars: A Tour of the Human Imagination*. Westport, CT: Praeger, 2005.

Schwarz, Berthold E. "Gary Wilcox and the Ufonauts." In Charles Bowen, ed. *UFO Percipients: Flying Saucer Review Special Issue No. 3*, (September 1969): 20–27. London: Flying Saucer Review.

Swords, Michael D. "Astronomers, the Extraterrestrial Hypothesis, and the United States Air Force at the Beginning of the Modern UFO Phenomenon." *Journal of UFO Studies* 4 (new series, 1992): 79–129.

Extremophile Living: Life and Love on the Outer Planets

The fifth planet from the sun, Jupiter, is the largest in the solar system, accounting for two-thirds of the system's planetary mass. It has nearly 320 times the mass of the earth, though much of it consists not of solid substance but of gases. Most of the atmosphere is made up of hydrogen sulfide. At the outer extreme are ammonia-ice clouds, beneath them hydrogen-sulfide crystals. The atmosphere is subject to fierce and frequent storms. Closest to the surface, watery ice and—it is thought—liquid water may proliferate. Astronomers are uncertain whether Jupiter has a core that is solid or densely liquid. It has at least 15 moons, including Europa, the focus of speculation about a subsurface liquid-water ocean in which life—probably microscopic—may exist.

As life forms are regularly being discovered thriving in the most extreme circumstances on Earth (thus the adjective "extremophile"), scientists have grown ever more open to the notion that seemingly inhospitable conditions on other worlds do not in themselves rule out the prospect of any and all life; in fact, the earliest life on Earth may have evolved out of similar chemical and climatic circumstances. Still, scientific theorists who concern themselves with such matters take care to express themselves in the most cautious terms. Perhaps the last exercise in more extravagant speculation from mainstream astronomers appeared in a 1976 *Astrophysical Journal* paper in which Carl Sagan and Edwin E. Salpeter hypothesized that immense floating creatures, comparable to gas bags, sail through the atmosphere, expelling helium. The biggest of them may be of such proportions that they are visible from outer space.

To mystic Emanuel Swedenborg, Jovians are sweet-natured folk, little interested in science, who walk about unclad, enjoying long conversations over extended meals. During his psychic visit there, Swedenborg read scripture to them, and they were duly impressed. Bernard le Bovier de Fontenelle, author of a highly popular 1686 work on extraterrestrial life, thought that Jovians are likely to be "phlegmatic" and humorless. "They take a day's time to answer the least question," Fontenelle wrote.

Life on Jupiter, if possible, would be completely unlike Terran life. Carl Sagan and Edwin E. Salpeter speculated that balloon-like creatures might exist by floating high above the planet's surface (*BigStock*).

In *Harmonies de la nature* (1815) Jacques Henri Bernardin de Saint-Pierre reported Jovians to be the Northern Europeans of the solar system: "Provided with light by constant auroras, which mingle with the soft brightness of the moons, when they milk their large herds in their vast grasslands, or spread out their nets, richly filled with fish, on their sandy beaches, they bless Providence and cannot imagine any more beautiful days or happier nights." From his work with spirit mediums, French psychical investigator Hippolyte Léon Denizard Rivail (1804–1869)—better known by his pseudonym, Allan Kardec—deduced that of all the planets "Jupiter is superior in every respect," a cosmic Paris where the most advanced and enlightened spirits dwell.

Traditionally, scientists, occultists, and theologians who put intelligent entities on Jupiter did not focus on that planet in particular. For philosophical reasons they judged all planets—as well as the sun, meteors, and comets—to harbor populations. (As the French writer Louis Cousin-Despréaux [1743–1818] put it in an 1802 book, "All these worlds are populated by an infinite multitude and infinite variety of sentient, intelligent beings who make the name of Omnipotence resound in all the spheres.") Thus, while nearer worlds such as Mars and Venus, where the possibility of breakthrough via observation or even direct communication always seemed imminent, treatment of Jovian life tended to be abbreviated.

It was well known long before the twentieth century that Jupiter, located far from the sun (a mean distance of 483,780,000 miles [778,570,000 kilometers], specifically), was likely to be intensely cold. So speculators sometimes held that the Jovian population was confined to the planet's most relatively temperate zone, the equator. Paul Gudin (1738–1812) imagined that because of turbulence in the planet's atmosphere caused by the gravitational influence of its moons, Jovians lay low and hid in caves to protect themselves.

There were, however, lots of them, according to the Scottish clergyman and astronomy buff Thomas Dick, who in an 1837 book cited startlingly precise population figures for each of the known planets, including their satellites and Saturn's rings. Jupiter houses, in Dick's eerily confident pronouncement, some 6,967,520,000,000 persons, with the moons—presumably representing suburban and provincial regions—holding a smaller but still impressive 26,673,000,000 residents. Writing in 1854, Sir David Brewster (1781–1868) judged Jovians to be superintelligent, able to employ "a type of reason of which the intellect of Newton is the lowest degree."

Jupiter Speaks

In the flying-saucer era of the mid-twentieth century, contact claimants, or at least a good many of them, borrowed the naïve model of a solar system in which all planets are inhabited. Usually, though not quite always, Jovians—who, as in the speculative literature above, tended to get short shrift—do not figure as a primary focus in contactee narratives. (George Hunt Williamson, however, claimed to have received communications from Etonya of Jupiter. The capital city of that planet is Adee, Williamson learned.) Jovians function as extras, while Venusians, Martians, and Saturnians occupy center stage.

The great age of contactees was mostly farce, but on (fortunately rare) occasion there was tragedy, too. The case of Gloria Lee (1925–1962), a Los Angeles woman, undercut the widespread belief that such claimants were charlatans without exception.

By the account published in her 1959 book, *Why We Are Here,* Lee—a former child actor, airline stewardess, and model interested in psychic phenomena—first heard from the Jovian "J.W." via a voice speaking inside her head one day in 1953. A few days later, after she had insisted on proof of J.W.'s existence by physical demonstration, she heard him speak, "Look up!" A flying saucer was passing overhead.

From there, following J.W.'s guidance, she became part of a psychic-development group. "I was utterly flabbergasted," she would write, "when someone described a person who claimed to be a 'space man' and identified himself as J.W.!" That clinched the case for his reality, as far as she was concerned. In due course she would see him but only as a "manifested light form."

She created the Cosmon Research Foundation in order to distribute J.W.'s teachings, whose earthly sources in Theosophy were not hard for informed observers to detect. Nonetheless, Lee organized her life around the channelings. In September 1962, when J.W. directed her to take channeled blueprints for a spaceship to Washington, D.C., to give to officials, she obeyed. Not surprisingly, no one would see her. J.W. expressed outrage. Lee said, "They're disturbed up there because of fighting in the world and the fact that nuclear bombs might upset their planets. The space people are going to invade the earth and establish a peace program. J.W. has ordered me to go on a fast for peace until he sends a 'light elevator' down to take me to Jupiter."

The fast began in a Washington hotel on September 23 and ended on November 28, when she was rushed to a hospital. She died there on December 2. Within two months the Miami-based contactee group Mark-Age MetaCenter reported that Lee was communicating with it from Jupiter.

Saturn

Sixth planet from the sun, the largest planet (95 times the earth's mass) after Jupiter, Saturn is famous—even among the otherwise astronomically illiterate—for its rings. It has an atmosphere consisting largely of hydrogen and helium, and at least 18 moons orbit the planet, whose mean distance from the sun is 887 million miles (1.427 billion kilometers). So far as all available evidence and scientifically imaginable possibility attest, no intelligent life resides there.

Before the twentieth century and advances in astronomy, though, some scientists, philosophers, and theologians held that the planet was inhabited. To the English physician John Peter Biester, who like a number of his contemporaries thought intelligent life to be ubiquitous throughout the solar system, Saturn harbors a population that moves with the seasons to keep warm, while the planet's rings provide reflected light and heat. Sir William Herschel referred casually to "the inhabitants of Saturn" and to "inhabitants of the satellites of ... Saturn." He also thought Jupiter and Uranus' moons are home to sentient races. His son John Herschel wrote in an 1830 book:

> The rings of Saturn must present a magnificent spectacle from those regions of the planet which lie above their enlightened sides, as vast arches spanning the sky from horizon to horizon, and holding an invariable situation among the stars. On the other hand, in the region beneath the dark side, a solar eclipse of fifteen years in duration, under their shadow, must afford (to our ideas) an inhospitable asylum to animated beings, ill compensated by the faint light of the satellites. But we shall do wrong to judge of the fitness or unfitness of their condition from what we see around us, when, perhaps, the very combinations which convey to our minds only images of horror, may be in reality theatres of the most striking and glorious displays of beneficent contrivance.

In 1837 Thomas Dick reported that Saturnians number 5,488,000,000,000, and that did not count the even more abundant suburbanites and provincials on the ring:

Although Saturn's environment is completely unlike Earth's, Saturnians are often described as human-like in appearance (*iStock*).

8,141,963,826,080. That's a total of more than 13.6 *trillion* Saturnians. As historian of astronomy Michael J. Crowe explains, Dick based "his calculation on the population density of England ... 280 persons per square mile," though he neglected "the possibility of oceans elsewhere."

As late as the latter 1800s Camille Flammarion, once a world-famous astronomer and best-selling author of popular-science books, speculated about "aerial beings" who make their home in the Saturnian atmosphere.

The eminent French biologist Comte de Buffon (1707–1788) and, a century and a half later, the Catholic priest and scientist Joseph Pohle (1852–1922) proposed that beings may live on Saturn's satellites.

✳

Meeting Saturnians

If you credit the testimonies of mystics and contactees, Saturnians are physically like us, though smarter. Perhaps the first to report on them from claimed firsthand observation was Emanuel Swedenborg, who found that the people of Saturn "are persistently tormented by evil spirits." From his in-spirit observations, he said, Saturnians do not judge their rings to be a "magnificent sight," in Herschel's later words (above). The ring, he wrote, "does not appear to them as a belt, but only as somewhat whitish like snow in the heavens in various directions."

Most business with Saturnians has been conducted in recent decades as contactees have met them, traveled in their spaceships, and sometimes gone with them to their home planet. For example, George Adamski met a Saturnian, in the company of a Martian, in Los Angeles on February 18, 1953. As Adamski would relate in *Inside the Space Ships* (1955), space people don't have names as we understand them, but for his own reasons he gave the Saturnian the appellation "Ramu." Ramu and the Martian Firkon drove Adamski to a spaceship piloted by Orthon, the Venusian whom Adamski allegedly met in his original November 20, 1952, contact. That small craft flew them to a larger mothership, on which Adamski met other space people.

The next meeting with Ramu took place on April 22, 1953, again in Los Angeles. (Anyone inclined to accord this story a degree of truth is encouraged to note Adamski's assertion [*ISS*, p. 117], "It was a blustery night, but I scarcely noticed the storm." Indeed, it would have been remarkable if he had, because no storm existed. Some years later, skeptical ufologist Richard Heiden, checking weather records, found mild conditions that evening.) Ramu and Firkon led Adamski to the same Pontiac they had driven during the previous meeting, and in due course they entered a Saturnian scoutship (small saucer) on their way to another mothership and another meeting with assorted offworlders.

After Adamski's claims grew ever more outlandish, events climaxed in early 1962, when Adamski informed associates around the world that he would fly to Saturn to attend a conference to be held between March 27 and 30. (Prior to this, Adamski had claimed a trip into space around the moon, but no visits to other planets.) The following June, he circulated "Report on My Trip to Saturn," giving details.

On March 24, he related, a spaceship from Saturn had landed at an air force base "where a high official of the US Government had a conference with the crew." Adamski himself boarded the craft on the 26th. Flying at 20,000,000 miles (32,000 kilometers) per hour, it took nine hours to get to its home planet. He went on:

> On the 29th the main conference was held in a building of exquisite design, equipped with push-button controls. After the conference we were shown how it operated. The floor was cleared, then by pressing certain buttons, the set-up for the conference appeared from beneath the floor, all in order. The walls were also adjustable to suit the need. For the conference they were a delicate purple with gold designs and very tall pillars. The table around which we sat was long with six representatives on each side [representing the 12 inhabited planets of the solar system] and the head counselor, the 13th, seated at the end. Extending the length of the table, through the center, was an indentation in which 12 small fountains played, one in front of each representative. Each was a different color and odor which blended as one, producing a pleasant atmosphere throughout the building. Music seemed to be coming from the fountains, ceilings and walls, such as is never heard on Earth. It was a blend of all actions in the Cosmos and could be likened to the breeze blowing through the trees or the ripple of water. Every sound known to man on Earth, and many more that are not known, were blended together in a perfect harmony; and whatever the melody was it would be beyond earthly comprehension. It was, as I understood, an expression of creation unto its Creator.

Everyone was given a robe to wear at the conference table. The one given to me was a delicate blue, in fact I cannot describe the color, with a rose embroidered on the right sleeve. The rose was like none I have seen on Earth, which reminded me of Jesus['s] saying: "My path is full of thorns." The chairman of the conference wore a robe of opalescent reflections representing Cosmic principles. During the 18 hours of the assembly (Earth time) it seemed to me that I no longer had a mind of my own nor did I feel as a person, but rather as an important part that fitted into a complete being expressing itself in the highest degree of its knowledge with a Cosmic feeling.

If Adamski expected the story to revive a flagging career, he had severely miscalculated. All it did was to fuel growing qualms about Adamski's truthfulness among the heretofore-faithful. Certain aspects of the tale struck them as more consistent with a psychic experience than a physical voyage to another world. Here, as elsewhere, Adamski had betrayed alarming impulses toward occultism, of which he had been fiercely critical in the past, warning enthusiasts that persons who reported mediumistic contacts with extraterrestrials are frauds. Or perhaps Adamski had been the victim of a sinister mind-control experiment by government operatives allied with the Silence Group (an Earth-based, international conspiratorial group seeking to frustrate the work of friendly space beings). Or, worst of all, the new group of space people who, according to no less than Adamski himself, had replaced the old Orthon/Firkon/Ramu generation. Conceivably, they were a more devious bunch with suspect motives. Or, finally, the unthinkable: Adamski had concocted the yarn out of whole cloth.

Another contactee who claimed to have befriended Saturnians, Reinhold Schmidt, witnessed—so he informed local law-enforcement authorities—a landing near Kearney, Nebraska, on November 5, 1957. The spaceship's occupants, four men and two women, communicated in "high German" to one another and in German-accented English to him. The conversation was brief, mostly focused on the U.S. space program, but other meetings, including rides in their ships, followed over time as Schmidt's star rose on the contactee circuit. Schmidt said that his space friends were from Saturn.

Schmidt, who had a background in confidence crime (scam artist) and whose saucer allegations must be understood in that context, ran afoul of the law in 1961, accused of bilking an elderly widow out of $5,000 for a bogus mining venture related to his extraterrestrial adventures. Tried in Oakland, California, for grand theft, he denied all charges but was convicted and sentenced to one to 10 years in prison on two counts. A young astronomer, Carl Sagan, testified that Saturn cannot sustain human life.

Being Saturnian

Still, these kinds of Saturn yarns were fairly modest in comparison to the ones that enlivened the contactee repertoire of Howard and Connie Menger. Howard

Howard and Marla Menger (shown here in 1959) testified that they were aliens. Howard said he was from Saturn and Marla was a Venusian (*Mary Evans Picture Library*).

Menger, who lived on a farm outside High Bridge, New Jersey, was among the contact claimants whose stories echoed Adamski's. To contactee advocates that amounted to confirmation; to detractors, it was simply imitation. In any event, Menger announced himself on October 29, 1956, on a New York City radio show hosted by Long John Nebel of WOR. Soon he was being called, both favorably and otherwise, the "East Coast Adamski."

In his telling of the tale, he began experiencing "flashbacks" of life on another world while he was a child, too young to have any idea what they meant. Then he saw flying saucers years before the phrase "flying saucers" was coined (in 1947). In 1932, when he was 10, he met a beautiful blond woman who was sitting on a rock by a forest brook. He was overcome with a "tremendous surge of warmth, love and physical attraction" even before she spoke to tell him that she had "come a long way to see you, Howard, and to talk with you." She knew who he was, she said cryptically, "from a long, long time." She talked of her "people" who had been observing him and of a life purpose he would learn later. "We are contacting our own," she said.

From time to time, Menger encountered other mysterious figures, and then in 1946 he watched as the woman he had met on the rock step out of a spaceship. This time he learned that she was 500 years old, even though she looked only 25. Perhaps most important in terms of what was to come in the area of consensus reality Menger inhabited, he was told that while he would never see her again, he would meet her sister one day. The sister was a Venusian living on Earth in her current incarnation. "She will work with you and be with you for duration of this life span," the spacewoman stated. "You will recognize her the moment your eyes fall upon her."

In any case, this was the story in his *From Outer Space to You* (1959). In real life, after he began holding gatherings at his farm in the wake of his coming-out as a contactee, the married Menger met an attendee, an attractive Jersey City blond dancer named Connie Weber, with whom he soon was conducting an affair. Eventually, he divorced his wife and married Weber.

This ordinary human story took on, not surprisingly, extraordinary—well, extra-terrestrial, specifically—dimensions when the Mengers told it. Howard said he had recognized Connie immediately as the Venusian sister as soon as his eyes fell on her. His "memory block" disintegrated on the spot, and he recalled that they were lovers in another life, when he was a Saturnian spiritual teacher named Sol da Naro and she a Venusian beauty named Marla. He had met her when his work took him to Venus. "Our love on Venus was intense and overpowering," he reported, "but it was fated we should not stay together, since I knew I must travel to Earth and complete a mission which had been outlined from my day of birth on that planet."

Writing as "Marla Baxter," Connie released a steamy book titled *My Saturnian Lover* (1958) detailing her love life with "Alyn" (her pseudonym for Howard). When they had sexual relations, she claimed, "Alyn" sometimes returned to his old Saturnian self:

> Alyn bent down to kiss my brow. I felt the undulating tremors of his body again, and then began a strange and fascinating transformation, right before my eyes. Alyn began to grind his teeth, and turn and twist and stretch. He appeared to be getting taller and stronger. He breathed in deeply, and I felt his chest expand greatly. It seemed as if he had grown a head taller. Not only did he grow taller and stronger, but his facial contour changed. His face seemed to get longer and triangular shape, and his eyes grew larger and deeper. Even his voice was different—deeper and lower. He had ceased to be Alyn and had become a Saturnian.... The next thing I knew he, as a Saturnian, had placed his hands under my armpits and slowly raised me at arm's length as if I had been a doll, and without so much as a muscle strain or change in breathing or the slightest exertion of any kind. He held me thus, high above his head for a moment, looking up at me with the most wondrously loving eyes, then slowly drew me down toward him until our lips met. It was this individual, this Saturnian, this strange being who revealed himself to me as he really was, with whom I fell in love.

In the fall of 1956, Howard encountered two Venusians and a Saturnian in an isolated cabin in the woods near his home. The Saturnian, who was playing what amounted to an extraterrestrial version of a piano, taught nonmusician Howard a tune popular on the sixth planet. Howard thought it a "beautiful, haunting melody"—rudiments of which, in fact (well, in his account anyway), had been playing in his head for many years as a residual memory of his years on Saturn—and in due course he released it on a long-playing album as *Music from Another Planet*. No one but Menger has ever thought of it as memorable, much less otherworldly.

By 1960 Menger had more or less recanted his claims, hinting that he had participated in a government experiment intended to prepare Americans for landings one day by actual space visitors. In the early 1990s he and Connie, still married and now living in Florida, reappeared, with Howard sort of recanting his recantation. A 1992 television documentary, *Farewell, Good Brothers,* produced and directed by Robert Stone,

FROM OUTER SPACE TO YOU

by HOWARD MENGER

*An account of visitors from space
. . . documented by actual photographs*

In this 1959 book, Howard Menger—who later recanted his claims—ennumerated a lifetime's worth of encounters with friendly space people (*Mary Evans Picture Library*).

featured the Mengers recapping their original story and Howard promoted an ET-technology scheme he was seeking to market. Menger died on February 25, 2009.

Uranus

Discovered in 1781 by Sir William Herschel, Uranus, the seventh planet, orbits at a mean distance of 1,783 million miles (2,869 million kilometers) from the sun. It is one of the four gas giants, and at least 18 moons orbit it. Its core consists of water, ammonia, and methane, and hydrogen and helium dominate the atmosphere.

Unarian life has never been a major theme in pluralist literature. Typically, it was treated in passing fashion, as in a posthumously published book by the French naturalist Jacques Henri Bernardin de Saint-Pierre, who could not imagine that nature would leave any planet—not to mention satellite, sun, or comet—uninhabited. On Uranus, he declared, lives an "animal of the reindeer kind, feeding on moss and combining in itself the advantages of the fleece of sheep, the milk of the cow, the strength of the horse, and the lightness of the stag." The intelligent inhabitants are the cosmic equivalent of Laplanders, with dogs with which they tended to reindeer herds. Oil lamps illumined the long, dark nights. Uranians are as uninterested in warfare as they are in cultural and intellectual pursuits. The Rev. Dick estimated that—at least in his time—a staggering 1,077,568,800,000 persons lived on the planet itself and 47,500,992,000 on its moons. Looking at those figures, one can only conclude that there cannot have been a lot of leftover land for those reindeer herds.

The contactee movement that emerged in the mid-twentieth century held as a matter of course that all solar planets are inhabited. Uranians as such, however, play a very small role in contact lore. They appear most prominently in the stories of the contactees George Hunt Williamson and Frances Swan.

Williamson, who died in 1986, was a maverick, an anthropologist with a considerably inflated resumé, with wide-ranging interests which in the early 1950s coalesced into an obsession with flying saucers and extraterrestrials. Soon after he moved to Prescott, Arizona, in 1952, he, his wife, Betty, and their friends Alfred and Betty Bailey sought to communicate with space people. Before long, they were receiving messages through the ouija board—then, more controversially, via Morse code-like messages on radio—from assorted off-worlders. One, who showed up on August 25, was Affa of Uranus. Affa was unenthusiastic initially, since he thought "Saras" (Earth) was too evil to deal with. A second Uranian, Zrs, also appeared on occasion. And Zo, from Neptune, informed the Arizona group, "We hold certain councils on Uranus. We must now decide what to do about your planet Earth. Your bombs will destroy Universal balance."

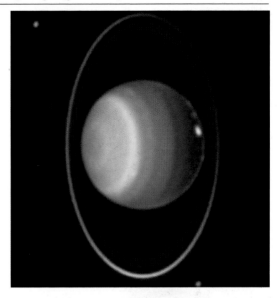

A 1998 image of Uranus taken by the Hubble Space Telescope's Near Infrared Camera shows a frozen, inhospitable, cloud-covered world surrounded by rings, yet Scottish clergyman Thomas Dick (1774–1857) speculated it was home to over a trillion inhabitants (*NASA*).

A Maine woman, Frances Swan, claimed actually to have seen Affa, though she did not recognize him at the time they met. Then he was just a distinguished-looking stranger whom she encountered at a 1953 Halloween party at the Grange Hall in Eliot, where she lived. He acted as if he didn't know anybody, so out of courtesy she engaged him in conversation. The conversation consisted of nothing outside of the usual banalities people utter in such circumstances, but for some reason he left an impression on her.

He came to mind the following April 30, when Mrs. Swan, who had long been interested in psychic matters, was driven to write these words: WE COME WILL HELP KEEP PEACE ON EU DO NOT BE FRIGHTENED. Three days later, a second message came, this one from Affa, who reported that he was communicating from a giant spaceship which had arrived from Uranus. Soon other beings from other worlds that comprised the Universal Association of Planets spoke up, but Affa remained the most voluble one. At one point he told her, "This Earth is really going to end as stated in the Holy Bible around 1956."

On May 18, Affa instructed her to write a letter to the U.S. Navy, to urge it to be open to the reception of radio messages from the space visitors.

As it happened, Swan's neighbors included a retired admiral, Herbert B. Knowles, to whom she went to relate these events. The Knowleses heard her out but expressed

(Continued on page 182)

NIBIRU

Arthur C. Clarke's short story "The Sentinel" was turned into the classic 1968 motion picture *2001: A Space Odyssey* (*Ronald Grant Archive/Mary Evans Picture Library*).

Nibiru is another of those alternative-reality planets unrecognized by astronomy, but to an international readership of books by Zecharia Sitchen (1920–), it was and is a real place, soon to make its presence known to all the world.

Born in the Soviet Union, raised in Palestine, and educated in England, Sitchen, now an American, came to prominence in the 1970s, publishing *The Twelfth Planet* (1976) just as the "ancient astronauts" fad of the earlier part of the decade was cresting. The movement took its inspiration from the best-selling *Chariots of the Gods?* (1969), in which Swiss writer Erich von Däniken (1935–) argued that extraterrestrial visitors to Earth long ago left evidence in the form of archaeological structures, religions, and mythology; using genetic engineering, they also created the modern human race.

Most of Von Däniken's claims were unoriginal. Notions of alien influences on history can be traced, at least in nascent form, to nineteenth-century occultism, to passing references in the works of the influential anomalist Charles Fort, and—perhaps most notably—mid-century flying-saucer books (for example, George Hunt Williamson's 1953 *Other Tongues—Other Flesh*). The theme of ancient visitation had for decades provided plots for science-fiction tales, perhaps the most famous of them Arthur C. Clarke's "The Sentinel" (1951), which inspired the celebrated 1968 Stanley Kubrick film (with screenplay co-written by Clarke) *2001: A Space Odyssey*.

Unlike the autodidact Von Däniken, Sitchen had some claims to serious formal education, though in economics, not in astronomy, linguistics, or ancient history, in all of which—in common with Von Däniken—he was self-taught. Sitchen was, however, literate in old languages, including Sumerian. From ancient writings, using his own translations (sometimes disputed by the relatively small number of academic experts who have paid attention), Sitchen has fashioned a complex hypothesized history in which the astronomically and physically dubious planet Nibiru, the twelfth in the solar system and orbiting far beyond Pluto, plays a key role.

According to Sitchen, Nibiru's elliptical orbit takes it around the sun every 3,600 Earth years. Its travels will take it to a position between Mars and Jupiter in the near future, at which point its inhabitants, the advanced extraterrestrial race known as what the ancient Sumerians called Anunnaki ("those who from heaven to Earth came," in Sitchen's translation; "the fallen ones," in the standard one), will appear to twenty-first-century humanity and reveal their role in the creation of *Homo sapiens* and of human civilization.

In Sitchen's account, it all began 450,000 Earth years ago when the people of Nibiru faced the realization that their planet's atmosphere was in decline, threatening all life. The realization sparked political unrest, and the deposed ruler Alalu fled into space. He ended up on Earth, where he found gold, which would fix his home world's atmospheric problems. In time other Anunnaki followed, creating Earth Station #1 for the purpose of mining gold from the waters of the Persian Gulf. This took place as political conflicts, warfare (including one waged with nuclear weapons), and genet-

ic engineering of slaves to work in the gold mine (the ancestors of present-day humans) went on over a period of several hundred thousand years.

Sitchin weaves Middle Eastern mythology, biblical stories, and more into the mix, operating on a principle, common to ancient-astronautical writing, that mythology is history in disguise and that "gods" are to be understood as space visitors. Sitchin's erudition has won him a following outside the diminishing band of Von Dänikenites. In common with other such theorists, though, Sitchen is something of a conspiracy theorist, maintaining that what should have been clear account of extraterrestrial interventions in the Ancient East got garbled because of scholars' "mistranslations," some of them deliberate. Over time, he has created what one critic characterizes as an alternative education system, awarding degrees in "Sitchin studies" to especially dedicated acolytes.

Further Reading

Sitchin, Zecharia. *The Earth Chronicles Handbook: A Comprehensive Guide to the Seven Books of The Earth Chronicles.* Rochester, VT: Bear and Company, 2009.

Zecharia Sitchin's Ancient Astronaut Theories—A Skeptical Archive. http://echo.gmu.edu/node/1908.

A CITY ON URANUS
Metalis, the amazing metal and glass city of the Seal Men of Uranus. Read its story on page 144
★

A 1941 story by Frank R. Paul, published in *Amazing Stories,* posits the theory of a highly advanced civilization on Uranus (*Mary Evans Picture Library*).

(Continued from page 179)

reservations about the reality of the space people. Swan responded that Affa had promised to show up in person at 1:12 PM on May 26.

Affa failed to appear, and the incensed Mrs. Swan swore that she would thereafter cease all dealings with unreliable interplanetarians. Within minutes—by 1:26—Affa (through automatic writing) was offering profuse apologies. Knowles proceeded to ask questions and was sufficiently satisfied with the answers that the next day he wrote Rear Adm. C.F. Espe, head of the Office of Naval Intelligence (ONI), to urge a communication attempt through Band CMM-306, repeating the signal M4 M4 A F F A. At Espe's failure to respond, Knowles wrote again. "Believe me," he asserted firmly, "the messages *are* real.... Communication *has* been established with Earth through Mrs. Swan.... Can you read these communications and believe they are the product of Mrs. Swan's imagination?"

On June 8 two ONI officers arrived in Eliot and sat down with Swan for an interview with Affa. The Uranian said he could not appear personally, but he would speak with them via radio at 2:00 PM on the tenth. Again he was a no-show, and that was it, Espe subsequently informed Knowles. The file of letters went to the Navy's Bureau of Aeronautics. There a security officer, John Hutson, read them through and got in touch with Knowles, who invited him up for a visit. Hutson visited between July 24 and 26, staying with the Knowleses and, of course, sitting with Swan as Affa intoned.

Back in Washington, Hutson reported to the FBI about his visit, and an agent interviewed him. A few days later FBI director J. Edgar Hoover forwarded an account to the Air Force's Office of Special Investigation (AFOSI), with copies to the Director of Naval Intelligence and to the Assistant Chief of Staff, G-2, U.S. Army. "No further action is being taken in this matter by this Bureau," Hoover wrote.

Matters rested there for five years. Then in 1959 U.S. Navy Cmdr. Julius Larsen, an ONI liaison officer to the CIA's Photographic Intelligence Center in Washington, happened upon the file. Larsen, who had a taste for paranormal mysteries, decided to look into the curious business. On July 5 he and a Navy pilot flew to Maine and spent the evening at the Knowles residence speaking with Swan. Larsen attempted his own automatic-writing experiment and scrawled a message signed "Affa," though Swan rejected the idea that this was her Affa. She judged Larsen a gullible and foolish sort.

The following day Larsen took his story to Center director Arthur Lundahl—who had a private interest in UFOs—and Lundahl's assistant, Lt. Cmdr. Robert Neasham, on loan from the Navy. Neasham had some familiarity with the subject of UFOs, having analyzed a film taken of alleged unidentifieds over Trementon, Utah, in July 1952. At their urging Larsen went into a mild trance state, writing down questions that soon were "answered" inside his head by—of course—Affa. When Neasham asked for proof that this was more than mere delusion, Larsen suddenly shouted (apparently as Affa), "Go to the window!"

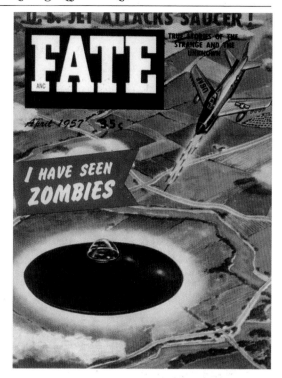

A summer 1952 issue of *Fate* includes a report from the U.S. Air Force's Project Blue Book in which an F-86 pilot attacked a UFO, but the alien craft was unharmed (*Mary Evans Picture Library*).

Lundahl and Neasham rushed there and gazed into the sky. Lundahl would later insist that he had seen nothing but clouds, while Neasham expressed a conviction that a spaceship could be glimpsed inside some of those clouds. According to his later testimony, the latter contacted the radar office at Washington National Airport, which told him that part of the sky—the part where the supposed UFO hid—was "blocked out." Neasham spoke urgently with Maj. Robert Friend, then of the Air Force's UFO-investigative body, Project Blue Book. When Friend came to talk with Larsen and Neasham on the ninth, Larsen demonstrated his space-contact technique, but Affa refused an invitation for a flyover.

In later years this forgotten little episode was rediscovered and, improved with the telling, became a kind of minor Space Age legend. In the legend the incident was moved to "CIA headquarters," and three leading CIA officials watched a UFO sail by as it deflected radar waves.

More specific information about Uranians comes from the late British writer W. Raymond Drake, author of several fringe books that trace alleged space visitors from the present into ancient times. Drake observed:

Dim green Uranus shone with baleful influence, its distant inhabitants were feared as wizards conjuring their darksome spells in greenish twilight. This picture seems confirmed by Space Intelligences who are said to describe the Uranians as tall with large eyes and overdeveloped heads, possibly hermaphrodites, having blood and organs different from our own. Lest we smile with arrogance, it is said that the Uranian spaceships disdain the warring creatures of Earth and seldom visit our skies.

Neptune

Neptune, the eighth planet in the solar system, is not a place that one would expect any sort of intelligent life, imaginable or unimaginable, to exist. The smallest of the four gas giants (the other three are Jupiter, Saturn, and Uranus), it is 60 times the diameter of the earth, and its atmosphere consists of hydrogen, helium, and methane. A layer of water and melted ices covers the planet's Earth-sized liquid core, and it is buffeted by the fiercest winds that blow on our neighboring worlds: 1,500 miles (2,414 kilometers) per hour. Neptune has eight known moons. Discovered in 1846, it gets its name from the Roman designation for the sea god whom the Greeks called Poseidon.

Within a very few years some spirit mediums were speaking of the new planet's inhabitants. In a book published in 1857, for example, British seer J.G.H. Brown, who claimed as a spirit guide no less than the Angel Gabriel, said that Neptune harbored the spirits in innocent babies who had died before the world could corrupt them.

On the other hand, in *Scientific Certainties of Planetary Life; or, Neptune's Light as Great as Ours* (1855), Thomas Collins Simon, an Englishman and amateur scientist, contended that all planets, including Neptune, are exactly like Earth, with "the same vegetable, animal, and intellectual life." A century later, contactee lore would allege much the same, counting Neptune among the 12 inhabited planets in the solar system. Its people are human and handsome, and they dwell in an ideal society without the assorted social ills that afflict the earth.

A few Earthlings have claimed contact with residents of Neptune. The prominent early flying-saucer contactee George Adamski, whose yarns included assertions of meetings with extraterrestrials living in our midst, claimed that while visiting Mexico in 1957 he met a man from Neptune. In all, he said, he had met individuals from five planets in the solar system, and they differed in appearance no more than do individuals from different terrestrial nations.

W. Raymond Drake declared that the ancients called the sea god Neptune because they knew he had come from the planet Neptune. "Since the planet [Neptune] receives only one nine-hundredth of the sunlight on Earth," Drake observed, "our astronomers believe it to be fantastically cold; in contrast Space Intelligences assert that chemical light from the atmosphere illumines advanced Beings similar to their neighbors on Uranus."

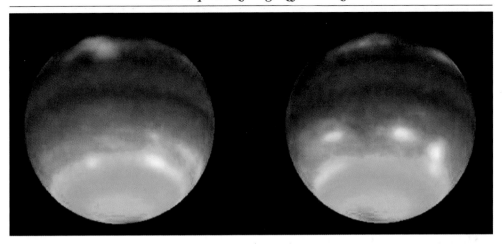

Neptune, like the other gas giant planets in our solar system, now appears to be yet another unlikely home for either alien or human life (*NASA*).

Confusingly, in the same decade another leading contactee, Orfeo Angelucci of Los Angeles, chronicled his interactions with an interplanetary/interdimensional being whom he called Neptune, though the planet was not his place of origin.

Pluto

Pluto was discovered in 1930 by Clyde Tombaugh (1906–1997) of the Lowell Observatory. Regarded for decades as the ninth and most distant planet from the sun, it was also the smallest in the solar system, and on occasion some astronomers even challenged its claim to being a planet in ordinary sense of the term. In the early twenty-first century, Pluto was downgraded to the status of "dwarf planet" and removed from the august company of the eight full-sized worlds. At its equator it is a mere 1,442 miles (2,320 kilometers) in diameter. Its atmosphere consists in large part of nitrogen which turns to frost as the planet's orbit takes it away from the sun. Pluto has one large moon, Charon, and in 2005 two smaller moons (each only about 10 miles [16 kilometers] in diameter) were also discovered.

In contactee literature Pluto is, like virtually all planets, an inhabited one. In 1952 Williamson and his small band of saucer communicants received messages from, among others from other worlds, the Plutonian Touka. Williamson and his associates thought Touka was a pleasant sort, but a few years later, in a 1964 book, W. Raymond Drake, citing "Space Intelligences" as his source, took a darker view: "The Plutonians are said to misuse their advanced science and dark occultism for evil," he stated; "their alien spaceships are reported as threatening Venus, Mars and Earth. Perversion of sex and psychic

(Continued on page 188)

CLARION

A drawing by illustrator Carol Rodriguez and published in Ashtar Command's 1952 book, *The New World Order*, shows the alien Aura Rhanes as described by Truman Bethurum (*Mary Evans Picture Library*).

Clarion is a planet in our solar system, but we never see it because its orbit keeps it always on the opposite side of the sun from the earth. So maintained contactee Truman Bethurum (1898–1969), who allegedly gleaned this information from meetings with travelers from that planet in 1952 and later.

As he told the story in a book, on lecture platforms, and on radio and television shows for the next decade and a half, Bethurum's encounters began in the early morning hours of July 28, 1952, in the Nevada desert. Employed as a heavy-equipment operator, he was sleeping between shifts when eight olive-skinned little men awoke him, then led him to a landed spacecraft (he was soon informed that it was called a "scow"). Inside the ship he met a "gorgeous woman, shorter than any of the men, neatly attired, and also having a Latin appearance.... She appeared to be about 42 years old," though it turned out that she had lived several centuries. She introduced herself as Captain Aura Rhanes from Clarion.

Other nocturnal conversations with Rhanes and her Clarion crew followed over the next several months, 11 in all. On a few other occasions Bethurum saw her in daylight, walking down streets or sitting in restaurants, passing herself off as a human being. Bethurum went public with his contact tales for the first time in August 1953, at a conference sponsored by the Los Angeles-based Flying Saucers International.

While most observers judged Bethurum to be a hoaxer, he attracted a small, devoted following. In the later 1950s he established the short-lived communal "Sanctuary of Thought," housed in Prescott, Arizona, from donations made by the faithful.

Clarion is a planet devoid of violence and other ills. Its people are Christians.

"Here, God has saved us from inclemencies and has spared us many social misfortunes, adultery and infidelity to the dangerous degree that it exists on the Planet Earth," according to a letter Aura Rhanes allegedly wrote—the original is in French—to a friend of Bethurum. All property on Clarion is owned in common, and there is no economic inequality.

Another contactee claimed to have actually visited Clarion, though he had little to say about it and the visit was only a cosmic pit stop on the way to other planets. Chief Frank Buck Standing Horse, an Ottawa Indian from Oklahoma, boarded a *Vea-o-mus* (spaceship) late one evening in July 1959, then zipped off to Mars and Venus. On Venus a female pilot, Mondra-o-leeka, from that planet relieved the original pilot, and the ship flew off to Clarion and landed there briefly before heading off to the real destination, the planet Oreon (pronounced *O-ree-on,* not to be confused with the constellation Orion). Standing Horse had little to say about what he saw and experienced while on Clarion. Apparently he did not meet the lovely Aura Rhanes. Few other contactees have ever mentioned the planet.

For reasons manifestly more frivolous than serious, the University of Colorado UFO Project, which investigated and analyzed reports on contract for the U.S. Air Force between 1966 and 1969, commissioned the Naval Observatory to determine whether a planet on Clarion's alleged orbit, staying forever invisible to earthly gaze, is physically possible. A scientist at the observatory concluded that it was not.

In April 1954 Sananda—otherwise known as Jesus—initiated what would prove to be four decades of automatic-writing communications, ending only with her death, through Dorothy Martin, an Oak Park, Illinois, woman with a consuming interest in occult matters. Sananda identified his home planet as Clarion, but this was not Aura Rhanes' Clarion. Sananda's Clarion existed in an ethereal, other-dimensional realm. Over time Sananda would regale Martin—who later renamed herself Sister Thedra at his urging—with cosmic wisdom and a host of unfulfilled prophecies.

Further Reading

Bethurum, Truman. *Aboard a Flying Saucer.* Los Angeles: DeVorss and Company, 1954.

Clark, Jerome. "The Odyssey of Sister Thedra," 25–41. In Diana Tumminia, ed. *Alien Worlds: Social and Religious Dimensions of Extraterrestrial Contact.* Syracuse, NY: Syracuse University Press, 2007.

FLYING WING OF PLUTO

Although Pluto has no atmosphere, this plane can travel above the surface of the planet using an electro-magnetic force for propulsion.
(See page 238 for complete story)

The ingenious Plutonians solve the problem of flight on a world almost devoid of an atmosphere in this 1942 *Amazing Stories* tale by Frank R. Paul, but ancient-astronaut theorist W. Raymond Drake described them elsewhere as a menacing race (*Mary Evans Picture Library*).

(Continued from page 185)

force are said to be dooming their brilliant but decadent civilization to destruction; their degenerate planet will soon be whirled into outer space."

These charges are inconsistent with the testimony of Kelvin Rowe. Friendly with ground-breaking contactees such as George Adamski and Truman Bethurum, Rowe gradually entered in contact himself when vague voices sounded in his head. The first clear signal came on March 9, 1954, as Rowe drove to San Bernardino, California, and the word "Pluto" sounded inside his head, loudly and precisely, three times. Later in the month there were other brief psychic messages, to which Rowe responded with a request for a personal meeting.

On April 4, 1954, as Rowe wandered through a contactee convention in southern California with his friend Bethurum, he encountered three cordial individuals, two men and a woman, and had a conversation with them. In due course, because of something they had said they could not have known, Rowe wondered if they were space people, a suspicion subsequently confirmed in a telepathic message from the young woman, who turned out to be from Pluto. Thereafter, he called her the "Lady of Pluto."

Eventually, he began meeting space people, and in January 1955 he encountered the Lady again. A beautiful woman standing slightly more than five feet (1.5 meters) tall, she wore a blouse, jacket, and slacks "in contrasting tones of a beautiful, pansy-blue, similar to royal blue, and a shade of red-wine in a scintillating, deep intensity." Her occupation was spaceship captain, and currently she and her fellow space people, prominently including Jovians, were tracking an asteroid that was approaching the earth at a dangerously close range. Not to worry, though; the Lady and her friends would prevent it from harming Earth. In his *A Call at Dawn* (1958) Rowe recounted voyages into space with the Lady or with her friends from Jupiter. Their literary inspiration, one suspects, was Bethurum's neither more nor less believable alleged interaction with the lovely Aura Rhanes of the hidden solar planet Clarion (see sidebar).

An English woman, Mrs. Lainchbury, who lived in a village near Manchester, was awakened one night in the spring of 1964 when a brilliant light sprayed through her bedroom window. Its source was a fiery orange sphere that apparently had exploded. This may well have been a meteor, but two months later, when a human-looking space-man manifested in her bedroom, she believed him when he said it had been his ship. He was now, alas, stranded on earth. Subsequent meetings with him and others like him led her to understand that all had been on the same craft. In the course of conversation, always telepathic, she was shown letters that materialized in the air in front of her eyes. They read PLUTO. Mrs. Lainchbury claimed that at the time she did not know the significance of the word, not having heard of the planet. One day in 1967 a familiar-looking orange sphere appeared over her home, a manifestation that she interpreted to mean that her friends were at last going home. In any event, she did not see them again.

Further Reading:

Adamski, George. *Inside the Space Ships.* New York: Abelard-Schuman, 1955.

Angelucci, Orfeo. *The Secret of the Saucers.* Amherst, WI: Amherst Press, 1955.

Brown, J.G.H. *A Message from the World of Spirits, Shewing the State of Men after Death.* London: Holyoake and Company, 1857.

Crowe, Michael J. *The Extraterrestrial Life Debate: The Idea of a Plurality of Worlds from Kant to Lowell.* New York: Cambridge University Press, 1986.

Drake, W. Raymond. *Gods or Spacemen?* Amherst, WI: Amherst Press, 1964.

Fitzgerald, Randall. "Messages: The Case History of a Contactee." *Second Look* 1, 12 (October 1979): 12–18, 28–29.

Good, Timothy. *Alien Base: Earth's Encounters with Extraterrestrials.* London: Century, 1998.

Menger, Howard. *From Outer Space to You.* Clarksburg, WV: Saucerian Books, 1959.

Williamson, George H., and Alfred C. Bailey. *The Saucers Speak! A Documentary Report of Interstellar Communications by Radiotelegraphy.* Los Angeles: New Age Publishing Company, 1954.

PART THREE

Between This World And the Otherworld

The Road to Fair Elfland: Fairies Experienced

Celtic seers ... say that Fairyland actually exists as an invisible world within which the visible world is immersed like an island in an unexplored ocean, and that it is peopled by more species of living beings than this world, because incomparably more vast and varied in its possibilities.

—W.Y. Evans-Wentz, in *The Fairy-Faith in Celtic Countries* (1911)

Moyra Doorly describes herself as "someone who was actually invited to go and live in Elfland and turned down the offer." To every appearance she is serious and sane. She is, moreover, not what one might expect—a breathless New Ager—but a well-regarded British journalist whose writings on medical history, women's issues, architecture, and Catholicism have been published in such eminently respectable outlets as *The Guardian* and *New Statesman*.

The experience happened on the island of Arran, off the southwest coast of Scotland, apparently a few years ago. (In her 2004 account in *Fortean Times,* she never mentions a date, though the reader is left with the impression that the incidents happened in the relatively recent past.) She writes that she had become a practitioner of meditation, devoting a part of every day to a simple relaxation technique that led her to sit gazing out at the island's rich natural landscape without, however, focusing on anything in particular.

Her first encounter with extraordinary entities took place some months into her meditation program. On a pleasant summer evening, in a garden fed by a stream that flowed down from a tree-covered hillside, Doorly noticed a silvery light. Inside the light was a procession of dimly perceived, diminutive figures, led by a creature she characterizes as a faun—traditionally considered a nature spirit with a goat's hind legs and horns but otherwise humanlike features. "The faun was ... about three feet [one meter] tall and seemed pleased with himself," she stated. "I saw short legs strutting with pride and heard tiny hooves clip-clopping on the paving stones. He had horns, too, about six inch-

Fauns, fairies, and elves live in Fairyland, a world Moyra Doorly claimed to have entered in person (*Mary Evans Picture Library*).

es long, and a wrinkled face. He could have come straight out of a book of fairy tales or myths."

As the creature passed near her, Doorly grew frightened, dashed inside the house, and summoned her male companion Peter, who also saw it clearly. Like her, he had an imperfect impression of other small figures.

There were subsequent encounters, including ones with an elf who, though the size of a six-year-old boy, had the "face of one who had lived for a thousand years." This entity, clothed in an outfit of spotted green and brown, regularly showed up in the couple's house, sometimes with a facial expression bespeaking "sinister mirth."

The invitation to Elfland came one day when Doorly spotted a procession of tall, thin entities, clothed in "wildly striped" garments, with thick, dull, gray hair on their heads.[1] As they glided along the banks of the stream, accompanied by a band of merry, garrulous imps in bright green, she decided to follow them. Along the way the imps tried to talk her into putting on clothes like the striped entities', but for some reason she declined.

Soon she found herself inside a hall set inside carved rock walls. A long table with prepared food on it stretched in front of the assembled group. The "stripies," as Doorly thought of them, gazed at her as if anticipating something, presumably her sitting down and joining them in the meal. When she remained standing, she heard a voice say, "You are the first person to come this way for 200 years. Come and be with us."

"At that point I turned away and found myself at the stream," Doorly would write. "My impression was that there was nothing in the stripies to 'connect with,' that there was something 'absent' about them and an emptiness in their languorous, dreamy air. My impulse was not to linger in their presence or at their table. I might forget too much, too quickly." Subsequently, Peter told her that he, too, had been asked to join the fairy folk but had also refused the invitation.

There were other sightings. One of the last, in early autumn, was with an unfriendly group that resembled leafless trees. They made it clear that they did not desire her presence. "Why are you here?" they demanded. "This is no place for you."

Away with the Fairies

Stories like these are exceedingly difficult to believe, of course, because they constitute a radical challenge to our sense of the possible. Still, they are consistent with many centuries not only of legend and mythology but of claimed personal experiences of the elfin realm. Perceived experiences have played a significant role in driving the tradition. Though in this skeptical age few are so bold (or foolhardy) as Doorly as to go public with testimony to the effect, alleged meetings with fairy folk still occur in the experience of humans worldwide.

They are, in other words, "real"—at least they have the resonance of reality to those individuals—though they leave open the question of whether "experience" is always synonymous with "event." Certainly, the testimony is sometimes puzzling, as is testimony to a wide range of other kinds of extraordinary and improbable phenomena that fall into a kind of twilight zone of ambiguous epistemology. In a recent survey of Scottish fairy traditions, two prominent academic folklorists remark with no small hint of exasperation, "It should be possible to believe one's informants without believing their explanations."

The fairy folk are encountered in what has been called liminal—threshold—space, a nebulous, transitional realm between the known and the unknown, or between consensus reality and a magical otherworld, or perhaps between individual awareness and cultural imagination. In Elfland, neither sun nor moon can be seen, and time flows differently from ours. What seem like minutes can be years in the ordinary world. In this liminal state—fittingly, as the seventeenth-century chronicler of fairy and other supernatural lore, the Rev. Robert Kirk (1644–1692), noted, fairies are usually seen at twilight, the liminal space between day and night—ordinary landscape features are transformed into magical places occupied by supernatural entities. Hillsides, trees, lakes, rivers, caves, and mountains become entryways to Elfland, usually described as beautiful, strange, and treacherous, or at least fickle. It could vanish in an instant, with the human visitor returning to awareness in a perfectly familiar local landscape.

In the richly documented fairy traditions of Northern Europe (none more so than—to a misleading degree, folklorists sometimes complain—those in the Celtic regions[2]), rural people go to some lengths to avoid interactions with their supernatural co-inhabitants. In strict obedience to a popular taboo, they refer to the fairies via neutral phrases ("They," "The Others") or flattering euphemisms ("Good People," "Good Neighbors," "Fair Folk")—less out of respect than out of sheer fright. The fairy folk, some small or tiny, others human-sized or larger, dislike being spoken of or having their secrets revealed, and concealed or invisible, they may be listening, prepared to repay loose lips with nasty tricks. The fairies of tradition—who, by the way, do not sport wings, gossamer or other, and are nothing like Tinkerbell—are as unlike the twee characters of Victorian children's literature and Walt Disney films as bitter is unlike sweet.

Among the malicious tricks fairy folk could play on the careless or unsuspecting was abduction into Elfland. The tradition's most famous victim, a thirteenth-century

The fairies of tradition are rarely winged and charming little people as in animated Disney films; and some can even be threatening, according to a few witnesses (*BigStock*).

Scot named Thomas Rymour de Erceldoun, was an actual historical figure (1226–1297, according to folklorist MacEdward Leach; according to others, Rymour died no later than 1290), surviving legal documents attest. He was the subject of a famous ballad, "Thomas the Rhymer," which his countrymen were singing possibly even before his death. ("Rymour" or "Rhymer" refers to Thomas' reputation as a versifier.) We do not have his direct word on the matter, but we do have the ballad, as well as subsequent poems and popular legends, concerning what many people believed or imagined to have been the fate of Thomas Rhymer—perhaps more seduction than abduction. As is the custom with traditional folk songs, nearly every singer had his or her own variant, with sometimes additional or even discordant details. (For example, in some instances the fairy queen turns into a hag after a sexual romp with Thomas, to be restored to beauty only after she returns to Elfland.) Nonetheless, the narrative—at least in broad outline—is comparable in all of them. The summary below paraphrases the most commonly recited storyline.

In the ballad Rhymer is lying "on Huntlie bank" (on the Leader River near the town of Erceldoun) when he sees a striking, green-clad woman approach atop a white horse with ringing bells around its neck. Immediately perceiving that she is no ordinary human, he bows to her as the "Queen of Heaven"—the Blessed Virgin Mary—but she hastens to correct him; modestly, she informs him that she is "but the Queen of fair Elfland." She invites him to kiss her lips, then her body, and after matters take their inevitable course, she declares that he owes her seven years' service and obedience to her every command.

They mount her horse, which flies "swifter than the wind" until it reaches a sort of desert landscape. The queen directs him to lay his head on her knee, an act that affords him supernatural vision. He is able to see three roads. One, narrow and thorny, leads to heaven. The second, broad and inviting, is the "path of wickedness." The third occasioned the ballad's most-often quoted verse:

And see not ye that bonny road,
That winds about the fernie brae?
That is the road to fair Elfland,
Where you and I this night maun gae.

The queen warns Thomas not to speak, even when addressed directly, to anyone but her once they have entered Elfland, or he will never be allowed to return to his own country. For three days, in deep darkness with neither sun nor moon in view, though they can hear the roaring of the sea, the two cross rivers and finally approach a stream of blood, fed by "a' the blude that's shed on Earth." They wade knee-deep in that blood until, on their arrival in Elfland, they observe a green garden harboring fruit-laden trees. Famished, Thomas reaches to pluck an apple but discards it when the queen discloses that this is literal forbidden fruit, consumption of which will deliver him to hell. (In other versions, however, the queen gives him the fruit to eat because it will give him the gift of prophecy. When he demurs, she demands that he follow her order, and he does so.)

Thomas dwells in the queen's court for seven years. After seven years, knowing that it is time for the elfin people to pay their periodic tribute to hell, the queen fears that the handsome Thomas will catch the devil's eye and be carried off to the nether regions. She returns him to Earth—"middle Earth" (not to be confused with *The Lord of the Rings*' supernatural "Middle Earth") as our world was called in those days.

Beyond the ballad were poems and legends that attested to Thomas' poetic and prophetic gifts in his lifetime, the reason he was frequently called "True Thomas." One story relates the circumstances of his second and final disappearance. As he was feasting in his castle, a man burst in to report that an unearthly buck and doe had trailed him from the woods to the castle. Intrigued, Thomas rose to see the mysterious deer, followed them into the trees, and was seen no more, in the mortal realm anyway. He would appear in people's stories about their experiences in Elfland.

For instance, in the witch-trial testimony of the Scot Arno Man late in the sixteenth century—during that period the authorities were conflating fairies and demons, making those who claimed interactions with the former *de facto* collaborators with Satan—Man claimed that with the fairies were "sundry dead men," including King James IV (killed in battle in 1513) and Thomas Rhymer. Such testimony reinforces the traditional belief that one may encounter the dead in Elfland as well as the otherworldly fairy folk, but in Rhymer's case it was also generally thought that he had not died but simply changed residence from here (middle Earth/consensus reality) to there (supernatural otherworld). In some old tales Rhymer functions as a human advisor to the fairy folk. In others, he traffics in horses, as in a story, told as true, chronicled in Reginald Scot's *The Discovery of Witchcraft* (1584). A word of explanation first: according to one tradition, albeit with uncertain historical foundation, Thomas' surname was Learmonth:

> I could name a person who hath lately appeared thrice since his decease, at
> least some ghostly being or other that calls itself by the name of such a per-
> son, who was dead above a hundred years ago, and was, in his lifetime,
> accounted as a prophet or predicter, by the assistance of sublunary spirits; and

now, at his appearance, did also give strange predictions respecting famine and plenty, war and bloodshed, and the end of the world. By the information of the person that had communication with him, the last of his appearance was in the following manner. "I have been," said he, "to sell a horse at the next market town, but not attaining my price, as I returned home, by the way I met this man, who began to be familiar with me, asking what news, and how affairs moved through the country? I answered as I thought fit; withal, I told him of my horse, whom he began to cheapen [bid down], and proceeded with me so far, that the price was agreed upon. So he turned back with me, and told me that if I would go along with him, I should receive my money. On our way we went, I upon my horse, and he on another milk-white beast. After much travel, I asked him where he dwelt, and what his name was? He told me that his dwelling place was a mile off, at a place called Farran, of which place I had never heard, though I knew all the country round about. He also told me that he himself was that person of the family of Learmonths, so much spoken of as a prophet. At which I began to be somewhat fearful, perceiving we were on a road which I never had been on before, which increased my fear and amazement more. Well! On we went till he brought me under ground, I knew not how, into the presence of a beautiful woman, who paid the money without a word speaking. He conducted me out again through a large and long entry, where I saw above six hundred men in armour laid prostrate on the ground as if asleep. At last I found myself in the open field, by the help of the moonlight, in the very place where I first met him, and made a shift to get home by three in the morning. But the money I had received was just double of what I esteemed it when the woman paid me, of which, at this instant, I have several pieces to show, consisting of nine pennies, thirteen-pence-halfpennies, &c."

After quoting the above from Reginald Scot in *Letters on Demonology and Witchcraft* (1830), Sir Walter Scott, markedly more skeptical of the story than Scot apparently was, remarks dryly on the anonymous informant's casual treatment of the extraordinary, not to mention immensely valuable, coins from the fairy realm. Still, truth questions aside, he goes on to give voice to a thought that would have occurred to anyone who knew of the True Thomas legends: that the "beautiful lady who bore the purse must have been undoubtedly the Fairy Queen."[3]

Other legends hold that Thomas lies asleep in the Eildon Hills, or near Dumbarton, or in Inverness, like King Arthur waiting to return at the particular moment in history when his presence is most urgently needed.

Adventures in the Otherworld

Much less well known, but in some ways reminiscent of True Thomas' adventure, is a story related in *The Journey through Wales*, published in 1188. The author, Ger-

There are many tales of the Fairy Queen, who varies in appearance from tiny and pixielike (as in this 1875 illustration from *In Fairyland* by Richard Doyle) to tall and stately (*Mary Evans Picture Library*).

ald of Wales (also known as Giraldus Cambrensis and Gerallt y Cymro), Archdeacon of Brecon, accompanied Archbishop Baldwyn of Canterbury and 3,000 soldiers on an expedition to encourage Welsh men to join the latest Crusade to "free" Jerusalem. Gerald took the opportunity to learn as much as he could about the culture and character of the Welsh. Still in print, the resulting book is an enduring and valuable chronicle of what medieval Wales was like.

Among the persons with whom Gerald spoke was a priest named Elidyr (also rendered as Elidor and Elidurus). Elidyr told him of a strange experience he had in his youth, when he was 12 years old and ran away from home. Though in some details comparable to it, Elidyr's predates Thomas' alleged experience by a century. Interestingly, however, the priest at no point specifically identified the little men as fairies or by any equivalent supernatural name, though who they are seems clear enough.

As Elidyr told it, after his escape he hid in the hollow bank of a river for two days. Then two tiny men—"no bigger than pygmies"—approached him and invited them to join them in their land, where "all is playtime and pleasure." He followed them to their realm. The journey is virtually identical to Thomas':

> They led him first through a dark underground tunnel and then into a most attractive country, where there were lovely rivers and meadows, and delightful woodlands and plains. It was rather dark, because the sun did not

shine there. The days were all overcast, as if by clouds, for there was no moon or stars.

Once he was received at the court, he found that a king ruled the land, consisting of beautiful, fair-featured little people who wore their hair long and rode horses the size of greyhounds. They did not consume meat or fish, filling their diets with assorted flavored milk dishes. "They never gave their word, for they hated lies more than anything they could think of," Gerald wrote, paraphrasing Elidyr's account. "Whenever they came back from the upper world, they would speak contemptuously of our own ambitions, infidelities, and inconsistencies."[4] Their language, which Elidyr learned to speak fluently, bore a considerable resemblance to Greek. Gold abounded in this land, so common that it was used in all kinds of manufactured products, including sports equipment.

Gold abounded in this land, so common that it was used in all kinds of manufactured products, including sports equipment.

Elidyr visited his mother periodically. At first the "pygmies" accompanied him, and later he was allowed to go alone. Only his mother knew where he was spending most of his time. His stories about the ubiquity of gold particularly drew her attention—or kindled her avarice—and she pleaded with him to bring a golden present to her. To his everlasting regret, Elidyr set about to fulfill her request. The opportunity arrived soon afterwards, when he and the king's son were playing with a golden ball. Elidyr grabbed it and ran. His playmate and another "pygmy" set off in hot pursuit. As he was entering his parents' house, the young thief stumbled, and the ball slipped from his hands. His pursuers snatched it up and left, "spitting at and deriding the boy," according to Gerald's account. Later, when a deeply ashamed Elidyr tried to find his way back to their realm, he could not locate the tunnel that led to it even along a route that had become familiar to him. He searched for nearly another year with no more luck.

Gerald recorded, "Whenever David the Second, bishop of St. David's, talked to him in his advanced state of life concerning this event, he could never relate the particulars without shedding tears."

Another strange story of otherworldly visitation is recorded in an eighteenth-century parish book kept by a Reverend Vigelius of Ramsburg, Sweden, in an entry dated September 29, 1759. The incident began on September 16, when his father sent Jacob Jacobsson, 22, on an errand across a lake to the nearby village of Loünmora to visit a crofter named Anders Nilsson. On his return, as he was pulling his boat up to the shore, young Jacob saw something that had not been there when he departed: a broad, large road stretching in front of him. Curious, he followed it until he came to a settlement consisting of grand mansions.

He entered a red-colored building. "Soon," Vigelius recorded, "he found himself seated on a bench by the door in a big chamber. He saw a chubby little man, with a red cap on his head, sitting by the end of the table, and he saw crowds of little people, running back and forth. They were all in every like way like ordinary men, but of short stature."

In their midst was a fine-looking, taller woman—the Fairy Queen?—who urged him to eat and drink. He declined the offer. When other little people inquired if he would like to stay with them, he responded with a spoken prayer: "God, help me back home to my father and mother!" The man with the red cap ordered his compatriots to throw him out because of his rudeness.

In an instant he was back at the shore, and all the scenery was restored to its normal appearance. His parents greeted his appearance with joy. They told him they and their neighbors had been searching for him the past four days, a revelation he greeted with bafflement; he felt as if he had been gone only a few minutes. He had no appetite. The next day he felt uneasy but otherwise all right.

Vigelius wrote, "Jacob made this statement to me in the presence of his parents on St. Michael's Day 1759. This boy has quite a simple, pious, meek and gentle character. He is praised by everyone. All his life he has been known to take pleasure in reading and contemplating God's words whenever he has some spare time."

Around the turn of the last century, an Irishwoman told Lady Gregory that she had visited Elfland on a number of occasions. She described the entrance to the otherworld thus: "In the wood beyond the tree at Raheen I used often to see like a door open at night, and the light shining through it, just as it might shine through the house door, with the candle and the fire inside, if it would be left open."

✳

Fairy World

Robert Kirk wrote that the fairy folk are "of a middle nature between man and angel." They live in subterranean spaces, entering them through cracks and crevices. In traditional belief a supernatural landscape overlies the natural one; thus, visible hills conceal the (usually) invisible race that dwells inside, in what in modern times we would call another dimension or parallel world. One who passes, voluntarily or involuntarily, into the fairy realm has crossed the boundary that separates this world from the otherworld.

Inside that realm, according to Kirk's informants, one will enter homes "large and fair … having for light continual lamps and fires, often seen without fuel to sustain them." Others, as we have seen, have spoken of great royal courts. Fairy culture mirrors its human counterpart in many ways. There are armies, marriages, musicians. Obsessed with dancing, fairies are often observed carrying on in circles to the accompaniment of fiddlers, harpers, and pipers. In fact, or at least in allegation, a number of folk airs and tunes—for example, the often-performed "The Fairies' Hornpipe"—in the British Isles are said to be of fairy origin. And human beings brought into the dancing circle may vanish into Elfland for a long time or maybe forever. (Fairies may also steal babies; in the place of a kidnapped infant, they leave one of their own, known as a changeling, identi-

An 1886 illustration from *The Fairies* by William Allingham shows fairies engaged in their favorite pasttime (*Mary Evans Picture Library*).

fiable as sickly, sour-natured, and in other ways an unfair trade.) Dead persons, or at least some of them, may live on in Elfland. Fairy animals, notably horses, cattle, and dogs, are equivalent to our own, only sized to fit. To some degree (though not in all particulars), Elfland evolves along with the human culture with which it coexists. For example, whereas in pre-automotive times fairy folk rode horses, in the twentieth century there are at least two reports—one from around 1940, the other (by a group of English school-children) in 1979—of elflike figures driving tiny cars.

Fairy folk may be short in stature, or they may be human-sized, or—albeit rarely—they may be taller. They may appear in numbers ("trooping fairies"), or they may appear as solitary wayfarers. The latter were sometimes thought to be of a menac-ing temperament.

Though speculations about the origins of fairy beliefs are numerous (and often conflicting), the answers remain elusive. To some extent, as already noted, they were experientially based—though not in a way that would persuade us, as Kirk was per-suaded, that the culture and geography of Elfland are real, if peculiar, places in the social and physical landscape. If "real" does not apply, however, "peculiar" surely does, when one considers that, even as the fairy faith has vanished from most (though not quite all) of the earth[5], encounters with fairy folk—even when not recognized as such— continue in the experience of human beings.

Jim Butler, a retired University of Alberta conservation biologist and an ordained Buddhist monk, has founded the ELFEN Project, in the process identifying himself as probably the Western world's only scientist to investigate—sympathetically—elfin experiences in modern times. The acronym stands for Elemental Life Form Encounters in Nature.

The tribes repeatedly expressed concern about the potential impact such devastation would have on sacred areas populated by supernatural beings....

As a consultant to aboriginal groups in Western Canada and the Arctic Circle, Butler offered advice to marginalized non-white peoples who sought to protect their lands from the ravages of gas, oil, and timber interests. The tribes repeatedly expressed concern about the potential impact such devastation would have on sacred areas populated by supernatural beings usually described as little people.[6] These little people—the Cree call them Apiscinisak—have an existence outside traditional lore, according to the Indians; they can be encountered. Such testimony intrigued Butler sufficiently that he commenced a formal investigation which took him to other traditional societies around the world in search of reports from seemingly credible experiencers of such incredible entities. He also collected reports from middle-class Europeans and North Americans not raised in the fairy faith but whose accounts resemble those of persons who were.

Butler borrows the term "liminal personae" to characterize these "'real', not imaginary, beings and societies." He adds: "These encounters seem to occur in a multiple presence environment, a parallel reality on the fringes of human perception." His ongoing survey work leads him to conclude, "Forty-six percent of encounters are in natural landscapes, and a surprising 27% are inside houses and an additional 23% in the vicinity of houses. In three different reports they have been present at the bedside when a person awakened."

One of his informants allegedly had an encounter in a forest in southern British Columbia, apparently around 1970. The young man and a female companion happened to be resting silently on a log in a clearing when suddenly they observed, coming from their right, a small, thin, muscular man, barely more than three feet (about one meter) high, with dark, leathery skin. His limbs looked "more like tree roots," the male witness told Butler many years later. As the strange entity stood in front of them, so close that they could have touched him if they dared, the couple felt an intense energy and powerful emotion emanating from him. He also gave off a sense of menace, enhanced when the figure hit the ground with his right foot, bent over, and waved a fist at them. Then it was gone, leaving as it had come, with confoundingly, unnatural speed. Bewilderingly, the entity had appeared both naked and clothed at once, and solid and insubstantial. Though the entire experience had lasted only about five seconds, the informant insisted that he could still recall, decades later, every detail of the being's face.

A Welshman told a similar story to folklorist Robin Gwynddaf. No date is attached to the encounter (such things are nearly always treated as nebulous anecdotes as opposed to "reports" or "sightings"), but apparently it took place in the early half of the twentieth century, when the informant was an eight- or nine-year-old boy. He had taken his bicycle and a cart to a wooded area to collect firewood. While engaged in his task, he heard something moving through the leaves. "Then I saw a little old fellow coming from the direction of some green bushes," he recalled. "Well, it was a little less than a yard tall perhaps.... The only other thing I remember clearly is that from his waist down it was green and some reddish color about its face. That's it. Green and red and a tiny little man. He didn't say anything.... I can't remember him leaving.... I remember him coming.... I know that it was [real], there's no doubt about it. It wasn't just some twig moving, or my imagination or anything of the sort. It was there, sure enough, that little old fellow."

Some strange stories occur—or at least are reported—outside the context of living traditions. If they had been noted, say, in the west of Ireland, they would have been subjected to an unambiguously culture-specific interpretation (as opposed, as with the first one below, to a more or less tongue-in-cheek one) and incorporated into an existing body of supernatural lore. Two examples allegedly took place in the state of Wisconsin not quite a quarter-century apart.

The first of these was printed in the *Milwaukee Sentinel* for December 20, 1896, datelined Deerfield, related as a "ghost story told by Widow Olson." Mrs. Olson and her 14-year-old son lived on the south shore of Stump Lake. One day a boy they did not know showed up at their door to inquire how he could get to the residence of a certain farmer whose house was on the opposite shore. Because the trip involved a three-mile walk, the mother directed her son to take the stranger by boat, a much shorter, less time-consuming trip. The Olson boy had his passenger sit at the stern (rear), while he picked up the oars and began rowing across the water. Oddly and rudely, the stranger sat with his back to his host. Worse, he did not respond to Olson's efforts to engage him in small talk. Then, as the newspaper account had it:

> His strange behavior made Olson observe him more closely and the more closely and the more he looked at him the more did he appear unlike a human. His attention was first attracted by the stranger's ears, which were abnormally large, reaching almost to the top of his head, where they came to nearly a point or sharp angle and were covered with a fine downy hair. His head was small and angular, something like that of a dog and covered with short, black curly hair that hugged the skin tightly. The hands were small, shriveled and covered with hair similar to that on his ears. Young Olson was now becoming almost frightened out of his wits at being alone in the boat with such an unearthly looking being and rowed with all his might. On

arriving at the opposite landing he got out of the boat hastily to let out his uncongenial passenger. The stranger arose to leave the boat, but instead of facing about to walk out, he backed and carefully kept his face from view.

The rattled young Olson rowed back home as fast as his arm and oar would take him. The moment he was inside the house, he began to tell his mother about his bizarre adventure. She looked over to him to see if he was serious, and as she did so, her glance fell over into his shoulder and out the window behind him. There, running up a hill close to the house, was the strange boy last seen on the other side of the lake, though he could not possibly have made the return trip that anywhere nearly that quickly. The stranger was chasing the Olsons' sheep.

> Mother and son both made after him, but on arriving at the crest of the hill nobody was to be seen while the sheep stood down the slope a little way huddled together as if recently chased by a wolf or dog. There was nothing within eighty rods that the stranger could have hid behind. Why they did not notice his strange appearance before starting in the boat, how he got back so quickly and where he disappeared to was more than the frightened widow and son could have been able to account for and they firmly believe there are still a few left of the old-time elf family.

In 1978 the author of this book interviewed Helen M. Anderson, the widow of Harry Anderson, in her home north of Fort Atkinson, Wisconsin. Mrs. Anderson vividly recalled a story her husband had told her. It happened to him, he claimed, late one night in 1919 when he was 13 years old. As he was riding east of Barron, with two friends and their father, the car ran out of oil and stalled. Awhile later a farmer who had been out fishing and was now walking home happened upon the party. On being informed of the problem, he offered to supply some oil if one of the group went with him to his farm, two miles away. Young Anderson accompanied him, secured the oil, and headed out alone to return to his friends.

With the full moon illuminating the surrounding landscape, Anderson noticed something unexpected: a group of figures approaching him on the road. That was unusual enough at this hour of night in a rural area, but the closer they got, the more odd the whole experience seemed. The figures—20 in all—proved to be little men, all bald, all dressed identically in leather knee-pants held up by suspenders over white-skinned bare shoulders; they were not wearing shirts. They were "mumbling" but apparently not communicating with each other. They paid no attention to Anderson, who was by now terrified. They walked past him, and he fled without looking back.

Anderson's friends laughed at him when he told them what he had seen, but in later years he confided the story to his wife, Helen. In an interview his widow insisted, "My husband was not an imaginative person at all. He had no imagination whatsoever. This absolutely happened, as far as he was concerned. I mean there was no question about it."

The same could be said of an April 1950 report from Canby, Oregon, where a woman named Ellen Jonerson, working on her lawn, happened to glance over to her

GOBLIN UNIVERSE

"Goblin Universe" is a term of nebulous origins—sometimes attributed to biologist and cryptozoologist Roy P. Mackal—to denote, often though not always disparagingly, the otherworldly realm of anomalous and paranormal phenomena. The term is not meant to be literal or precise but metaphorical. It can mean that since the likes of goblins don't exist, the specific extraordinary entity alleged in someone's sighting report can be rejected without further consideration or conversation. Alternatively, it can suggest that since the claimed experience is inexplicable and thus surpasses language's capacity to describe, "goblin" as quasi-serious/quasi-humorous effort to plug the linguistic hole is as good as any other word.

F.W. Holiday (1921–1979) was an investigator of, and witness to, the fabled monsters of Loch Ness. For a time—though his friend Colin Wilson said he changed his mind before his death—he was persuaded that the creatures are not unknown animals in the zoological sense; rather, they are demonic dragons that threaten the well-being of humankind. At one point he arranged for and participated in an exorcism of the loch. (The exorcism itself was conducted by an eccentric Anglican clergyman, the Rev. Donald Omand, who already believed the creatures to be evil based on a previous experience with a water monster in a Norwegian fjord.) During this period he was convinced that he had seen a dark-suited supernatural figure on the lochside, presaging a subsequent heart attack.

Like other observers, Holiday saw the Goblin Universe as eternally tricksterish, offering enough to suggest its existence while denying investigators and experiencers anything like conclusive proof that it is there. "The Goblin Universe is a hall of distorting mirrors," he wrote, in which nothing appears in its actual form but as things shaped, at least on their surfaces, out of our dreams.

Unfortunately, unable to resist the temptation to move beyond these sorts of broad generalities, Holiday moved into intellectual incoherence when he wrote in specifics. Writing in England's *Flying Saucer Review* (March/April 1972), for

neighbors' yard. There, to her considerable surprise, she spotted a tiny male figure, perhaps a foot tall, with his back to her. The figure was of stocky build, clad in overalls and a plain shirt, with a skullcap on his head. Moments later, when he turned around, Jonerson saw that his face looked heavily tanned. She dashed inside to call a friend, then ran out to see the figure walking away with a waddling motion toward a parked car. He vanished underneath it. The story is sometimes cited in the UFO literature.

example, he attempted to link a well-known, still-unexplained UFO encounter from a few years earlier and fossilized prints found in Texas. The former occurred on April 24, 1964, near Socorro, New Mexico, when a police officer reported the landing of an unknown aircraft. Nearby, he briefly glimpsed two small figures. In the ensuing investigation law-enforcement and Air Force representatives found footprints apparently left by the ostensible crew members.

From this well-publicized aspect of a famous UFO case, Holiday declared that the occupants had not stepped out of a craft but out of a "tempic field different to [sic] the one inhabited by ourselves." The tracks were like ones discovered near Glen Rose, Texas—fossilized human prints found alongside those of dinosaurs—evidence, in Holiday's reading, that supernatural beings shoot freely through time. In prosaic reality, the allegedly human prints—once championed by creationists as evidence that people and dinosaurs coexisted—are also from dinosaurs; these prints get their distinctive appearance from the fact that

sediment filled in the toe marks before hardening into rock. Besides that, the prints are significantly larger than those at Socorro. Nonetheless, though his argument was nonsensical from any perspective from which one cared to observe it, he went on to express sneering contempt for anyone who dared raise so much as an eyebrow:

> Personally, I wouldn't trust an establishment scientist further than I could throw him as regard interpreting the "holy footprint" business objectively. Too much is at stake including all the accepted machinery of causation. You would hardly expect high priests of the scientific *status quo* to take part in the slitting of their own throats.

Further Reading

Holiday, F.W. *The Dragon and the Disc: An Investigation into the Totally Fantastic.* New York: W.W. Norton and Company, 1973.

———. *The Goblin Universe.* St. Paul, MN: Llewellyn Publications, 1986.

From Folklore to Flying Saucers

In the latter twentieth century, claims like these were interpreted as encounters with occupants of UFOs, even though the claimants fail to mention the presence of mysterious flying objects. In 1969, however, the influential French-American ufologist Jacques Vallee, author of *Passport to Magonia: From Folklore to Flying Saucers,* insisted that

Little folk are popular figures in fairy tales, such as the French story of Abeille, but the late Harry Anderson told his wife how he met little men back in 1919 (*Mary Evans Picture Library*).

all UFO phenomena are aspects of a latter-day fairy lore. In his analysis the "modern global belief in flying saucers and their occupants is identical to an earlier belief in the fairy-faith." By this Vallee did not mean to dismiss UFO sightings as silly fairytales but to propose that a single, undefined paranormal source accounts for both.

It is true that on infrequent occasions fairy-encounter claims do call close encounters of the third kind—at least in a very broad sense—to mind. The British folklorist Jeremiah Sullivan collected a story from Cumberland, apparently set in the late eighteenth or early nineteenth century, involving "an inhabitant of Martindale, Jack Wilson by name," a real individual. Crossing Sandwick Rigg one night, he allegedly came upon a large group of fairies engaged in vigorous, if otherwise undescribed, activity. According to Sullivan:

> He drew near unobserved, and presently descried a stee [ladder] reaching from amongst them up into a cloud. But no sooner was the presence of mortal discovered than all made a busy retreat up the stee.

> Jack rushed forward, doubtless firmly determined to follow them into fairyland, but arrived too late. They had effected their retreat, and quickly drawing up the stee, they shut the cloud, and disappeared. And, in the concluding words of Jack's story, which afterwards became proverbial in that neighborhood, "yance gane, ae gane, and niver saw mair o' them." The grandson of the man who thus strangely witnessed the last apparition of the fairies,

himself an old man, was appealed to not long ago on the truth of this tradition. Having listened to the account of it already printed, he declared "it was a' true, however, for he heard his grandfather tell it many a time."

Walter Yeeling Evans-Wentz printed the account of an Oxford classmate, a native Irishman, who with a companion reported this encounter:

> Some few weeks before Christmas, 1910, at midnight on a very dark night, I and another young man (who like myself was then about twenty-three years of age) were on horseback on our way home from Limerick. When near Listowel, we noticed a light about half a mile ahead. At first it seemed to be no more than a light in some house; but as we came nearer to it and it was passing out of our direct line of vision we saw that it was moving up and down, to and fro, diminishing to a spark, then expanding into a yellow luminous flame. Before we came to Listowel we noticed two lights, about one hundred yards [91 meters] to our right, resembling the light seen first. Suddenly each of these lights expanded into the same sort of yellow luminous flame, about six feet [two meters] high by four feet [1.2 meters] broad. In the midst of each flame we saw a radiant being having human form. Presently the lights moved toward one another and made contact, whereupon the two beings in them were seen to be walking side by side. The beings' bodies were formed of a pure dazzling radiance, white like the radiance of the sun, and much brighter than the yellow light or aura surrounding them. So dazzling was the radiance, like a halo, round their heads that we could not distinguish the countenances of the beings; we could only distinguish the general shape of their bodies; though their heads were very clearly outlined because this halo-like substance, which was the brightest light about them, seemed to radiate from or rest upon the head of each being. As we traveled on, a house intervened between us and the lights, we saw no more of them.

Another fairy encounter, this one encompassing the missing time associated with modern alien-abduction reports, with UFO-like elements appears in an 1896 book by Elias Owen, *Welsh Folk-Lore: A Collection of the Folk-Tales and Legends of North Wales.* Though undated as these stories nearly always are, it is presumably from the early to mid-nineteenth century. Its specificity as to names, places, and geography affords it more surface plausibility than a vague once-upon-a-time folktale:

> The Rev. R. Jones' mother, when a young unmarried woman, started one evening from a house called Tyddyn Heilyn, Penrhyndeudcraeth, to her home, Penrhyn isaf, accompanied by their servant man, David Williams, called on account of his great strength and stature, Dafydd Fawr, Big David. David was carrying home on his back a flitch of bacon. The night was dark, but calm. Williams walked somewhat in the rear of his young mistress, and she, thinking he was following, went straight home. But three hours passed before David appeared with the pork on his back.

Some folklorists and ufologists have voiced the view that the humanoids described in close-encounter reports amount to fairies in appropriately modern guise (*Mary Evans Picture Library*).

He was interrogated as to the cause of his delay, and in answer said he had only been about three minutes after his young mistress. He was told that she had arrived three hours before him, but this David would not believe. At length, however, he was convinced that he was wrong in his time, and then he proceeded to account for his lagging behind as follows:

He observed, he said, a brilliant meteor passing through the air, which was followed by a ring or hoop of fire, and within this hoop stood a man and woman of small size, handsomely dressed. With one arm they embraced each other, and with the other they took hold of the hoop, and their feet rested on the concave surface of the ring. When the hoop reached the earth these two beings jumped out of it, and immediately proceeded to make a circle on the ground. As soon as this was done, a large number of men and women instantly appeared, and to the sweetest music that ear ever heard commenced dancing round and round the circle. The sight was so entrancing that the man stayed, as he thought, a few minutes to witness the scene. The ground all around was lit by a kind of subdued light, and he observed every movement of these beings. By and by the meteor which had at first attracted his attention appeared again, and then the fiery hoop came to view, and when it reached the spot where the dancing was, the lady and gentleman who had arrived in it jumped into the hoop, and disappeared in the same manner in which they had reached the place. Immediately after their departure the Fairies vanished from sight, and the man found himself alone and in darkness, and then he proceeded homewards. In this way he accounted for his delay on the way.

Even with (relatively infrequent) stories like these, Vallee's reading is surely overstated. Fairy lore and UFO lore overlap at points but are hardly "identical." It is more certainly true, however, that UFOs, or at least some experiences of them, occupy the same imaginative/experiential space that fairies once occupied. Perhaps they raise the same kinds of questions about anomalous perception and states of consciousness. In our time visitors, in any case, to an otherworldly realm are more likely to describe an extraterrestrial environment. Claimed trips to Elfland are hard to come by in our time, perhaps making understandable the complaint from one of Moyra Doorly's elfin contacts, that no one had come their way for two centuries.

Further Reading:

Bord, Janet. *Fairies: Real Encounters with Little People.* New York: Carroll & Graf Publishers, 1997.

Briggs, Katharine. *An Encyclopedia of Fairies: Hobgoblins, Brownies, Bogies, and Other Supernatural Creatures.* New York: Pantheon Books, 1976.

Child, Francis James, ed. Mark F. Heiman and Laura Saxton Heiman, eds. *The English and Scottish Popular Ballads.* Volume I. Northfield, MN: Loomis House Press, 2001. Original edition published in 1877.

Doorly, Moyra. "Invitation to Elfland." *Fortean Times* 179 (2004): 38–42.

Evans, Alex [Jerome Clark]. "Encounters with Little Men." *Fate* 31, 11 (November 1978): 83–86.

Evans-Wentz, Walter Yeeling. *The Fairy-Faith in Celtic Countries.* New York: University Books, 1966. Reprint of the 1911 edition.

Henderson, Lizanne, and Edward J. Cowan. *Scottish Fairy Belief.* East Linton, Scotland: Tuckwell Press, 2001.

J.H.C. "Chaucer's 'Canterbury Tales.'" *Notes and Queries* Vol. 2, 4th S. (35), August 29, 1868: 197.

Kirk, Robert. Stewart F. Sanderson, ed. *The Secret Common-Wealth & A Short Treatise of Charms and Spels.* Totowa, NJ: Rowman & Littlefield, 1976. Original edition published in 1691.

Lenihan, Eddie, and Carolyn Eve Green. *Meeting the Other Crowd: The Fairy Stories of Hidden Ireland.* New York: J.P. Tarcher, 2003.

Picasso, Fabio. "Infrequent Types of South American Humanoids. Part III: Gnomes and Little Green Men." *Strange Magazine* 19–21 (1993), 60.

Scott, Sir Walter. *Letters on Demonology and Witchcraft.* New York: Ace Books, 1970. Reprint of the 1830 edition.

Sullivan, Jeremiah. *Cumberland and Westmoreland, Ancient and Modern, the People, Dialect, Superstitions, and Customs.* London: Whittaker & Company, 1857.

Svahn, Clas. "Missing Time." Posting on Magonia Exchange e-list (June 11, 2007).

Vallee, Jacques. *Passport to Magonia: From Folklore to Flying Saucers.* Chicago: Regnery Company, 1969.

GHOST RIDERS IN THE SKY: SPECTRAL ARMIES ON THE MARCH

According to sworn statements made two weeks later, something very difficult to believe or comprehend unfolded before stunned onlookers in Oxford township, Sussex County, New Jersey, early on the evening of August 21, 1818.

When she heard her children shouting animatedly from outside, where they were playing, Wille Harman stepped out the door to ask what the outcry was about. The children pointed to neighbor Andrew Raub's field. There, according to her statement before Justice of the Peace William Ribble, she "saw a large number of men in white apparel, formed in three lines, moving across the field not far from a burying ground adjoining said field."

The figures seemed "rather to fly than to walk," judging by the motions of their "arms or wings.... After viewing them for some time ... [she observed as] five others appeared amongst them of a larger size, who seemed to be more actively engaged than the rest, [who were] moving about the field in great confusion for a considerable time, as if they were climbing over each other." The five newcomers were also clad in white, but their clothing shone more brilliantly. All of them—apparently over a few minutes' time—rose into the sky. Soon, Mrs. Harman observed a "second company in the air, which appeared to move in the same direction as the first." They were wearing white clothes like the others, but these were "not so white as the first," and they were fewer in number than the original group. They remained in sight for half an hour.

Her husband related that he had been working in the house that evening when his wife called to him to look at something in Raub's field. Once out the door, he saw "men dressed in white, who appeared to be in great confusion, hurrying over the ground." A short time later, they "ascended into the air, and disappeared by degrees." Then a group of approximately 200 of the figures appeared in the sky, seemingly on the trail of the first group. The entire episode occurred over half an hour, he estimated.

The appearance of spectral beings was once assigned religious and even political meaning (*iStock*).

The third witness to speak to another legal authority, in this instance Justice of the Peace John Summers, was Maj. Samuel Raub, evidently a relative of Andrew Raub. As the major was returning from the latter's mill, he heard David Harman call his name. Directed to turn his gaze to the field, Raub scanned the area rather casually without seeing anything out of the ordinary at first. Harman then pointed to an area of the sky 50 feet (15.25 meters) or so above the ground, where Raub immediately discerned "nearly one hundred men in white apparel, floating along in the air, in a northerly direction." Over the next 10 to 15 minutes "they by degrees disappeared."

As stories of the strange occurrence circulated through the neighborhood, John Clark, who knew the witnesses, interviewed them and then took them to legal authorities to whom they could make sworn statements (the illiterate Harmans signed with Xs). Though he refused to speculate about what they had seen, Clark said he believed them because they were "persons of integrity."

Beyond the Merely Extraordinary

In the year 1014, according to medieval historian Rudolphus Glaber (985–1047), one quiet Sunday evening in the French village of Tonnerre, a priest named Frotterius, awaiting dinner, happened to look out his window, where he saw

> an enormous multitude of riders drawn up as though in a battle-line, moving steadily from north to west. After he had watched them closely for some time, he became alarmed and called out to a member of his household to come and see them, but as soon as he had called out, the figures had dissolved and dis-

appeared. He was so shaken by the sight that he was hardly able to keep from tears. Later that same year he fell ill and died, ending his life in the same godly manner that he had lived. He was taken away by the portent which he saw, and this has been attested by witnesses.[1]

Tales of spectral armies—"counterparts of our flying saucers," according to English historian Keith Thomas[2]—are to be found in many ancient and medieval chronicles, where they are usually called "prodigies" and variously interpreted as divine, demonic, or delusional. While actual spectators were mostly shocked, frightened, or befuddled, outsiders drew grand inferences from their occurrence, as often political (indicating, for example, God's favor for their side in a power dispute) as religious. Others saw them as God's omens or Satan's tricks.

Sightings of ghost ships have been part of nautical legend for centuries (*Mary Evans Picture Library*).

That people believed they had seen these things is beyond dispute. In other words, these were not, as a general rule, mere literary concoctions passing as authentic accounts. Such sightings—which, if taken literally, are hard to square with any conceivable notion of the possible—continued well past the Middle Ages and into at least the nineteenth century. If they had not, there would be little reason not to view them with suspicion. After all, the medieval world was full of fantastic visionary phenomena hard for us even to imagine, and without analogue in our post-Enlightenment times. Moreover, people of that era were perfectly able to observe and interpret phenomena they knew to be natural as supernatural, too. For example, a thirteenth-century English chronicle records this sighting:

About midnight of the day of our Lord's circumcision, the moon being eight days old, and the firmament studded with stars, and the air completely calm, there appeared in the sky, wonderful to relate, the form of a large ship, well-shaped, and of remarkable design and color. This apparition was seen by some monks at St. Alban's, staying at St. Amphibalus to celebrate the festival, who were looking out to see by the stars if it was the hour for chanting matins, and they at once called together all their friends and followers who were in the house to see the wonderful apparition. The vessel appeared for a long time, as if it were painted, and really built with planks; but at length it began by degrees to dissolve and disappear, wherefore it was believed to have been a cloud, but a wonderful and extraordinary one.[3]

An often-cited early March 1706 flood of sky-army reports is plausibly explained as an observation of aurora borealis (northern lights), not often seen in England, enflamed by widespread anger at the execution of the popular Jacobite leader James Radcliffe, Earl of Derwentwater, the previous February 24.[4]

The older reports recount two types of spectral armies: those with consensus-reality counterparts (in other words, ghosts in the more or less conventional sense) and those without (beings representing no known nation, army, or social order). In some instances the details are too sparse for us to discern which is being described. Because of their potential for political exploitation, the former seem more dubious, and often less documented, than the latter. Nonetheless, this one is—at least superficially— more intriguing than most. It is alleged in a contemporary account to have taken place at the English Civil War battlefield of Edgehill in Warwickshire:

On the Saturday before Christmas Day, 1642, about midnight between twelve and one o'clock at Kineton there was heard afar off the sound of drums beating, and of soldiers groaning. Then on a sudden there appeared in the air the ghostly soldiers that made those clamours and immediately with ensigns displayed, the beating of drums, muskets going off, cannons discharging, and horses neighing, the signal for this game of death was struck up, one army, which gave the first charge, having the King's colours, and the other the Parliament's, in the head or front of their battles, and thus pell-mell to it they went. The King's forces seemed at first to have the best of the battle, but afterwards to be put into apparent rout; and thus till two or three in the morning, in equal scale continued this dreadful fight—the clattering of arms, the crying of soldiers, and the noise of cannons so terrifying the poor beholders that they could not believe they were mortal, or give credit to their eyes and ears. After some three hours' fight, the army which carried the King's colours appeared to fly; the other remaining as it were master of the field, and staying a good space, triumphing and expressing all the signs of conquest, and then, with all their drums, trumpets, ordnance and soldiers, vanishing. The poor beholders who had stayed so long against their wills, made with all haste to Kineton and knocked up Master Wood, a Justice of the Peace, who called up his neighbor, Mr. Marshall the minister, to whom they gave an account of the whole battle, and averred it upon their oath to be true. At which, being much amazed, they would have conjectured the men to be mad or drunk had they not known some of them to have been of approved integrity; and so suspending their judgments till the next night, which being Sunday and Christmas night, about the same hour, with the same men, and with all the substantial inhabitants they drew thither. About half an hour after their arrival there appeared in the heavens the same two adverse armies, in the same tumultuous warlike manner, who fought with as much spite and spleen as before, and then departed. Much terrified with these horrible visions, the gentlemen and all the spectators withdrew themselves from those prodigious enemies. They appeared not the next night, nor all that week; but on the following Saturday night they were seen again with far greater tumult—fighting for four hours and then vanishing. On Sunday night they appeared again, and performed the same actions of hostility and bloodshed, insomuch that Mr. Wood and others forsook their habitations thereabout, and betook themselves to more secure dwellings; but Mr. Marshall, the minister, stayed. The next Saturday and Sunday the same tumults and actions were seen again. The rumours whereof coming to his Majesty at Oxford, he immediately dispatched thither Colonel Lewiskirke, Captain Dudley, Capt. Wainman, and three other gentlemen of credit, to take full view and notice of ye same business, who, first hearing the true attestation of Mr. Marshall and others, stayed there till the Saturday night following, when they themselves saw the fore-mentioned prodigies, and on Sunday night knew distinctly divers of the apparitions by their faces, as that of Sir Edward Varney and others that were slain in this delusive fight, of which upon oath they made testimony to his Majesty. What this doth portend God only knoweth, and time perhaps will discover; but doubtless it is a sign of His wrath against this land for these civil wars, and may He in his good time send peace between his Majesty and the Parliament.[5]

Phantom armies aren't necessarily skybound. An apparently unrecognized phantom army marched, it is said, in June and July 1686 near Lanark, Scotland, along the banks of the Clyde. "Numerous spectators" witnessed the spectacle. Seeing nothing, one man ridiculed the others and denounced them as "damned witches and warlocks with the second sight." Suddenly, however, he sighted them, too. Also in Scotland, in Glenary, Inverness, in 1760, a man identified as a "respectable farmer" and his son witnessed the passage of at least 16 pairs of columns of red-clad soldiers, accompanied by numerous women and children carrying cooking utensils. One mounted officer, riding a gray horse, led them. Father and son saw him so clearly that later they swore they would have recognized him anywhere. "In the midst of them," Catherine Crowe wrote, "was an animal—a deer or a horse, they could not distinguish which—that they were driving furiously forward with their bayonets." Fearing that they would be hurt or impressed into service, the two had just started to flee when the entire army vanished before their eyes.

The most famous—and deservedly famous—of phantom-army cases is a story, or several related stories, from Cumberland (since 1974, incorporated into the county of Cumbria) in northwestern England. The figures were seen at various times on a mountain known as Souter-fell, 17 miles (27 kilometers) to the south-southwest of Carlisle. Of the mountain, an anonymous correspondent for *Gentleman's Magazine* called it "distinguish'd.... The West and North are barricaded with rocks, the East is more plain but with-

In 1760 a man reported seeing ranks of red-clad soldiers, followed by women and children, who then suddenly disappeared (*iStock*).

al steep, and seemingly 900 yards [823 meters] in height, but every where of difficult access." Not, in other words, a place where one is going to see hordes of human beings and where the sight even of one is, if not unheard of, at least out of the ordinary.

In late June 1735, on Midsummer's Eve, an unnamed servant who worked for John Wren, owner of a small estate on the eastern side, claimed to have seen a marching army, divided into "distinct bodies of troops," moving on the mountain. The soldiers were clearly visible. Since no such thing seemed possible and "as no other person in the neighborhood had seen the like," no one believed him. Two years later—again on Midsummer's Eve, this time between eight and nine o'clock—a nearby landowner named William Lancaster noticed what he thought were a few hunters walking behind some horses. On looking again 10 minutes later, he was taken aback to see them now on horseback, followed by "a vast army ... five in rank." Alerting family members, the Lancasters, according to the first published account (*Gentleman's Magazine*, November 17, 1747), "frequently observed that some one of the five would quit rank, and seem to stand in a fronting posture, as if he was observing and regulating the order of their march, or taking account of the numbers, and after some time appear'd to return full gallop to the station he had left, which they never fail'd to do as often as they quitted their lines, and the figure that did so, was generally one of the middlemost men in the rank."

As darkness fell, the formal marching ended, and the figures began walking in more casual configurations as would civilians engaged in commonplace activities. With the passing of light, they were lost to sight.

In his *Survey of the Lakes* (1787) mapmaker James Clarke collected testimony concerning what appear to be later sightings from 1743 and 1745. In the former instance, John Wren and his servant Daniel Strickett were gazing out on Souter-fell on a summer evening when they were puzzled to see a horse at full gallop on an extremely steep slope.[6] They were surprised that a horse could have managed to get there, much less travel at such a sharp incline at such a clip. Then they spotted a man and a dog running—again at inexplicable speed—behind the horse.

Strange as the sight was, apparently it did not occur to them that these were anything but creatures of flesh and blood. In fact, the next morning they scoured the site on the theory that the horse must surely have lost a horseshoe or two which they could recover and recycle. Or maybe, they further reasoned, the man had fallen and been killed. Neither horseshoe nor body was to be found, and when they recounted their experience to friends, they found themselves at the receiving end of derisive laughter.

Two years later, on the evening of June 23, figures appeared on Souter-fell again. Strickett, who now worked for Lancaster on his adjoining estate, was the first to see them. He kept quiet for a while but finally, after they continued in view, he spoke to his employer. When he looked, he saw them, too, and over the next two and a half hours, a total of 26 witnesses watched a vast army march south and west around the mountain. According to Clarke, "Frequently, the last, or last but one in a troop would leave his place, gallop to the front, and then take the same pace with the rest, a regular swift walk; those changes happened to carry every troop (for many troops appeared), and oftener more than once or twice, yet not at all times alike. The spectators saw, all alike, the same changes, and at the same time, as they discovered by asking each other questions as any change took place."

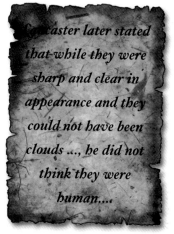

...caster later stated that while they were sharp and clear in appearance and they could not have been clouds ..., he did not think they were human,....

Amid the troops rolled the occasional carriage. The *visible* part of the column was at all times half a mile long, and since the army was moving all the while, it had to have consisted of a staggering number of troops. Lancaster later stated that while they were sharp and clear in appearance and they could not have been clouds (as skeptics had suggested), he did not think they were human "because of the impractability of a march over the precipices, where they seemed to come on." He also recalled that "horse and man upon strict looking at appear'd to be but one being, rather than two distinct ones." Activities continued, as before, until the light faded and nothing more could be seen.

As we will see, one curious theme running through some of the accounts holds that the number of spectral troops is beyond counting.

✳

All Clad with Brilliant White Raiment

A story with features in many ways like those that would characterize the 1818 encounter in New Jersey took place in a rural Rutherford County settlement in western North Carolina. There were two reported incidents.

The first occurred on the evening of July 31, 1806. Around 6:00 PM, as eight-year-old Elizabeth Reaves stood in a cotton field near the family house, she noticed a host of figures on nearby Chimney Rock Mountain. She shouted to her older brother and sister as well as an unnamed "negro woman" (apparently a slave), who rushed to alert Patsey Reaves, the mother. According to a statement Mrs. Reaves filed subsequently before attorney David Dickie:

> Mrs. Reaves ... turned towards the Chimney Mountain and saw a very great crowd of beings resembling the human species, but could not discover any particular members of the human body, nor distinction of sex; they were of every size from the tallest men down to the least infants; they were all clad in brilliant white raiment; but they could not describe any form of raiment; they appeared to rise off the side of the mountain south of the rock and about as high. A part of the mountain top was visible above the shining host; that they moved in a northern direction, and collected about the top of Chimney Rock. When all but a few had reached the rock two seemed to rise together and behind them a third. These three moved with great agility toward the crowd and had the nearest resemblance to men of any they had seen. While looking at these three, they saw three more rising from the same place, and moving in the same order and direction. Then several others rose and went towards the rock. This lasted about an hour, when Mrs. Reaves sent for Mr. Robert Searcy, who said that when he came he saw more glittering white appearances of human kind than he had ever seen of men at any general review; that they were of all sizes from that of men to infants; that they were of all sizes from that of men to infants; that they moved in throngs round a large rock not far from the Chimney Rock; they were about the height of Chimney Rock and moved in a circular course between him and the mountain; two of full size went before a general crowd about the space of twenty yards [18.3 meters].

In the wake of their sudden vanishing, witnesses felt strangely drained and physically wasted. Surviving records are unclear on whether there was an additional observer, a local Presbyterian pastor, the Rev. George Newton, or whether he merely witnessed Mrs. Reaves' swearing to the statement. In any event, the good reverend declared that if the phenomenon did not have some natural explanation (presumably a mirage), it could well be a "prelude to the descent of the holy city." In that, the reverend proved himself, if not a prophet, at least a good medieval thinker.

A sequel of sorts occurred five years later. In September 1811 an elderly farm couple stated they had seen "two opposing armies of horse-men, high up in the air all mounted on winged horses." Sounds accompanied the eerie sight, commencing with a ringing cry of "Charge!" from the commander of one army. Swords flashed, and shouts, groans, and screams followed as one side routed the other. It was all over in 10 minutes, and the figures were gone.

They were back, however, over subsequent evenings. Watched by the old couple and "three respectable men," the ghosts—perhaps because they had won the battle—were no longer engaged in combat. Exactly what they were doing is not clear from available

During the Civil War, witnesses in West Virginia watched as a large ghostly army marched before their eyes in broad daylight (*iStock*).

accounts. It is known that the reports caused considerable local excitement. A delegation from a nearby town included a magistrate and a clerk, who took notarized statements.

✳

A Splendid Panorama

In February 1862 G.W. Kinney of Barnston, Québec, wrote a local newspaper[7] to describe something that he had seen while standing on the banks of a lake near the settlement. Not especially clear or lucidly written, the letter leaves a number of questions unanswered, but it is the only record of the alleged incident:

> Two weeks ago to-day in the morning [evidently sometime in mid- to late-January], I discovered that the mountains on the west side of the lake looked very different from what they usually do. It came to my mind what I had heard had been seen a few days before this in the same place. I stopped and saw, apparently, a train of cars, four in number; presently they changed their position and came together, forming into one body, one side of which was perpendicular to a great height; and then another similar form made its appearance at a short distance, I then saw as it looked to me, an army of men advance towards each other and then disappeared; it then passed away into some different position. I then saw a ship come in sight, turn broadside to the apparent army of men, and thus they appeared and disappeared for six hours, passing before my eyes like a splendid panorama. There were no clouds to be seen in the sky that day in that direction, or any

fog. This is no idle dream or fancy, and I can substantiate it with the testimony of a very good number of people, who were with me in the morning, and saw the same sight.

✴

A Weaponless Shadow Army

West Virginia came into the union on June 20, 1863, carved out of Virginia, one of the original 13 states and the eighth to align itself with the Confederacy, following President Lincoln's election. Residents of mountainous western Virginia, culturally, economically, and politically at odds with their fellow citizens to the east, voted to secede from the secession and to cast their lot with Lincoln and the original American republic. Even so, the Greenbrier County town of Lewisburg, now legally in West Virginia, still considered itself a part of old Virginia, just a few miles to its east. Thus, Lewisburg amounted to Confederate territory. So the curious occurrence of October 1 that year attracted the interest of rebel authorities and Southern newspapers.[8]

On that hot and dry afternoon, no wind blew, and not a cloud dotted the sky. In the stillness, some residents sat or stood idly by as they took in the day. (An account identifies the others as "four respectable ladies and a servant girl.") As he sat on his porch, Moses Dwyer noticed objects floating in the sky just over the treetops on the hills to the south. As they came into clearer view, they arrived in the thousands, looking like "rolls like cotton or smoke, apparently the size and shape of doors ... passing ... in beautiful order and regularity." The same contemporary account reports, "The rolls seemed to be tinged on the edge with light green, so as to resemble a border of deep fringe.... They were perhaps an hour in getting by."

Finally, the sky cleared, but the strange sights were not over. If anything, things were about to get even more interesting:

> In the deep valley beneath, thousands upon thousands of (apparently) human beings (men) came in view, traveling in the same direction as the rolls, marching in good order, some 30 or 40 in depth, moving rapidly—"double quick"—and commenced ascending the almost insurmountable hills opposite, and had the stoop peculiar to men ascending a steep mountain. There seemed to be a great variety in the size of the men; some were very large, whilst others were quite small. Their arms, legs, and heads could be distinctly seen in motion. They seemed to observe strict military discipline, and there were no stragglers.
>
> There was uniformity of dress, white blouses or shirts, with white pants; they were without guns, swords, or anything that indicated "men of war." On they came through the valley and over the steep road, crossing the road, and finally passing out of sight, in a direction due north from those who were already looking on.

Exactly two weeks later, "eight or 10 of the Confederate pickets at Runger's Mill" along with many civilians in the area ("about four miles east of Percy," an apparently no-longer extant settlement) viewed an identical procession. Again, it took an hour to pass by.

✳

Mysterious Warriors of the Heavens

In *Last-Day Tokens* (1904) a deeply devout man named J.N. Loughborough collected accounts of marvelous phenomena that in his interpretation amounted to evidence of the imminent Second Coming of Jesus Christ. Of course, they didn't, but among the remarkable phenomena he recounts one that came to him via a June 13, 1901, letter he received from a correspondent identified only as "Reverend Schultz" from Oakland, California:

> In the month of September, in the year 1870 — I do not remember the exact day of the month, but it was in the dark of the moon — I was visiting with my uncle in northwestern Illinois, in the locality then known as Green Vale, now Stock Post-office. One evening, my uncle and I were up until nearly midnight, and before retiring went out-of-doors, and noticed a great red light, lighting up all things lighter than a bright moonlight. The sky was perfectly clear, and as we looked into the heavens to see what caused this great light, we saw a large bright circle of golden red, with streaks of red from the edge of it all around. These outer circles seemed to be moving upward, and finally the object we were viewing assumed the form of a beautiful crown, apparently as large as a good-sized washtub. From the body of the crown there went up sharp prongs about eighteen inches [45 centimeters] in length. All was vivid red. There were no jewels on this crown, but all was of one color. This view lasted about ten minutes after we first saw it. I do not know how long it may have been in the heavens, before we noticed it. It opened up as it appeared and disappeared from view, leaving all in dense darkness for a moment. Then it was immediately replaced by a streak of red light about four feet [1.2 meters] wide, extending over the entire heavens from east to west, with prongs out on the lower or south side of the band. These prongs were about two feet [0.6 meters] long, all pointing to the southwest. The prongs were also of deep red. The band then looked much like a timber saw, as all of these sharp points were pointed one way.
>
> While we were looking wonderfully upon this, there arose from the north, as far up as the sun would be when two hours high, a perfect army composed of thousands of men, fully equipped, arms shouldered, and then, from the south, another army just like the first arose. Both of these armies were clad in deep red, and marched toward one another. When they reached the red band — and that extended, as I said, from east to west — they leveled their guns, and both sides fired at once. We heard no report, but saw the barrels,

and with the breach of the guns began beating one another, using their guns as clubs. I was in the Civil War, 1861 to 1865, and saw skirmishes where this very mode of warfare was resorted to, but this scene in the heavens was the most awful battle one could ever want to witness. It was immensely greater than anything I ever witnessed in the war. In this sky battle the clubbing went on until there was not a person left standing. All were killed and prostrate on the ground. We heard no noise, as before stated, but saw the thick smoke and confusion of the battle.

The battle being thus over, the whole scene again disappeared, but only for a short time, when there arose from the east a bright flaming red light, extending from east to west across the whole heavens. This band of light was about one rod wide, and went from the east to the western horizon over the zenith of the heavens. This wave of light lasted about five minutes, revealing a terrible scene of dead bodies and broken guns, covering the whole Earth as far as the eye could extend. This whole scene, with its varied changes, lasted from thirty to forty-five minutes.

When I was in Missouri some years later, hunting land, I met a man to whom, in the course of our conversation, I quoted from Scripture the text about there being "signs in the heavens," when he at once described to me the very scene which I have here related, he having also seen it in Missouri at the same time I saw it in Illinois.

Three months later, on the evening of December 1—so the *St. Joseph Herald* reported—residents of Nashville, Michigan, saw black-clad soldiers, "mysterious warriors of the heavens," in large numbers appear in the clouds, visible in the faint moonlight that shone through the mostly overcast sky. The newspaper account is short of details but claims that the soldiers were not marching—apparently they were either motionless images or standing at attention in "perfect ... military style and order." They passed through the night with the clouds as they moved from east to west over a three-hour period. "The phenomenon was observed by the families of several different farmers who reside in the neighborhood," the paper stated. "The people of that neighborhood take it to be the prognostication of war, and have gone to prophesying and predicting terrible things."

The Late President in the Clouds

Less than two decades after the murder of Abraham Lincoln, a second president fell victim to an assassin's bullet. Republican James A. Garfield, who had narrowly won the election of 1880, was in office less than five months when on July 2, 1881, a failed job-seeker named Charles Guiteau shot him as the president was walking through a Washington train station on his way to a speaking engagement. Garfield lingered in precarious health until he died on September 19. The tragedy left the nation in shock and anguish. In the days after his death, apparitions of angel armies, and sometimes of

Garfield himself, figured in spectacular visions reported—mostly skeptically, attributing the sightings to grief-driven hysteria—in the press.

In one story, a group of people observed "a whole platoon of angels marching and countermarching to and fro in the clouds after nightfall." Elsewhere in Maryland, a farmer claimed to have seen giant soldiers in the sky. They wore dazzling uniforms and held muskets as they marched "in the pale, weird light that seemed to be everywhere ... presenting arms at the sound of unheard commands." The same bizarre sight was observed by others "many miles away." Some even alleged—"in spite of the ridicule of their associates"—that the ghost of President Garfield was plainly visible in the soldiers' midst.

"There is no doubt ... that there are many who thought they saw Garfield in the clouds," a nationally distributed newspaper story asserted.

Not long after President James A. Garfield died in 1881, aparitions of soldiers, angel armies, and the president himself were reported (*iStock*).

"In Talbot county [Maryland] the illusion was seen by many. A farmer living near Clara's Point, on going out into yard after dark, saw ... angels and soldiers marching side by side in the clouds, wheeling and going through every evolution with military precision and absolutely life-like and natural."

On the evening of May 3, 1891, at Metz, France, a group of workers walking along a highway noticed a small, dark, densely packed cloud hovering just above a nearby meadow. Its closeness to them made it an unusual sight. Over the next minutes the cloud thinned out and spread over the sky. In some fashion it transformed into a vast aerial battlefield in which soldiers, horses, artillery, and more came into unambiguous view. As more than a hundred witnesses watched over the next hour and a half, a full-fledged battle ensued, vanishing from view as night fell. The Paris correspondent of the *New York Mercury* wrote, "A number of intelligent and trustworthy people, including a couple of priests, have come forward and attested to the genuineness of the facts given."

A Christian periodical, the *Evangelic Visitor*, printed the 1894 experience of H.W.J. Smith of Dickinson County, Kansas. In Smith's telling, he and a neighbor, B.W. Blue, were visiting their mutual friend Andrew Thompson, who lived three miles from Manchester. At some point in the evening Smith and Blue stepped outside, presumably to take in the fresh air, when their eyes fell upon "something like a large luminous ball" about 30 degrees above the eastern horizon. The light then appeared to move slightly, then return to its original position. That would be a common optical illusion if not for what happened immediately afterwards:

> It [the light] opened as a casket with a hinge, presenting on its right a cross—most beautiful, golden, corrugated and furbished. At the left of this was a living man clad in citizen's style, with a plain crown on his head. His form was symmetrical, his countenance bright and permissive—a perfect son of man.
>
> The casket closed, and away it went to the eastern horizon like a meteor. Then it oscillated as if for a time to be emptied and refilled, returning on the same path to its original place. It opened, presenting a portly man, with sword and scabbard on his thigh, a cross on his breast and on his head a crown of many glittering jewels, like stars. He looked beautiful, but was partly hidden by an obtrusive rider on a black or dark horse.
>
> These were hidden or overshadowed by a haughty woman in costly royal attire, who seemed to rule over both. Then these were eclipsed by the coming of a military leader with sword in right hand, elevated ready to strike, the scabbard cast away, a cross on his right breast and a square and compass on his left. On his head was a military hat, the crown blended with the man's hair. On each side of the man's head was a horn, and a cross was erect behind him. He stepped out and forth and began action, never stopping to rest or turning his back on the enemy. He retreated eastward to within about five degrees of the horizon, then began to advance with heavy martial tread, like one tramping the wine press and wielding his sword.
>
> About 11:40 PM as we stood watching the phenomenon, blood was seen to stream forth from the casket and spread far and wide, apparently two-hundred miles [322 kilometers] in extent. Mr. Blue, who is a veteran of the [Civil] war, said it was like the blood of the battlefield, only a deeper red. The warrior seemed at times to be in blood to his knees and above.
>
> At 12:15 I retired, but Mr. Blue remained watching until 2:00 AM and says the warrior was yet parading the skies and was joined by another, who advanced to meet him from the east. The casket vanished after this warrior stepped out. Myself [sic] and Mr. Blue saw the first and second scenes. Others saw the second. Mr. Thompson and Mr. Blue saw all the second.[9]

If this strange story is to be taken as a description of an authentically perceived experience, it—like other sky-phantom accounts—had to have been strictly localized. Giant figures and a 200-mile blood spill would have been massively observed and reported, of course. These are products of the visionary imagination, leaving no lasting evidence of their presence in anything other than memory and testimony. What makes them interesting is that they are not figments of a single, subjective imagination but of a collective one.

Angels We Have Seen on High

On the evening of August 20 or 21, 1893, citizens of Covington, Indiana, claimed that "angel forms in solemn procession" (in the words of one witness, a woman who taught at Indiana Normal College) passed over their town.

The vision commenced with a circle of light in the northern sky. Soon, that changed into the sight of human-looking figures in white, flowing robes marching two abreast, 10 to 15 pairs at a time. When one company disappeared, another would take its place. Over 10 minutes' time meant the passage of 100 to 200 figures in total. "The occurrence took place between 9 and 10 o'clock," a press account asserted. "The forms of the spirit visitors were to all appearances covered by gauzy substance."[10] They were at about 30° elevation in the northwestern sky.

Into Silence

Our last record of a sky battle is reported briefly and inconclusively, at least in American newspapers, in central Europe in 1909, and then the atmosphere returns to its usual mysterious elements: unknown airships and aircraft, UFOs, cryptozoological flying things. Armies in the sky are no longer fashionable, and it appears that people's fantastic visions take other forms these days. Or it may be that those who experience such things know better than to speak of them. If decades into the controversy about UFOs one can still be ridiculed for having seen something so—relatively speaking—prosaic, perhaps those who have viewed even more appallingly incredible aerial phenomena know better than to ask for it.

Further Reading:

Crowe, Catherine. *The Night-Side of Nature or Ghosts and Ghost-Seers.* New York: Redfield, 1853.
McCue, Peter. "Phantoms of the Battlefield." *Fortean Times* 210 (2006): 42–45.
Reid, Frank John. "Phantom Riders on Souter-Fell." *Fate* 31, 12 (December 1978): 46–51.
Rickard, Bob, and John Michell. *Unexplained Phenomena.* New York: Penguin Putnam, 2000.

Sky Serpents: The Horror of the Heights

One day in early 1833, a native chief approached two Western missionaries serving in Sumatra, a large Indonesian island, to relate a bizarre experience. The chief, whose name was Tam Basar, swore that he and a companion had seen a snake flying through the air. Fearing that it was dangerous, they killed it when it landed near them. In the face of missionaries' manifest incredulity, the chief insisted firmly that he was telling the truth, supplying the additional detail that the snake, four feet (1.2 meters) long, had no wings. To the listeners that only made the story more far-fetched.

A year later, in January 1834, one of those missionaries, N.M. Ward, happened to be walking through a forest near the Pedang-Bessie River, a mile or so from the location where the flying snake had allegedly appeared. He and a companion stopped to study a particularly tall tree. Looking up, they were shocked to sight a flying snake, exactly as described by the native informant. Four feet (1.2 meters) long and wingless, it was moving rapidly through the air from the tree they were standing under to another about 240 feet (73 meters) away.

"Thus," Ward wrote in *Missionary Herald* for March 1841, "was I convinced of the existence of flying serpents; and, on inquiry, I found some of the natives, accustomed to the forest, aware of the fact."

Ward went on to write that Dutch naturalists working the area didn't believe him, any more than he had believed Tam Basar. The skeptics, however, were wrong. There are five species of "flying" snakes in South and Southeastern Asia; flying is in quotes because the creatures are actually gliding or parachuting. Herpetologists do not dispute their existence, and many photographs, films, and videos exist, as do collected specimens. What Ward saw, in other words, was nothing otherworldly.

But what about this?

Stories of flying snakes in South and Southeastern Asia are based on fact. Though lacking wings, there are several species of snake that have adapted their bodies to gliding from tree to tree (*iStock*).

In June 1873 a farmer identified as Mr. Hardin, who lived a few miles east of Bonham, Texas, along with workers in nearby fields, observed an "enormous serpent ... as large and long as a telegraph pole ... of a yellow striped color," in the words of the *Bonham Enterprise*. That would have been remarkable enough, except that this was floating in a cloud heading in an easterly direction.[1] The witnesses "could see it coil itself up, turn over, and thrust forward its huge head as if striking at something, displaying the maneuvers of a genuine snake."

At Fort Scott, Kansas, not long afterwards, at mid-morning on the twenty-sixth of the same month, two persons, unnamed but described as "reliable parties" willing to swear to it by affidavit, reported seeing a "huge serpent, apparently perfect in form," encircle the sun. It was clearly visible for a short time, then vanished from sight.[2]

The *New York Times* took note of the two stories in successive editions on July 6 and 7. It called the Bonham sighting "the very worst case of delirium tremens on record." In the following edition, noting the Kansas report in the wake of the equally implausible one from Texas, an editorial writer sputtered, "It will soon be time for a national prohibitory liquor law, if this sort of thing is to continue."

Or this:

In late July or early August 1887, near Bedford, Iowa, some kind of flying creature appeared overhead. When Lee Corder—the one named witness—noticed it, he first took it to be a buzzard, but as it began to descend, he grew less sure, and soon he was certain that it was nothing he had ever seen before. When it finally got close enough so that he could get a clear look at it, the contours of a great writhing serpent with glistening scales and a forked tongue came into view. It was as much as a foot wide. When it landed with a thud in a corn field, nobody ventured into the stalks to see more. Apparently, it slithered off via more conventional mode of transportation, since the *Bedford Times-Independent* account mentions nothing about the snake's ascension.

Or this:

The late historian Mari Sandoz wrote in her *Love Song to the Plains* (1966), "Back in the hard times of 1857–58 there were stories of a flying serpent that hovered over a Missouri River steamboat slowing for a landing. It was like a great undulating serpent, in and out of the lowering clouds, breathing fire, it seemed, with lighted streaks around the sides." She quotes a period ballad:

'Twas a dark night in Sixty-six
When we was layin' steel
We seen a flyin' engine come
Without no wing or wheel.

It came a-roarin' in the sky,
With lights along the side ...
And scales like a serpent's hide.

A word of caution: No independent verification for these claims, either the flying-serpent sightings or the folk song they are said to have inspired, has been demonstrated to investigators. On the other hand, Sandoz did not have a reputation as a mere yarn-spinner. A respected writer in her time (best known for *Cheyenne Autumn,* on which John Ford's 1964 film of the same name, starring Richard Widmark, was based), she is unlikely to have conjured this up out of her imagination, but unhelpfully, her book provides no source citations. Perhaps they will show up one day in the pages of a mid-nineteenth-century frontier newspaper.

✶

Fantastic Serpents

Even so, there can be no doubt that sky serpents, if not so ubiquitous as sea serpents, were present—in print anyway—in the America of the 1800s, and not just in America. In earlier centuries these things were called dragons,[3] which were the subject of a body of international folklore, mythology, and even (sometimes) sighting reports.[4] Another surviving remnant of the dragon tradition can be found in a long-forgotten genre once called the "snake story." "Snake stories" were a kind of shorthand for "preposterous tall tales from rural districts."

To understand how implausible snake stories were, consider that the largest documented snakes are reticulated pythons, which make their home in Southeast Asian jungles. The longest of them measure 30 feet (nine meters). Possibly, very rare and undocumented specimens may exceed that (certainly, occasional intriguing anecdotal

Sea monsters have long dwelled in the imaginations of sailors all over the world (*Mary Evans Picture Library*).

testimony suggests as much), but probably by no more than a few feet. And if so, they live in places human beings hardly ever enter.

Any account of an American snake alleged to be more than six or seven feet (about two meters) long is suspect. Yet old newspapers are crowded with accounts that strain belief. Some random examples:

- A serpent estimated by some to be 100 feet (30 meters) in length frightened people in the Upper Sandusky, Ohio, from the 1850s into the 1890s.

- A snake 28 feet (8.5 meters) long made appearances through the 1870s into the early 1880s near Milk Creek, Maryland.

- The trail of an immense, unseen serpent, discovered by fishermen in Maine's Chain of Lakes in 1882, indicated that the creature was 90 feet (27 meters) long and weighed 30 tons.

- A snake 40 feet (12 meters) long was observed near Muncie, Indiana, as it crashed through fence rails one scary day in August 1895.

Another modern dragon was—and is (reports continue, but in significantly reduced numbers and places)—the water monster. One variety, of course, was the sea serpent, reports of which thrilled and intrigued newspaper readers and sparked furious debates among scientists. Even more fantastically, however, if you were to believe the papers of the time, you'd have to believe that a significant percentage of North America's lakes and rivers housed giant reptiles, usually serpent-like. For instance, from the 1880s alone (and not a complete list by any means):

- "Two huge animals that resembled lizards" observed fighting in a stream flowing into Long Lake in what is now eastern North Dakota one night in 1883. The witness claimed that they were 20 feet (six meters) long, each with an alligator-like head, four feet (1.2 meters) with long toes and sharp claws, and fire-red eyes, with a spinal ridge that "resembled a saw."

- A monster as big around as a stovepipe with a serpent's head seen in Narrow Lake, south of Charlotte, Michigan, in 1886.

- "Something like an immense log, 20 feet [six meters] long," swimming, sinking, reappearing, and behaving "in a legitimate sea serpent fashion" observed in the summer of 1886 by "reputable citizens" in Lake Kampeska near Watertown, Dakota Territory (in present-day South Dakota).

- In a lake in Ohio's Ottawa County in May 1887, a monster described as looking like either a sturgeon or a serpent, 20 to 30 feet (six to nine meters) long, a brilliant light covering its entire body, which shined in the evening darkness. The creature had "arms which it tossed wildly in the air." It left enormous tracks along the beach.

Well, so it says—and more—in the papers, whose fidelity to strict factual reality in those freewheeling days of journalism could be shaky. It is curious, however, that lake-monster stories were so recurrent that, far from being treated as an object of sensationalism in all cases, they were just as often mentioned with disarming casualness, sometimes merely as a passing sentence or two in a local-items column. Some of the tales, on the other hand, are so outlandish that it is doubtful they were ever meant to be credited. As for the rest, all we can say is that lake monsters once were a highly fashionable anomaly and that—for reasons about which we can only speculate—they are less so today, confined now to a paltry handful of North American fresh-water bodies.

✳

Serpents in the Sky

But let's get back to the more or less classic dragons of nineteenth-century America: the ones that flew, with or without wings. In honor of their marine counterparts, we'll call them sky serpents, though all of them were not serpents, strictly speaking. Consider this tale, credited to lumberjacks Thomas Camp and Joseph Howard. The two were cutting wood five miles northeast of Hurleton, California, at 4:00 PM on March 10, 1882, when events took a decidedly odd turn. The *Gridley Herald* (March 10) quotes their testimony from a letter they wrote to the newspaper:

We were startled by the sound of many wings flapping in the air. Looking up, we perceived passing over our head, not more than forty feet [12

Mention the word "dragon" and one typically pictures a Medieval European mythical beast, but dragons—or sky serpents—were also a staple of America's nineteenth-century press (*iStock*).

meters] above the tree tops, a creature that looked something like a crocodile. It was, to the best of our judgment, not less than eighteen feet [6 meters] in length, and would measure two feet [0.6 meters] across the body from the head to the tail, a distance of probably twelve feet [3.7 meters]. The tail was about four feet [1.2 meters] long, and tapered from the body to a point probably eight inches [20 centimeters] wide. The head was in the neighborhood of two feet [0.6 meters] in length and the jaws (for its mouth was open) could not have been less than sixteen inches [41 centimeters] long. On each side of the body, between the head and the tail were six wings, each projecting between eighteen inches [46 centimeters] or two feet [about a half meter] from the body. As near as we could see, these wings were about fifteen inches [38 centimeters] broad and appeared to be formed similar to a duck's foot. On the other part of the body we counted twelve feet, six on a side.

When Howard fired a shotgun round, the pellets rattled as if they had struck sheet iron. The creature uttered a "cry similar to that of a calf and bear combined but gave no sign of being inconvenienced or injured." A "number of Chinamen" also allegedly saw the thing. The *Herald* concluded the account with a statement affirming that Campbell and Howard were "reliable men" who could be taken at their word.

Another story from 1882 California, however, reduces the flying crocodile to no more than a modest diversion from the usual. In early February, in a dispatch which saw print in many newspapers, the *Los Angeles Times* related "one of the most startling snake stories ... told in these parts for some time," crediting it to "the engineer and fire-man who came in last night on the Southern Pacific express." Their testimony was "corroborated by the passengers." That testimony recounts something like a thrilling scene from a 1950s monster movie.

As the train passed Dos Palms (now a nature preserve in the Mojave Desert in extreme south-central California), the engineer's gaze turned to the east. There, what appeared to be a column of sand blowing in the wind was heading slowly westward, not far from the railroad track. It was clear that it and the train would soon cross paths. As they got closer to each other, the cause proved to be nothing so prosaic as a dust devil. It was a huge serpent, positioned vertically with its tail dragging the ground. "Pro-pelled by two large wings near the head," the *Times* said, the creature "seemed to be about thirty feet [10 meters] long and twelve inches [30 centimeters] in diameter."

Somehow, the train accidentally clipped off part of the tail. Displeased, the ser-pent rapidly turned and gave chase. It dived down and smashed several windows, roar-ing all the while and frightening the passengers. The pistol-packing among them fired repeatedly, but if any of the bullets found their target, no evidence of same could be discerned. The creature flew off and was lost to view.

"This is vouched for by every one who was on the train," according to the *Times,* "and is given for what it is worth." No follow-up followed, nor was a single witness named. Good story, though.

It's uncertain whether the improbably monikered Jefferson Rawbone, "a well-to-do farmer living near St. Louis," really did claim (in April 1890) to have had a run-in with a host of "white snakes with pink eyes and yellow wings," or whether this was some correspondent's idea of a joke about the effect of excessive alcohol consumption. The newspaper account is short and devoted as much to ridicule as to specifics.

Three years earlier, the *Pittsburgh Chronicle* gave straightforward treatment to a sighting said to have been made by workers at a pipe mill in Etna, an industrial settle-ment across the Allegheny River from that Pennsylvania city, in mid-September 1887. As a number of men stood outside the factory, welder William Stewart happened to glance up into the sky, where a curious sight at (so he estimated) 2,000-foot (610 meters) altitude caught his attention. It looked like a snake—perhaps, he guessed, five feet (1.5 meters) long.[5] Reasonably enough, he doubted his senses and elected to say nothing. But then it got close enough that there could be no mistake, and he alerted his companions to its presence. At this point it was only about 500 feet (152 meters) away, and now at this distance it proved to be at least 25 feet (7.6 meters) in length. According to the *Chronicle:*

It was jet black and in thickness looked like an ordinary keg. The ponderous jaws of the reptile were frequently seen to open, from which emerged a large tongue. It sailed in a regular course, but when the jaws opened it then took a downward course and seemed as though it would fall to the ground below. On the descent the mouth remained open, and after a fall of about 100 feet [30 meters], the jaws would close and the snake would raise its head and slowly wend its way up to its former height.

The course of the monster air snake was in a northwesterly direction. During its stay of about an hour it seemed to long for a visit to every part of Etna. From the mill it moved like a snake on land westward about a mile to a point on the Allegheny river, from where it took a back course to the place where it was first seen by the naked eye. From there it took an upward direction and it was watched until it disappeared behind the mill, sailing somewhat toward the southeast.

Several generally similar reports appear in newspapers in the Carolinas over a span of two and a half decades, from 1880 to 1904.

The first, if relevant only in a broad way, appears in a North Carolina account, published in the December 3, 1880, issue of the *Statesville Landmark* under the bland heading "Meteoritic Displays." Though it is merely unusual, not anomalous, it seems curiously prescient, given the odd phenomena that would in time present themselves in Statesville and environs:

A meteor of surpassing brilliance was seen about midnight [on December 1] ... almost 8 miles [13 kilometers] east of Statesville. It made everything very light about the presence of the observer. It had the shape of a huge spotted serpent, 75 yards [68.6 meters] long, as large as a pine tree, with eyes very distinct and mouth open toward the north pole. About ten feet [three meters] back from the head it seemed to rest on the sky and the head part to be elevated, then a little further back it was raised in a kind of loop, and the tail reached down toward the tops of the trees. It was seen by the man and his family about a half hour, and then it gradually passed away. The observer thought that it portended some terrible calamity, and was very much frightened.[6]

No less than the *New York Times*—even then as sober as any newspaper in the land—took note of a Carolinas-based sky serpent in the classic sense. (The *Times* story was widely reprinted in newspapers throughout the country in the following days.) A short article in the May 27, 1888, issue tells the story of three Darlington County, South Carolina, sisters—Ida Davis and unnamed younger siblings—who, while walking in the woods, spotted a hissing serpent, 15 feet (4.6 meters) long, sailing above the treetops. The creature was moving at the speed of a hawk or buzzard. The *Times* remarked that other residents of the area had reported the same phenomenon earlier in the day, though it provided no details.

An expanded story providing at least some of those details appeared in other newspapers, using the portion the *Times* had printed but going on to recount the (or at least a) sky serpent's appearance in Grassland, 10 miles (16 kilometers) to the southeast:

Some reports of sky serpents describe these creatures as snakelike and wingless, which is highly reminiscent of how they are portrayed in Chinese art (*iStock*).

> A panic was caused among the inhabitants by the approach of the creature. The steeple of the Methodist Church is crowned by a weathercock in the form of a gilded dove. The last rays of the sun caused this dove to glisten brightly, and the eyes of the serpent were attracted by it. Descending in its flight, it soared to within a few feet of the dove, and circled slowly around it, as if moved either by curiosity or a desire for prey. Suddenly it appeared to discover the inanimate and inedible nature of the dove, and, with a furious swash of its tail, knocked the weathercock from its fastenings and sent it to the ground below in a hundred pieces. Some of the fragments picked up are stained with blood, showing that the monster's tail came into contact with the stout iron rods by which the dove was held in place.

The article asserts that the Rev. Richard Medway and his wife witnessed the incident as they were approaching the church for the evening service. Mrs. Medway fainted at the sight. Her husband swore that it was some kind of flying snake. "His description of it agrees essentially with that given by the Davis girls," the account concludes.

Apparently, such phenomena continued to be seen, or at least reported. Further digging through newspaper archives will eventually recover the others that undoubtedly exist. In July 1897 the *Charleston News and Courier* mentioned the most recent sighting of "the flying snake"—not, note, "*a* flying snake." It was sighted twice on the eleventh, near Newman Swamp 10 miles (16 kilometers) south of Hartsville, at 6:00 and 7:00 PM.

The second witness, identified as Henry Polson, is quoted: "The monster was low down, just above the tree tops, had its head thrown back in a position to strike and was just floating through the atmosphere lengthwise." It could have been anywhere from 25 to 40 feet (7.6 to 12.2 meters) in length. Allegedly, the creature was also observed, in the *News and Courier*'s words, "near Chesterfield court house and also in several towns in North Carolina."

The skies of mid-1897 America were crowded with still-unexplained mystery airships, but there apparently there was also room for a sky serpent or two. One was recalled 64 years letter in a letter composed by lifelong Detroit resident John B. Rosa (an eight-year-old paperboy at the time of the sighting) and published in the *Detroit News* for July 15, 1961:

> Going down Grand River for my papers, about 4 in the morning ... the policeman I was with and I saw an object that looked to be about three feet [one meter] in diameter. It was about 1,000 feet [300 meters] in the air and was heading east. It was a silvery color and had a tail about three blocks long. It traveled like those big sea serpents you read about skipping over the top of the water. It made a low hissing noise that we could just hear. My dad, who was leaving our home for work, also saw it as it seemed to pass right over our house....

In any event, the next findable Carolina sighting is only briefly detailed—unfortunately, because it sounds more impressive than most. On the afternoon of September 16, 1904, in the countryside near Troutman, North Carolina, Mrs. John B. Lippard and her children saw "30 or more large snakes sailing through the air" over their farm. Each was about five feet (1.5 meters) long and four to five inches (10 to 13 centimeters) wide. "They watched the snakes sail around and alight in a piece of thickety pine woods.... Most assuredly these people saw something" (*Statesville Landmark,* September 20).

Presumably the stolid, sober Mormon folk did not invite a serpent into Eden, Utah, but on July 20, 1894, one flew over their town. It was around sundown when an immense flying object—some 60 feet (20 meters) from head to tail, 18 inches (46 centimeters) in diameter—sailed from the mountains to the north over the town. It did not wriggle but floated tranquilly through the sky, at a speed estimated to be around 40 miles (64 kilometers) per hour.

After descending to 20 to 30 feet (six to nine meters) above ground near a store on the edge of a park, it swerved left and "disappeared up over the mountains in the direction of Middle Fork canyon. The movement of the monster was like a snake in water and it seemed to acquire speed without any effort whatever. Its skin seemed to be formed of scales like an alligator," as the *Ogden Standard* told it in its July 23 edition. It went on to assert that the account was "vouched for by a number of Eden's reliable men who saw the grim specimen. It was seen by half the inhabitants and created great excitement."

In May 1899, passing through a wooded area, Robert McDougall of Waterford, New Jersey, was startled—an understatement, doubtless—when a winged snake, five feet (1.5 meters) long, darted from a low branch of a pine tree, uttering guttural cries. "It had the look of a bat in its face," an apparently sincere McDougall told a clearly disbelieving *New York Journal* correspondent, "but it was a flying snake sure enough, one of the venomous kind, I should say. Its skull resembled that of a puff adder.... It had no hair, and it had a tapering tail and eyes that flashed fire."

Another named witness, Hiram Beechwood, claimed a daybreak sighting near a swamp. The snake was crossing a road, apparently in the conventional snake fashion, when it noticed Beechwood. Evidently annoyed by his presence, it emitted an "angry bleat" and promptly spread heretofore-unnoticed wings which carried it aloft. It flew slowly into the swamp.

The reporter wrote that to locals "flying snakes are an established fact. They stick pretty closely to the thick undergrowth." When provoked, they let loose with a frightening scream.[7]

One 1899 sighting allegedly occurred from a porch in White County, Tennessee, in August. The *Knoxville Sentinel* remarked, "H.C. Cotton ... reports seeing a flying snake the other evening.... Several persons who were with him also saw the snake." The rest of the paragraph is taken up with the predictable stale jokes about the quality of the alcohol in the neighborhood.

A last report from that active year comes from a letter written by a friend to "Policeman O'Brien of New York." According to a widely distributed newspaper story, a friend in Florida had communicated a series of sightings from the town of Everglades. Among them were the McCorkle brothers, allegedly known to O'Brien. The correspondent— apparently not himself a McCorkle—said the witnesses were in their orange grove when suddenly a "snake rose from the top of an old orange tree and started circling westward. It was about thirty-five feet [10 meters] long and had four wings, a skull like a puff adder [see New Jersey report above], a bald pate, tapering tail, eyes that flashed fire [ditto], a tongue that was clearly venomous, and a look of dark blue annoyance."

✳

Dragons of California

For some reason, a number of the wildest sky-serpent tales are set in California. In the first of these, however, the dragon-like creature is less giant snake than another kind of monstrous reptile: the long-extinct pterosaur.

In August 1886, the *Ventura Free Press* related, a stranger who identified himself as Peter B. Simpson entered the newspaper office to unburden himself of a terrifying story. In reporting his account, the paper noted simply, "He says that these things are facts. We give the statement for what it is worth."

The previous month, he had left the Esmeralda mining country in Nevada with his wife, three children, and a dozen head of cattle. The party's destination was Santa Barbara County in California. On the evening of July 15, under a nearly full moon, the Simpsons set up camp along the upper end of Elizabeth Lake, half a mile or so from Bakersfield, then a small village. The campers noted an odd, pungent odor which seemed to be emanating from the water and floating through the valley in a faint mist.

The beast that Peter Simpson described seeing in 1886 was a reddish monster with jagged teeth, a snout, and wings (*iStock*).

Simpson put the cattle out to graze, and he and his family settled in for a night's sleep. Around midnight strange sounds—thunderous roars and eerie hisses—emanating from somewhere out on the lake roused him from slumber. He could barely make out something that looked like a black cloud, beneath which the water bubbled and boiled. Puzzled but not frightened, he returned his blanket and soon started to doze. Moments later, hell broke loose.

Simpson's first impression was that a cyclone had hit. A mighty rushing of wind stirred the air, awakening everybody. The wagon rose up and sailed 20 feet (6.1 meters) before it was dropped, the wheels badly damaged. The cattle were stampeding. A shadowy shape—which proved to be the source of the rushing sound—was flying away until it disappeared in the distant darkness. For a short time, as everything turned silent, Simpson stood, rifle in hand, trying to sort out what had just happened. At that point other sounds, something like the crashing of battering rams, or at least some terrific conflict, came to his ears. Something was happening on the other side of the hill. The *Free Press* provides this unnerving description:

> The monster had come upon a drove of antelope sleeping in the gulch and had at once attacked them. About ten feet [six meters] from where Mr. Simpson stood a fine buck lay bleeding, bitten clean through at one stroke of the "thing's" horrid jaw. Around another buck the monster's wings

seemed folded, while its long tail, barbed at the end, played around the air incessantly. Two other antelope were vigorously trying the effect of their short horns upon the scaly sides of the monster. Mr. Simpson's description of this "thing" is very succinct: "It was about thirty feet [ten meters] long over all, I should judge," he said, "and of a warm, reddish color, with a long snout and jagged, yellow teeth. It had enormous wings, rigged like those of a bat, evidently, long hind legs and a long tail, with a seemingly hard, barbed point. From its head and neck fell a shaggy mane, and its huge eyes gleamed like horrid fires."

Simpson put his rifle to his shoulder and fired at the monster. He could hear the bullet strike it, but it did not penetrate the flesh. Still, it must have had some effect because the creature took flight, the dead antelope still in its beak. It headed toward the lake, then plunged into it with a mighty splash.

The next morning, Simpson returned to the scene and collected round, translucent scales about the size of dinner plates. He inferred that either his shot or the two antelopes' horns had knocked them off. The newspaper account noted that they were "of a reddish glazed appearance, somewhat similar to ground glass," though it is not clear if Simpson actually showed them to representatives of the *Free Press*.

> *The dragons rose out of the water and flew so low over the men … that they keenly felt the backwash from the wings….*

In 1895 the *St. Louis Republic* opened a long dispatch with these alarming words:

> A number of persons living in the vicinity of Reedley, Fresno county, Cal., all reputable citizens, too, swear that they have seen and hunted two dragons with wings 15 feet [4.6 meters] long, bodies without covering of hair or feathers, head broad, bills long and wide, eyes not less than 4 inches [10 centimeters] in diameter, and with feet like those of an alligator somewhat, though more circular in form. They have five toes on each foot, with a strong claw on each, and its tracks is 11 inches [28 centimeters] wide and 10 inches [30 centimeters] long.

At least the writer doesn't feel the need to employ euphemisms. He calls them what they were: good old-fashioned dragons. In any event, so the story (involving monsters slightly reminiscent of the one in the 1882 California tale already recited) goes, the creatures were spotted first southeast of Selma early on the evening of July 11. Their "peculiar cries and the rushing of their mammoth wings" continued to be heard even after they were no longer visible.

On July 13 the creatures feasted on farmer A.X. Simmons' chickens. Well, maybe, maybe not. The account is vague on whether they were actually seen doing so; possibly more to the point, the account says that on examination the teeth marks on the victims "resemble those made by a very large dog," the logical inference being that they *were* made by a very large dog. Anyway, on the evening of the nineteenth, picnickers in a buggy saw the dragons pass overhead, visible in the moonlight and generating serious unease with their eerie wails and snapping jaws. Two hog farmers near Selma saw the creatures under a bridge. The dragons rose out of the water and flew so low over the men (said to be Maj. Henry Haight and Harvey Lemon) that they keenly felt the back-wash from the wings.

Soon a six-man party commenced a night-long vigil, hoping to capture or kill the monsters, but the long hours passed uneventfully. Then in the morning one Emanuel Jacobs came into town to report his discovery of dead ducks, apparently slaughtered by the dragons, in High Valley in the mountains four miles away. Two of the party, J.D. Daniels and a Mr. Templeton, returned and hid themselves in holes they'd dug near a pond where the ducks had been killed. What happened next is attributed to Daniels:

> About 11 o'clock the cries were heard in the direction of King's river, seeming two or three miles away. The ominous yells drew nearer, and in a few moments we heard the rush and roar of wings, so hideous that our hair almost stood on end. The two dragons came swooping down and circled round and round the pond in rapid whirls, screaming hideously all the while. We had a good view of them while flying.
>
> They passed within a few yards of us and their eyes were plainly visible. We could also see that instead of bills like birds, they had snouts resembling that of the alligator, and their teeth could be seen as they snapped their jaws while passing.... They were probably examining [the pond to determine] if any food was to be had, such as ducks, mud hens and fish. At length they came down with a fearful plunge into the pond, and the mud and water flew as though a tree had fallen into it. They dived around in the water, and as nearly as we could judge at the distance of thirty yards [27.4 meters], they were something over six feet [two meters] long, and while wading through the water they looked not unlike gigantic frogs. Their wings were folded and appeared like large knobs on their backs. Their eyes were the most visible parts and seemed all the time wide open and staring. They were very active and darted out among the tulles and rushes catching mud hens....
>
> As soon as we saw a good opportunity, we leveled our guns at the one nearest [sic] us and fired. One rose in the air, yelled and flew away. Every stroke of the wing showed great strength. The other floundered about in the water until it reached the end of the pond, when it crawled out, dragging along its wounded wing after it, and started across the plain. We loaded our guns and gave chase. We soon lost sight of it, for it went much faster than we could. However, we were able to follow by its dismal cries in the distance. We followed it half a mile, when it passed out of our hearing. The next day a company went in pursuit and trailed it by the blood in the grass. It was followed three miles to Jumper slough, which was entered, and all trace of it was lost. When it passed down the bank it left several well formed tracks in the mud.

One of the best was cut out with a spade, and after drying was taken to Selma, where it is in the possession of Mr. Snodgrass.

Ah, yes, Mr. Snodgrass, who hereafter dissipates into the mists of history. Old newspapers are full of Mr. Snodgrass and his equivalents, last seen in possession of Earth-shattering secrets and revelations.

Monstrosities and Visions

Two fantastic stories told as true are of creatures which, though not exactly sky serpents, share some characteristics with them.

In its June 18, 1853, edition the *Brooklyn Daily Eagle* carried a piece by Elizabeth Oakes Smith, then a well-known writer, drawing on the reminiscences of Peter Embury, a lifelong resident of New York. Embury could recall a time in the pre-Revolutionary years when a large, deep pond, called the Collet, occupied a prominent place in the then-small city before it was drained and buildings were constructed on the site. "I rarely relate this," he said, "and do not expect people to believe it, being so like the old stories of dragons."

As Embury told it, he and some playmates were engaged in boys' activities along the banks of the Collet when one shouted out that they should look at something:

> They all gathered to the spot, and there found up near a large branch, but clinging to the body of the tree, a creature so nearly of the appearance of the bark itself, that it was scarcely distinguishable from it—a creature that gave them full time to examine him. He was of a lizard shape and more than a foot in length, his long hands clinging fast to the tree, and his tail curved partially round a twig. His eyes were red and fiery, and the boys declared they emitted sparks, like Old Nick himself. But the strangest part was a pair of filmy, bat-like wings, which he kept moving up and down, producing a rapid current of air. The boys stayed round him for several hours and called on others to see the strange beast, but forbore to molest him. They never saw him but this once. Turtles, lizards, and snakes of all sizes were numerous in the pond.

One of the most fantastic stories of the nineteenth century first appeared in the March 27, 1868, issue of a newspaper in Santiago, Chile. A translated version was published in the *Milwaukee Daily Sentinel* (May 18) and other North American newspapers in the weeks that followed:

> Yesterday, about five o'clock PM, when every one had finished work at this mine (Garin Mine), and the workmen in a group were awaiting their evening meal, we saw coming through the air a gigantic bird, which at first sight we supposed to be a cloud surrounded by the atmosphere, and divid-

At first appearing to be a foot-long reptile, the strange animal seen by New York residents in 1853 emitted sparks and flapped leathery wings (*iStock*).

ed from its companions by a chance current of air.

As the object in question came nearer, filling us with a very natural feeling of surprise, we were able to note that it was an unknown creature of the air—the *roc* of the "Thousand and One Nights" perhaps. From whence did it come? To where was it going? Its direction was from northeast to southwest; its flight rapid and in a direct line. On passing a short distance and over our heads, we were able to note the rare structure of its body. Its great wings were clothed with a brown plumage; the head of the monster was in shape similar to that of the grasshopper with enormous eyes wide opened and brilliant as stars, and covered with something like hair or bristles; the body, lengthening itself out like that of a serpent, was covered with brilliant scales, which emitted metallic sounds as the strange animal moved itself along.

Surprise resolved itself into fear among the workmen in the presence of such a strange phenomenon. The whole stock of ornithological science possessed by the good miners was in vain exhausted to find the name and qualities of the strange bird which had just passed without leaving a sign. Some assert that in those moments they perceived a detestable smell, like that given out by arsenic on being burned. Others [say] that their senses were not offended by any unusual odor. The superstitious believe that it is the devil in person they have just seen pass, while others recollect having been witness, some years ago, in the same place, of the passage of a similar monstrous bird.

As the whole affair is in the extreme curious, we have thought it our duty to communicate it to you, withholding all useless comment, for the truth is that we cannot explain satisfactorily to ourselves what we have seen for the first and probably last time in our lives.

The tale was reprinted even in Britain's respectable scientific journal *Zoologist*.[8] The celebrated anomaly chronicler Charles Fort discusses it in his *Lo!* (1931) next to the 1873 sky-serpent sightings mentioned early in this chapter. Fort, who was seeking evidence of interplanetary visitation, thought the supposed creature was in truth a "construction that carried lights, and was propelled by a noisy motor." Since nobody has reported anything like it since, though, a more than usual dose of doubt seems in order.

Somebody identifying himself simply as "T.R.B." of Frederick, Maryland, sent a letter, dated November 19, 1883, to the town's newspaper, the *News,* where it appeared on the twenty-seventh. There is no way of knowing, of course, whether the writer was joking, deluded, or sincerely trying to communicate a visionary experience which could have easily been dropped into, or inspired by, the Book of Revelation.[9] The editor featured the letter on the front page under the heading CAN ANYONE EXPLAIN IT? He expressed the plaintive hope—met, alas, by silence—that "perhaps it might act phantasmagorically on some one of our readers, enough to deduce a reply":

About half-past six this morning, while out driving, just as I reached the top of Red Hill on the Jefferson Road ... I happened to glance towards the Catoctin Mountain at my right, and there witnessed the most singular and fearful sight it has ever been my fortune or misfortune to behold. The sky had a fierce red appearance (like as if the departing sun of the day before had stained it with an indelible and fadeless hot fury) and trailed its brilliant rays low down amid the trees upon the mountain-top. The dark bodies of the trees were vividly outlined against this fiery back-ground and formed a series of grotesque, startling and diabolic pictures. Beginning at the extreme right a monstrous dragon with glaring eye-balls and mouth wide open, displaying a tongue, which hung like a flame of fire from between its jaws, reared and plunged as if seeking to reach some object beyond its grasp. Then came a troop of horned and cloven demons marked all over with spots like a leopard, each spot gleaming out with a dazzling radiance, and each demon bearing in his hand a blazing brand which he moved wildly over his head while the entire troop danced in a weird and rapid manner. Next followed a vast and appalling cavern that lifted up its glaring entrance, from out which streams of burning oil seemed to flow and huge boulders of incandescent cinder were belched with a vigor and a roar that at once blinded and deafened one. The next and last picture of the series revealed a gallows, tall, and gaunt, and threatening, that stood up as if possessed with life, and in the fingers of a long skeleton arm which it held forth grasped about the neck the body of a man upon whose haggard face the lustrous hues of the sky placed with terrific force and brought out with frightened emphasis the woe, misery, and suffering that threaded its every lineament. As I looked the scenes increased in integrity and swiftness of action until my brain swam in a delirium of horror and my heart thumped like a trip hammer. Just as I had reached the verge of fainting from pure excitement the sun rose in all its golden glory from out the valley to my left hand bathing the world in a warm flood of welcome light and driving from view the bewildering pictures which had so lately frozen the blood in my veins. Having always led a thoroughly sober and straightforward life I am at a loss to explain the cause and portent of this alarming phantasmagoria. Can you interpret it for me?

In the Twentieth Century

Anyone inclined to relegate sky serpents to dubiously factual nineteenth-century newspaper yarns has to acknowledge the reality—however one defines "reality" in this context—that the press continued to feature reports into the next century. Two flying-snake reports from the Midwest are especially intriguing.

A contemporary press account, published in the *Washington Post* and elsewhere, relates an experience said to have occurred to a woman identified as Mrs. John Bishop in late August 1911. As she and her children occupied themselves in the backyard of their St. Charles, Missouri, house, they heard a whirring sound. Its source proved to be a spotted snake three feet (one meter) long, propelled by wings moving so fast that they never got a clear impression of what those wings looked like. When they first spotted it, it was flying away from them, but suddenly it reversed direction. The Bishops fled into the house and watched through doors and windows as it sailed around the property for some 20 minutes. Eventually, it disappeared to the east.

"If we didn't know Ford Ewalt quite as well as we do," the *Adams County Union-Republican* (Corning, Iowa) observed in its May 5, 1926, issue, "we might be tempted to ask him 'who is your favorite bootlegger?'" Ewalt, however, was no drinker, and he was with his wife, who also attested to the strange sight, on a drive the previous Sunday evening (May 2). Ewalt claimed that when he first saw the flying snake, he was stunned speechless. Mrs. Ewalt, however, spoke up to pronounce, "That was a snake."

The incident took place on a rural road west of Corning. The snake flew in front of them and was soon lost to sight. The article does not say whether it had wings or not, only that it was sailing about five or six feet (about a meter) off the ground.

Aside from the North Carolina reports mentioned earlier, press references allude to sightings in Pennsylvania, Ohio, and the Ozarks in the early 1900s, but further details have yet to be unearthed.

Serpents of Sea and Sky

If sky serpents are analogous to sea serpents, a few—if we are to credit the reports, naturally—are both. American papers, for example, carried this story in late August 1911 (around the period of Mrs. Bishop's Missouri encounter):

> Passengers and crew of the steamship *Celtic* brought with them to New York a revival of the sea serpent tales of other years. They reported having passed the other day a formidable looking creature which was going at high speed in pursuit of a school of young whales. The monster, they said, had wings, although it appeared to be an aquatic animal, and rose frequently ten

Mrs. John Bishop and her children witnessed a flying, spotted snaked in their backyard in the summer of 1911 (*iStock*).

feet [three meters] or more from the water. Whales and pursuer faded from sight within a few minutes.

The *Syracuse Herald* of September 15, 1922, printed this item:

The Constantinople correspondent of the [London] Sunday Express says armed launches belonging to the Greek fleet are scouring the Sea of Marmora for a winged sea monster which is reported to have appeared off the Princes Isles.

It was first sighted in the Aegean, off the island of Negroponte, and it so frightened the fishermen that the Greek government had to send out an armed launch in pursuit. It now seems to have passed unseen through the Dardanelles.

Persons who claim to have seen the monster declare that it measures 40 feet [12.2 meters] and that the flappers alone would smash a ferry boat. The passengers and crew of the Siri Sefain boat saw it halfway between Pendik and Cartal, a station of the Anatolian railway. There was a violent commotion on the surface of the otherwise tranquil sea, and then appeared the vague form of an enormous winged monster of which first the head and then the tail was seen.

The Siri Sefain boat, they declare, danced "like a toy ship" in the disturbed waters until the monster dived and disappeared towards the islands.

Naturalists believe the monster to be a whale.

Although emerging from the sea, sea monsters have been seen with wings, clearly an unusual adaptation that one would never see on an animal of the natural world (*Mary Evans Picture Library*).

According to another dispatch, the "winged marine monster ... had been sighted circling Dog Island at great speed for three or four days. When it rose from the sea and flew over San Stefano toward the city of Stamboul it was reported to have made a booming sound like the German tri-planes that flew over Paris during the war." Allegedly, the creature could fly thousands of feet above the surface. "The head of the nautical reptile," the account continues, "was fully ten feet [three meters] across, with two enormous reddish green eyes butting out on either side."

More ambiguously, reports from 1922 of sea monsters off Ireland's west coast described things shaped like porpoises, except 100 feet (30 meters) long, moving with express-train speed through the ocean. Always appearing at night, they were regarded as an omen of bad luck. Further: "Occasionally [one] would leap out of and forward over the water a distance equal to its own length.... When [fishermen] see one flying near the surface of the ocean, [the creatures] leap out of the water 40 or 50 feet [12 or 15 meters] and gliding, by the aid of their large winglike fins, guided by their vertically set tail, bring down the bird."[10]

A winged freshwater monster stars in a wild tale set in Grunderville, Pennsylvania, in the early part of August 1906. As reported in the *Washington Times* and elsewhere, Rachel Talbot, "the young daughter of W.A. Talbot, president of the Piso Company," happened to look out from her summer villa to observe something strange in the middle of the Allegheny River: the head of a large reptile protruding several feet above the water, a thousand feet across at this part of its course. She called to Hank Jackson, a ferryman for a local lumber company. Jackson grabbed a rifle and blazed away, a poor choice of action which only worsened things. Rearing its head 10 feet (three meters) in the air, the creature headed for shore in a rage, moving at an alarmingly rapid rate of speed "partly by lashing the water with the tail end of its body and partly by two enormous, finlike wings spreading out from either side of the neck, with which it fanned the air furiously."

Instead of fleeing, Jackson took the time to take a carefully aimed shot. This one hit one of the wings, causing the creature to be at least temporarily disoriented. It began circling in the water "like a loon," all the while flicking its tongue and hissing.

When barge workers on the other side saw what was happening, they, too, started shooting. The monster alternately dived under the water or flew a short distance above it. The account goes on:

> Jackson says the snake finally jumped, or flew as high as the ferry cable, which hangs twenty feet [12 meters] above the water, and it was there, by a well-directed shot, he succeeded in disabling the serpent's other wing, and with a shriek resembling the cry of a wild bird it flew clear over the cable, struck the water with a mighty splash and darted down the river, leaving a wake as wide as the wash of a steamboat.
>
> It is believed by those who saw the monster it is the same one reported as being seen in Oil Creek at Titusville on August 1, and it probably entered the Allegheny at Oil City. Two boys, Jackson Miller and Harold Boynton, saw the serpent while they were camping on the river near Irvington, but the story told by these lads was not believed until the experience of the Grunderville people.

✳

Bodies of Reports

If reports are one thing, bodies—actual physical evidence—ought to be another. As it turns out, though, bodies exist, in common with the sightings, only as reports. For whatever it is worth, let us note that the body reports are not of immense dragon-like serpents but of smaller flying snakes. In that sense, while still hard to credit, they at least don't *feel* grossly impossible.

The first known American report of a slain flying snake predates the existence of the United States itself. Naturalist Hieronymus Benzo of Milan accompanied a French expedition to the future Florida in the mid-sixteenth century. In his chronicle of his experiences, he recorded, "I saw a certain kind of Serpent which was furnished with wings, and which was killed near a wood by some of our men. Its wings were so shaped that by moving them it could raise itself from the ground and fly along, but only at a very short distance from the earth."

Three centuries later, during the summer of 1875, a woman in Leavenworth, Kansas, claimed to have seen a flying snake near her house. A few weeks later, in a brief note, the editor of the *Leavenworth Times* laconically remarked that an unnamed friend had alerted him to a curious item. Two boys named Remington and Jenkins, hunting in the woods, had captured a snake. No ordinary snake, this one was sailing four feet (1.2 meters) above the ground. One boy swooped it up in his hat, brought it to the ground, and killed it. "It is over one foot long, spotted, and has wings about the size of a man's hand," the editor said. "The boys have the serpent preserved in alcohol." There is no evidence that the editor did anything to document the story except to write down what his friend had told him.

In March 1885 a filler paragraph in various newspapers alleged that a flying snake could be viewed on exhibition at some unspecified location in Virginia City, Nevada. The creature was said to be four feet (1.2 meters) long, and its wings were located four inches (10 centimeters) behind the head.

Unlike his Kansas counterpart, an Australian editor asserted that he had examined a captured specimen. American papers such as the *St. Louis Republic* cited this 1895 report from the *Queensland Mercury:*

> James Bass of the sandy flat lying beyond the Blue hill, near the head waters of Carns' creek, has brought another specimen flying serpent to this office. It is somewhat smaller than the one exhibited by him at Gulley last year and larger than the one which he presented us on Christmas day. Like the other two, it has four three jointed legs, each 7 inches [18 centimeters] long. Between these legs, which are situated two on each side of the body, is a leathery membrane, much resembling a bat's wings. Mr. Bass declares that he has often seen them fly across Carns' creek at places where it is 60 feet [20 meters] wide.

Plantation owner John S. Dickinson of Comorn, Virginia, allegedly shot and killed a flying snake in September 1905. Prior to that, locals had spotted the creature—something heretofore unobserved in the area—as it ate birds and landed on tree branches. On being brought to Earth, it was determined to be five feet (1.5 meters) in length, an inch in diameter. Even more unlikely, its wings were covered with feathers.

✳

A Snake that Flies

Far and away the most provocative sky-serpent reports are to be found among the Navajo and the Hopi of rural Arizona. There, both traditions and sightings keep belief in something called by the Navajos *Tłiish Naat'a'i* (snake that flies) and by the Hopi *Tłiish Naat' Agii* (snake among the flying animals). Cryptozoologist Nick Sucik has investigated the phenomenon in the field and via interviews with native informants.

The creature "is described as a snake (or at least a snake-like reptile) possessing the ability to fly," Sucik writes, "as opposed to simply gliding, through aid of membranes or expanded skin extending behind the head and fanning out along the body, not unlike the exaggerated display of a cobra's head." Witnesses insist that it is in all ways like a snake except for the membranes, said to be transparent and to move so rapidly in flight as to be all but invisible, often creating the impression of a snake sailing through the air without support. Generally, the membrane wings are apparent only when the creature is uncomfortably close.

Sucik collected reports of the creature's manner of flight. Most observers said it stretched out horizontally at full length and moved straight ahead. In other cases, though, it was said to slither exactly as it would if on the ground or to engage in rolling loops and twists. "Such claims defy logic," Sucik rightly remarks, since "anything that becomes airborne and remains so must force air forward, downward and aside for aerodynamic lift. The horizontal undulations of reptiles would be worthless" in this regard. Yet, he says, the witnesses were firm in their conviction of what they saw, or anyway thought they saw.

Observers also speak of sounds associated with the creatures. One is a hissing, a snake characteristic caused by the expelling of air through the nostrils. Decidedly uncharacteristic is a kind of hooting sound. A humming—sometimes compared to an engine's roar—evidently is associated with the wings' movement.

Witnesses insist that it is in all ways like a snake except for the membranes, said to be transparent and to move so rapidly in flight as to be all but invisible....

It is further alleged that the creatures live within rock crevices and that—in a particularly fantastic detail—they build nests, a physically impossible task for snakes as conventionally understood. They may also act aggressively, swooping dangerously close to witnesses, even—on apparently rare occasion—biting them. The Navajo differ on their nature, some holding that they are really a variety of snake, others that they are something unnatural.

In an introduction to Sucik's 2004 paper, Kiowa writer Russell Bates refers to his "own tribe's winged snakes.... Sightings of flying snakes have occurred here in Oklahoma where I live."

✸

Imaginary or Not?

Some things resist explanation, even theory. Some of the stories are flat-out fabrications, clearly, while others ... well, who knows? There are no serpents in the sky, of course, in any herpetological sense—which is fortunate for us confirmed herpetophobes—any more than there are other impossible creatures that nonetheless apparently sane, honest souls perversely insist on reporting. Some things jump from the imagined to the experienced, and other things don't.

The purely imaginary are broad variations on a broad theme. The stories that arise from experience (however defined) seem to draw on a narrower range of detail, themes repeated over time and space. The flying snakes known to Southwestern Indian tribes very much resemble those reported in the Carolinas in the latter nineteenth and early twentieth centuries. Perhaps the ones in Iowa in 1926 and New Jersey in 1899, too, and maybe others. Unfortunately, further information is absent and unrecoverable. We can only infer that however inadequate, the newspaper coverage was well meant, the witnesses sincere. Even more impossible in any biological sense, unthinkable to any sensible person, are the immense, dragon-like creatures in the atmosphere. They are just as inconceivable in lakes, rivers, and oceans, whatever else superficial reflection might lead one to judge.

About such things perhaps all we can say is that—in some paradoxical fashion—the certainty of their nonexistence can provide us with no assurance that they cannot be experienced. Those of us who quail at an encounter with a harmless garter snake may not want to linger on that prospect.

Further Reading:

Evans, Jonathan D. "The Dragon." In Malcolm South, ed. *Mythical and Fabulous Creatures: A Source Book and Research Guide,* 27–58. New York: Greenwood Press, 1987.

Shuker, Karl P.N. "In the Spotlight: Flying Snakes." *Strange Magazine* 17 (Summer 1996): 26–27.

Sucik, Nick. "Exploring the Prospect of an Unidentified Species of Reptile within Navajo and Hopi Lands: In Search of Tłʼiish Naatʼaʼt." Kykotsmovi, AZ: privately printed, 2004. Online at anhttp://www.azcentral.com/12news/pics/dragonsofthedine.pdf.

Mystery Airships: Aeronauts from the Twilight Zone

A balloon passed over New York City at a considerable altitude late on the afternoon of October 5, 1861. Passing from west to east, it carried two men, witnesses attested. No one knew where it had come from. The event was strange enough to warrant coverage in the *New York Times*.

Over several days in mid-July 1875 residents of Chicago and neighboring Indiana watched the passing of a mysterious high-altitude balloon. It—the presumption being that a single vessel was responsible—was variously reported as flying southwestwardly (in Illinois) and southeasterly (in Indiana). Its origin unknown, it was the subject of speculation in newspaper accounts. A month later, on the evening of August 16, an unidentified balloon was seen, again at a great height, sailing westward over Minneapolis.

Late on the afternoon of September 28, 1879, a balloon called the *Pathfinder* ascended from St. Louis, carrying two men. One was 71-year-old aviation pioneer "Professor" John Wise, known in his lifetime as the Father of American Ballooning. In early July 1859, in his balloon *Atlantic,* he and his three-man crew had flown 1,200 miles (1,931 kilometers) in 19 hours, from St. Louis to upstate New York, the longest such voyage made in America till then, unmatched until 1910. The last known sighting of the *Pathfinder* in flight took place near midnight that same day, when two railroad men in Miller Station, Indiana, 30 miles (48 kilometers) southeast of Chicago and half a mile from the southern shore of Lake Michigan, spotted it in the moonlight as it moved rapidly toward the water. After that, a month's worth of mystery and press theories closed when the badly mangled remains of Wise's traveling companion George Burr were recovered on the lake shore near Miller Station. The balloon had apparently crashed and sunk in the water. Wise's own body was never found.

Curiously, before the men's fate was known, what was thought to be their balloon, though it could not have been, was reported on at least two occasions. At 3:00 PM

Witnesses saw a balloon they assumed to be the *Pathfinder* piloted by John Wise, but at a time and distance far from where Wise's balloon apparently crashed into a lake in 1879 (*iStock*).

on October 2, at Pontiac in east-central Michigan, a man claimed to have seen a large balloon in the western sky. It flew overhead and vanished in the east. It carried a basket underneath it, but the witness could not see the occupants, if any. "He thinks it was the Wise balloon," a Michigan press account noted. Twice—first in the morning, then in the afternoon—in the northern Illinois city of Rockford, residents spotted an unidentified balloon. On the first occasion it was high in the sky, sailing toward the northwest. On the second, it was at a low altitude, thus permitting witnesses to see the car and "dark objects" inside. It was, according to a press wire report, "supposed to be the *Pathfinder*," though that very day the balloon's tragic end four weeks earlier had been established.

Two years later, alleged eyewitnesses also swore they had seen a balloon that should not have been there. Amid much area publicity, a large balloon, carrying an aviator identified in press accounts as Professor King, was scheduled to be launched from the Twin Cities fairgrounds on September 12, 1881. Slightly delayed by wind conditions, the launch took place at 5:40 PM, and the balloon ascended to 4,000 feet (1,219 meters) and drifted four miles until it came down in a cow pasture not far from St. Paul, to the intense disappointment of those who had expected a much longer flight heading points east. Soon recovered, it was secured to trees to keep it earthbound.

Nonetheless, nearly 190 miles (306 kilometers) to the east, at Stevens Point, Wisconsin, observers claimed to have seen a large balloon on two occasions over a six-hour period. It was first sighted at 9:00 PM heading northwest, then again at 3:00 AM sailing eastward.

There was, moreover, a curious sequel. King and a companion attempted a second launch a month later, this time from Chicago. As they sailed in a northwesterly direction over Wisconsin, they lost control of their vessel and fell out of contact, occasioning concerned speculation about their fate. Before the answer was known, a report came out of Fargo, in present-day North Dakota, that a "balloon, probably Professor King's airship," had been seen hovering in the sky on the evening of October 17. It turned out, however, that King's ship was nowhere near Fargo; it had gone down in heavily wooded, thinly populated Barron County, Wisconsin. The two men were unharmed, but it took them two days to find their way to a town and reassure the anxious public that they were all right.

✳

The History and Mystery of Flight in America

The first small-balloon flight, carrying no passengers, took place on June 4, 1783, from Annonay, in the south of France. The following November 21, a balloon launched from Paris carried two men aloft for 25 minutes on a five-mile trip.

America joined the balloon craze on June of the next year. Though he had never personally observed a balloon and was forced to construct his own out of sketchy descriptions he had come upon in his reading, lawyer and saloonkeeper Peter Carnes launched a tethered flight from a park in Baltimore on the fourteenth. He repeated the experiment on the morning of the twenty-fourth, in front of an enthralled crowd, and made several launches lasting into the afternoon. As the last of them was about to ascend, Edward Warren, 13, stepped forward to volunteer to board the "splendid chariot"—a basket attached to the underside of the silk balloon. (Carnes, who weighed 234 pounds, astounding for a time when people were shorter and thinner than they are now, may have judged himself too hefty to do the same himself.) To the crowd's resounding cheers, which he acknowledged with "a significant wave of his hat," he rose into the air with the balloon until Carnes brought it and him back to Earth a few minutes later. On-lookers took up a collection to reward the plucky young man.

Though ballooning—typically practiced as a public spectacle from fairgrounds and other social spaces—was popular in 1800s America, significant advances in aviation overwhelmingly were taking place in Europe, especially in France, England, and Germany. While American inventors did not lack for imagination and ambition, their creations, if they got off the drawing boards, had a way of not abiding long in the air, if they could manage to rise into it, and sometimes took their pilots and crews with them. Around 1850, in England, the first manned glider flew, and on September 24, 1852, French engineer Henri Giffard sailed the first successful dirigible—a lighter-than-air, 144-foot vehicle with a steam engine and three-blade propeller that enabled the pilot to control its movement. Traveling at 17 mph, the airship covered five miles before landing.

In the next years and decades other dirigibles, with greater engine power and the capacity to traverse longer distances, were developed. Not until the very late nineteenth century did America—where dirigibles (also known as airships) were all but unknown until the early twentieth century—take the lead in aviation progress, culminating a few years later with the greatest breakthrough of them all: the flight of the winged, heavier-than-air machine developed by Wilbur and Orville Wright and suc-

(Continued on page 261)

DEMONIC UFOs

The UFO phenomenon became part of American pop culture in the 1950s, when stories like this one from a November 1954 issue of *Fate* were easy to find in magazine stands (*Mary Evans Picture Library*).

Unidentified flying objects—"flying saucers"—came to international attention in 1947, and the sightings continued unabated over the next years. By the 1950s the notion that UFOs might be extraterrestrial spacecraft became widely popular. A minority of hard-core UFO enthusiasts, however, were drawn to more exotic occult readings of the phenomenon.

The early 1950s saw the rise of the contactee movement in southern California. Contactees grafted metaphysical doctrines onto flying saucers. Contact messages, which came via face-to-face meetings, channeling, automatic writing,

dreams, or voices in the head, had unambiguous religious overtones, including prophecies and moral lessons. The Space Brothers recruited contactees and their followers to spread the saucer gospel and to prepare disbelieving humankind for the day the skies will fill with spaceships and extraterrestrials will bring peace and harmony to our galactic backwater.

Early on, however, a few participants in the contactee subculture feared that all was not what it appeared to be. Longtime occultist and newly turned contactee Trevor James Constable warned that some ostensible space beings were really malevolent entities who were lying about their true nature. Noting that several contactees had been led astray, leaving families and jobs at the direction of "unethical invisibles," Constable wrote that "the 'spacemen'" exert "a psychic despotism over innocent and well-meaning people." According to Constable, good and evil entities are locked in battle for the soul of the human race. The evil entities dwell inside an astral shell beneath the earth's surface, allied with near-physical beings based on the moon. They have earthly associates, prominently including advocates of nuclear disarmament. Only atomic bombs can penetrate the astral shell, posing a threat to the astrals' sinister plans.

In the 1960s occult journalist John A. Keel (1930–2009) picked up on Constable's theories (though without crediting him) and painted UFOs and paranormal phenomena as evidence of a demonic invasion. Keel called the demons "ultraterrestrials" but did not hesitate to identify himself as a latter-day demonologist. "The quasi-Angels of Biblical times have become magnificent spacemen," Keel wrote. "The demons, devils, and false angels were recognized as liars and plunderers by early man. These same impostors now appear as long-haired Venusians."

Unlike Constable, who saw at least some UFO entities as kindly intentioned, Keel believed they are uniformly evil. Once upon a time they exerted direct control over the human race when the ruling classes of the world married ultraterrestrials disguised as humans. When democratic movements entered the world, however, and royal dynasties were overthrown, the ultraterrestrials were forced to mount a direct counterattack to restore their domination. They are behind cults, secret societies, and other movements, and under a wide range of guises they have affected the lives of human beings and the course of human destiny. Any human being who deals with them will end up destroyed. "We are biochemical robots helplessly controlled by forces that can scramble our brains, destroy our memories and use us in any way they see fit," Keel thundered. "They have been doing it to us forever."

Similar ideas were beginning to appear in the pages of England's *Flying Saucer Review* (also known as *FSR*), a widely read and influential magazine among the world's ufologists. Editor Charles Bowen had begun to wonder if contactees were having real experiences—heretofore, conservative ufologists had dismissed them as hoaxers or victims of psychiatric disorders—but being misled by a "façade deliberately created by alien entities whose objectives are in no way connected with our welfare." These entities come from "universes parallel with ours but with a different time stream." Though some of the beings are benevolent, most were not, and the bad guys are winning. The magazine's assistant editor, Dan Lloyd, explicitly identified Satan as the moving force behind the UFO phenomenon. Satan wants people to believe that UFOs are of extraterrestrial origin, because that is a materialist concept and materialistic concepts encourage a "one-sided development of man's intellect.... There could be no greater distortion of what is actually happening at the present time in man's relation to the spiritual world than to spread the delusion that physical machines are coming to Earth with physical beings from outer space."

Another forceful, even—as his critics had it—unhinged proponent of demonological ufology was Gordon Creighton, a retired British diplomat long associated with *FSR* and its editor after Charles Bowen stepped down. There is hardly a human misfortune or evil, from wars to street crime to disease epidemics that Creighton does not ascribe to demonic UFO entities, which he calls jinns after traditional Islamic lore. (There are good jinns and bad ones, but demonological ufology is focused exclusively on the latter.) Jinns were behind the making of Steven Spielberg's popular film *E.T.: The*

A scene from the 1982 film *E.T.: The Extraterrestrial*. Former British diplomat Gordon Creighton believed that aliens were in no way as benevolent as depicted in this popular Steven Spielberg movie (*Ronald Grant Archive/Mary Evans Picture Library*).

Extraterrestrial, whose depiction of friendly aliens was calculated to mislead human beings about the true, decidedly unfriendly intentions of the aliens. In Creighton's judgment (and his italics) the movie was "*a subtle way for facilitating a take-over by something out of the Pit.*" The jinns own the earth, treating us as animals from whose gene pool they can borrow as the occasion suits (thus UFO abductions). They are also responsible for the AIDS epidemic. In 1990 he warned that demonic entities were soon to engineer a third world war for their own inscrutable but nefarious purposes.

Though many ufologists saw Creighton's views as extreme and unbelievable, one prominent American abduction investigator, Ann Druffel, not only endorses them but draws on them in her counseling of abductees. Convinced that Creighton's jinn "hypothesis" is a "logical ... answer [to] all the puzzles abducting entities pose," Druffel, a conservative Roman Catholic, proposes techniques of resistance in which prayer figures prominently. The gray aliens often associated with abduction stories "are not a new phenomenon," Druffel writes. "They are an order of creation with the ability to shape-shift and harass human victims for their own playful or malicious motives. They have appeared in various types of garb throughout the centuries." She urges persons suffering alien harassment to call on "angels, saints, and other spiritual personages" who "are available to human beings." The archangel St. Michael, she says, is a particularly effective banisher of demonic UFO entities.

Mainstream Christian denominations have paid relatively little attention to the UFO phenomenon, but some fundamentalist writers have seen UFOs and their occupants as fallen angels— demons, in other words. Besides the inevitable scriptural citations, they cite secular theorists, especially Keel, as authority for such conclusions. Evangelical writer Clifford Wilson expresses sentiments that could easily have been stated by Keel or Creighton: "[A] great pattern of brainwashing is taking place. Are men and women being influenced, even 'possessed,' so that when the signal is given they will be ready to give total allegiance to these beings who will then show themselves as their masters? Is this why there is such greatly increased activity in UFOs, and Ouija boards, Satan worship, séances, and all sorts of dabblings that even a generation ago were regarded as foolish and evil?"

Like Keel and Creighton, evangelicals accept as accounts of actual events fantastic stories of interactions with space people that many ufologists reject as conscious fabrications or as psychological

episodes. For example, Kelly L. Segraves is convinced that channeling entities such as the ubiquitous Ashtar, widely revered in contactee circles as the head of a vast space command here to transform human consciousness, are quite real, serving— beneath their benevolent exteriors—the anti-Christ. Their true purpose is the "massing [of] all of their forces in a great deception to lead as many as possible away from the truth God. These fallen angels are therefore appearing unto man in the guise of visitors from other planets."

Some evangelicals interpret the coming of UFOs with prophesied signs of the end times, while others believe them to be just one more manifestation of Satan's continuing malignant interference in human affairs. Among advocates of the former is a website devoted to the subject. Taking note of abduction stories in which witnesses claim sexual contact with aliens, apparently to create hybrid beings, it declares that UFOs and their occupants are "under the authority of the Prince of the Power of the Air, Prince of the Aerial Host, Lord of those that fly [—] Satan. Jesus warned that one of the signs of the end times was that it would be 'just as it was in the times of Noah'. In Genesis we see the account of non-human intelligent beings 'breeding' with humans, creating hybrids and contributing to the proliferation of evil against God. The messages we see from contact with extraterrestrials and other advanced beings contain claims that *they are the*

Many of those who report being abducted by aliens have said they have been subjected to scientific experiments, some of which involved breeding with the aliens (*Mary Evans Picture Library/Michael Buhler*).

ones who created us, through genetic manipulation."

Further Reading

Alnor, William M. *UFOs in the New Age: Extraterrestrial Messages and the Truth of Scripture.* Grand Rapids, MI: Baker Book House, 1992.

Clarke, David. "Flying Saucers from Hell." *Fortean Times* 211 (2006): 34–38.

James, Trevor [pseudonym of Trevor James Constable]. *They Live in the Sky.* Los Angeles: New Age Publishing Company, 1958.

Keel, John A. *UFOs: Operation Trojan Horse.* New York: G.P. Putnam's Sons, 1970.

Segraves, Kelly L. *Sons of God Return.* New York: Pyramid Books, 1975.

"UFOs, Aliens and Antichrist: The Angelic Conspiracy and End Times Deception."

Early ballooning began in eighteenth-century France before becoming a popular curiosity in the United States (*Mary Evans Picture Library*).

(Continued from page 255)

cessfully flown (for 12 seconds) at Kitty Hawk, North Carolina, on December 17, 1903. From then on, the world and the skies surrounding it would never be the same.

If there is a historians' consensus narrative that follows the course of aviation in the nineteenth century, there is also another story, preserved not in the credible official documents on which much of our understanding of the receding past depends but in yellowed clippings from the often freewheeling, not always trustworthy American newspapers of another era. At least as analogy—a literal reading is an iffier proposition (see below)—these may be thought of as proto-UFO sightings, in other words, reports of craft-like aerial objects that should not have been there, "there" being, usually, the sky but—even more puzzlingly—sometimes the ground.

The sightings of unidentified balloons with which this chapter has opened may or may not be related to the question of mystery airships. We know no more about them than what old press accounts provide. With rare exception the papers are unsatisfactory, but nobody took the effort to interview witnesses in an effort to reconstruct what they were actually seeing, as a modern investigator would do with a UFO report. We have no idea, for example, what was meant when the 1881 claim of a balloon over Fargo was withdrawn. We have only this cryptic press statement: "The rumor that Prof. King's balloon had been seen in this vicinity is entirely unfounded." By that time, the fate of King's balloon was known, and so it was known that it did not sail over Fargo. Therefore, it is unquestionably true that "Prof. King's balloon" could not have been seen. But was another balloon seen?

It is unlikely that we shall ever be able to answer that question, and it is only one of many unanswerable questions. Still, through the fog and mist, the outline of a fantastic alternative-reality aviation history comes mysteriously into view. First, however....

Shapes in the Sky

On December 6, 1887, the *Free Press* of Gouverneur, New York, carried this letter from a correspondent, identified only as G., from the nearby village of Fine:

> Perhaps I might interest some of your readers, if I should tell them of a strange phenomenon I saw at sunset Oct. 24th. I was sitting at a window, looking towards the east, watching the clouds as they rolled up from the west, giving us a clear sunset. At the south the forest sparkled and glistened, as if clad in what looked to me like sparkling silver. I began to look around for the cause; and coming from the north was—what? I can only describe it like this: About midnight between the heavens and Earth, and coming at a rapid rate, was [sic] what looked like silver balls, reminding me of silver coin of all denominations, bright and sparkling, tumbling and rushing through the air going towards the east, and finally disappearing beyond the lower stratus of clouds. Two winds were prevailing at the time. The upper stratus of clouds going towards the east, the lower towards the west, and this bushel of sparkling balls, below the lower clouds, towards the east also. This grand phenomenon was visible about 4 minutes, and was seen by several persons here in town. Can any one tell me[,] from my discription [sic], what it was, and the cause of it? The day had been dark and gloomy.

The modern UFO phenomenon dates from a much-publicized sighting on June 24, 1947, in which private pilot Kenneth Arnold reported nine silvery craft—flying in formation at something like 1,700 miles (2,735 kilometers) per hour—over Mount Rainier, Washington. From his report and the many that followed in the next days and weeks, the phrase "flying saucers" was coined. Skeptical pundits then and since have argued that UFOs are delusions of post-World War II popular culture, false reports driven by images from modern science fiction and aerospace technology. As the report quoted above indicates, however, UFOs in the modern sense were being observed and described long before the concept even existed. Mystery airships were not proto-UFOs because UFOs, whatever they may or may not be, were already present in nineteenth-century skies, suggesting an independent phenomenon with an independent existence that manifests regardless of particular cultural context.

Some other examples:

On an evening in early June 1898, when observers at Chippewa Falls, Wisconsin, watched a strange object in the western sky, one described it as "having the appearance of an illuminated board, its dimensions being about 16 feet [4.9 meters] long by 9 inches [23 centimeters] broad, suspended in mid air." It cast a "lurid, glaring" light which made its presence impossible to overlook, according to the *Centralia* [Wisconsin] *Enterprise and Tribune*, June 11.

IMPOSSIBLE BUT TRUE

On Nov. 12, 1887, the British steamer *Siberian* saw an enormous ball of fire rise from the sea off Cape Race, move against the wind toward the ship, then move away to be lost from sight in five minutes. What was it? Fire does not rise from the sea, it does not move against the wind. Was it really a submersible-aircraft-spaceship the *Siberian* saw?

A November 1947 *Amazing Stories* issue reported on a fireball witnessed in Siberia in 1887 that was much like the one seen by E.W. Campbell and his son in 1898 in Texas (*Mary Evans Picture Library*).

A few months later, at 9:00 on the night of October 3, persons in and around Garland, Texas, saw a "meteor" heading slowly in an easterly direction. It abruptly reversed that direction and moved on a vertical course before breaking into "three distinct bodies, each taking its own course. The first one was a bright red, the second a white light and the third a bright blue. The red and blue lights soon died out, but the white one continued on its way a few seconds, when it burst, emitting a shower of stars, which were extinguished almost immediately."

That same night, at the same time, just a few miles to the south, E.W. Campbell and his 12-year-old son, George, riding along a rural road, were puzzled when everything became illuminated. The source was a big ball of fire descending from the sky. When it got to within three feet (one meter) of the ground, it stopped and hovered for a period of time (unspecified), emitting a buzzing sound all the while. Approximately 10 feet (three meters) in diameter, the object cast so intense a light as to hurt the eyes. It then shot off into the sky and was quickly lost to view.

Both of these reports were carried in a single article in the *Galveston Daily News*, October 6.

HIDDEN REALMS, LOST CIVILIZATIONS, AND BEINGS FROM OTHER WORLDS

Investigating sightings of a "fire ghost"—a luminous aerial object seen in the countryside in the Geneva, Iowa, area—a wealthy farmer named L.H. Spangler loaded a shotgun on the evening of February 12, 1895, and rode his wagon out half a mile from his residence to the place where the phenomenon was being reported. The *Waterloo* [Iowa] *Daily Courier* of four days later gave this account:

> Mr. Spangler saw a huge mass of fire about the size of a sugar barrel hanging in the atmosphere about twenty rods [330 feet, or 100 meters] distant. The immense orb was slowly receding and Spangler whipped up his team until he was within three rods [approximately 50 feet or 15 meters] of the strange object. He then leveled his gun, took good aim and fired both barrels almost simultaneously. There was a loud report and the air was filled with millions of luminous glittering fragments which lighted up the country for miles around…. The fragments began to slowly come together and in a short time had again formed into one large body, which shot straight up into the air and disappeared behind a large black cloud. A long vivid streak of light was left across the sky which gradually faded away. After seeing the last strange phenomenon Mr. Spangler returned to his home, and the "fire ghost mystery" still remains unsolved.

Mystery Airships over North America

Meanwhile….

Officially, there were no airships in Ontario in 1891. But on July 12 a dark structure hovered over a neighborhood in Ottawa. Observed through binoculars, "the object appeared somewhat in the shape of a huge cigar," according to an account in the *Ottawa Free Press,* "at one end of which there appeared to be a revolving fan, while the other end was enlarged, from which a bright light was plainly visible. Lesser lights were visible at intervals in the center." Witnesses thought that the object was much too large and too oddly shaped to be a balloon. It headed northward and was shortly lost to view.

Officially, there were no airships in Texas in 1892. Even so, at 11:00 PM on August 30 residents of Waxahachie's north side heard a voice calling out from the darkness and apparently from above. Rushing to their windows, they saw a strange object, with colored lights attached, passing northwestward at some distance above their rooftops. The voice was presumed to emanate from the flying craft, though the speaker was unseen. "Nobody knows how far it traveled or the nature of its mission," the *Galveston Daily News* remarked in its September 2 edition. "Those who saw it are responsible, truthful people."

At the time such sightings were rare, though if experience is any guide more surely remain to be uncovered as research in period newspaper records continues. By mid-

Not all UFOs look like discs; a number of reports describe cigar-shaped objects in the sky (*Mary Evans Picture Library/GEOS*).

November 1896, however, mystery airships had become so ubiquitous a presence over central and northern California that they soon became a topic of national discussion and wonderment. Though apparently there were unreported and unrecorded sightings in the region from as much as a month earlier, the first to attract wide notice occurred over Sacramento early on the evening of November 17, when a light characterized (in the next day's *Sacramento Evening Bee*) as resembling an "electric arc lamp propelled by some mysterious force was seen by hundreds of people." Some swore they were close enough to hear voices emanating from it. Among the latter group, though, accounts differed. In some reports the voices were arguing about something, in others they were singing in a rousing chorus. In any event, the coverage encouraged residents of Sacramento suburb Oak Park to come forward to claim that the previous evening an object at high altitude had circled the town, trailing smoke.

For the next two weeks sightings, speculation, and excitement ran rampant. As witnesses recounted closer encounters, they usually reported unambiguously airship-like devices. One of the best sightings took place in Oakland, where electrician Case Gilson and three other men observed an airship coming from the southeast and heading north through a clear sky at an estimated 1,000 feet (300 meters), bearing no lights. The *Oakland Tribune* (December 1) quotes Gilson as saying it "looked like a great black cigar with a fishlike tail.... The body was at least 100 feet [30 meters] long and attached to it was a triangular tail, one apex being attached to the main body. The surface of the airship looked as if it were made of aluminum, which exposure to wind and weather had turned dark." Moving at "tremendous speed," it effected a sudden change of direction and shot west across the bay toward San Francisco. It reappeared at 8:30, "when it took about the same direction and disappeared." Percy Drew saw the same or a very similar object over Oakland two nights later, the only difference being that this one carried a red light.

On a smaller scale, the California airship scare presaged the events, prominently including bewildering claims and counterclaims, that would ripple through the North American interior in the spring of the next year. The press reported stories of alleged airship inventors and attributed assertions to attorneys who allegedly represented them. These attorneys had a hard time keeping their stories straight, and the most celebrated supposed inventor—one Elmer H. Benjamin, a dentist from Maine—denied responsibility for the sensational invention. History attests to his truthfulness in this regard. There were also hoaxes (press inventions, tall tales, lighted kites) and misidentifications (usually of Venus and meteors) that would soon become all too familiar in numerous sections of the country.

After the first week of December, the California chapter of the airship scare had closed, though sightings continued sporadically for a few more weeks, almost exclusively in rural areas. Over the winter reports moved eastward into the farmlands and tiny villages of Nebraska (and perhaps elsewhere; at least one published report from Pennsylvania in March has come to light). On February 2, 1897, in a dispatch out of Hastings, the *Omaha Daily Bee* noted that the previous fall, persons in the south-central part of the state had seen a light, which they thought was from an airship, though the few details provided point toward an astronomical explanation. The *Bee* also recorded a sighting from the day before, February 1, of a maneuvering light that flew at a "most remarkable speed."

The first sighting close enough to expose details occurred on the fourth at Inavale, 40 miles (64 kilometers) south of Hastings, when a small band of worshippers leaving a prayer service spotted a light passing through the night sky at a considerable distance. A few minutes later, it returned, this time at a much lower altitude, enabling observers to see a cone-shaped structure some 30 to 40 feet (12 meters) in length, "with a bright headlight and six smaller lights, three on a side, and ... two sets of wings on a side, with a large fan-shaped rudder" (*Bee,* February 6). After a mid-month sighting near Big Springs in western Nebraska, the *Kearney Hub* (February 18) ventured to suggest that the "now famous California airship inventor is in our vicinity."

Reports spilled over into neighboring Kansas that month and grew ever more dramatic until by late March airships allegedly appeared over the state capital in Topeka. On March 29, responding to charges that the "airship" was nothing but Venus, the *Kansas City Star* asserted, "The light seen last night ... was certainly neither a star nor a planet. The light moved parallel with the horizon and with great rapidity.... And then when the strange light was reddest there was Venus, a short distance to the right.... Again, when the midnight watchers caught another glimpse of the light, Venus had long before sunk to rest."

The sightings over the well-populated Midwestern cities of Topeka and Omaha were sufficiently dramatic and credible to go onto the press wires and to show up in newspapers in other states. After that, airships were seen throughout the American interior as well as Texas and the Deep South. (Some evidence, awaiting further research and documentation, hints at sightings in Mexico.) Some representative reports:

Belleville, Kansas, March 26 and 28, evening. "Friday night J.A. Rae, telegraph operator, ... reported that the light hovered over the city three-quarters of an hour and then moved rapidly away. It looked half the size of a locomotive head light and was of a bluish tint. Last night hundreds of Belleville people watched for the light and it appeared about 10 o'clock. This time the light was so strong that it reflected brightly through the windows. At times it would disappear and then in an instant flash out again. While over the town its course was erratic. It remained half an hour and then darted off toward the north and soon disappeared. Several who saw the light through a strong glass say they could distinguish the outlines of an airship" (*Chicago Daily Tribune,* March 29).

Albia, Iowa, April 2, 10:00 PM. "The mysterious airship ... came from the west, and then passed toward the north, moving in an erratic manner. It appeared as a brilliant reddish light, and was seen by many reliable people" (*Iowa State Reporter,* April 8).

Wilmington, North Carolina, April 5, evening. "Hundreds of people were out on the streets and wharves ... looking at a brilliant floating mass in the heavens to the west of the city. It was moving very rapidly, and many persons saw the aerial wonder.... The ship moved to the west at a rapid rate. It seemed to have something like a searchlight, facing earthwards.... The ship appeared to come from the ocean.... Some gentlemen who saw the ship through field glasses inform us they could see wires and ropes of rigging about it. To the naked eye many colored lights were visible. Even those who looked at it without glasses admit of no doubt that it was an airship" (*Wilmington Messenger,* April 6).

Guthrie, Oklahoma, April 7, 11:00 PM. "The attention of Landlord Trumbull of the Arlington hotel was attracted by a dark looking object moving through the air above the city.... Mr. Trumbull called a number of people, who watched the strange shadow object for a long time.... Its outlines were indistinct, but a light was thrown out from the front, and at times there were flashes of light along the sides. It moved swiftly backward and forward, sank almost to the ground just north of the city, and then rose straight into the air at great speed and disappeared" (*Galveston Daily News,* April 8).

Louisville, Kentucky, April 12, early morning. "Augustus Rodgers ... claims it passed over Louisville last night.... Rodgers, who lives two miles south of the city, came out of his cabin an hour before daylight to attend to his stock. There immediately above him at a distance of 400 feet [122 meters], according to his story, was a terrifying and yet a beautiful sight. A huge, oblong shape ... apparently about 40 by 15 feet [12 by 5 meters], brilliantly lighted, for it was yet dark, and flying through the air at a speed of 100 miles [160 kilometers] an hour, met his eyes ... in the form rather of a barge than a ship, with massive proportions and solidarity. Rodgers called to his wife ... and together they watched the strange sight as it disappeared to the southeast. Before it vanished uncouth and enormous shadows flickered from all parts of the ship, and both Rodgers and his wife saw a form, like that of a man, standing at the front of the ship and directing its course" (*Louisville Evening Post*, April 13).

Deadwood, South Dakota, April 12, late evening. "One young man ... distinctly saw queer lights floating in the air above him and the dim outline of a mysterious something sailing over the city. It moved in a leisurely manner and was in sight sailing slowly for at least twenty minutes. The same thing was observed by four other gentlemen, and each gives a different account of its appearance. The gentlemen are personally unacquainted with one another" (*St. Paul Pioneer Press*, April 13).

Deadwood, April 15, evening. "C.A. Peckinpaugh ... and a companion say they saw an air ship alight on Terry Peak. It is said that it was also seen by fifteen or twenty others, some of whom started up to investigate[,] but before they reached it, it rose and flew away. It was cigar-shaped with enormous wings" (*Sioux Falls* [South Dakota] *Argus-Leader*, April 19).

Canton, South Dakota, April 13, evening. "The airship passed high above this city, headed due north. In the light [of] the moon it was plainly seen and appeared as large as a good-sized tent. It had a red light at the head and a green one at its stern. It seemed to be propelled by huge wings or fans, which look like wind mills with the sails placed horizontally, and to rise and fall in the air by changing the angles of the fans. The ship was seen by Mayor Seely, ex-Mayor Laxson, Dr. Lewis, Dr. O'Neil and Colonel Stanley" (*Omaha Daily Bee*, April 15).

Fort Snelling, Minnesota, April 15, evening. "That little community is much exercised over the appearance ... of a phenomenon bearing a red, a white and a blue light, the white being, perhaps, as large as a locomotive headlight, the others somewhat smaller. When first seen the celestial visitor seemed to be, perhaps, 1,500 feet [500 meters] in the air, and was directing its course toward Minneapolis. It followed that direction until it reached a point perhaps two miles northwest of the forest, when it reversed direction, and returning toward the fort, descended earthward. The commandant at the fort sent a guard to meet the visitor, but they were unable to keep close tab on its whereabouts and could not find it" (*St. Paul Pioneer Press*, April 17).

Odd lights were seen at Deadwood, South Dakota, on April 12, 1897, a month when there were numerous reported sightings all over America (*Mary Evans Picture Library*).

Pierre, South Dakota, April 15, evening. "A number of citizens of this city, East Pierre and Fort Pierre are certain they saw the mysterious airship about 9 o'clock last night passing rapidly over toward the west, several hundred feet in the air and traveling at a rapid speed. Most of them only claim to have seen a bright light, resembling a locomotive headlight, but others are just as certain they saw a long dark object, supplied with long arms extended from each side" (*Omaha Bee,* April 17).

Birmingham, Iowa, c. April 16. "William H. Walters, living near this city, is responsible for the statement that he and several others saw an air ship settle down on a meadow a mile from this city. They ran toward it, but when they were within 100 yards [91 meters] it rose into the air. Two men could be seen in the car. The machine was about 100 feet [30 meters] long and 20 feet [6 meters] thick at the center, tapering to a point at each end. When it rose it made a whirring sound like that of a circular saw" (*Syracuse* [New York] *Daily Standard,* April 17).

Derry, Pennsylvania, April 17, evening. "The air ship ... passed here ... according to many prominent persons, who claim to have sighted it. It is cigar-shaped and has red and green lights and a very small center light, white and very brilliant. The ship was headed east, traveling very rapidly and about

500 feet [152 meters] high. A car is hanging about ten feet from the airship entirely enclosed" (*Indiana* [Pennsylvania] *Messenger,* April 21).

North Central Missouri, April 19, late evening. "Near midnight, F.R. Pryor, James Freels and Wm. Barnes saw the much talked of airship, near said F.R. Pryor's residence on Shoal Creek. The ship came from the direction of Chillicothe, and after alighting near Mr. Pryor's residence where it remained for a few minutes seemingly in the interest of generating electricity it again took flight, going in a northwest direction.... It was a monster; the sails or wings being spread as those of a South American Condor, and the head light as dazzling to the eyes as the rays of the noon day sun, while the green and red lights shown [sic] as the lights at a church festival. The ship seemed to move through the air with as much ease and rapidity as the fleet winged carrier pigeon" (*Hamilton* [Missouri] *Farmer's Advocate,* April 28).

Sabinal, Texas, April 20, 2:00 AM. "The famous airship ... was seen directly over this place ... by Charles McClar, night operator of the Southern Pacific company.... He says that the ship was not more than 300 feet [100 meters] above the earth and traveling in a westerly direction... The bottom much resembles the keel of a steamboat. Its passage through the air was accompanied by a strange whirring sound, not unlike the buzzing of an electric battery" (*Galveston Daily News,* April 23).

Columbia Heights, Ohio, April 22, 9:20 AM. "Mrs. Burkhart, who was hanging out clothes, was the first to discover the ship and she pointed it out to Mrs. Case. The son was called and the trio watched it until it disappeared from view. Mrs. Case ... describes [it] as being shaped like a yacht. It carried a small sail and was propelled by a wheel, which Mrs. Case claims was similar to a windmill, which was attached to the rear. This glistened brightly in the sun light as the ship soared by. Bert Case thinks the ship was 1,500 or 2,000 feet [457 or 610 meters] from the earth" (*Massillon* [Ohio] *Independent,* April 22).

District of Columbia, April 23, morning. "The mysterious airship ... came down the Potomac and gradually disappeared from view over the hills of Virginia, sailing southeast. It was plainly seen by the officers and soldiers at Fort Myer, by the attachés of the Analostan Boat Club and by hundreds of other reputable citizens who are willing to make oath that it was the genuine thing. To the naked eye it seemed like an oblong balloon floating upon its side, with a slight pitch in the direction in which it was going. Those who were fortunate enough to have glasses declare that it was a double-barreled arrangement, shaped like a catamaran [boat with two parallel hulls] hanging vertically, rocking from side to side, and often shifting its position as if it was drifting in the atmosphere. Sometimes one of the ends would be toward the observers and then they would see it full broadside. No smoke or smokestack or wings or other means of propulsion could be detected, nothing more than the two cylinder-like objects that were coupled to each other fore and aft" (*Salem* [Ohio] *Daily News*, April 24).

San Antonio, Texas, April 25, 12:00– 1:00 AM. "The airship ... passed over San Antonio.... The course that the bright object took was from northwest almost due east and then south, passing over the city apparently about two miles east of the city hall. The sky was heavily clouded and not a star was visible. This brought out all the stronger the keen white light of the airship head- light, together with the shim- mer that the strong illumina- tion cast about it. It prevented, however, anything like a view of

Bright beams of light emanating from objects in the sky sometimes made it difficult for "airship" witnesses to get a clear view of the phenomena (*iStock*).

the structure itself, but as the strange object wheeled about and came near- er a dozen or more dim lights among them a cluster of green lights on the side of the ship toward the city, and another immense cluster of red lights at the stern, plainly indicated its artificial nature.... The maneuvering of the object in lowering and rising, as well as the arrangement and color of the lights[,] left no doubt but that the object was the airship which has been hovering over the central portion of Texas for the past several days. No stop was made, but an almost southeasterly course was pursued by the ship. The aerial visitor passed out of sight by degrees, the red stern lights growing dimmer and dimmer until they seemed to gradually dissolve into the black- ness of the night" (*San Antonio Daily Express,* April 26).

Cincinnati, Ohio, May 8, 8:00 PM. "What was supposed to be an airship sped across this city from the southeast to the northwest at a great height and with incredible speed. It showed a brilliant light and some who saw it are unable to describe its form; others say it was cigar shaped.... Its speed was not less than 100 miles [160 kilometers] per hour" (*Fort Wayne* [Indiana] *Gazette,* May 9).

Donald Keyhoe's *The Flying Saucers Are Real* (1950) was the first UFO-era book to look back on the mystery airships of the late nineteenth century (*Mary Evans Picture Library*).

✳ *Airships as UFOs?*

Charles Fort (1874–1932) was the first writer to collect airship reports and preserve them between book covers. Though frustrated by the many transparent pranks, hoaxes, and mistaken observations, he thought that beneath all the foolishness, arguable evidence of interplanetary visitation possibly could be discerned. If that were the case, that evidence would emerge less ambiguously in the future. "If, in April, 1897, extra-mundane voyagers did visit the earth," he wrote in *New Lands* (1923), "likely enough they will visit again, and then the alliance against the data [the confusion generated by jokesters and dismissive astronomers] may be guarded against."

In *The Flying Saucers Are Real* (1950), the first book to discuss the airship phenomenon in the context of the then-new UFOs (if not called by that name quite yet), Donald E. Keyhoe set down a sensationalized, misleading account. Its effect, as was surely its intention, was to blur differences between mystery airships and flying saucers. Thus, while the original press accounts clearly reported that the objects sported "large" and "magnificent" wings, Keyhoe wrote that such were "stubby" and "short" in the fashion of those recorded in more recent years, and—not incidentally—more consonant with an extraterrestrial interpretation.

Since then, the mystery-airship question has generated several whole books (both commercially published and privately circulated), chapters in general works on UFOs, and numerous magazine articles, mostly—of course—in the ufological literature. A concentrated effort to unearth accounts from aged newspapers began in the mid–1960s, and even now researchers are finding previously unknown reports. Thomas E. Bullard's massive collection *The Airship File* (1982) is the essential document, but even it does not complete the recovery operation. Countless other stories have been found since then, while surely hundreds more await conscientious researchers.

The first thing that needs to be said is that, with exceedingly rare exception, we are dependent on press accounts for what we "know" of this episode. These accounts—at least those from the American press—are frequently not credible. It took early researchers a while to figure out that in 1897 what passed for journalism would not begin to pass muster today. Some of what saw print was conscious fiction, somebody's idea of a joke, an editor's need to fill space. Other accounts, however, are apparently so accurate that the stimulus for the sighting, usually a planet, a star, a meteor, or a kite, is identifiable simply from what we are told, even if the witness and the reporter represent it as an airship.

The bright planet Venus in the night sky has sometimes been mistaken for an airship (*iStock*).

From these common realizations airship students proceed to differ. Throwing up their hands, some have concluded that a great deal was being made of nothing, that the entire airship affair was newspaper hype and nothing more. However tempting, this is almost certainly not true, since airship sightings were confined neither to America nor to the late nineteenth century; more sober newspaper accounts from Canada, New Zealand, Australia, and the British Isles from the mystery-airship era attest to sightings of phenomena strikingly comparable to those recounted in the more matter-of-fact American stories. Something was happening.

A literal, uncritical reading would lead one to believe that various secret inventors, apparently independently, had mastered powered flight and were soon to announce their marvelous constructions to the world and to the patent office. The early history of aviation is well known and firmly documented, and—as we have seen—it does not include records of flights—and innumerable ones at that—over North America in 1897.[1] The names of alleged aeronauts cited in newspaper stories, recounting alleged encounters with the crews, do not match the names of real persons.

A few of the stories reflect a secondary current of speculation: that the pilots of the airships were Martians. (In those days, in the middle of the frenzy about alleged canals on the Red Planet, nearly all hypothetical extraterrestrials were presumed to be

Martians.) Some of the tales have been conclusively exposed as hoaxes, and others have the appearance of thinly—or not so thinly—veiled yarns.[2]

So if they weren't terrestrial aircraft or extraterrestrial spacecraft, what were the airships? Ufological theorists John Keel and Jacques Vallee have laid out interpretations that, while not exactly identical (Keel's leaning more toward the openly demonological), drew on the explicitly supernatural, speculating that shape-shifting entities from other realities were posing as late-nineteenth-century American aeronauts.

A more conservative interpretation holds that the mystery airships, more apparent than real, were like modern UFOs, except misinterpreted by witnesses viewing them through their particular cultural lens or carelessly reported in the press. Sightings were overwhelmingly nocturnal, and many were of lights that, it was presumed, were attached to dirigible-like structures whose shadowy shapes witnesses may or may not have glimpsed. Some post-1947 reports describe generally dirigible-like forms (and for various reasons are unlikely to be of *actual* dirigibles). Moreover, the rare surviving testimony of turn-of-the-last century witnesses—recovered, admittedly, decades after the fact—seems consistent with that analysis.

✳

A Landing in Texas

The mystery airships of a century or more ago may be a prime example of the experience-anomaly phenomenon, there for the duration of a sighting, gone forever afterwards. Perhaps more revelatory than reports of distant craft are the landing and contact stories in April 1897, which on their face appear neither more nor less credible than their UFO-era correlates, though from this distance it may be all but impossible to prove one thing or another with anything like certainty. Nonetheless, one such story from Texas is particularly intriguing.

Late on the evening of April 19, J.R. Ligon, agent for a Texas brewing company, and his son Charley, having just returned to their rural home near Beaumont, were unhitching the horses when they noticed lights in a nearby pasture. They walked the few hundred yards to the site, where they allegedly found "four men moving around a large dark object" that proved to be a landed airship estimated to be 180 feet (60 meters) long and 20 feet (six meters) wide, with four large wings, two on either side; propellers were attached to the bow and stern. The aeronauts indicated that they needed water. Ligon is quoted in the *Houston Daily Post* (April 21) as saying, "They came to my house, each bringing two buckets." The only crew member to provide information, and then only when asked, identified himself as Wilson. He said he and his companions had flown their machine to the Gulf of Mexico and were returning it to Iowa, where they came from and where the craft had been constructed.

On April 25, the *New Orleans Daily Picayune* carried an interview with a man identified as Rabbi A. Levy, who was visiting the city to attend his niece's wedding. Levy, said to be a Beaumont resident, told the reporter that on a recent night, having heard of an airship landing on a farm two miles from town, he rushed to the site. In the darkness he glimpsed the outline of an airship—in his judgment something like 150 feet (46 meters) in length, with large wings. Levy said, "I spoke to one of the men when he went into the farmer's house, and shook hands with him.... Yes, he did say where it was built, but I can't remember the name of the place, or the name of the inventor. He said that they had been traveling a great deal.... I was so dumbfounded that I could not frame an intelligent question to ask."

It is often difficult, even impossible, to establish that the alleged witnesses to these sorts of fantastic claims were real people, much less that they were credible individuals. In this instance, contemporary press, census, tax, and other records have established conclusively that J.R. Ligon (who apparently died c. 1899) lived in Beaumont. Moreover, two subsequent items in the *Houston Post* attest to his continuing association with the airship encounter. On June 20, 1897, the newspaper noted that Ligon planned to participate in a Beaumont trade show on July 3 "by exhibiting an airship.... True, this will not be the same flying machine that Mr. Ligon saw but it will be a fair simile of that remarkable vessel and will be complete in every detail. At the grounds the ship will be placed on exhibition and no charge will be made for examination of the plans of construction of the method of operation." The *Post*'s July 4 issue listed the floats that had participated in a big parade associated with the show. One is "Ligon's airship, poised over twenty little girls singing National airs." It must have been quite a sight.

The Ligon family had long been established in Beaumont and nearby communities. A Joseph Ligon (apparently not J.R.) lived in Beaumont in 1897. Charles J. Ligon, born around 1875, is noted as living in Ellis, Texas, an apparently no-longer-extant community, though there is an Ellis County now part of the Dallas-Fort Worth metroplex. Marine Corps Maj. Charles Ligon of Beaumont, obviously not the Charley in the story but perhaps a relative and namesake, was killed in Vietnam in 1967. At least one J.R. Ligon (who did not respond to an inquiry) currently resides in Texas.

There is no question about the presence of a Rabbi A. Levy in Beaumont in 1897. Beaumont historian and newspaper columnist W.T. Block has written of the city's small but thriving Jewish community, dating from the 1870s. In September 1895, Temple Emanuel was established, and its members "immediately engaged Dr. Aaron Levy as the city's first resident rabbi.... In 1901, Dr. Levy left for a new assignment."[3] Block notes that during his stay in Beaumont "Rabbi Levy, as the voice of the congregation, plunged headlong into community affairs.... In September, 1896, he won much acclaim from Christians for an eloquent address at the opera house, entitled 'The Jews versus Christians.' He also contributed many newspaper articles and taught a school."

Sadly, the Beaumont newspapers of the period, which would have been enormously useful in sorting out this curious business, have been only spottily preserved. (Probably, it bears noting, Ligon's original story was published there on April 20. Whether it was the same as or different from the one the *Houston Post* printed the next day is at present undeterminable.) Nonetheless, references to the rabbi, all flattering, can be found in

(Continued on page 278)

MAGONIA

Ufologist Jacques Vallee calls Magonia "a sort of parallel universe, which coexists with our own. It is made visible and tangible only to selected people." It is a reflecting realm in which those who experience it see what they expect to see—in other words, whatever the particular society in which they live imagines a supernatural encounter to be. Thus, rural Celtic peoples meet fairies and our own civilization reports technologically sophisticated extraterrestrials. Magonia is another catch-all phrase for what some call the Goblin Universe.

Vallee outlined his ideas in an influential book titled *Passport to Magonia*, which examines what the author maintains are the threads that connect fairy lore, demonology, religious visions, and occult entities to UFO beings. In his view:

> When the underlying archetypes are extracted from these [UFO-derived] rumors, the saucer myth is seen to coincide to a remarkable degree with the fairy-faith of Celtic countries, the observations of the scholars of past ages, and the widespread belief among all people concerning entities whose physical and psychological descriptions place them in the same category as the present-day ufonauts.... The mechanism of the apparitions, in legendary, historical, and modern times, is

standard and follows the model of religious miracles.

Vallee does not deduce from this all such phenomena are merely illusory. He argues that a purposeful intelligence lies behind them, but that the intelligence is elusive and incomprehensible. But not all who subsequently grappled with comparable concepts would agree. For example, the longstanding London-based UFO journal *Magonia* holds that such phenomena are cultural and psychological constructs with only purely human reference points.

The term came into ufology via an article in the May/June 1964 issue of England's *Flying Saucer Review*, where W.R. Drake mentioned a ninth-century French reference to a "ship in the clouds" that arrived from a place called Magonia. The full account, not reproduced in Drake's brief account (which removes details uncongenial to a ufological interpretation), is from a manuscript written in 833 C.E. by Agobard (779–840), the archbishop of Lyons. Translated from Latin, the title is "Book against False Opinions Concerning Hail and Thunder." It is essentially a long condemnation of folk beliefs that Agobard viewed as contrary to Christian doctrine, among them the "mad and blind" notion of a "certain region called Magonia, from which ships, navigating on clouds, set sail to transport back to this same region the fruits of the earth ruined by hail and destroyed by the storm."

On one occasion, Agobard notes, "senseless fools" held in captivity "three men and one woman who they said had fallen from these ships." These unfortunates were trotted out in front of a mob, which would have stoned them to death if the archbishop had not intervened to save them. He persuaded the angry crowd that the charges were ridiculous. "The truth finally triumphed," he recalled.

In UFO literature, taking off from Drake and Vallee, the incident has been characterized as a medieval encounter in which the four would-be victims are either extraterrestrials or escaped abductees. In some mangled versions the four are killed. The legend has been variously interpreted over the centuries of its recycling in print.

In a comprehensive analysis, however, Jean-Louis Brodu rejects ufological interpretations as anachronistic, urging a reading that makes sense in the context of its time and place. In the ninth century it was believed that the earth was flat and that ships—sailing ships—floated through cloud oceans. "Magonia" may be a corruption of "Magonianus," meaning "from Port-Mahon," then a flourishing harbor on the Balearic island of Minorca. Folklorist Miceal Ross, on the other hand, notes the medieval belief that the ocean is curved "somewhat like a Moëbius strip. This latter curiosity resembles the fanbelt of a car, except that it has twists in it

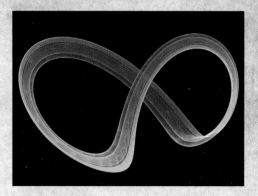

In medieval times many thought the oceans were curved like a Moëbius strip (*BigStock*).

which impart to it the property that a resolute movement forward from any point inside the lower belt will bring the traveler over the starting point outside the belt and ultimately back to the original position. Put on a cosmic scale, ships sailing westward before the European discovery of America could, by this process, it was believed, 'shoot the gulf' and sail across the sky."

Further Reading

Brodu, Jean-Louis. "Magonia: A Re-evaluation." In Steve Moore, ed. *Journal of Fortean Studies: Volume 2*, 198–215. London: John Brown Publishing, 1995.

Ross, Miceal. "Anchors in a Three-Decker World." *Folklore* 109 (1998): 63–75.

Vallee, Jacques. *Passport to Magonia: From Folklore to Flying Saucers*. Chicago: Henry Regnery Company, 1969.

(Continued from page 275)

the *Galveston Daily News,* for example this: "Rabbi Levy has won many friends during his stay in Beaumont" (November 30, 1896). (Galveston is just to the southwest of Beaumont in the far east-central part of the state.) Interestingly, each press mention of him is consistent with the *Picayune*'s in identifying him as "Rabbi A. Levy."

The significance of Levy's testimony was not lost upon the *New York Times.* "The story about an airship will not down," an editorial writer remarked in the April 28, 1897, issue, "if there is any confidence to be placed in the evidences of witnesses, whose trustworthiness on other subjects would not be doubted. The *New Orleans Times Picayune* has been interviewing Rabbi A. Levy of Beaumont, Texas, and quotes him as declaring, with all the solemnity a ministerial position and unimpeachable character will give, that he has himself seen the sky boat close at hand and has conversed with its passengers. Levy would have been a mature 49 years old at the time.

Wilson Redux

The Ligon claim of an encounter with an aeronaut named Wilson does not stand alone. It is one of several recounted in Texas newspapers that April of 1897. Wilson's name is not mentioned specifically in all of them, but in those instances details within the accounts link them to others in which the name appears.

For example, in a letter published in the *Dallas Morning News* for April 19, C.G. Williams of Greenville wrote that around midnight on the sixteenth, as he was out for a late-night stroll two miles south of town, he encountered an "immense cigar-shaped vessel" on the ground. He saw three men step out of the ship. While two engaged in what looked like repairs, the third approached Williams to ask if he would mail some letters but promise to keep names and addresses secret. Williams, a former newspaper reporter, took notes during the conversation that followed, recording that "electricity" powered the airship, which the speaker said he had constructed after years of labor "at a little town in the interior of New York state." A few minutes later, the crew reentered the craft, and Williams went into Greenville to put the letters into the post.[4]

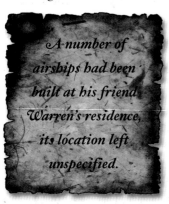

A number of airships had been built at his friend Warren's residence, its location left unspecified.

According to another letter, this one printed in the *Morning News*'s May 16 issue, an aeronaut named Wilson ("the owner") and three crew members (identified as Scott Warren, Mr. Waters, and an unnamed "Mexican or Spaniard") landed in an airship near Lake Charles, Louisiana, at noon on April 19 (the same date as Ligon's encounter).[5] Allegedly, the letter was composed the next day by an unnamed young man, who sent it to his friend D.H. Tucker. Passing in the sky half a mile away, so the letter related, the airship had let loose with an "unearthly whistle" that caused the anonymous informant to be tossed from his buggy. The ship then landed, and the occupants rushed over to inquire about his well-being.

In the course of the ensuing conversation, Wilson replied that the ship was propelled by a gas after the witness asked him if electricity powered the craft. "I learned," the letter asserted, "that Mr. Wilson (though I doubt if that is his correct name) formerly lived in Fort Worth, but I do not remember to have ever seen him. He is apparently a young man and has the typical face of a genius or an inventor" (whatever that means). A number of airships had been built at his friend Warren's residence, its location left unspecified. One day soon, Wilson hoped, he would be able, with proper financing, to establish a "line of air ships to be operated between New York and San Francisco and other points."

Tucker, who had given the Dallas paper the report, claimed in a note that the young witness was no longer living, having perished in a Grenada, Mississippi, flood since writing it. (A massive flood engulfed Mississippi from early April into the next month.) He does not refer, as he might have, to Ligon's story, which the Lake Charles tale both confirms and contradicts. Fort Worth as Wilson's residence, however, would come up in other newspapers in distant south Texas, as we shall see.

At 10:00 PM on April 20, at the town of Uvalde—300 miles (483 kilometers) southwest of Beaumont as the airship flies—Uvalde County Sheriff H.W. Baylor, a hard-bitten, longtime lawman and a well-known figure in south Texas, noticed a bright light and voices coming from the alley behind his house. On investigation he was surprised to see a landed airship, with large finlike wings and three crew members. One introduced himself as Wilson, adding that he was a native of Goshen, New York.[6] In 1877, he went on to say, he had lived in Fort Worth, where he befriended former Zavala County Sheriff C.C. Akers. (Zavala County borders Uvalde County to the south.) Told that Capt. Akers was now a customs officer in Eagle Pass (along the border with Mexico in Maverick County, directly west of Zavala, immediately southwest of Uvalde) but frequent visited Uvalde, Wilson asked to be remembered to Akers. After Wilson and his crew drew water from Baylor's hydrant, they boarded the ship, which then sped north in the general direction of San Antonio. County Clerk Henry J. Bowles, who lived just north of Baylor, witnessed the ship's departure.

"Mr. Baylor is thoroughly reliable, and his statement is undoubtedly true," the *Galveston Daily News* affirmed in its April 23 edition. "His description of the ship does not differ materially from that given by Mr. J.R. Ligon of Beaumont and the gentleman who saw it at Greenville."

The *Daily News,* however, did not leave it at that. It sought out Capt. Akers and secured this statement from him, published in its April 28 issue:

> I can say that while living in Fort Worth in '76 and '77 I was well acquainted with a man by the name of Wilson from New York state and was on very friendly terms with him. He was of a mechanical turn of mind and was then working on aerial navigation and something that would astonish the world. He was a finely educated man, then about 24 years of age, and seemed to

have money with which to prosecute his investigations, devoting his whole time to them. From conversations we had while in Fort Worth, I think that Mr. Wilson, having succeeded in constructing a practical airship, would probably hunt me up to show me that he was not so wild in his claims as I then supposed.

I will say further that I have known Sheriff Baylor many years and know that any statement he may make can be relied on as exactly correct.

As his eyes swept the southwestern sky, he saw a brilliant, multi-colored light moving rapidly in his direction.

At midnight on April 22, as a *Houston Daily Post* story had it (April 26), a "whirring noise" awoke farmer Frank Nichols, who lived two miles east of the tiny settlement of Josserand, approximately 75 miles (121 kilometers) northwest of Beaumont. Through his window he observed a large, well-lit airship landed in his cornfield. Throwing on some clothes, he stepped outside and started toward the ship, but before he got there, he encountered two bucket-bearing men who requested permission to draw water from his well. In return for his permission, the men allowed Nichols to examine the vessel, which carried a six- to eight-man crew and employed "highly condensed electricity" as its motive power. One member told the farmer that five airships had been constructed in a village in Iowa and that a big stock company would build more so that airship travel would be common within the year.

In a letter printed in the April 30 issue of the same newspaper, H.C. Legrone[7] of Deadwood (130 miles [209 kilometers]) directly north of Beaumont and now essentially defunct) recounted an alleged encounter that took place either on or about the evening of April 28. It should be noted that Legrone was the town's leading citizen. The village (originally called Linus) began with a homestead built and run by Adam Legrone, H.C.'s father. Deadwood's nucleus and economic foundation were the mill and gin that H.C. Legrone built. He was also the town's first postmaster.

As he would tell the story, around 8:00 PM, hearing sounds from his horses, Legrone stepped outside to investigate what the problem was. As his eyes swept the southwestern sky, he saw a brilliant, multi-colored light moving rapidly in his direction. Soon it slowed, then stopped, hovering for a few minutes before alighting on a field nearby. As he hastened to the site, Legrone wondered if this was the airship that had everyone talking. Its five-man crew stood outside. Two carried rubber bags 100 yards (91 meters) to Legrone's well, from which they extracted water, while he spoke with the other three.

They informed me that this was one of five ships that had been traveling the country over recently; and that this individual ship was the same one recently landed near Beaumont, in the State, after having traveled pretty well all over the Northwest. They stated that these ships were put up in an interior town in Illinois. They were rather reticent about giving out information in regards to the ship, manufacture, etc., since they had not yet secured everything by patent, but stated they would soon be secure in this, and expected to establish a factory in St. Louis at an early day and would at once enter into active competition with the railroad for passenger traffic, especially in transcontinental travel. They stated that they could shorten time from Atlantic to Pacific two to three days.

Wilson's name is evoked in the *San Antonio Daily Express* on April 26, and for the first time, he gets a first name. Citing no source, an article about a recent local airship sighting states, "The inventors are Hiram Wilson, a native of New York and son of Willard H. Wilson, assistant master mechanic of the New York Central Railroad, and a young engineer, C. J. Walsh of San Francisco." Allegedly, the airship was the product of several years' labor, with the parts shipped to the Bay Area from various parts of the country. Initial experiments were conducted in California and Utah. "It is believed," the article concludes, "that the present trip of the machine is for further experimental purposes."

The only period airship patents filed were by C.A. Smith of San Francisco (August 11, 1896) and by Henry Heintz of Elkton, South Dakota (April 20, 1897). Neither machine ever flew, though one turn-of-the-last-century witness claimed to have witnessed a test flight of Heintz's machine: "The inventor [Heintz] tried out the machine in front of the blacksmith shop and was the pilot. The machine actually got up about eight feet [2.4 meters] or so, then plopped to the ground."[8]

In spite of efforts, no Hiram Wilson has ever been established in nineteenth-century Goshen, New York. Except for the *Daily Express* claim, however, Wilson apparently lost his first name sometime between 1877 and 1897. A search of the 1877 Fort Worth directory yields seven Wilsons, none beginning with Hiram. The occupations of four are listed (blacksmith, cook, shoemaker, grocer); none is consistent with Akers' assertion that his friend Wilson was of sufficient means to pursue his aviation interests full-time. The others are R.L. Wilson, C.C. Wilson, and W.P. Wilson. Presumably, Akers was not lying when he claimed to have known a Mr. Wilson in Fort Worth in the latter 1870s, but just who he was remains unknown. Because would-be airship inventors were ubiquitous in America in those days, his interest in flight technology hardly makes him someone special.

It is certain, however, that nobody named Wilson—at least in any event-level-reality sense—was flying around Texas and Louisiana in the spring of 1897. And we will never know why the phantom Wilson in 1897 knew of the real-life Wilson's friendship with Akers two decades earlier—unless this was all a big elaborate but purposeless hoax involving a web of conspirators conducting intrigue over nothing of consequence and placing their well-earned public reputations at risk.

Furthermore, even if that were the case, why didn't the conspirators get their stories entirely straight? Possibly, if someone had done a real investigation of these matters long ago, when the informants were still alive, we might have some answers. Or possibly not. Oddly and frustratingly, the core details both conform and conflict:

HIDDEN REALMS, LOST CIVILIZATIONS, AND BEINGS FROM OTHER WORLDS **[281]**

Williams: three crew members; ship "built at a little town in the interior of New York state"; Fort Worth and Wilson's name not mentioned.

Tucker's friend: four crew members; ship "built ... at different places"; Fort Worth and Wilson mentioned.

Ligon: four crew members; ship one of five built in small Iowa town; Wilson, but not Fort Worth, mentioned.

Baylor: three crew members; Fort Worth and Wilson mentioned.

Nichols: six to eight crew members; ship one of five built in Iowa; Wilson and Forth Worth unmentioned.

Legrone: five crew members; one of five ships "put up in an interior town in Illinois"; Wilson and Fort Worth unmentioned, but Beaumont landing is cited.

ey rode another half mile before their horses refused to continue. As they stood there, Sumpter and McLemore noticed "two persons moving around with lights"....

Perhaps the differences are more apparent than real. The argument might run like this: Not all of the witnesses saw all of the crew members, just those who stepped outside or who otherwise chose to reveal themselves. Perhaps Legrone's memory or hearing was imperfect; the aeronauts told him Iowa, but he heard Illinois—two distant but adjoining Midwestern states, both starting with "I," probably indistinguishable in this Texan's mind. Maybe one of the crew members told him he was from "a little town in the interior of New York state," not that he built airships there. Since—literally—all we know is what we read in the papers, such rationalizations are necessarily speculative and neither provable nor disprovable.

✳

A Landing in Arkansas

As reported in the *Helena Weekly World,* on May 13, 1874, as well as other state newspapers, Constable John J. Sumpter, Jr.[9], and Deputy Sheriff John McLemore, working out of Hot Springs, Arkansas, were riding north of the city late on the evening of May 6, pursuing fugitives. When they spotted a brilliant light moving through the sky, they kept their silence, fearing that their voices could be overheard. The light vanished suddenly, and the two resumed their search for another four or five miles. Now the luminous object reappeared, descending behind a hill.

They rode another half mile before their horses refused to continue. As they stood there, Sumpter and McLemore noticed "two persons moving around with lights" about 100 yards (91 meters) ahead. They drew their rifles, dismounted, and challenged the strangers.

A man with a long dark beard came forth with a lantern in his hand, and on being informed who we were proceeded to tell us that he and the others — a young man and a woman — were traveling through the country in an airship. We could plainly distinguish the outlines of the vessel, which was cigar-shaped and about sixty feet [18 meters] long, and looking just like the cuts that have appeared in the papers recently. It was dark and raining and the young man was filling a big sack with water about thirty yards [27.4 meters] away and the woman was particular to keep back in the dark. She was holding an umbrella over her head. The man with the whiskers invited us to take a ride, saying that he could take us where it was not raining. We told him we believed we preferred to get wet.

A short conversation ensued, during which the old man related that he and his associates were working their way to Nashville but would take their time so that they could tour the country. The officers, in a hurry to resume their search, left soon. When they returned to the scene empty-handed 40 minutes later, the airship was gone.

This, in any event, was the account they gave in a sworn statement before Justice of the Peace C.G. Bush on May 8. The *Fort Smith Daily News Record* remarked that in the face of ridicule the officers "most seriously maintain that it is absolutely true, and their earnestness is puzzling many who ... see that the men are not jesting." The *Arkansas Gazette* affirmed their "undoubted integrity."

Many comparable stories published in the 1897 press are not credible on textual evidence alone. Like the tall tales that would load the classic contactee literature more than half a century later, the aeronauts are quoted *verbatim* in lengthy discourse, as if the alleged witness were taking detailed notes (though such conscientious record-keeping is, of course, unmentioned) so as not to miss a word. The nonsensical content is a lesser consideration. Even apparently sincere claimants to extraordinary beings and entities describe exchanges that do not make a whole lot of sense; those claimants, however, don't profess to repeat the exact words. Only fiction writers and liars do that.

Sumpter and McLemore, who only paraphrased what the old man reportedly told them, did not provide suspiciously excessive detail. Clearly, as other Arkansas newspapers indicate, they were known to people who lived in their jurisdiction. C.G. Bush was a Clark County court officer during the period in question. Hot Springs is located in Garland County, just north of Clark, in the west-central part of the state.

This conclusion seems, if unsatisfactory, inescapable: Craft-like structures were being perceived in the sky and, more rarely, on the ground. They were not UFOs as we understand them, though UFOs in our sense were being recorded at assorted times and places in nineteenth-century America. The mystery airships were a profoundly anomalous experience phenomenon, its content supplied by images from the experiencers' culture, just as in traditional societies vivid experiences of supernatural entities (gods, fairies, monsters) take their shape from prevailing beliefs about otherworldly encounters.

It is likely, in other words, that if mystery airships are not poorly described UFOs, they are something almost infinitely stranger.[10] To all available appearances, the airship sightings and related experiences of the latter 1800s are not just unexplained but inexplicable—an impenetrable enigma, a shadow fallen on history, its source invisible to science and understanding, vanished but for the testimony of the long dead.

Further Reading:

Bullard, Thomas E., ed. *The Airship File: A Collection of Texts Concerning Phantom Airships and Other UFOs, Gathered from Newspapers and Periodicals Mostly during the Hundred Years Prior to Kenneth Arnold's Sighting.* Bloomington, IN: privately printed, 1982.

Chariton, Wallace O. *The Great Texas Airship Mystery.* Plano, TX: Wordware Publishing, 1991.

Clark, Jerome. "Airship Sightings in the Nineteenth Century," 44–63. In *The UFO Encyclopedia: The Phenomenon from the Beginning.* Second edition. Detroit, MI: Omnigraphics, 1998.

Cohen, Daniel. *The Great Airship Mystery: A UFO of the 1890s.* New York: Dodd, Mead and Company, 1981.

Eberhart, George M. "The Ohio Airship Story." *Pursuit* 10,1 (Winter 1977): 2–8.

Evans, Hilary, and Robert E. Bartholomew. "Great American Airship Wave: United States, 1896–97," 214–224. In *Outbreak! The Encyclopedia of Extraordinary Social Behavior.* San Antonio and New York: Anomalist Books, 2009.

Fort, Charles. *The Books of Charles Fort.* New York: Henry Holt and Company, 1941.

Welsch, Roger L. "'This Mysterious Light Called an Airship,' Nebraska 'Saucer' Sightings, 1897." *Nebraska History* 60, 1 (Spring 1979): 92–113.

End Notes

PART ONE: EARTH'S SECRET PLACES

Lemurian Mountain: Outpost of the Lost Continentals

1. Comte de Saint Germain (c. 1710–c. 1780) was a real historical figure, a man of murky origins known in the European courts of his time. Prone to self-mystification and a charlatan's narcissism, he claimed to be an alchemist and hinted that he was an immortal being. More prosaically, he may have been a French spy. He was almost certainly some species of confidence artist. In the enormously influential mystical school known as Theosophy, invented by Madame Helena Pretrovna Blavatsky (1831–1891), Saint Germain is identified as a Tibetan Master. Occultists have also pegged him as a (pre-AMORC) Rosicrucian.

2. Nom de plume of the late Jim Keith, author of books advocating various conspiracy theories and alternative realities.

Cities of the Poles: Voyages by Exclamation Point

1. One woman wrote Palmer that in 1929 she had seen a newsreel, narrated by Byrd himself, recalling his trip over the North Pole. Footage showed "a warm water lake surrounded by conifers, with a large animal moving about among the trees, and what Byrd described as a mountain of coal, sparkling with diamonds." Unsurprisingly, no evidence that such a newsreel ever existed has come to light.

The Living Hell: The Demons beneath Us

1. In the early 1970s, not long before he died, Shaver had a different story about his introduction to the reality of a hidden race of earthbound entities. While employed as a fisherman in Delaware Bay, he "noticed that the clouds were doing paintings," as he related to interviewer Gene Steinberg, "and somebody was painting on the clouds with some apparatus, and I could talk to them, and I did talk to them ... mentally. And over a period of time, a whole summer and fall, I got quite well acquainted with the people of the underworld, just by talking to them with cloud pictures and mental voices."

2. In *Underground Alien Bases* (1990) "Commander X" (pseudonym of the late Jim Keith) informs us that Mount Lassen "is a portal to a sizeable underground city, which includes

a UFO base that has been taken over in the past by the greys, but is now back in the hands of the Ashtar Command [an interstellar military alliance], who are using the base to operate a vast command post from which they can launch their disc-shaped vehicles into the air at a moment's notice. Several individuals have apparently made it to the outermost fringes of this city, but only one or two that I know of have actually been to the base inside Mount Lassen. On warm summer evenings when the midnight sky is clear, I'm told that brilliant 'orange fireballs' can often be seen streaming in and out of the peaks of Lassen as the saucers venture to and fro from the underground home port."

3. This part of the story is reminiscent of accounts from older traditions, in which a captive of the fairies reappears—almost always in some supernatural fashion—to plead for rescue from a friend or family member. In 1692 fairy lore collector Robert Kirk died suddenly near the Fairy Knowe of Aberfoyle, Scotland. Locals believed the fairies were responsible because the Rev. Kirk had betrayed their secrets. A subsequent legend attested that an apparitional Kirk appeared to a relative, directing him to contact a cousin, Graham of Duchray, with instructions on how the reverend could be saved from confinement in fairyland. When Kirk's ghost appeared in front of Graham, however, the witness was so unnerved that he failed to do what he was supposed to do—namely, throw a knife over Kirk's head—that he was lost forever.

PART THREE:
BETWEEN THIS WORLD AND THE OTHERWORLD

The Road to Fair Elfland: Fairies Experienced

1. An elderly woman identified as Mrs. Sheridan told Lady Gregory of her visits to Elfland: "The others [a euphemism for fairies] had striped clothes of all colors" (*Visions and Beliefs in the West of Ireland,* 1920).

2. For reasons of space and concision, this chapter draws mostly, albeit not quite exclusively, on British Isles fairy traditions. Of other traditions, folklorist Stewart F. Sanderson has written, "There appears to be no country in the world where fairies by one name or another are not found, no traditional society, whatever its cultural patterns or historical development, where some such creatures do not figure in folk belief. Yet there is no clear and specific agreement in the testimony of tradition as to who or what the fairies are, nor even on their general characteristics in different parts of the world." Douglas Hyde, who studied Irish otherworld beliefs in the late nineteenth and early twentieth centuries, observed that even within that country, "different parts of the Irish soil cherish different bodies of supernatural beings. The North of Ireland believes in beings unknown in the South, and North-East Leinster has spirits unknown to the West." Yet, he added, "Of course there is nothing inherently impossible in all these shapes existing any more than in one of them existing, but they all seem to me to rest upon the same kind of testimony, stronger in the case of some, less strong than in the case of others, and it is as well to point out this clearly."

3. The Queen reappears in a nineteenth-century account represented as a direct experience. In an 1868 issue of *Notes and Queries,* a correspondent cited the testimony of a "clergyman of the Church of England, and a graduate of the University of Oxford, well known to the writer.... He firmly believed in fairies; indeed he could not well do otherwise, for

he assured me that with his own eyes he had seen the Queen of the Fairies and all of her court pass before him through a field and pass over a stile. They were all dressed in green, and of the traditional size—the common people being something better than half a foot in height, the queen being taller. I questioned and cross-questioned him about his health before and after this vision, but I could not shake him in the least. He was a sober, thrifty, unimaginative man, and I have known no one less likely to indulge in any freaks of fancy."

4. On the other hand, the Rev. Kirk wrote in the late seventeenth century that fairy folk are susceptible to "envy, spite, hypocrisy, and dissimulation," though largely innocent of cursing and drunkenness. Over the centuries the Welsh fairies apparently lost their noble character. At least by the nineteenth century, according to John Rhys (*Celtic Folklore: Welsh and Manx,* 1901), they were judged to be "of a thieving nature."

5. As the late Katharine Briggs, a world-class authority on the subject, wrote in 1976, "However often they may be reported as gone, the fairies will linger. In Ireland the fairy beliefs are still part of the normal texture of life; in the Highlands and Islands the traditions continue. Not only in the Celtic areas, but all over England scattered fairy anecdotes are always turning up. Like the chorus of policemen in *The Pirates of Penzance,* they say, 'We go, we go,' but they don't go."

6. On their celebrated Corps of Discovery exploration of President Jefferson's Louisiana Purchase, Meriwether Lewis and William Clark learned of fierce "little people" said to menace anyone who threatened their domain (a hill six miles north of present-day Vermillion, South Dakota, preserved as Spirit Mound Historic Prairie). "It is supposed to be the residence of devils," Clark recorded. "They are in human form with remarkable large heads and about 18 inches high. They are very watchful and armed with arrows." Members of the Sioux, Omaha, and Otoe tribes shared an unshakable conviction of their reality and independently conveyed as much to the expedition. On the sweltering day of August 25, 1804, Lewis, Clark, and 10 of their fellows managed with difficulty to complete a four-hour trek to the site, where they spotted masses of bison and birds and an impressive expanse of prairie, but no little people.

Ghost Riders in the Sky: Spectral Armies on the March

1. Translation courtesy of Yannis Deliyannis.

2. *Religion and the Decline of Magic.* New York: Charles Scribner's Sons, 1972, p. 89.

3. Cited by Carolly Erickson, *The Medieval Vision: Essays in History and Perception.* New York: Oxford University Press, 1976, p. 31.

4. See Vladimir Jankovic, "The Politics of Sky Battles in Early Hanoverian Britain." *Journal of British Studies* 41, 4 (October 2002): 429–59.

5. Cited by W. Sydney, "The Mysterious Appearances in the Heavens during the Seventeenth Century." *Notes and Queries,* February 11, 1888, pp. 104–05. Grounds for skepticism of this story, perhaps too good to be true, exist, according to investigator Peter McCue, who argues that the report is "possibly fictitious." He and a colleague, the parapsychologist Alan Gauld, "found no independent source confirming that Charles I had sent a delegation to investigate ghostly events in the Kineton area." No evidence of a minister named Samuel Marshall could be unearthed either.

6. In the most searching modern reconstruction of the incident, Frank John Reid remarks that the accounts of the 1730s were published in the following decade, while the stories set in the 1740s did not see print until 1787, after Clarke interviewed still-living witness Strickett and William Lancaster's son. Given the similarities of the paired accounts, he considers the possibility that these are simply versions of the same story, but with the passage of time and the dimming of memory, an incorrect 1730s date has been assigned to them. For various reasons he concludes that this is probably not the case, that "the phantoms seem really to have acted much the same in their last two appearances." For our purposes we have assumed Reid is correct in his surmise.

7. *Stanstead Journal.* The letter is reprinted in the *Montreal Witness* for February 13, with this cogent editorial comment: "It was evidently what is termed a *mirage,* but the question is, where was the army thus reflected?" That question applies, obviously, to other efforts to explain such appearances thus.

8. The story first appeared in the *Staunton* [Virginia] *Spectator* for September 15 and was widely reprinted. It also appeared in Frank Moore, ed. *Anecdotes, Poetry and Incidents of the War: North and South 1860–1865.* New York: Arundel Print, 1882, p. 373.

9. This article was reprinted in California's *Woodland Daily Democrat* on October 3, 1894.

10. Newark [Ohio] *Daily Advocate,* August 22, 1893.

Sky Serpents: The Horror of the Heights

1. In November 1892 the American press circulated a story quoted from a periodical identified as the *Calcutta Indian Gentleman,* citing the testimony of a wealthy Bengalese farmer named Atkama Yatzry. Yatzry claimed that he had seen an enormous serpent, with yellow and black stripes, floating in the clouds. The article continues: "Over a score of men, women and boys who were working along the flat the time of the phenomenal occurrence attest that they plainly saw the same hideous monster in his ethereal flight. One witness describes the serpent as at least four 'tsongs' (two hundred feet) in length and as big around as a man's body. All witnesses concur in saying that the head and foreparts of the creature resembled an alligator more than anything else. It ... kept its body in continued motion as long as it remained in sight."

2. It has been suggested, reasonably enough, that this was merely an auroral phenomenon to which unbridled imagination—or a correspondent's frontier sense of humor—had been applied.

3. For an interesting early effort to consider dragons from a zoological (or proto-cryptozoological) point of view, with material of relevance to the present discussion, see Chapter II of Edmund Goldsmid, ed., *Unnatural History, or Myths of Ancient Science,* published privately in Edinburgh in 1886. The chapter in question is a reprint of a paper (translated from the Latin) by European university professor George Caspard Kirthmayer (1635–1700), "On the Varieties of the Dragon, and Chiefly on Flying Dragons."

4. And not just in ancient and medieval times. An 1885 volume by scientist Gunnar Olof Hylten-Cavallius—its title translates as *On the Dragon, Also Called the Lindorm*—collected 48 sighting reports, half of them attested to by multiple witnesses, of immense snake-like reptiles. Some were alleged to be up to 20 feet long, though usually closer to eight or

10. Hylten-Cavallus summarized the descriptions of lindorms, said to have bodies "as thick as a man's thigh ... black with a yellow-flamed body ... a flat, round or squared head, a divided tongue, a mouth full of white, shining teeth." Lindorms were also alleged to have horse-like manes and big, saucer-shaped eyes with a hypnotic effect on observers. In September 1927 a prominent Saskatchewan newspaper, the *Regina Leader,* told of sightings near Killaley of a similar creature. A local official wrote the province's minister of education to ask what the creature was and "whether or not it is dangerous. The creature travels like a snake and when it is molested it rears up its head and makes a noise similar to a cow roaring but coarser. When stones that were thrown at it struck the creature it roared loudly and jumped about four feet towards the man who threw the stone.... The creature has a forked tongue.... At the thickest part of the body it is about one foot in diameter and it is estimated to weigh between 100 and 150 pounds. Down the back of its head and neck it has thin hair about an inch long. It has four small legs close up to its body. The back of the creature is of a brown color." Several residents said they had seen something like it two or three decades earlier.

5. The object had to have been barely visible (at best) at that distance, leading the reader to wonder how Stewart even could have estimated its size or, for that matter, discerned the phenomenon's serpentine contour.

6. On November 15, 1862, Iowa's *Davenport Daily Gazette* related the sighting, at 2:00 AM the previous day in neighboring Rock Island, Illinois, of a fiery meteoritic ball that "burst into a serpentine coil of light, resembling a huge serpent with its head erect and body gracefully wreathed in a coil, in which position it remained for a short time and gradually wreathed in a coil ... and gradually disappeared."

7. One would like to know the details behind these casually cryptic two sentences in a long article in an Indiana paper, the *Fort Wayne Gazette* (May 27, 1883), concerning the discovery of a vast quantity of mammal fossils in Wabash County: "This is near the same location where Justice Keagle, of Laketon, saw the large flying serpent a few years ago. The squire has lost his interest in all science and attends strictly to his office affairs." The sky serpent is a secondary marvel in a local-items column in the June 16, 1900, edition of the *Greenville Evening Record of* Pennsylvania: "Venango county papers note the appearance of a flying snake and also a feathered snake. The latter was captured by Arthur Savage, of Canal township, and is said to have a fine coat of feathers and a head like a chicken. It is about three feet in length. It eats nothing but grain and drinks an abundance of water. Mr. Savage intends to take it to some zoological garden." A column on local affairs in Ohio's *Athens Messenger and Herald* (May 24, 1907) casually observes, "The boys were telling snake stories down in front of Brooks & Hibbard's pool room the other evening, when a big burley fellow chimed in and told about a huge flying snake often seen out about Luhrig."

8. "A Strange Bird," 1868. *Zoologist* 2, 3 (July): 1295.

9. Revelation 12:7–9: "And there was war in heaven; Michael and his angels fought against the dragon; and the dragon fought and his angels, and prevailed not; neither was their place found any more in heaven. And the great dragon was cast out, that old serpent called the Devil, and Satan, which deceiveth the whole world; he was cast out into the earth, and his angels were cast out with him."

10. *Kingston* [New York] *Daily Freeman,* June 17, 1922.

Mystery Airships: Aeronauts from the Twilight Zone

1. "A Chronology of Flight," documenting real-life aviation history from 1709 into 1947, appears as an appendix (pp. 203–16) to Gordon I.R. Lore Jr. and Harold H. Deneault Jr.'s *Mysteries of the Skies: UFOs in Perspective* (1968). It is a useful guide to the evolution of flying machines, from balloons to dirigibles to airplanes.

2. One story, heretofore unpublished between book covers, is related in one long paragraph in a column otherwise devoted to pedestrian local news, published in Wisconsin's *Eau Claire Leader* for April 17: "The airship was sighted on Thursday night [April 15] by Albert Crawford, John Powers, John Crawford, Elder Stanton and his son. The ship came along with great speed, showing a red, green and white light. The ship touched ground near Marsh's farm and a curious looking man in a fur coat, after fastening the wonderful apparatus to a stump[,] walked across to Melvin Bannister's house and rapped at the door. Bannister's dogs set up a fearful barking but the visitor pulled a strange kind of a lantern out of his pocket which had the effect of sending the curs a-howling with their tails between their legs. The airship man talked a very queer language and the noise was so peculiar that it left Mr. Bannister to believe he was a being from another world. The strange visitor made signs he wanted a hammer and some shingle nails which Mr. B. soon provided him with. Also filled a can for him with skim milk. Melvin made signs he would go with the stranger to help to mend the ship, but the man shook his head ... so Mr. B. forebore. After the mending was all done, the strange man handed back the tools to Mr. B., waved his hand to him very politely, tossed him a coin and mounted with his ship over the trees. Mr. B. says the thing made a fearful whizzy noise as it shot upwards, but after awhile [sic] it sailed away in great style. Mr. B. describes it as a long cigar shaped device with wings and fans and fixings attached. The Crawfords, Stantons and [others] ... came up just as the ship set sail, but they got a good look at it. They also carefully examined the coin left by the heavenly visitor. It was unlike anything they ever saw before. A beautiful metal of a very strange color and much heavier than gold. They are all of the same opinion as Mr. Bannister that the airship and the man came from another world."

The notion of an otherworldly visitor who leaves a miraculous artifact (sometimes a coin) as last proof of its passing presence is an old folklore motif. More creative, perhaps, is the reference to the visitor as clad in a fur coat, a detail that would be revived in the 1909 testimony of C. Lethbridge, who claimed (according to the *London Daily Mail,* May 20) that while driving a wagon along a mountain road in Wales he spotted a landed cylindrical craft, next to which stood two "young men ... officers" wearing fur coats. They were conversing in a language Lethbridge did not understand, but when they saw him, they fled into the ship and flew away. Here, however, no otherworldly associations are advanced; we are to believe that the aeronauts were German spies, which they could not have been. For cogent reasons the claim is usually thought to be a hoax. In *Lo!* (1931) Charles Fort, who thought so too, at least brought the claim into an extraterrestrial context, if only to dismiss it: "Anybody else [who] wants to think that these foreigners were explorers from Mars or the moon" was welcome to do so, he remarked, but he would not be among them. Curiously, during a UFO wave in France in the autumn of 1954, a railroad worker reported coming upon a tube-shaped object. Just outside it was a man "either covered with hair or wearing a long, hairy overcoat," in the words of a *Christian Science Monitor* account (October 15). When he spoke to the stranger, the latter replied in a language unknown to the questioner. As the witness left to report the incident, the figure reentered the craft and flew away.

3. The rabbi's first name is spelled "Aron" in a profile published in a volume titled *The Advantages and Conditions of Beaumont and Port Arthur of Today* (1901). It states: "Dr. Aron Levy was born in Sarrebourg, Meurthe, France, on the 14th of September, 1848. Graduated in the St. Jermain University in 1865 in Paris, and entered the Rabbinical College and graduated in Metz Moselle, in 1871. In the same year, by a ministerial degree, Dr. Levy was called to Lischeim, and afterwards removed to the United States of America. In 1874 he officiated for a short time at the Rampart Street Temple, in the city of New Orleans. In 1875 he organized a congregation in Brasheon, now called Morgan City. In 1878 he left for Jefferson, Texas, where he organized and became the Rabbi of Mount Sinai Congregation. In 1884 the Dr. organized the present Congregation in Texarkana. In 1892 the Rabbi was elected in Austin, Texas, their spiritual leader, W. Moses being then the President of Bethel Congregation, and in 1895 the reverend gentleman was called to Beaumont to officiate. On Oct. 1st of the same year, on New Year's of the year 5655, at residence of Mr. Hirsh about 14 Jews assembled and there organized Emanuel Congregation, with Dr. A. Levy as its Rabbi. He organized the Sabbath school, and today he is also the teacher of his private English Elementary School, which is highly regarded by the community."

4. C.G. Williams, known by the nickname "Tuffy" in his life, is buried in Caddo Mills, near Greenville.

5. Lake Charles is 60 miles east of Beaumont.

6. In Orange County in the southeastern corner of the state, north of New York City.

7. The name is spelled "LaGrone" in some records.

8. Quoted in Ruth Becken, et al., *A History of Elkton*, Elkton, SD: privately printed, c. 2000, p. 94.

9. In 1874 John Sumpter Sr. founded the first bank in Hot Springs, called the Arkansas State Bank. Following a serious town fire three years later, the bank was forced out of business. Prior to that Sumpter, with George Latta, ran the short-lived newspaper *Hot Springs Times* (1873–1874).

10. On August 27, 1973, the *Albany* [Oregon] *Democrat-Herald* reported the testimony of a local resident, Herbert DeMott, who recalled a strange encounter in 1906, when he was 10 years old and living near Mitchell, South Dakota. He said he had seen a "craft" land near a well. A door opened, and "I was welcomed inside" by two ordinary-looking men sitting on "camp stools." In conversation with him, they discussed (in the fashion of 1897 aeronauts) the ship's propulsion system, offering the usual pseudoscientific bafflegab. In DeMott's paraphrase: "The outer shell of the craft was filled with helium gas, and when the lever was moved the magnetism from the earth was cut off, allowing the craft to rise." The occupants drew water from a horse trough "to be used in making electricity." They refused to reveal anything about themselves or their place of origin.

Index

Note: (ill.) indicates photos and illustrations.

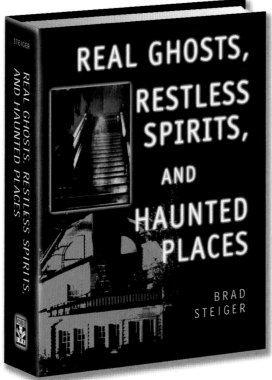

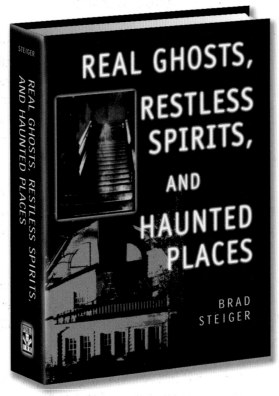

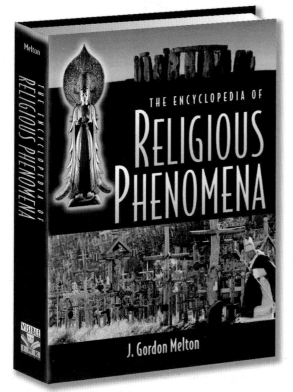

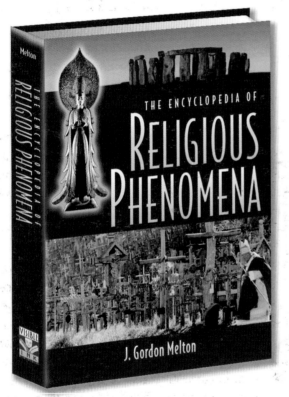

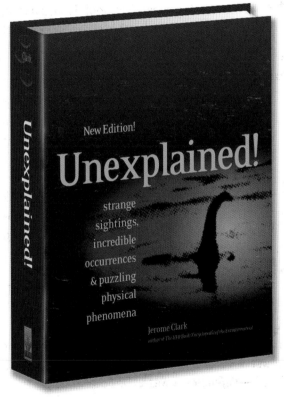

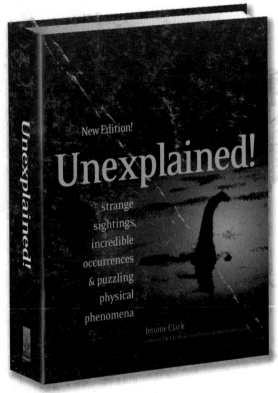